Does the Center Hold?

Text and Illustrations

by

Donald Palmer

Does the Center Hold?
An Introduction to Western Philosophy
Third Edition

Donald Palmer

Visiting Assistant Professor
at North Carolina State University

Professor Emeritus at College of Marin

Boston Burr Ridge, IL Dubuque, IA Madison, WI New York
San Francisco St. Louis Bangkok Bogotá Caracas Kuala Lumpur
Lisbon London Madrid Mexico City Milan Montreal New Delhi
Santiago Seoul Singapore Sydney Taipei Toronto

McGraw-Hill Higher Education

A Division of The **McGraw-Hill** Companies

1 2 3 4 5 6 7 8 9 0 MAL/MAL 0 9 8 7 6 5 4 3 2 1

Library of Congress Cataloging-in-Publication Data
Palmer, Donald.
    Does the center hold? : an introduction to Western philosophy/
    Donald Palmer.—3rd ed.
      p.   cm.
    Includes bibliographical references and index.
    ISBN 1–7674-1580-9
    1. Philosophy—Introductions.   I. Title.
BD21.P24 2001
190—dc21   2001018043

Sponsoring editor, Ken King; production editor, Melissa Williams; manuscript editor, Karen Dorman; art director, Jeanne M. Schreiber; design manager and cover designer, Jean Mailander; art manager, Robin Mouat; illustrations, Donald Palmer; permissions editor, Martha Granahan; manufacturing manager, Randy Hurst. The text was set in 11/14 Tekton by TBH Typecast and printed on acid-free 45# Scholarly Matte by Malloy Lithographing, Inc.

Text credits are on a continuation of the copyright page, p. 447.

www.mhhe.com

To Leila

Preface

I've met students whose parents pressured them to major in business or biology, or to enroll in pre-law courses, but I can't remember ever meeting students whose parents insisted that they become philosophy majors. Certainly, nobody ever went into this field motivated by greed, unless he or she was laboring under a serious misapprehension. Plato may have gone into philosophy impelled by a frustrated lust for power, but few make that mistake anymore. Most students end up in their first philosophy class with little or no idea of what they are about to engage in. They are there because "philosophy" fulfills a requirement, and it fits conveniently into their schedule—or because they were *able* to get into it (the class wasn't closed!). Happily, it is not unusual for students to sign up for a philosophy class because of a friend's recommendation and the good reputation of a particular instructor. This is good, because we certainly need good philosophy teachers. To the uninitiated, philosophy is hard. It's also intimidating. It's not clear what the *point* of philosophy is. Its uses are not easy to detect. Its arguments are often very abstract; it is difficult to see how they relate to "real life." Though its practitioners often seem out of touch with the world (they "have too much time on their hands," as some of my students say), they are obviously very smart, and it seems as though what they claim to be the most important points often depend on the subtlest of distinctions. Students are expected to read whole paragraphs—and sometimes, whole books—written by these philosophers in arcane or highly technical English, often in translation. Such reading assignments happen almost nowhere else in one's college career except in literature classes. But at least novelists write for a general audience, because nobody pays them if nobody understands them. For the most part, philosophers seem to write exclusively for each other. (Who pays *them?*) Worst of all, philosophers are contentious. They each seem to disagree with most other philosophers, so it's hard to know what's really true or whether any progress is ever made.

These barriers are just some of what philosophy teachers are up against. In the face of them, it's amazing that college campuses have as many introductory philosophy classes as they do, and that anybody is ever enticed to major in philosophy. Some philosophy teachers are geniuses—or at least magicians. Everything they touch turns to gold. Most of us, however, need some help. I have written this book hoping that it would be such an aid. Besides helping to teach the Western canon—the "great" philosophers and great philosophical ideas, arguments, and debates—I have tried to address the typical queries, puzzlements, and objections introductory students have vis-à-vis philosophy. I have presented these questions both in the Introduction and *in media res*. I have tried to leave the impression that philosophy is the legitimate legacy of each student as a citizen of the world. Its history and ideas are there to be appropriated by all. Rather than being an odd and esoteric endeavor, philosophy hovers around all other activities and occasionally bursts through into them. I want students to recognize that we are all philosophers—that what Sartre says about freedom is true of philosophy—we are condemned to philosophize—and, in conjunction, that what their grandmother told them is true: anything worth doing is worth doing well. I hope students come to feel that the problems of philosophy have an existential import in their lives.

I also hope that students will realize that there is a certain kind of philosophical analysis and form of argumentation whose skills can be learned and applied in other areas of their lives, not just in philosophy classes, and that there are different kinds of payoffs here—even financial ones. (Law schools like philosophy majors.) Also, some students—but not all—will come to realize, once they get the hang of it, that philosophy is fun. As the anthropologist Claude Lévi-Strauss says, just as some food is good to eat, some ideas are good to think. So I hope that this book is a contribution to not only a lively, interesting philosophy class, but also one that *is* fun. I've tried to write it in an engaging manner without watering down difficult ideas too much and without pandering to simplicity. The vocabulary may sometimes be just a notch beyond the students' familiarity but not so much as to be a turnoff. Students want to be challenged, after all. Do I need to justify using cartoons and jokes in order to make the book more entertaining? I hope not. As I say, philosophy should be fun.

Unlike the authors of many philosophy texts, I've taken personal positions on most of the topics I discuss. This approach probably needs more of a justification than do the cartoons. Well, frankly, a philosophy book that simply lays out the various alternative ideas end to end in a purely antiseptic way is a book I find inherently dull and suspect. You'll no doubt disagree with some of my conclusions, but at least I don't think you'll find them doctrinaire. I'm a hopeless eclectic—or perhaps a Jamesian. (If it works, use it!) Not only that, but according to my experience as student and teacher, part of the dynamics of a good philosophy course, unlike courses in Spanish or biology, consists in slight antagonisms between the text and the class. Think of this antagonism as an opportunity! I'm sure I've given you plenty of fodder.

I hope one of the strengths of this book is found in the connections it makes between philosophy and other fields in which students are interested, especially art, literature, physics, sociology, psychology, and psychoanalysis. Philosophy may no longer be the queen of all disciplines, but she is certainly their consort.

Despite certain appearances to the contrary, the text is fairly conventional in the selection of material. The topics are themes typically taught in introductory philosophy courses on this continent. I think the chapter divisions and subdivisions speak for themselves in this respect. I try to establish continuity throughout the book both by providing a Glossary with a system of cross-references and by keeping certain themes alive from chapter to chapter so that ideas once learned do not simply evaporate. (Here, "use it or lose it.")

The changes in the second and third editions are the consequence of numerous communications to me from professors, students, and general readers. I am grateful for the many suggestions proffered, especially for the extensive comments, criticisms, and recommendations made by philosophy teachers who had used the first edition as a college text and who were in a good position to detect the book's strengths and weaknesses. The readers for the preparation of the second edition were David Carl, Diablo Valley College; Andrea Grace Diem, Mt. San Antonio College; Daniel Kealey, Towson State University; Wesley Kobylak, Monroe Community College; Glenn McCoy, Eastern New Mexico University; Edward Slowick, Ohio University; and Steve Wilkens, Azusa Pacific University. For the third edition, the readers were Gregory Comnes, Hillsborough Community College; Robert Fudge, Syracuse University; Joseph W. Huster, University of Utah; and Loren E. Lamaksy, Bowling Green State University. I thank them all. They were acute critics, and the book has been improved because of them.

For the second edition, the many suggestions I received resulted in scores of minor alterations, deletions, and corrections scattered throughout the body of the book and in several major changes as well: a more extensive treatment of the pre-Socratic philosophers, a new section on Aristotle and one on Spinoza, a section on mysticism and one on the feminist critique of Western moral philosophy, and a section on the deep ecology movement. Each chapter is now followed by a list of inexpensive and readable paperback books for those who would like to delve further into philosophy's deep waters, and at the end of each chapter there are a number of "topics for consideration" to aid students and teachers who are using this book as a college text. I also reorganized the structure of several chapters. There have been fewer major changes for the third edition. I added some new drawings, corrected some mistakes, clarified some fuzzy language, updated some older material, and further developed topics where critics agreed among themselves that I should do so. A substantial addition was made to the section on the mind-body problem in Chapter 4, and by popular demand I have more to say about the problem of evil in Chapter 5.

I hope that all these changes and additions have produced an improved version of *Does the Center Hold?*

And now to the acknowledgments. If a long list of names bores you, skip this paragraph because I intend to pay my debts here and thank many of the people who participated in the construction of this book (most without their knowledge or consent). First, the philosophers. . . . Well, that's all the philosophers I've ever studied but particularly Wittgenstein, Kierkegaard, Sartre, Marx, Freud, Nietzsche, Plato, Descartes, Spinoza, Hume, and James; you'll hear from them again. (Some may be rolling over in their graves.) Next, my own teachers, including Virginia Orkney, Cornelius Weber, George Duncan, Howell Breece, John Searle, Stanley Cavell, Benson Mates, Stephen Pepper, Jerry Clegg, Juan Rodríguez Rosado, and Leonardo Polo, and (by osmosis) the cartoonists Charles Addams and Virgil "Vip" Partch. Next, thanks to all my students over a thirty-year period at the College of Marin—all six thousand of them. (Well, perhaps not *all* of them. One student demanded publicly that I be fired after it dawned on him that some of the philosophers he studied in my class contradicted each other. In his letter to the college president he said he only had time to study what was known to be true.) To this list of six thousand I can now add a few hundred more students whom I have since taught at North Carolina State University here in Raleigh. Just as I initially thanked Jim Bull, my editor at Mayfield for the first two editions, I now express my gratitude to Ken King, editor of the third edition, along with other diligent members of the excellent team at Mayfield who coached this edition along: Marty Granahan, Jean Mailander, Robin Mouat, and Melissa Williams and also Julianna Scott Fein, whose intelligence and wit are deeply appreciated.

Also, though it may seem odd, I want to thank the great American desert, where many thoughts were hatched and pages written—the Smoke Creek Desert, the Black Rock Desert, the Mojave, the Organ Pipe National Monument, the Anza-Borrego, and therewith (of course) the late Edward Abbey, wherever you may be. Once again, let me thank my true source of energy, inspiration, and love, the person to whom this book is dedicated, my wife, Leila May. Without her, even philosophy would be worth much less to me.

Contents

Introduction

This book is an introduction to philosophy. Such a book should not need much of an introduction, which would be merely an introduction to an introduction. Still, a few preliminary comments are appropriate. First, a word about the style. Everybody's style is both unique and imitative. Consciously or unconsciously, I've imitated the styles of my teachers and of the philosophers I've studied. (I've thanked them in the preface.) This book is written in something of a unique style despite all these influences. I hope philosophy teachers, philosophy students, and the general reader will find my style compatible with their own styles of teaching, learning, thinking, and enjoying. My style attempts to be both lighthearted and serious at the same time. It is lighthearted because of my deep conviction that joy and knowledge are not mutually exclusive (Nietzsche's "joyful wisdom"). I hope you'll find at least some of the jokes funny without being distracting. I dare to hope that a few of them might be illuminating. But the book is also serious because it asks serious questions. Several philosophers (e.g., Dewey, Sartre, Heidegger) tell us that to be human is to confront the world with questions. And all of our smaller questions are framed by the bigger questions, such as "What is reality?" "What is knowledge?" "What is value?" "What is it to be human?" These are philosophical questions. They are what philosophy (and life) are about. What annoys some people about philosophy is that these questions never seem to receive a final answer. Each generation appears to answer them; then each new generation rephrases them in such a way as to require new answers. But that's also what is annoying about life (and what's exciting about it as well). We will find one philosopher—Bertrand Russell (p. 35)—saying that our ability to pose these questions is more important than our own inability to arrive at completely satisfactory answers.

Nevertheless, I have been so presumptuous as to try to draw my own tentative conclusions at the end of each chapter. This isn't always done in introductory philosophy books because students are supposed to be allowed to draw their own conclusions—but I suspect that one way or another students will manage to survive my conclusions (especially with the help of their professors). And if you don't want to be contaminated by my ruminations, just skip them. (Although who's fooling whom? Writers' conclusions are usually subconsciously smuggled into the formulation of the questions they pose and, indeed, even in the structure of the material they exhibit. Be on guard!)

Another feature of this book to which students should be alerted is its exclusively Western orientation. The philosophers and philosophies studied here are all in the Greco-Roman-European tradition. Rich philosophical veins exist in other cultures, but I do not have the expertise to mine them. Not only are most of the philosophies in this book Western philosophies, but they are systems of thought that have been put forward for the most part by males. This is a weakness in my book for which I am only partly at fault. I agree with feminist philosophers who claim that in the past women have been systematically discouraged from attempting to participate in the history of philosophy and that when women did make such attempts, they were marginalized or even suppressed. I am heartened to note that today the system of barriers that has discouraged women from a philosophical vocation is being dismantled.

Now, what about the title of the book, *Does the Center Hold?* I borrowed the idea from the poet William Butler Yeats, who, in "The Second Coming," says, "Things fall apart; the centre cannot hold." Yet in prereflective thought (life before philosophy), the center certainly seems to hold most of the time for most of us. The world we inhabit presents itself to us in a fairly orderly and predictable manner in both its physical and social manifestations. But occasionally, natural or social disasters burst forth (such as earthquakes and wars), the order and reasonableness of things disappear, and there is chaos. Also, at some point in their lives, most individuals suffer bouts of "mini-madness," where the center does not seem to hold. (Such an experience may have inspired Yeats's poem.) Furthermore, as Descartes reminds us, every night we each slip into a dream world that is madder than madness. Then we wake up and minimize the experience of unreason by relegating it to a sphere of unreality.

When I was a child, I liked to go to Playland at the Beach in San Francisco (now covered over with townhouses). One of my favorite spots was the Dizzy Dish. You sat at the center of a large disk that slowly began rotating. As it moved faster and faster, only the person sitting at the exact center, marked by an orange circle, was safe (by virtue of centripetal force). All others inevitably began sliding off the disk at first inch by inch; then suddenly, amid much shrieking, they were hurled to the perimeter (centrifugal force). When you first felt yourself slipping, you clawed to reach the middle, but inexorably it seemed to pull away from you. The center did not hold. I suspect that the onset of insanity sometimes provokes similar sensations but so does the study of philosophy. Under the philosophical scrutiny of thought, knowledge, reality, and values, the commonsensical center and normal orderliness of the world seem to slip away. As Nietzsche said, while philosophizing we sometimes feel as though we have cut our moorings and are floating off into the cold darkness of outer space.

A less picturesque way of posing the central question I am asking is this: When we address the problems about reality, knowledge, and value to which I alluded a moment ago, can we put together solutions that hold? Do these solutions have to last forever, or do time and context require all answers to be partial and relative? Should we, like the medieval and early modern philosophers, demand answers that are *sub species aeternitatus* (from the point of view of eternity)? Is the alternative simply eternal ignorance? Or, to the contrary, can carefully worked out provisional answers still be good answers?

Philosophy, I believe, will prove to be such an always-provisional attempt to achieve a view of "the bigger picture"—to see how, as someone has said, "things hang together," if they do. Returning to the book's title, we can say that *Does the Center Hold?* asks whether a scrutiny of human experience reveals some kind of unity, or does it plunge us into chaos? Each of the chapters in this book attempts to be an aid to the reader in answering that overarching question, and each does this by scrutinizing a different feature of experience. Of course, readers must draw their own conclusions. Mine, flavored with what I hope is a healthy skepticism, is that the center does hold, but only *roughly*. And some days it seems to hold better than others. The truth is that the history of Western philosophy does not play itself out in terms of a debate between those philosophers who think that the center does hold and those who think that it does not. There are, of course, a few philosophers who think that it does not hold—Friedrich Nietzsche is the most dramatic of these—but the real debate is between those who claim that it holds absolutely and those who claim that it holds relatively well. (Though, ironically, in the absolutists it is sometimes possible to detect an anxiety driving the argument, as if still fearing that the center may not hold despite their protestations to the contrary. One of the absolutists—René Descartes—admitted that his own philosophical questions frightened him.) The debate is already clearly articulated in ancient Greece.

Heraclitus (ca. 470 B.C.E.), about whom I will have more to say in Chapter 1, wrote what would prove to be one of the most famous aphorisms in philosophy, "You can't step in the same river twice." No two moments or events are the same. Things fall apart; new things are born. Everything becomes its own opposite. However, Heraclitus believed he had discovered a hard center in the midst of the apparent chaos in the fact that there is one thing that does not change, namely, change itself. But Heraclitus's philosophy was interpreted historically as a form of deep pessimism, something that had to be refuted. The attempted refutation came in a book by Parmenides (ca. 515–ca. 440 B.C.E.), whom we will also encounter again in Chapter 1. He defended the astounding thesis that nothing ever changes at all. Everything is eternally still and immutable. Motion and time themselves are illusions whose deception would be swept away by philosophy. The center holds . . . with a vengeance.

Parmenides' theory deeply influenced a philosopher in the next generation who is recognized even by his opponents as one of the two or three most important thinkers in Western history—Plato (427–347 B.C.E.). As you read this book you will see that he, more than any other individual, will represent the paradigm of a philosopher who wants to prove that the center holds—that there is a rational unchanging core at the center of reality and that all apparent chaos is held at bay by its certainty. If you check the index you will see that Plato's name appears here more often than that of any other philosopher. He will represent a certain standard to which others aspire or from which they slowly drift or hastily retreat. Even anti-Platonists (like myself) are parasitic on his thought. You will get quite a dose of Plato before you are done studying philosophy.

1

What Are We Doing in This Class?
Is Philosophy Possible?

Very few academic courses devote a big part of the class time to agonizing over what the subject matter of the course is or whether the discipline to be studied even exists. Yet such is the case with philosophy. Philosophy poses a series of questions that it then tries to answer, and one of these questions is "What is philosophy?" This fact itself tells us something about philosophy because it informs us of philosophy's self-reflective nature. It is part of philosophy's task to think

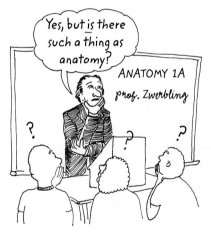

about itself, because philosophy is an activity whose purpose involves questioning the assumptions of every system of thought, including its own. It is this perhaps overly introspective aspect of philosophy that annoys some people and causes them to think of philosophers the way they think of neurotics and psychotics—who also spend a lot of time creating bizarre, convoluted explanations of how they relate to the world and to themselves. (We shall see that the line between philosophy and madness is sometimes

Thought Thinking about Itself

5

The Thin Line between Philosophy and Madness

very thin indeed, and more than one philosopher has concluded that what is needed is a cure for philosophical problems, not a solution to them).

The Origins of Philosophy

One way of trying to understand philosophy is to look at its origins, both linguistic and historical. The word "philosophy" is from the Greek *philosophia*, meaning "the love of wisdom." Plato took this definition very seriously and saw the philosopher as a kind of lover; hence Plato spent a lot of time trying to determine the meaning of love in order to demonstrate that *true* lovers *always* love wisdom. But the activity we call philosophy went back hundreds of years before Plato. It is generally agreed that the first recorded philosopher in the Western tradition was THALES of Miletos (c. 580 B.C.E). Looking briefly at what he had to say may reveal something about the nature of philosophy, though it might also prove to be a bit disappointing because Thales' main theory is so obviously false (his theory: *everything is water!*) and

Everything Is Water

because his "activity" does not seem so unusual—at least not to us. It is known that, while visiting Egypt, Thales formulated a hypothesis to explain why the Nile, unlike almost every other known river, tended to dry up in the winter and flood in the summer. His hypothesis was that winds were the cause of these phenomena. What's so remarkable about this theory (other than the fact that we now know it to be false)? What catches our attention is that all of Thales' predecessors had tried to explain these facts about the Nile by attributing them to supernatural events. Thales, rather than talking about miracles or the will of the gods, explained the one natural phenomenon (the flooding of the Nile) in terms of other natural phenomena (the desert winds).

Even his outrageous claim that everything is water is an attempt to explain natural phenomena in terms of other natural phenomena (and not so outrageous a claim—the leap

The Leap from "Everything Is Water" to "Everything Is Atoms"

from "Everything is water" to "Everything is atoms" is smaller than it may seem, and this leap took only a hundred years).

From the perspective of our desire to learn something about the nature of philosophy, Thales' erroneous answer is much less significant than his *question* (namely, "What is everything composed of?"), and what is even more interesting than either Thales' question or his answer are the presuppositions behind his question. Like most Greeks, Thales was acutely aware of the dramatic changes that took place in the observable world: day changes to night, then back to day again; summer changes to winter, then to summer again; hot changes to cold and then to hot again. And then that most mysterious of all changes, life to death, which somehow

produced life again. Thales' question assumes that if there is change, then there must be something behind change that itself does not change. Thales also observed that the world was composed of many individual things: rocks, lizards, toothpicks, rainbows, and people. Yet the world was somehow a whole and not just a loose collection of unrelated objects. Thales' question assumes that if there are "many," then somehow there must be a "one" behind the "many." That is, Thales' question

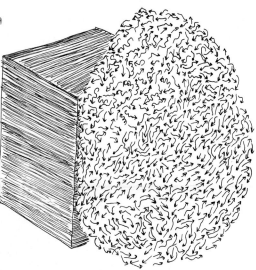

Something behind Change That Itself Does Not Change

presupposes that the concept of difference is logically dependent on the concept of sameness, which is more basic, and that difference must somehow be reducible to sameness. Furthermore, Thales' question assumes that the human mind is capable of fathoming that unchanging one behind the many, and having fathomed it, the mind would understand what makes the center hold, would understand the sense in which things hang together. This was Thales' concern twenty-six hundred years ago and continues to be the concern of philosophers and scientists today.

Once again, it is important to stress that for Thales, the answer to his question would have to be natural, not supernatural. This is primarily what separates Thales' mode of thinking from the mythic form of thought that preceded him. Myths explain why things are the way they are by tracing these things to their origins. In this respect, **Mythos** (the mythic way of thought) is no different from **Logos** (the philosophic/scientific way of thought). But myth traces the origins of things to supernatural time, sometimes called "strong time" by mythologists, and to supernatural ancestral beings. Strong time is the period of the early beginnings before "normal" time existed. The magical beings that existed then were unrestricted by the limitations of time and space that constrain people in normal time. The heroic or dastardly actions of those magical beings are the source of our own world. The order of the social and natural worlds is explained by showing how these worlds relate to strong time and to the divine beings that inhabited that time. Myths are usually conservative. They justify the status quo by revealing its relation to strong time ("We do these things because our ancestors did them. . . ."). Myths often begin with a formula that refers to the beginning of the world ("Once, a long, long time ago, when the earth was very young . . ."). The recitation of the myth removes both the speaker and audience from natural time and returns them to strong time.

The Center Does Not Hold—Things Fall Apart

Furthermore, the ritual surrounding the recitation of a myth reconstitutes the social and natural worlds. The mythical mind believes that if these myths were not recited, if these rituals were not performed, the world would fall into chaos, the center would not hold, and things would fall apart. Societies based on myth are traditionally "unhistorical." They do not record history because "history" implies change, and myth-oriented societies deny change. The only change was the fall from strong time into daily time. Since then, nothing has changed. In the Greek world, the two main transmitters of Mythos were the poets Homer (ninth century B.C.E.) and Hesiod (tenth century B.C.E.), two masterful tellers of heroic tales. Furthermore, many of the theatrical dramas of Greece were based on ancient myths. The depictions by the poets and dramatists of the origins of the world and the activities of the gods on Mount Olympus would be the background against which the newly emergent Greek philosophy came to operate.

Like mythical explanations, Thales' "philosophical" theory traces things to their origin—not to their chronological origin but rather to their *ontological* origin, that is, their origin *in being*. What is the relation of observable objects in the world to ultimate reality itself? What must be the hidden truth behind natural objects for them to exhibit the forms they do exhibit and to undergo the changes they undergo? Thales' hypothesis contains no reference to strong time or supernatural entities (though one curious fragment from his book says, "All things contain gods"). Rather, it involves logical analysis of the discernible facts drawn from observation. The Greeks were aware of the four elements: earth, water, air, and fire. Thales concluded that one of these elements must be more basic than the others and asked himself which of the four was capable of taking on the greatest number

The Fall from Strong Time

of forms. Water seemed the most likely candidate. When heated, water changes to steam, then to air. When frozen, it changes to a solid. It disappears both down into the earth and up into the sky and then bubbles back up from the earth and falls from the sky. Thales saw that rivers deposit deltas at their mouth and (incorrectly) deduced that water was being turned to earth. He saw dew on the ground in the morning

and (incorrectly) deduced that earth was being changed to water. He saw the Mediterranean phenomenon called "the sun drawing water" (in which, during certain kinds of storms over the sea, clouds seem to swirl in a vortex around the sun), and he (incorrectly) deduced that the fire in the sun was fed by water.

Then water was the basic element! And not supernatural water—though perhaps very super natural water.

The distinction between Mythos and Logos helps determine the nature of philosophy, but it is not without its problems. First, the viability of the distinction itself has been questioned by some. The psychologist C. G. Jung and the anthropologist Claude Lévi-Strauss have both argued that so-called Logos is simply our modern, Western way of mythmaking and is in some respects inferior to other forms of Mythos. For example, they pointed out, the abstractions of Western Logos are too distanced from the actual textures of everyday experience. Scientific theories seem to deny the reality of the sensuous features of the world with which we are in daily contact or mystify them in their attempt to reduce them to invisible entities like atoms, electrons, and neutrons— **theoretical entities** that take on the status of the magical entities of strong time. To other critics, Western science

has become politically contaminated, and its claim to superiority over other forms of Mythos is a version of **ethnocentrism** and cultural colonialism. Although these critics occasionally score some points, they are in a distinct minority among writers on the topic, most of whom defend the view that science represents genuine progress away from Mythos. Still, the separation between Mythos and Logos may not be as clear as we would like.

Scholars have reminded us that many philosophers who followed Thales—philosophers known today as the pre-Socratics because they flourished in the years before Socrates' death in 399 B.C.E.—still displayed decidedly mythical trends in their thought. An example is Thales' immediate philosophical descendent, ANAXIMANDER of Miletos (ca. 545 B.C.E.) who criticized his master's theory, saying that if any one of the four elements were fundamental, then everything would have collapsed back into that element long ago. So for him there must be an aboriginal, nameless, formless element behind all things, and he called this primordial stuff "the Indeterminant" or "the Unlimited." The most famous fragment still extant from Anaximander's lost book says:

> From what source things arise, to that they return of necessity when they are destroyed; for they suffer punishment and make reparation to one another for their injustice according to the order of time.

Some scholars say that in using moral categories such as "injustice" and "reparation" to explain the world, Anaximander is clearly pursuing a form of explanation similar to

Water Suffering Punishment for Its Injustice

that of the great mythmakers. Furthermore, it is easy to point out many great Western philosophers who flourished hundreds of years after Anaximander and who had recourse to divine beings in their accounts of reality. (See Chapter 5.) So the rejection of supernatural explanation cannot be the essence of defining philosophy.

A brief summary of the views of some of the other main pre-Socratic philosophers will highlight the strengths and weaknesses of attempts to define philosophy in terms of the Mythos/Logos distinction, and it will provide us with more information about the activities of the earliest Western philosophers.

A school of philosophy dedicated to a kind of mathematical contemplation was founded by PYTHAGORAS (ca. 572–ca. 500 B.C.E.) and it lasted almost 400 years. Four prominent philosophers in this school were THEANO, Pythagoras's wife, and their three daughters, MYIA, DAMO, and ARIGNOTE. This shows that women philosophers were important in the ancient world even if little by way of precise information about them has come down to us. (Indeed, one historian in the eighteenth century was able to list sixty-five women philosophers in the two-hundred-year period after the Peloponnesian War alone.)

Pythagoras did not seek ultimacy in some material element, as his predecessors had done. Rather, he held the curious view that all things are numbers. Literally understood, this view seems absurd, but Pythagoras

Four Pythagorean Philosophers

meant, among other things, that a correct description of reality must be expressed in terms of mathematical formulas. Furthermore, he anticipated the bulk of Euclid's writings on geometry and discovered the ratios of concordance between musical sound and number. From this, he deduced a mathematical harmony throughout the universe, a view that led to the doctrine of "the Music of the Spheres."

If this part of Pythagoras's view looks mostly like Logos, another side looks more like Mythos. He was the leader of a religious cult whose members had to obey a strict number of esoteric rules based on asceticism, numerology, and vegetarianism. Despite their vegetarianism, Pythagoreans had to forswear eating beans, because eating beans is a form of cannibalism. A close look at the inside of a bean reveals that each one contains a small, embryonic human being (or human bean, as the case may be).

Another pre-Socratic philosopher of note was HERACLITUS (ca. 470 B.C.E.), whom we have briefly met in the Introduction. He looked for ultimate reality not in some particular physical element (as did Thales), nor in an invisible indeterminate element (as did Anaximander), nor in numbers (as did Pythagoras); rather, he sought it in the structure of change. "Everything changes but change itself," he wrote. And change, or *process*, is a system of destruction and creation. "All things," he said, "come into being through opposition, and all are in flux like a river."

This modern-sounding view—that reality is composed not of things but of ever-changing relationships of attraction and opposition governed by law—could

Nothing ever remains the same.

Heraclitus

certainly be called Logos (and indeed he called the law that governs all things Logos). Yet Heraclitus was known as "the dark one" because of his oracular style and mysterious epigrams. For example, he said, "Thunderbolt steers all things," and "Justice is strife," and "War is the father and king of all," and "You cannot step in the same river twice."[1] Are these sayings part of Logos or Mythos? And was he an optimist or a pessimist? We have already seen that for many generations after Heraclitus's death he was seen as a philosopher of despair. Most paintings of him for the next eighteen hundred years depict him with tears in his eyes. He was incorrectly viewed as believing that the center does not hold—that there is, in fact, no center to hold. (I say that this view of him was incorrect because Heraclitus clearly believed that, despite the fact that only change and movement existed, it was not chaotic, pointless change, but one governed by Logos.)

Heraclitus's counterpart, PARMENIDES (ca. 515–440 B.C.E.), whom we've also briefly met in the Introduction, appeared to assert exactly the opposite of the dark one. Parmenides held that motion is an illusion and that nothing ever changes. Thus, not only can you not step in the same river twice, you can't step in it at all. The world as perceived by the senses is a delusion. Why? Because change requires that "what is" come from "what is not"; but nothing can come from "what is not," so change is impossible. Only Reason can reveal the truth. And what does Reason tell us? That Being is itself. "A" = "A."

"A" can never be other than "A." The idea of change is conceptually incoherent. Being *is*. That means, Being is uncreated, indestructible, unmovable, and completely full (the idea of "empty space" is a self-contradictory idea), a *plenum*. This rigorous application of Reason to Being is perhaps Logos at its most extreme, and the most strident defense of the view that the center holds. (Failure to hold would entail a kind of change, which is logically impossible—the opposite of logical **necessity**.)

So far I have been talking as if the Mythos/Logos distinction tries to separate systems of myth from systems of rational thought. But even within the latter category we must seek to distinguish between what we today call philosophy and other forms of rational thought such as scientific thinking. (This is not a distinction that the pre-Socratics could have made. Indeed, Thales seems to be the first entry in both the history of Western philosophy and history of Western science.) Some writers accept this fact and, stressing the speculative nature of philosophy, claim that science is what happens when certain branches of philosophy find a way of becoming **experimental** and empirical. For example, Sir Isaac Newton, whom we consider an exemplary scientist, titled his main work *The Mathematical Principles of Natural Philosophy*. And in truth much of what was once touched only by philosophers' speculations has been taken over today by physicists, sociologists, and psychologists.

However, designating philosophy as merely immature science not only diminishes philosophy but also misses much of what is interesting about it. I suspect (but cannot prove) that many philosophical questions by their very nature cannot be made experimental—particularly those having to do with values. (When the first Soviet cosmonauts communicated to earth that they had surveyed the skies and discovered that there was no god to be found up there either, one must think that they were joking or that they badly misconstrued the problem of God's existence.) Furthermore, philosophical questions often arise within science. When physicists claim that certain particles are fundamental, the question comes up, By what criteria do we determine that something is "fundamental"? Or what criteria shall we use in medicine for determining death? What counts as the confirmation of a theory? These kinds of philosophical queries, which constantly crop up in science, cannot be ignored; and they prove that philosophy is not just unenlightened science.

I think our brief journey to the historical origin of philosophy has been helpful though not definitive. A number of philosophy's features will probably not get addressed by simply returning to the Greek source of philosophy. Another approach, which will get at some of those features, is to list and characterize the various branches of philosophy generally recognized today.

Contemporary Branches of Philosophy

If you pick up the catalogue of a typical four-year college or university in the United States and look under the "philosophy" heading, you will find courses offered in the following areas, among others: epistemology, ontology (or metaphysics), logic, ethics (or moral philosophy), political philosophy, and aesthetics, along with a group of courses whose titles begin with the words "philosophy of _____," for example, philosophy of science, philosophy of religion, philosophy of mind, philosophy of sport. Let's take a look at what you would study if you signed up for these courses.

Epistemology

Epistemology is theory of knowledge. It concerns questions like these:

> What is knowledge, and how does it differ from opinion? Does knowledge require certainty, or can something be known without being known for certain? Does knowledge in fact exist, or must we be satisfied with mere opinion? If there is knowledge, how do we come by it?

Notice that these questions are conceptual rather than experimental. Only the last of these questions could be made the object of an experiment, strictly speaking, and hence could be claimed to be the dominion of psychology; yet we shall shortly see that even this question is not exclusively, or even mostly, experimental.

Ontology

Ontology is theory of being. (Some writers prefer to call this **metaphysics.**) It concerns the following questions:

What is it for something to be real? What is the nature of existence? What is the difference between appearance and reality?

Notice that these questions are not experimental because you would already have to have made some tentative decisions about them before you could begin any experiment. The questions, "Do minds exist?" and "Are prime numbers real?" are not like the questions, "Do unicorns exist?" and "Are ghosts real?" To answer the latter questions, experiments and explorations can be imagined. But philosophy classes take few field trips because there is no place to go—or, to put it more accurately, no matter where you are, you are already there!

Philosophy Field Trip

Logic

Logic is the most specialized branch of philosophy. It is sometimes defined as the science of valid inference. This science, which was founded by Aristotle in the fourth century B.C.E., is a purely formal study. That is to say, it wants to know what forms of argumentation are valid, and it does not concern itself with the truth status of the arguments' conclusions or with their supporting statements. Look, for example, at the argument:

> All men are mortal.
> Socrates is a man.
> Therefore Socrates is mortal.

This is a *valid* argument. That means that the first two statements (the argument's premises) **logically entail** the third statement (the argument's conclusion). The argument would still be valid even if it turned out that the first or second premise of the argument was false. Even if we discovered that some men are immortal and that Socrates was actually a fish, the argument would be valid purely because of its *form*, which is the following:

> All As are Bs.
> S is an A.
> Therefore S is a B.

This brief summary has not done justice to the breadth and depth of the influence that logic has had on contemporary philosophy. There

How old are you, anyway?

9,627 years old.

Then obviously you are _not_ Socrates.

**All Men Are Mortal.
Socrates Is a Man.**

were great advancements in the field in the nineteenth century, and in the first decades of the twentieth century a lexicon of symbols had been developed that gave logic a precision it had formerly lacked. Once the relation between logic and mathematics had been carefully studied, logic—or symbolic logic, as its new form is called—became almost a branch of calculus and provided a powerful tool of analysis and criticism that finds a home in most other fields of philosophy.

The next three branches of philosophy—ethics, political philosophy, and aesthetics—all overlap the rather amorphous concept of axiology, the study of value. Ethics is moral philosophy and as such is interested in moral value. It deals with concepts like goodness, duty, and right and wrong. **Political philosophy** studies social value and explores the justification of political institutions and political relations. Aesthetics studies the value of beauty and related qualities that provoke judgments about art and nature. It encompasses the **philosophy of art,** which is the major part of aesthetics, and also the value of natural beauty.

Ethics

Ethics, or moral philosophy, asks questions like these:

> What is the good life? Are there such things as moral duties and obligations that bind us? That is, is there something we truly _ought_ to do? Are some moral arguments "better" than others, or are all of them equally valid or invalid? Are values absolute, or are they relative to time and place?

Again, notice that these questions are not experimental or empirical. Psychologists may be able to tell us why people hold the moral values they do hold. Sociologists and anthropologists may tell us whether any values are held by all cultures and what the social consequences are of holding certain values. But these questions are not the same ones philosophers ask, though empirical information about values provided by the social sciences may be pertinent to philosophical questions about morality.

> Look, I'm not saying I _disapprove_ of your values or that mine are _better._ I'm just saying that mine are _different!_

Political and Social Philosophy

Political and social philosophy ask questions about the state's legitimate authority over its members and about social values such as justice. Typical questions are:

> Can the idea of government be rationally justified, or must all governments be irrational? Do humans have any political duties or social obligations? Under what conditions? Are there such things as natural social rights? Can such rights be justifiably overridden as a form of punishment?

Once more, notice that these questions are related to questions asked by political scientists and sometimes they overlap them—as in the question "Are some forms of government superior to others?" But generally they are not identical to the questions asked by political scientists, the latter of which are basically empirical.

Aesthetics

Aesthetics is the branch of philosophy that explores the nature of aesthetic objects and of aesthetic judgments. That definition doesn't help much, of course, unless we have some idea what these latter two terms mean. Historically, the main component of the concept of aesthetic objects has been beauty, and the central theme of aesthetic judgments has been judgment about beauty. However, other qualities that are occasionally discussed as objects of aesthetic judgment are the sublime, the ugly, and the comic. Therefore, aesthetics is wider than the philosophy of art because many of its objects are associated both with art and with nature. Nevertheless, in terms of both the history of philosophy and the contemporary scene, most discussions within aesthetics relate to art. In the mid-eighteenth century, the German philosopher Alexander Baumgarten coined the term "aesthetics" from a Greek word having to do with sensation. Yet what we call aesthetics goes back at least as far as Plato in the fourth century B.C.E., and some historians claim that he originated it. Contemporary aestheticians ask, just as Plato did, about the nature of artistic or aesthetic value. They want to know the source of and justification for aesthetic judgment and whether certain necessary features of art or perception exist that make some artwork or perceptions objectively more valuable than others. Aestheticians also want to see how artistic activity fits in conceptually with the rest of human activities.

As I mentioned earlier, besides these traditional branches of philosophy, you will also find in college catalogues courses called "Philosophy of X," where X is some field or activity that itself is *not* philosophy, such as science, law, sport, religion, or even love and sex. (In fact, aesthetics is such a branch when it is defined as containing the "philosophy of art," for art itself is *not* philosophy. Yet it is possible to philosophize about art, and when one does that, one engages in aesthetics.)

The reason such fields as these are possible has to do with a feature of philosophy that has been called its "second order" level of analysis. Take a look at this attempted definition of philosophy by William Capitan. I think it fails as an exhaustive definition (they all do!), but it has the virtue of revealing the side of philosophy we are discussing now. Capitan says philosophy is "rational inquiry into the structure of any thought system, its presuppositions, concepts, and the status of its claims."[2] This definition shows why it is possible to have the "philosophies of _____" and also shows why a course on Marx or Freud might well be taught in a philosophy department even though neither Marx nor Freud is thought of primarily as a philosopher. Freud, for instance, employs certain key concepts, like "sublimation," "projection," "transference," "displacement," and "reaction-formation"; and psychoanalysts look for instantiations of these concepts in human behavior. This is first order analysis. Philosophers do not engage in this hands-on approach but take a step back and ask *second order* questions like "What is the logic of these concepts?" "What presuppositions do these concepts make about the mind, knowledge, and value?" "What would count as establishing a case for or against these claims?" Capitan's definition stresses what we can call the analytical or critical aspect of philosophy, what has already been designated here as its second order status. A tendency to emphasize this analytical feature of philosophy is also seen in the definition of Stuart Hampshire, a well-known contemporary British philosopher. According to Hampshire, "Philosophy is a free inquiry into the limits of human knowledge and into the most general categories applicable

**Marx and Freud Are Discovered
in a Philosophy Class**

to experience and reality."[3] With the term "free inquiry," I take it that Hampshire is laying out an *ideal* condition for philosophy—that its inquiry should be unconstrained by the dictates and requirements of politics, religion, personal advantage, or the demands of other "special interests." I say it is an ideal condition because surely a great deal of what passes for philosophy has bowed one way or another to the demands of extraphilosophical agenda. This "ideal" seems to imply that there is, or ought to be, such a thing as pure reason, or pure logic, and that philosophy should be the pursuit of this unfettered rationality. But in truth it is not likely that the human mind ever functions purely objectively and disinterestedly, independent of nonphilosophical encumbrances, at least concerning issues of any importance. Nevertheless, Hampshire is right—philosophy must engage in self-vigilance and be suspicious of its own motives if it is even to approximate its goal.

Hampshire's definition refers to "the most general categories applicable to experience and reality." This intentionally vague part of his characterization calls attention both to the fact that certain key categories are of interest to philosophy (such as time, space, existence, sociality, beauty, love, and death) and also to philosophy's interest in their *general* character. By their general character, Hampshire means something like this: I may ask you what time it is, and in doing so, I am certainly not asking a philosophical question. Or you may tell me that it takes less time to fly from San Francisco to Reno than from Reno to St. Louis, and in doing so, you are not making a philosophical assertion. But if I ask you not "What time is it?" but

"What is time?"—then I am asking a general question that is probably a philosophical question. (Unless, for example, I am simply asking you for the dictionary definition because my English isn't too hot, and I'm not familiar with the word "time.") Similarly, if I ask you what it means for something to be located in space, I am asking a philosophical question, but not if I ask, "How many chairs will fit around the dining room table?"

In this book, I call these general questions "the big questions." This is slightly pompous but not quite so pompous as calling them "the most important questions," as some philosophers do. (It should be admitted forthwith that what makes a question "important" are the circumstances in which it is asked.) One could also call these philosophical questions *deep* questions, yet they are deep not in some presumptuous sense but in a metaphorically archeological or geological sense. They are deep in that they

lie beneath other questions and support them. When I talk about the amount of time it takes to get from point A to point B, then underlying my meaning is some general conception of time, and philosophy critically investigates that underlying general conception.

Let me add yet another attempt to define philosophy. This one is from Professor Craig Channell. According to him, philosophy is the "ongoing critical activity of developing theories to describe, explain, or account for certain aspects of human experience."[4] Though the last part of his definition is so vague as to be practically useless, his reference to philosophy as an "activity of developing theories" emphasizes a feature of philosophy that the other definitions have understressed—philosophy's constructive and creative side. Some philosophers (especially in the first half of the twentieth century) have thought that philosophy should not develop theories but should be satisfied with engaging exclusively in criticism and analysis; yet, as we shall see, the history of philosophy abounds with grand theoretical schemes trying to show how everything relates to everything else. Most of the individuals studied in the history of philosophy developed such schemes. This feature of philosophy is well captured in Wilfrid Sellars's perhaps slightly facetious definition of philosophy as "an attempt to see how things, in the broadest possible sense of the term, hang together, in the broadest possible sense of the term."[5]

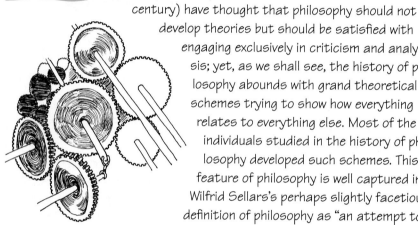

How Things Hang Together

So why are there so many *attempts* to define philosophy? Why not a straightforward, definitive statement made once and for all? After all, we can do that with words like "triangle." "A triangle is a three-sided closed figure." Anything that is a triangle has those features, and anything that has those features is a triangle. Anything that lacks them is not a triangle—*period!* The reason we can give an exhaustive definition of "triangle" but not "philosophy" is probably that the former is a closed concept, and the latter is an open concept. That is, we can state the conditions that are both **necessary** and **sufficient** for something to be a triangle, but such conditions probably do not exist for something being a piece of philosophy. Philosophy is not the only open concept. Some of the best are—such as "love" and "art." Let me illustrate. A few years ago I was in a museum of modern art on an uncrowded weekday morning. I wandered into a large room and saw that it had only a pile of gravel in the middle. At first I thought I had mistakenly trespassed into a room where construction was going on. I started to back out when I noticed that there was a small engraved card on a stand in front of the heap of rock. It contained the words "The Gravel Pile." There were some museum visitors strolling around the pile quietly contemplating this "work." Others were scoffing at it. The question has to come up—"Is this *art*?" Only the most arbitrary definition can decide that question for us.

Art has recently gone through a critical period of exuberance and self-doubt. The outer edges of the concept expand and contract and sometimes seem to break. This is perhaps as it should be (more on this in

The Gravel Pile

Chapter 10). But even if we are unsure about works on the periphery, that does not prevent us from recognizing cases at the center of the concept. We may have doubts about Robert Barry's **conceptual art** (his work: *All the things I know but of which I am not at the moment thinking*—1:36 P.M.; 15 June 1969, New York), but there can be no doubt about Vermeer's *Girl with Turban*.

The case is similar with philosophy. Most of the questions we will examine are at the center of the concept, but a few will be on the periphery. We will discover that we cannot state any one characteristic or any set of characteristics that must necessarily be present to guarantee that we are doing philosophy and that, when absent, guarantee that we are *not doing* philosophy. Rather, philosophical inquiries will have what Ludwig Wittgenstein (much more about him in Chapter 10) called "family resemblances" when he tried to show what an open concept was like. He wrote the following about the open concept "game":

> And we can go through the many, many other groups of games in the same way; can see how similarities crop up and disappear.
> And the result of this examination is: we see a complicated network of similarities overlapping and criss-crossing: sometimes overall similarities, sometimes similarities of detail.

I can think of no better expression to characterize these similarities than "family resemblances"; for the various resemblances between members of a family: build, features, colour of eyes, gait, temperament, etc. etc. overlap and criss-cross in the same way.—And I shall say "games" form a family.[6]

The idea of philosophy is probably like the idea of game. The various activities the word "philosophy" designates are not related to each other by virtue of possessing one set of common denominators; rather those activities have "family resemblances" to each other.

Family Resemblance

The Philosophy of Socrates

Let us make one last attempt to understand what philosophy is by trying something different. We will turn to ancient Greece once more and examine the activity of one of the earliest and most famous philosophers, Socrates, and hope thereby to gain some insight into the nature of philosophy itself.

SOCRATES (469–399 B.C.E.), who spent his entire life in Athens, did not give lectures or write treatises. Not only did he not write treatises, he was opposed to writing philosophy in any form because he thought that the letter kills the spirit. Philosophy for Socrates was a kind of social activity, a kind of discourse between two or more people who were looking for the truth. Therefore, his philosophizing took place in the streets of Athens and in its shops and parks where Socrates would engage anyone who was interested in conversation about "higher things." Socrates' wife, Xanthippe, sometimes found his habits annoying because she would send him on a simple errand, and he would remain for long stretches of time pursuing his philosophical interests. Sometimes he would return hours later without the item he'd been sent out for. According to one story, Socrates had been stumped by a question posed to him during one of these conversations, and he remained standing on the spot all night, chin in hand, thinking. According to another

Socrates (469–399 B.C.E.)

(probably **apocryphal**) story, an exasperated Xanthippe hid her husband's robe so he could not go out and philosophize with the boys. But Socrates slipped out nude, so his disciples began bringing along an extra robe in case Socrates arrived naked.

Fortunately, Socrates' brightest disciple, Plato, did not heed his master's advice concerning the written word. Plato wrote down everything he could remember Socrates having said. He transcribed Socrates' words in the same conversa-

Socrates Arriving for a Philosophy Discussion

tional style in which he had heard them, and the result is about twenty famous "Platonic dialogues." If it were not for these, and for the briefer and less philosophical writings of another contemporary, Xenophon, we would know very little of Socrates' teaching. As it is, students of Socrates have certain problems to deal with. How can we be sure that Plato is really giving us the thoughts of Socrates and not his own thoughts? After all, even though Plato's philosophy is an expansion of Socratic thought, we know that Plato developed his own philosophy far beyond Socrates' formulations. There is probably no ultimate solution to this problem, but as a rule of thumb we can say that the earlier the dialogue the more authentic the record and the later the dialogue the more likely that Plato is simply using the figure of Socrates as his own spokesman.

Each of the main Platonic dialogues emphasizes one philosophical theme—for example, the nature of truth, beauty, justice, virtue, courage, piety, friendship, or the art of governing. Scholars have demonstrated that the typical Platonic dialogue of the early period can be schematically divided into three segments.

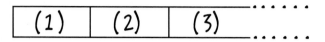

In the first segment, Socrates meets a young man who claims to know something about one of the aforementioned "big" topics. Socrates flatters the young man and compliments himself on his luck at having found someone who actually *knows* something that he, Socrates, has been seeking for fifty years—and a young man at that, usually eighteen, nineteen, or twenty years of age. Socrates begs the young man to impart his wisdom to him. When the young man does so, Socrates acts deeply impressed—sometimes awestruck. The young man's head begins to swell.

How wonderful that you know what virtue is—and to think, you're only 20 years old!

First Segment

What we can call the second segment of the dialogue begins when Socrates seems to notice some apparently minor problem with the formulation of the youth's argument. The young man thinks a simple cosmetic job can cover the blemish, but we readers know that Socrates' objection will become the small thread that, when pulled, unravels the garment. By the end of this second segment, the young man is confused and admits ignorance. In some of the dialogues, Socrates' cross-examination is quite gentle; in others, quite harsh. In one dialogue, the protagonist ends up in tears.

What we call the third and final segment of the dialogue begins when both Socrates and his partner have admitted ignorance. The young man

SOCRATES! What have you done to me?

Second Segment

Third Segment

does not know what "X" is (virtue, beauty, truth, etc.), and Socrates does not know either. At this point, Socrates will say to his despairing companion something like this: "Look, here we are, two ignorant men, yet two men who *desire* to know. I am willing to pursue the question seriously if you are willing." And in a certain sense, the real philosophizing begins at this point. It is as if, before any real philosophy can exist, the young man's earlier claim to knowledge had to be shown for what it was—an arrogant, blustering sort of defense mechanism whose function was to disguise the man's ignorance from himself and from others. This is the negative, destructive side of Socrates' method. Then the constructive side comes about in the third part of the dialogue, where Socrates and the young man try out numerous hypotheses meant to discover the truth. Yet in almost every case, the truth remains undiscovered. The Socratic dialogues end inconclusively. Why is this? Before we can answer, I will have to say more about "Socratic ignorance."

Socrates' irreverence offended a number of powerful men in Athens. They managed to have him arrested and tried for impiety, for teaching false doctrines, and for corrupting the youth. During his trial Socrates told the jury the story of his friend Chaerephon, who had gone to the temple of Apollo at Delphi to worship and had asked the god (through the oracle, the god's spokesperson) who was the wisest man in the world. The oracle answered that Socrates was the wisest. Socrates claimed to be absolutely

Socrates Lectures the Jury

perplexed by this response because he knew nothing, so how could he be the wisest man in the world? But eventually Socrates came to realize that in some sense, he was wiser than others. Others knew nothing but *thought* they knew something; Socrates knew nothing and *knew* that he knew nothing. Therefore, he knew more than others.

How seriously are we meant to take this story? It is obviously loaded with irony; Socrates is using it to inform his 501 jurors and his accusers that they were both wrong to charge him with teaching false doctrines (because he knows nothing, he teaches nothing) and wrong to believe that they were in a position to judge him (because as ignorant people, they were in a position to judge no one). And, indeed, Socrates' discourse is full of irony. It is clearly part of his method of philosophizing to communicate ironically, indirectly, using flattery, insult, humor, overstatement, understatement, misstatement, poetic allusion, and "old wives' tales" ("old husbands' tales"?). Professor Robert Paul Wolff, in his book *About Philosophy*, has a simple but ingenious analysis of "Socratic ignorance" that we will borrow.[7] Wolff says that we can think of the Socratic dialogue as having three audiences. The first is the most naive audience and is usually represented by the young man with whom Socrates discourses. When Socrates says, "I am ignorant," the young man takes this assertion literally and contrasts it with his own supposed state of wisdom. The second audience is more sophisticated and is represented either by characters who appear in the dialogue in some peripheral way or by the readers of the dialogue. This audience thinks, "He is *not* ignorant. His claim of ignorance is purely ironic." And in some sense, this second audience is surely right. Socrates obviously *does* know things and knows more than those to whom he professes ignorance. Yet a third audience exists, the

The Three Audiences

most sophisticated of all, represented, it is hoped, by the most sophisticated readers of the dialogue (namely you and me). This audience says, "He is ignorant." That is to say, in terms of the rigorous standards to which Socrates holds himself and others, he truly does not know. There is a *deep* sense of knowledge in which true knowers can give an exhaustive account of what they know and in which they understand how that knowledge relates to all other knowledge. Also, knowers have incorporated that knowledge into

TRUTH (trōōth): verity, conformity with fact. Honesty, integrity.

their lives in ways that have transformed them. In other words, for Socrates, the person who truly *knows* justice becomes just, the person who knows truth becomes truthful, and the person who knows beauty becomes beautiful. In certain kinds of knowledge, one understands how all things are linked, and, in this sense, when one knows anything, one knows everything. When one achieves this knowledge, one achieves human excellence—**aretê** in Greek— and one becomes an excellent human being. This is the knowledge Socrates has sought all his life, but it has always eluded him. And in this sense, Socrates does not know. He is *ignorant*. The irony thickens here because both the least sophisticated and most sophisticated audiences agree that Socrates is indeed ignorant but for very different reasons.

Now we can return to the question of why so many of the

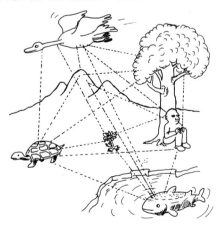

All Things Are Linked to All Things

Socratic dialogues end inconclusively. They must do so. If, at the end of the various dialogues, Plato had made Socrates finally define "X" (again, truth, justice, beauty, etc.), this result would have been completely misleading, for it would have implied that knowledge could be purely formal—that we could arrive at a dictionary-type definition and memorize it. Once we had memorized it, we could then say we *knew* it, even though this "knowledge" in no way affected our lives. For Socrates, formulaic definitions by themselves could not count as true knowledge.

"The Unexamined Life Is Not Worth Living"

Socrates went to his death still pleading ignorance, yet claiming at the same time that "the unexamined life is not worth living." At the end of his trial, he bade farewell to his accusers and the jury with these words: "The hour of departure has arrived, and we go our ways—I to die and you to live. Which is better God only knows." And when asked in his execution room what he would do in the afterlife, if indeed there was an afterlife, he said he would continue doing in death what he had done in life. He would ask the

Socrates Quizzing the Shades in Hades

shades in Hades if they had any knowledge. So is this not discouraging—that one of the greatest philosophers and deepest thinkers of all time went to his grave never achieving the knowledge he had spent his life seeking, a knowledge whose search is called "philosophy" and that we cannot even define? Is this not especially discouraging to introductory students on their first day?

Perhaps we will be a bit encouraged if we end the chapter with a famous passage from a philosopher who flourished twenty-five hundred years after Socrates, Lord BERTRAND RUSSELL (1872–1970):

> Philosophy is to be studied not for the sake of any definite answers to its questions, since no definite answers can, as a rule, be known to be true, but rather for the sake of the questions themselves; because these questions enlarge our conception of what is possible, enrich our intellectual imagination and diminish the dogmatic assurance which closes the mind against speculation; but above all because, through the greatness of the universe which philosophy contemplates, the mind is also rendered great, and becomes capable of that union with the universe which constitutes its highest good.[8]

Lord Russell (1872–1970)

Conclusion

Before winding up this chapter, let me remind you of something I said in the Introduction about objectivity. In the body of each chapter in this book I try to present the material in a fairly straightforward manner. Sure, my biases—conscious and unconscious—will have slipped in here and there, and I make some judgments about the philosophical ideas we study, but I have tried to achieve a balanced presentation. However, in the Conclusion to each chapter, I unabashedly give my own opinions. They may not be at all the conclusions you draw from the material you will have just read. If not, our disagreement will be an invitation to you to formulate your own positions clearly and to defend them with arguments. All right, now you've been warned (twice!). So let's continue.

Plato claimed that philosophy begins in wonder, and Aristotle, a student of Plato, commenced one of his books with this line: "All men by nature desire to know." According to this ancient Greek view, we are all philosophers by nature. We are *Homo philosophicus*. If that optimistic picture is true, then we have no need to justify an interest in philosophy. If someone sees you carrying your philosophy book and asks why you are studying philosophy, all you have to say is, "Because I am a human being."

And there is some truth to this ancient Greek view. One's soul would have to be very shriveled indeed never to have asked any of "the big questions." Most people do not become professional philosophers, of course. (And there is something odd about the notion of a "professional philosopher." From the Greek point of view, that would be something like becoming a professional human being. Socrates would have been horrified!) Nor do many of us spend most of our time philosophizing. Furthermore, some people are probably more naturally philosophical than others—such a thing as a philosophical temperament does exist. What provokes us to philosophize? Sometimes hormones. Sensitive adolescents spend much time agonizing over the meaning of Life, Death, Art (i.e., rock music), and Sociality; and many people seem to go through a classical midlife crisis in which the big issues are raised once again. But philosophical questioning doesn't have to be hormonal. Sometimes a most insignificant occurrence can

Sensitive Adolescent Agonizing over the Meaning of Life While His Father Goes through a Midlife Crisis

plunge us into a philosophical meditation, as can a dramatic or traumatic event such as the loss of a close relative, a friend, or a lover. These experiences make us feel that, at least momentarily, the center does not hold. But it is not only at moments like these that we philosophize. We will be philosophers all our lives, and I am partial to the Greek/Russellian view that philosophizing magnifies our humanity. I am guilty of holding the opinion that the person who never philosophizes is somehow less of a person.

So if one is necessarily going to philosophize, why not do it well? Why do we think that activities like eating, driving, and earning money should be done well but that thinking about the big questions can be done sloppily with impunity? Let's have a little *areté* here too. Therefore, I recommend that you give yourself over to the "professionals," if only for this semester. For many of you, this will be the only philosophy course you take in your lifetime. A bunch of philosophy courses is not everyone's cup of tea, and there are many pressures on one's college planning—even more reason to take this course seriously.

Philosophers and philosophical theories can be read like great novels. The great novelists (Cervantes, Flaubert, the Brontës, Dostoyevsky, Eliot, Proust, Joyce, Mann, etc.) hand you a pair of magical spectacles and invite you to look through them, saying something like "If you look at the world through these glasses, you will see things you have never seen before, and having once seen them, they will be yours to possess forever." So it is with really good philosophy. Philosophical concepts offer themselves as possible interpretations of the world. The world is very complex, and the more interpretations of it that make themselves available to us, the more free and more effective we will be in the world. Philosophical concepts are like tools. The bigger our repertoire of tools, the more effective our work.

In this vein, the twentieth-century Austrian philosopher Ludwig Wittgenstein made great use of a figure now usually referred to as

The Duck/Rabbit

"Wittgenstein's duck/rabbit." Is this a duck or a rabbit? Of course, it can be read either way. The question "What is it really?" does not apply here. The suggestion I am making is that the world is much more like Wittgenstein's figure than we first realize. Creative solutions to the problems with which life presents us require the ability to make multifarious interpretations of the world. Philosophy gives us some tools for just such creative interpretation. Often the world is much more varied than to allow even only two interpretations (duck or rabbit?). It is more like this figure, suggested by Virgil Aldrich, who says, "look at this figure under these five titles: (1) square suspended in a frame, (2) lampshade seen from above, (3) lampshade seen from below, (4) looking into a tunnel, and (5) aerial view of a truncated pyramid."[9]

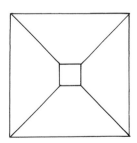

And if, after having inspected some of these philosophical tools, we choose never to use them as viable interpretations of the world, we still come away with an advantage, for they will have served as critical analyses of our ordinary beliefs. If we

conclude that our ordinary beliefs withstand philosophical scrutiny, so much the better. To paraphrase Aristotle (taking some liberties in doing so), in terms of getting you a job, philosophy may be the most useless of all studies, but it is nevertheless the best.

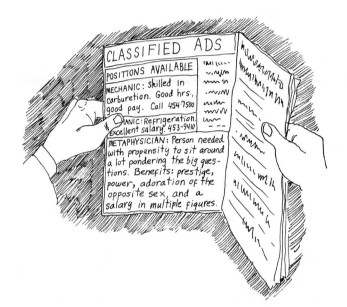

Topics for Consideration

1. In what way can the study of the origins of philosophy in the pre-Socratic thinkers illuminate the *nature* of philosophy?
2. Can you find any common denominators underlying the various theories of the pre-Socratic philosophers?
3. Defend one of these views:
   a. Philosophy and science as they are practiced in the West today are part of Logos and radically distinct from Mythos.
   b. Logos is just a kind of Mythos.
4. Defend one of these views:
   a. "Philosophy" can be defined.
   b. "Philosophy" cannot be defined.
5. If Socrates said he was ignorant but was in fact knowledgeable, was he simply a liar?
6. At this early stage of your philosophical career, would you say that any one of the branches of philosophy listed in this chapter (epistemology, ontology, logic, ethics, political and social philosophy, aesthetics) should have priority over others? Why?

Suggestions for Further Reading:
Paperback Editions

Donald Palmer, *Looking at Philosophy: The Unbearable Heaviness of Philosophy Made Lighter*, 3rd ed. (Mountain View, Calif.: Mayfield, 2001). A popularized overview of Western philosophy by a congenial guy. (Buy several copies. They make excellent gifts.)

Robert Pirsig, *Zen and the Art of Motorcycle Maintenance* (New York: Bantam Books, 1975). The modern odyssey of a motorcycle rider on a cross-country journey in pursuit of the answers to the questions posed by the ancient Greek philosophers. Particularly good about the Mythos/Logos question and the nature of *aretê*.

Plato, "Apology," in *Great Dialogues of Plato*, ed. Eric H. Warmington and Philip G. Rouse, trans. W. H. D. Rouse (New York: New American Library, 1956). Plato's account of Socrates' trial.

Merrill Ring, *Beginning with the Pre-Socratics* (Mountain View, Calif.: Mayfield Publishing Co., 1987). Contains extant fragments from the lost works of the earliest philosophers and a commentary filling in the gaps.

Bertrand Russell, *The Problems of Philosophy* (New York: Oxford University Press, 1975). Written in 1912, this insightful book by a brilliant philosopher is somewhat dated but well worth reading.

I. F. Stone, *The Trial of Socrates* (New York: Doubleday Anchor, 1989). A poor grasp of Socratic and Platonic philosophy is counterbalanced by excellent investigative skills and a passion for the defense of free speech by a foremost journalist who learned ancient Greek in his old age just so he could write this book.

Nancy Tuana, *Woman and the History of Philosophy* (New York: Paragon House, 1992). An impressive critique of those features of the history of Western philosophy that have demoted, demeaned, marginalized, or perpetuated the suppression of women.

Notes

1. All quotations of Heraclitus are taken from John Mansley Robinson, *An Introduction to Early Greek Philosophy* (Boston: Houghton Mifflin, 1968), pp. 89–93.

2. William H. Capitan, *Philosophy of Religion: An Introduction* (New York: Pegasus, 1972), p. 1.

3. Stuart Hampshire, *The Age of Reason* (New York: New American Library, 1961), p. 12.

4. Craig Channell, "The Advocacy Method: A Reply," *Teaching Philosophy*, Vol. I, No. 1 (Summer, 1975), p. 41.

5. Wilfrid Sellars, quoted in Richard Rorty, "The Fate of Philosophy," *New Republic* (Oct. 18, 1982), p. 28.

6. Ludwig Wittgenstein, *Philosophical Investigations* (New York: Macmillan, 1964), p. 32.

7. Robert Paul Wolff, *About Philosophy*, 4th ed. (Englewood Cliffs, N.J.: Prentice-Hall, 1989), p. 14.

8. Bertrand Russell, *The Problems of Philosophy* (New York: Oxford University Press, 1975), p. 161.

9. Virgil C. Aldrich, *Philosophy of Art* (Englewood Cliffs, N.J.: Prentice-Hall, 1963), p. 20.

2

Truth Is Beauty,
Beauty Is Truth
Rationalist Epistemology

Epistemology is theory of knowledge. These are the big questions in epistemology: What is knowledge? What is the difference between opinion and
knowledge? Does knowledge require certainty? What are the limits of knowledge? Is knowledge in fact possible? (This question is an epistemological version of the question Does the center hold?)

The word "knowledge" seems perhaps a bit highfalutin. Still, we are all
familiar with it, and we certainly use the verb "to know" many times throughout any day.

- Do you know what time it is?
- I used to know that word in French, but I've forgotten it.
- She knew all the material on the test.
- We didn't know he would arrive today.

In ordinary discourse, what do we mean by "know" when we make such
comments? I take it that when we say someone knows something, we mean
more or less that he or she could come up with a right answer on demand.
But, justifiably or unjustifiably, philosophers have not been satisfied with
this account of the meaning of "knowledge." In fact, this dissatisfaction
began early in the history of philosophy. We have already seen that in the
fifth century B.C.E., Socrates insisted on a more rigorous notion of knowledge than that provided by common sense. His demand came to fruition in
the epistemology of PLATO (427–347 B.C.E.). Plato will serve as an early
exemplar of what I am calling **rationalism** in this chapter.

40

The Philosophy of Plato

Plato's analysis of the concept of knowledge can be set forth in the following manner. Take the sentence "P knows X" (where "P" is any person and "X" is any fact). What must be the case before such a sentence could be true? First, it must be true that "P believes X." You can't claim that you know something if you also claim that you don't believe it. (I can think of only one kind of case to the contrary. If someone knocks on your door and you open it to discover a friend with whom you've been out of touch for fifteen years, you may exclaim, "Joe Smith, I don't believe it!" But, of course, you *do* believe it. Otherwise you would simply shut the door and go back to watching TV.)

Then *belief* is a necessary part of knowledge, but it is certainly not the *whole* of knowledge. (Just because I believe something strongly doesn't mean I know it, . . . not even if I believe it very, very strongly.) Then what more besides belief is needed? Truth is required. X must be the case. No one has ever known that the earth is flat for the simple reason that the earth is not flat. Even if thousands of people once claimed to know that the earth was flat, we know that all of them were wrong. (C. S. Lewis once suggested that, before

Believing Something Very, Very Strongly

Columbus, people did not think that the earth was flat—not because they thought it was round but because they didn't think about it at all.) So now we have this:

P knows X.

entails (a) P believes X,

and (b) X is the case.

Knowing That the Earth Is Flat

Here (a) and (b) are necessary parts of knowledge. But are they sufficient? That is, does true belief constitute knowledge? Plato denied it, more or less, for the following kind of reason. Suppose you ask me if I know that the earth is round, and I say I do. Do I believe that it is round? Yes. Is it round? Yes. (I am purposely ignoring here the fact that in truth the earth is slightly pear shaped—well, you would be pear shaped, too, if you were spinning at a thousand miles an hour.) So why doesn't this constitute knowledge? Suppose you ask me how I know that the earth is round, and I say, "Take a look at the bottom of your feet. Do you see how they are arched? Now I ask you, would God give us rounded feet if the earth were flat?" Suddenly you would realize that I didn't know at all that

Being Pear Shaped While Spinning at 1,000 Miles per Hour

the earth was round. I had just made a lucky guess!

So if true belief is not sufficient for knowledge, what would be?

P knows X.

(a) P believes X.

(b) X is true.

(c) P can give the Logos for X.

The Greek word "Logos" is the source of our word "logic" as well as the source of all those terms ending in "-logy" (biology, the theory or study of living things; sociology,

Proof That the World Is Round—Direct Method

the theory or study of society; and so on). So to give the Logos for X is to be able to give the theory, or the result of a study, that explains X. Logos also means "word" in Greek; one has to be able to say what that theory is. If someone told Plato or Socrates that she knew the answer to a question but just couldn't say it, Socrates and Plato would charge that precisely what was proved is that she did not know the answer.

For Plato, to give the Logos of X is to justify your belief in X; and, for him, knowledge is justified belief. This conclusion seems pretty sound, but the idea of justification is quite technical in Plato, as we have already seen. In fact, it is even more technical than the foregoing analysis revealed, as you will discover when we turn to Plato's famous Simile of the Line, which is the centerpiece of his most important work, the *Republic*. (It is called a simile because in it knowledge and reality are likened to a line that Socrates

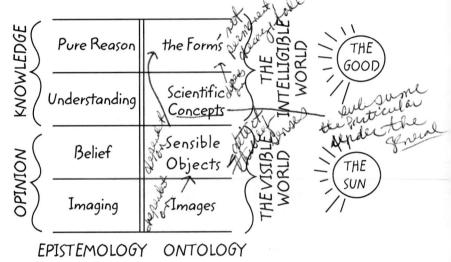

The Simile of the Line[1]

draws—presumably on the ground with a stick.) What we get here is Plato's whole metaphysical scheme. The right side of the line is his **ontology** (his theory of being). The left side is his **epistemology** (his theory of knowledge). There is also implicit here an **ethics** and an **aesthetics.** We will concentrate on the left side of the line because it corresponds with the topic of this chapter, but in order to do so, a few words must be said about the ontological side of the line as well.

The *visible world* (i.e., the physical world) can be thought of as representing Heraclitus's world of flux. It is composed of two strata: images and sensible objects. These two levels never remain the same from one moment to the next.

Images

Shadows and reflections are the examples Plato offers us of images. They are dependent on the sensible objects of which they are images. The shadow of a tree is for Plato *less real* than the tree both because the tree lasts longer than the shadow and because the tree can exist without the shadow, but the shadow can't exist without the tree. Now switch to the left side of the line. On this side, we have not *things* (like shadows or trees) but mental states—states of awareness. If the object of your state of awareness is an image, you are in a state of imagination. The implication in the *Republic* is that this state is one of deception. The person in this state confuses an image with a thing. (Have you ever been attracted to the *photo* of someone or yelled, "Go, Niners!" during a televised football game? No? It's never happened to me either—but then, *we* are philosophy students!)

Isolde Mistaking the Shadow of a Tree Trunk for Tristan

Sensible Objects

Sensible objects are the individual things in the physical world: trees, books, cats. They are more real than images, but they are not absolutely real both because they are not permanent (trees and cats grow old and die; books fall apart or are burned) and because they are dependent. They are dependent first of all on the sun. (If the sun were closer everything would burn up; if it were farther away, everything would freeze; if it did not exist, there would be no trees, books, or cats and no images of them either.) And as we will see shortly, sensible objects are also dependent on the Forms.

Back to the left side of the line. If the object of your

Trees and Cats Grow Old—Books Fall Apart (The Center Does Not Hold)

awareness is a sensible object, you are in a state of *belief*. Imagine seeing an animal in a field and asking a local farmer what the creature is. He says, "It's a horse." You ask him how he knows it's a horse, and he says (impatiently, no doubt), "It's a horse! Take a look. A horse is a horse!" OK. The farmer believes it's a horse (belief); it is a horse (truth); so why does Plato say that the farmer doesn't *know* it's a horse? Because the farmer hasn't given the Logos. What would that be like? Well, perhaps something like this: you ask the farmer:

Cats and Shadows Are Dependent on the Sun

How do you <u>know</u> it's a horse?

A horse is a domesticable quadruped with closed hoofs and 32 pairs of chromosomes; and <u>that</u> creature is such an entity. Ergo, it is a horse!

He knows!

Actually, it's a zebra.

This man *knows*. He was able to grasp the objects of individual perception at a higher level—the conceptual level. (There are lots of problems here, of course, including the problem of *elitism*. On this account, of all the millions of people who have dealt with horses, only a select few have actually known what one is—and Plato wasn't one of them! Furthermore, it's hard to see how you could know what a horse is without performing a biopsy and understanding biology and chemistry. Indeed, it's beginning to look as though one would have to know *everything* in order to know *anything*. Some interpreters believe that this dilemma is exactly what Plato had in mind. It would at least make sense of Socrates' claim to be ignorant.)

Concepts

So we've seen that one leaves belief for understanding (and thereby opinion for knowledge) by grasping the perception at the conceptual level, that is, by subsuming the particular under the general. In doing so one leaves behind Heraclitus's world of flux and enters into "the intelligible realm," a world of Parmenidean permanence. One elevates objects from the constantly changing physical world and stabilizes them by placing them in the context of Logos, of a theory or a science. Let's illustrate these levels. Imagine three different episodes: (1) Your pen rolls from the desk and falls to the floor; (2) a meteorite falls into the earth's atmosphere, splashing silver sparks into the night sky; (3) in the sixth round of a heavyweight boxing match, the champion receives a body-jolting uppercut on the chin and falls to the canvas like a load of bricks. In each of these cases, the imagery would be described very differently (this is the level of perception), but to understand the three events, we would need a theory, the very theory discovered by Sir Isaac Newton: given any two masses, these masses mutually attract each other in direct proportion to their mass and in indirect proportion to their distance. This is knowledge. But apparently for Plato it is not the highest kind of knowledge. There is still pure reason to be dealt with.

Gravity at Work

Forms

According to Plato, the concepts with which we have been dealing here (horse, gravity) are not mere abstractions from concrete cases. These concepts are images of higher truths, and he called these higher truths the **Forms.** These Forms are the archetypes of everything existing in the visible world. They exist outside time and space. They are not physical, but they aren't mental either. That is, they don't just exist as ideas in people's minds. Because they are not physical, they cannot be grasped by the senses; and even though they are not mental, they can be grasped only by the intellect, which has transcended the senses. These Forms are real in the sense that they are uncreated, indestructible, unchanging, and therefore eternal. Notice that they are not absolutely real because they are still dependent— upon something Plato calls "the Good"—dependent in the same way that sensible things are dependent upon the sun.

GOOD

TRUTH
BEAUTY   JUSTICE
VIRTUE
GENERAL NICENESS

The Heaven of Forms

The Good seems to be a kind of Super-Form, the Form of all Forms, which is an absolute value that grounds all reality and bestows worth on it, very much the way God would later do in the ontology of the medieval period. (Drop one letter, "o," from "Good" [= God], and change the "u" in "Sun" to "o" [= Son], and you have a crude version of medieval Christian Platonism.) It is the Good that is the center of the whole Platonic system. The center holds because the Good holds. It has a kind of Parmenidean permanence. If it did not hold we would be plunged into a world of Heraclitian flux.

Now how can the mind grasp the Forms? Only by *totally* transcending

Transcending the Five Senses

the senses, which are somehow committed to the world of Becoming, hence naturally hostile to the world of Being. Concepts, though definitely part of the intelligible sphere, are still image-bound and hence, somehow, still *contaminated*. (Notice the anti-body bias that enters into Western philosophy here with Plato. It is very uncharacteristic of the Greeks, whose social practices, art, and even religion showed no signs of disdain for the body.) Earlier, when you were presented with Newton's definition of gravity ("Given any two masses . . ."), you saw two masses in your mind's eye. However, the mind grasps the Form and not merely the concept when it frees itself from that visual imagery. This it does by

Hello, body. This is mind speaking. I hate you!

mathematizing its object. It is as if, for person P, the move from the definition ("Given any two masses . . . ") to the formula

$$\left(F = \frac{Gm_1m_2}{d^2} \right)$$

liberates the truth from the flux of the world, and to grasp the ultimate intelligible order of the universe is to grasp it purely formally, i.e., mathematically. If this interpretation of Plato is correct (and there certainly are other interpretations), then Plato believed that there existed not only a correct formula for Horse and Gravity, but for Love and Beauty as well.

Many of us today are prepared to grant the former, but we resist the latter. We point to the notorious relativity in the aesthetic taste of differ-

A Punk Beauty Arguing with a Ubangi Beauty about Beauty

ent individuals and cultures to refute Plato. (Parisians and Ubangis do not agree as to what beauty is.) But for Plato, if both the Parisian fashion model and the Ubangi princess are truly beautiful, a common denominator must exist. Perhaps it has to do with a mathematical account of "order" involving grace, balance, and "eros." Perhaps someday Beauty's Sir Isaac Newton will come along and finish this equation: "B = . . ."

Finally, concerning Plato, let's ask about the process of learning in his theory. The dialogue that deals with this process is the *Meno*. In it, Meno and Socrates have been discussing "virtue" and whether it can be taught. Socrates has forced Meno to admit that he doesn't know what virtue is, hence that he doesn't know whether it can be taught. (That is, Socrates has brought the dialogue to the end of the "second phase" referred to in Chapter 1.) Both Socrates and Meno admit that they are ignorant, and Socrates says that he is willing to pursue the issue seriously if Meno is willing. Here Meno states what has come to be called **Meno's paradox:**

MENO: And how will you try to find out something, Socrates, when you have no notion at all what it is? Will you lay out before us a thing you don't know, and then try to find it? Or, if at best you meet it by chance, how will you know this is that which you did not know?

SOCRATES: I understand what you wish to say, Meno. . . . as if a man cannot try to find either what he knows or what he does not know. Of course, he would never try to find what he knows because he knows it and in that case he needs no trying to find or what he does not know because he does not know what he will try to find.

MENO: Then don't you think that is a good argument, Socrates?

SOCRATES: Not I.[2]

In the dialogue, Socrates seems not to take Meno's paradox very seriously. This (false) impression is fortified by the fact that Socrates responds to Meno not with a philosophical argument but with a story he had heard from priests and poets:

They say that the soul of man is immortal, and sometimes it comes to an end—which they call death—and sometimes it is born again, but it is never destroyed; . . . Then, since the soul is immortal and often born, having seen what is on earth and what is in the house of Hades, and every-thing, there is nothing it has not learnt; so there is no wonder about virtue and other things, because it knew about these before.[3]

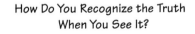

How Do You Recognize the Truth When You See It?

But the seriousness with which Socrates takes both Meno's paradox and the poetic rejoinder to it is seen in the episode that occurs immediately after in the dialogue. Meno and Socrates are strolling in a garden, and they come across the gardener, an untutored slave boy. Socrates asks the boy to solve a fairly complicated geometrical problem—that of doubling the square. The boy objects that he hasn't studied mathematics, but Socrates, undeterred, begins to ask him a series of questions: Should we solve the problem by using arcs or straight lines? (Try straight lines.) Should we put the straight lines inside or outside the square? (First outside, then, when that fails, inside.) After a long series of questions that the boy can answer with a "yes" or a "no," the boy eventually produces the correct answer—a diagram like this:

So, according to Socrates, the unschooled slave boy was able to answer a difficult mathematical question without being given any information he did not already possess. You and I may feel that Socrates' method in this case involved some intellectual sleight of hand. Plato's conclusion, though, is that the slave boy already knew the answer to the question, but he did not *know* that he knew it. The truth, according to Plato, existed in the slave boy's soul. It was a piece of unconscious knowledge, knowledge based on an **innate idea,** that is, an idea present at birth in the soul of the individual. On this account, all learning is truly remembering,

**The Slave Boy Knows More
Than He Knows That He Knows**

and it answers "Meno's paradox" (how will we recognize something we don't know?) by saying that in fact we do know what we don't know, and recognition is recollection. So, Plato, like Freud and Proust (author of the seven-volume novel, *Remembrance of Things Past*) takes the phenomenon of memory absolutely seriously and makes it a central feature of his theory of knowledge.

$$W\,A\,A\,A\,H$$
$$V = h\ cm^3$$
$$d = w/v$$
$$p = hd$$
$$KE = \tfrac{1}{2}\,mv^2$$
$$F = mrw^2$$

SLAP

Let's review some of the key features of Plato's epistemology. To know is to transcend the ever-changing flux of the physical world and to grasp a permanent rational order behind the flux, an order that will demonstrate the universal in the particular. This "grasping" is an intellectual act of the mind, which, in its purest manifestation, is exclusively formal (i.e., mathematical). Such an intellectual act can only take place if there are certain innate ideas upon which it can be based. Knowing, then, is an act of making the observable world intelligible by showing how it is related to an eternal order of intelligible truths. These features of Plato's epistemology are part of the program of rationalism, one of the two key epistemological poles in Western thought.

Platonic rationalism was immediately countered by Aristotelian empiricism (to be discussed in Chapter 3). Yet rationalism managed to dominate later Greek and Roman philosophy and all of the early Middle Ages, only to be countered once again by a revival of Aristotelianism in the work of St. Thomas Aquinas in the thirteenth century.

René Descartes's Rationalism

Rationalism may have achieved its fullest maturity in the seventeenth century in the work of RENÉ DESCARTES (1596–1650). We will inspect his version of rationalism before looking at rationalism's alternatives.

Theories of knowledge are never created in a vacuum. There are always psychological, economic, social, and political conditions behind them, acting as motives for them. In a certain sense each epistemology, rather than describing and accounting for

René Descartes (1596–1650)

some autonomous thing called "knowledge," perhaps actually creates and validates its own "knowledge," which is circumscribed and limited by the intellectual, economic, social, and political forces that motivated the epistemology in the first place. The external circumstances that motivated Plato were very different from those that motivated Descartes. Plato, a man of noble

Theories of Knowledge Are Never Created in a Vacuum

ancestry, lived at a time when the old aristocratic system of governing was collapsing in the face of the emergence of a new commercial class and an incipient democracy. In the two-hundred-year period before Plato's time, social and intellectual conditions had conspired to undermine the moral authority of the old aristocratic values, whose canon was the myths of Homer and Hesiod. As the old values of honor, loyalty, courage, and the natural right of the nobility to govern deteriorated, they were being replaced with what to Plato were plebeian values that thinly disguised greed and the thirst for power. These new values were taught in Socrates' and Plato's day by the professors of rhetoric known as "the Sophists," who, from the perspective of Socrates and Plato, seemed to celebrate perversely a world in which the center did not hold. In order to counteract the Sophists' corroding influence and to maintain some structure that justified rule by an

The Old Aristocratic Values Collapsing under the Onslaught of the New Rabble (Plato's View)

elite, Plato not only had to attack the Sophists, but he also had to oppose the authority of Homer and replace it with the authority of Pure Reason. The works of Homer had embodied the aristocratic values that Plato wished to support, but Homer had offered no defense of those values except an appeal to the emotions through his poetic discourse. If Plato was to defend values rationally, he had to replace the power of poetry (as manifested in Greek myth and drama) with that of philosophy, the spokeswoman for reason. The poetry/philosophy opposition is not the one that faced René Descartes in the seventeenth century; rather he was confronted by

The Contest between Philosophy and Poetry

the religion/science opposition. Descartes lived during a period that birthed new sciences. Copernicus had been dead only forty years when Descartes was born. Descartes was a contemporary of Galileo and Kepler. Newton was eight years old when Descartes died. In fact, Descartes himself had made a major contribution to the history of science while still in his twenties by discovering **analytic geometry.**

Now the ever-increasing power of the new science was beginning to challenge the waning authority of the Church, which had dominated for a thousand years but suffered several major setbacks in the two hundred years before Descartes's birth (a series of internal schisms, defeats at the hands of secular rulers, and the creation of the Protestant Reformation). The Church was fighting to retain not only what political power it still had but also its custody over the human *moral* self-image. It was in this sphere that the new sciences seemed to be most directly challenging religious authority, and the confrontation came to a head in 1632, when the Inquisition arrested Galileo, tried him, and found him guilty of impiety. The specific event that provoked Galileo's arrest was the publication of an essay reporting his discovery that there were four moons orbiting the planet Jupiter. Now, it may not be immediately obvious why the religious authorities would be threatened by such a claim. The traditional view of what was at stake in the Galileo affair is this:[4] For a thousand years, the concept of human dignity was closely bound to the idea that God had created the Garden of Eden in the very center of the universe and that the rest of the cosmos was formed as a series of concentric circles radiating out of Eden, the belly button of reality. This view meant that the human drama was the *key* drama in the cosmos and that every other being in the universe was simply placed here as a witness to the human drama. This concept had the effect of imbuing every human act with *meaning.* Even if one's life was filled with misery (and there was plenty of misery in the medieval world), at least that misery had significance; hence there was a certain dignity in even the most miserable human existence.

Ce ne sono quattro!

Now this heroic conception of human life was suddenly threatened by the Copernican theory that the earth was not the center of the universe—that in fact the earth and the other planets actually orbited the sun (that is, that the heliocentric and not the geocentric theory was correct). If the earth is just hurtling through space with no more and no less meaning than that of any other body in the universe, what would this finding mean for the concept of human dignity? (Freud once said that human dignity has suffered three mortal blows: first, Copernicus's discovery that the human is not at the center of the universe; second, Darwin's discovery that the human is an animal; and third, Freud's discovery that the ani-

mal is sick.) But there was one scientific fact that prevented the Coperni-can radicals from winning the day. It was the undisputed fact that the earth's moon orbits the earth. If the heliocentric theory were true, why would the moon orbit the earth? Why wouldn't it travel around the sun the same way the earth was supposed to do? Now you can see the significance of Galileo's discovery. If Jupiter's moons orbit Jupiter, that then proves moons can orbit planets that are not the center of the universe, and this proof kicked the last strut out from under the geocentric theory.

Somewhat like Galileo, Descartes found himself in an awkward situa-tion. He was a dedicated Catholic who did not look forward to a confronta-tion with the ecclesiastical authorities, yet he had just finished a manu-script on physics (*The World*), many sections of which he knew would agree with Galileo. So rather than publish his manuscript, he decided to write a book of philosophy that would create an intellectual climate of reconciliation between science and religion. He wanted to show that the idea of being a "religious scientist" was not self-contradictory. Indeed, he wanted to show that the possibility of science itself presupposed certain theological assumptions. He called this book *Meditations on First Philosophy* and dedi-cated it to "the Most Wise and Illustri-ous Men: The Dean and Doctors of the Sacred Faculty of Theology in Paris."

In his letter of dedication, Descartes fawned and groveled before the theologians at the Sorbonne, but to his friend, Father Mersenne, he wrote in a very different tone, "and I want to say, just between us, that these six *Meditations* contain all the fundamental ideas of my physics. But please keep this quiet, because if

they knew it, [the theologians] would be very reluctant to accept my views."[5]

In my own opinion, Descartes was successful in his undertaking. As far as I can determine, Catholicism never again had a head-on confrontation with science. Descartes had demonstrated that such a collision course was not necessary. It seems to me that today most religious opposition to scientific theories comes from certain Protestant camps (e.g., opposition to the teaching of Darwin's theory of evolution). Perhaps the Protestants are still waiting for their Descartes.

The Collision Course between Religion and Science

Well then, let us turn to Descartes's epistemology as he developed it in the *Meditations*. In the first paragraph of that book, Descartes announces his grandiose proposal: "I must once for all seriously undertake to rid myself of all the opinions which I had formerly accepted and commence to build anew from the foundation, if I wanted to establish any firm and permanent structure in the sciences" (p. 165).

Notice a key metaphor in this passage, one taken from carpentry. Knowledge is seen as a building in which all the superstructure is resting on a foundation, and the building is only as strong as the foundation. (You will observe as you proceed that philosophers often develop their ideas around a key metaphor. For instance, think of the role played in Plato's thought by the notions of sunlight and shadows.) Descartes continues:

> I shall at last seriously
> and freely address
> myself to the general
> upheaval of all my
> former opinions.

Now for this object it is not necessary that I should show that all of these are false—I shall perhaps never arrive at this end. But inasmuch as reason already persuades me that I ought no less carefully to withhold my assent from matters which are not entirely certain and indubitable than from those which appear to me manifestly to be false, if I am able to find in each one some reason to doubt, this will suffice to justify my rejecting the whole.[6]

Here we see Descartes's technique, which has come to be known as **methodological doubt.** It has a motto, *De omnibus dubitandum est* (Everything is to be doubted), and it requires Descartes to doubt any **proposition** whatsoever if he can find the slightest reason to do so. Notice that, unlike courts of law, methodological doubt does not require that the doubt be reasonable; rather, any possible doubt will be sufficient to put a proposition out of commission. And the point of all this doubting is to attempt to find something that cannot be doubted, something indubitable, absolutely certain. That absolute certainty, if it exists, will be the foundation of the house of knowledge.

> I shall proceed by setting aside all that in which the least doubt could be supposed to exist, just as if I had discovered that it was absolutely false; and I shall ever follow in this road until I have met with something which is certain, or at least, if I can do nothing else, until I have learned for certain that there is nothing in the world that is certain. (p. 170)

Descartes's rule, "Everything is to be doubted," is not recommended by him as a way of life. It is part of a philosophical game, but a *serious* game. The point of the game is to discover the foundation of knowledge, if there is such a thing to be discovered. And if there is no foundation to discover, then the game will be abandoned, and one will return to real life. But one will return with much more cynicism than one had before the game because one will "know" that there is no such thing as knowledge; only opinions, hearsay, prejudices, and passions exist. The "house of knowledge" is built on shifting sands. Descartes's method is his way of seeking a definitive answer to the question, Does the center hold?

Let us return to the project of the *Meditations*. Descartes continues:

> All that up to the present time I have accepted as most true and certain I have learned either from the senses or through the senses; but it is sometimes proved to me that these senses are deceptive, and it is wiser not to trust entirely to anything by which we have once been deceived. (p. 166)

Here we see that Descartes's dismantling of the rotten timbers from the house of knowledge is done more with a bulldozer than a crowbar. Because the senses are known deceivers, they will be doubted away, which means that all beliefs based on the senses (and that is *most* of them, after all) will be jettisoned. But suddenly Descartes himself suspects that perhaps his house bashing is moving too fast. He says:

> But it may be that although the senses sometimes deceive us concerning things which are hardly perceptible, or very far away, there are yet many others to be met with as to which we cannot reasonably have any doubt, although we recognize them by their means. For example, there is the fact that I am here, seated by the fire, attired in a dressing gown, having this paper in my hands and other similar matters. And how should I deny that these hands and this body are mine, were it not perhaps that I compare myself to certain persons, devoid of sense, whose cerebella are so troubled and clouded by the violent vapours of black bile, that they constantly assure us that they think they are kings when they are really quite poor, or that they are clothed in purple when they are really without covering, or who imagine that they have an earthenware head or are nothing but pumpkins or are made of glass. But they are mad, and I should not be any less insane were I to follow examples so extravagant. (p. 166)

**René Descartes—
Heavy Equipment Operator**

So there is René Descartes, sitting in his PJs alone at his desk in front of his fireplace. (Quite a different stage from that of old Socrates, who philosophized in the streets of Athens, seeing philosophy as essentially a social activity! It is clear that the notion of thinking has undergone a dramatic change since the Greek period.) Descartes stares at his hand and thinks, "This is my hand." How could he possibly be wrong? Only a madman could stare at his hand and wonder if it is his hand. If, after leaving your classroom, you see someone sitting on the campus lawn staring at his hand, and the person says to you, "I'm not sure this is my hand," you won't say to yourself, "A philosopher!" Rather, you'll say, "A lunatic!" Descartes knows this perfectly well, yet, following the strictures of **radical doubt,** he does indeed question whether what he is looking at is his hand. (By the way, did you notice Descartes's marvelous baroque description of madness? "... cerebella ... troubled and clouded by the violent vapours of black bile ...") Descartes continues:

> At the same time I must remember that . . . I am in the habit of sleeping, and in my dreams representing to myself the same things or sometimes even less probable things than do those who are insane in their waking moments. How often has it happened to me that in the night I dreamt that I found myself in this particular place, that I was dressed and seated near the fire, whilst in reality I was lying undressed in bed! . . . I remind myself that on many occasions I have in sleep been deceived by similar illusions, and in dwelling carefully on this reflection I see so manifestly that there are no certain indications by which we may clearly distinguish wakefulness from sleep that I am lost in astonishment. (pp. 166–167)

Do you get Descartes's point? Can you refute him? Can you *think of a test that will prove you are not dreaming now?* Obviously, pinching yourself (as they do in the comics) won't work because it is quite possible to dream that you are pinching yourself. For the same reason, you can't just ask your neighbor "Am I dreaming?" It is possible to dream whatever answer she gives. In fact, it seems that Descartes has us over a barrel because the only way to refute

Philosophy Student Dreaming about Dreams

him would be to think of a test that can't be dreamed. But any test you can *think* of, you can *dream.* (A student of mine once suggested that one can't dream that one is dead. This may be true, but I think that killing yourself to refute Descartes would be a rather extreme measure. And, of course, even such a philosophical martyrdom would fail because you would never know whether it had worked.)

Take this, René Descartes!

Descartes's conclusion is not that one should keep wondering whether one is dreaming, but that there is no philosophical proof that at any given moment one is not

Philosophical Martyrdom

dreaming. Therefore the senses and the commonsense picture of the world based on the senses cannot be the foundation of knowledge.

Let's start diagramming some of this:

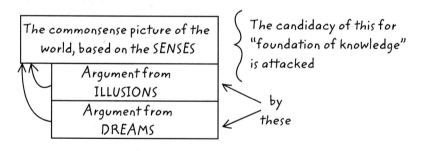

The commonsense picture of the world, based on the SENSES

Argument from ILLUSIONS

Argument from DREAMS

The candidacy of this for "foundation of knowledge" is attacked

by these

Can there be another candidate for some kind of certain knowledge? What about mathematics? Descartes says, "For whether I am awake or asleep, two and three together always form five, and the square can never have more than four sides, and it does not seem possible that truths so clear and apparent can be suspected of any falsity or uncertainty" (p. 168). Descartes's point here as he states it seems wrong. If I can make a mathematical error when I'm awake, I can jolly well make one when I'm dreaming!

But the real point Descartes is trying to make here is worth pausing over. It requires learning two technical philosophical terms that are of some value, **a priori** and **a posteriori.** An a priori claim is a claim whose truth or

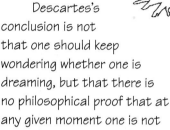

rationalist

falsity can be known independently of observation. An a posteriori claim is one whose truth or falsity can be known only by appealing to observation. Now Descartes's point can be put this way: the "argument from illusion" and the "argument from dreams" can attack only a posteriori claims. But mathematics is a priori; hence it should escape both of these skeptical arguments. One does not prove that 2 + 3 = 5 by taking a field trip or doing an experiment. Putting three pieces of chalk next to two pieces of chalk and counting them is no proof that 2 + 3 = 5, any more than finding five white swans is proof that all swans are white. (The way you prove that 2 + 3 = 5 is by demonstrating that that proposition is a version of the proposition A = A and then demonstrating that any denial that A = A leads to a self-contradiction. This kind of proof is not an act of perception but is what Plato would call an act of "pure reason.")

Mathematical Experiment

So what Descartes is asking is whether the a priori truths of mathematics might not serve as the absolutely certain foundations of knowledge. Descartes was a mathematician, after all, so he would no doubt have loved to answer that question affirmatively, but the rigors of methodological doubt forced him to answer in the negative, as we will see:

> Nevertheless I have long had fixed in my mind the belief that an all-powerful God existed by whom I have been created such as I am. But how do I know that He has not brought it to pass that there is no earth, no heaven, no extended body, no magnitude, no place, and that nevertheless I possess the perceptions of all these things and that they seem to me to exist just

exactly as I now see them? And besides, as I sometimes imagine that others deceive themselves in the things which they think they know best, how do I know that I am not deceived every time that I add two and three, or count the sides of a square or judge of things yet simpler, if anything simpler can be imagined? (p. 168)

This text is the introduction to one of the most curious chapters in the history of philosophy: Descartes's "evil genius" hypothesis. Descartes asks himself, How do I know that the universe was not created by a malevolent demon whose only goal is to deceive so that even when I make the most basic mathematical judgments, such as that $2 + 3 = 5$, I err; yet I never know that I am erring? Much to Descartes's chagrin, he realizes that he *cannot* disprove the existence of such a "god" (as Descartes calls it at one point). Therefore, even if it is not very likely that such a demon exists, its existence is **logically possible,** and from this it follows that mathematics is not absolutely certain. (Imagine a math teacher who tells her students "Two plus three is five, . . . unless there is an evil genius, in which case two plus three may not be five." If one has to add that qualification to math, then math is not unqualifiably true, and it cannot be the foundation of knowledge.)

Descartes and the Evil Genius

Rationalist Epistemology

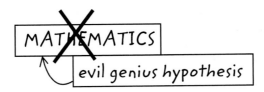

So, Descartes is stuck in the following state (which would surely be taken as the paradigm case of paranoia if methodological doubt were confused with real doubt):

> I shall then suppose, not that God who is supremely good and the fountain of truth, but some evil genius not less powerful than deceitful, has employed his whole energies in deceiving me; I shall consider that the heavens, the earth, colours, figures, sound, and all other external things are nought but the illusions and dreams of which this genius has availed himself in order to lay traps for my credulity; I shall consider myself as having no hands, no eyes, no flesh, no blood, nor any senses, yet falsely believing myself to possess all these things. (pp. 169–170)

This text is one of the most dramatic descriptions in philosophy of the prospect of the center *not* holding. As you see, at this point in Descartes's tale (a perfect overlapping of Mythos and Logos), he cannot prove that the center holds, but he does not give up in despair. He looks for a foothold that will allow him to climb out of the abyss into which he has fallen.

Well, then, is there a truth so certain that it can be known indubitably even if the senses deceive Descartes, even if he is dreaming, and even if there is an evil genius?

> I myself, am I not at least something? But I already denied that I had senses and body. Yet I hesitate, for what follows from that? Am I so dependent on body and senses that I cannot exist without these? But I was persuaded that there was nothing in all the world, that there was no heaven, no earth, that there were no minds, nor any bodies: was I not then likewise persuaded that I did not exist? Not at all; . . . without doubt I exist also if [the evil genius] deceives me, and let him deceive me as much as he will, he can never cause me to be nothing so long as I think that I am something. So that after having reflected well and carefully examined all things, we must come to the definite conclusion that this proposition: I am, I exist, is necessarily true each time that I pronounce it, or that I mentally conceive it. (p. 171)

This, then, is the absolutely certain foundation of all knowledge. In the *Meditations*, the version is "I am." In another work, the *Discourse on Method*, it is "I think, therefore I am" (*Cogito ergo sum*). This truth is certain under any possible conditions. Every time I make the assertion "I am," I am *right*. Not even an evil genius or madness can falsify this finding.

Now the nature of this "foundation" must be clarified.

is a thinking thing (ego sum)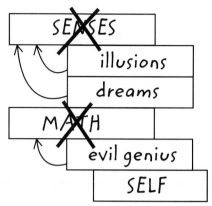

I am, I exist, that is certain. But how often? Just when I think; for it might possibly be the case if I ceased entirely to think, that I should likewise cease altogether to exist. I do not now admit anything which is not necessarily true: to speak accurately I am not more than a thing which thinks, that is to say a mind or a soul, or an understanding, or a reason, . . . I am, however, a real thing and really exist; but what thing? I have answered: a thing which thinks. (p. 173)

So selfhood's essence of which Descartes is so certain is thought or consciousness (which, as you see, Descartes conveniently equates with "soul." Perhaps his hidden religious agenda is sticking out a bit here). *thinking agenda*

This discussion is the beginning of Descartes's notorious mind-body dualism. The self is defined as mind or soul (a "thing which thinks"), and the body is not an essential part of the self. In order to see Descartes's argument that leads to this strange conclusion (strange because most of us have always assumed that our bodies are rather essential aspects of our selves and not baggage we take along with us when we go out), take a look at a couple of sentences:

1. "*I doubt that I have a body.*" Now this is an *odd* doubt, and if you ever heard anyone express it, you would think that person to *be* odd (either odd or a philosopher!). But it is *only* odd. It is not an impossible doubt. So Descartes's method requires this doubt.

2. "*I doubt that I have a mind.*" This is not only an odd doubt; it is an impossible doubt. To *doubt* that one has a mind is to *establish* that one has a mind because doubting is an activity of the mind. To Descartes, this proves that there is a *necessary* relation between self and mind—

I DOUBT THAT I HAVE A MIND.

and only a **contingent** (i.e., nonnecessary) relation between self and body.

I DOUBT THAT I HAVE A BODY.

This argument is a difficult one to evaluate, but let's let it slip by just to see what Descartes does with it. "But what then am I? A thing which thinks. What is a thing which thinks? It is a thing which doubts, understands, conceives, affirms, denies, wills, refuses, which also images and feels" (p. 174). Here Descartes is defining the mind in terms of its capacity to perform certain mental acts: to doubt, to understand, and so forth. To say that anything has a mind is to say that that thing can perform these acts. For Descartes, this conclusion seems to be a "package deal." If you

I doubt that I have a body.

Well, it's not a very good body...

can do any one of these, you can do them all. If there is any one of them you can't do, then you can't do any of them. It was for this reason that Descartes concluded that animals do not have minds. Dogs do not affirm or deny anything, so (appearances to the contrary notwithstanding) they must not will anything either. (Perhaps there is a religious motive here as well. To admit that dogs have minds is to admit that they have

I did not steal your chocolate-covered donut!

souls. Now do we really want dogs barking in heaven? Isn't it enough that they keep us awake and befoul our lawns here on earth?)

There is another feature of the mind that Descartes wanted to reveal. It comes out in the famous "wax example."

YAP YAP BOW WOW AROOOOO ARF ARF

Divine Barking

Let us begin by considering the commonest of matters, those which we believe to be the most distinctly comprehended, to wit, the bodies which we touch and see; . . . Let us take, for example, this piece of wax: it has been taken quite freshly from the hive, and it has not yet lost the sweetness of the honey which it contains; it still retains somewhat of the odour of the flowers from which it has been culled; its colour, its figure, its size are apparent; it is hard, cold, easily handled, and if you strike it with the finger, it will emit a sound. Finally all the things which are requisite to cause us distinctly to recognize a body, are met within it. But notice that while I speak and approach the fire what remains of the taste is exhaled, the smell evaporates, the colour alters, the figure is destroyed, the size increases, it becomes liquid, it heats. Scarcely can one handle it, and when one strikes it, no sound is emitted. Does the same wax remain after this change? We must confess that it remains; none would judge otherwise. What then did I know so distinctly in this piece of wax? It could certainly be nothing of all that the senses brought to my notice since all these things which fall under taste, smell, sight, touch, and hearing are found to be changed, and yet the same wax remains.

. . . We must then grant that I could not even understand through the imagination what this piece of wax is and that it is my mind alone which perceives it. (pp. 175–176)

René Descartes Inspecting His Hands, Which Suddenly Seem to Be Covered with Melted Wax

This example constitutes another attack on the claim that the senses are the source of real knowledge (the view called **empiricism,** which will be inspected in the next chapter), and Descartes has selected a brilliant example indeed. He goes through the five senses, cataloguing the information about the wax that the senses provide. Then, when he holds the wax to the fire, *every one* of those characteristics changes. Yet we know, he says, that it is the same wax. How can we know this if the senses tell us the opposite? Where do we get the concept of "sameness"? Clearly not from the senses because their data are in constant flux (like Plato's "Becoming"). Descartes's answer is very Platonic. According to him, the concept of "sameness," i.e., the concept of identity, must be an innate idea because it cannot be derived from observation. We are all born with the (apparently unconscious) knowledge of the "principle of identity," "A = A." This absolutely necessary and a priori truth is presupposed by any other knowledge whatsoever. If we did not know this truth, we could not know any truth.

The wax example also generates the innate idea of **substance** (i.e., of substantiality, of "thingness") and particularly of material substance (i.e., the idea of a physical body). According to Descartes, this idea cannot be derived from the senses alone. In order to understand Descartes's point, consider it this way. Imagine that we build a computerized robot. We install five sensors in it, one for tactile data, one for visual data, one for olfactory data, another for tastes, and one for sounds; and we teach it a language to name the data of all the sensors. Then we program it to record all the sensory data it receives, and we send it out into the world. Now the robot will send back reports like those in the illustration. What the robot could *not* say is "There is a blue pen on the table," and that's because it would be lacking the two key concepts, "identity" and "thingness." If we pre-programmed these concepts into our robot, they would organize the sensorial data into a coherent picture of the world.

Blue, cylindrical, hard, cold, here now.

So far, then, much of what we've discussed here is reminiscent of Plato, but Descartes's theory has the advantage of keeping the number of innate ideas down to a manageable handful. (Up to this point, we have only "self," "identity," and "substance.") For Plato, there seemed to be as many innate ideas as there were words, and that view is a bit implausible. But remember, in Descartes's system, before any innate idea can be accepted as true, it will have to be established that it was not placed there by the evil genius.

Now we are going to proceed with the construction of Descartes's house of knowledge, but we are going to speed things up quite a bit. One reason we are going to do so is that this chapter is about the rationalistic conception of knowledge, and we have already discovered its essence in our discussion of Plato's Simile of the Line and of Descartes's quest for the foundation of knowledge. The other reason is that it is generally thought that Descartes's upward building is not as tight as his argument leading down to his foundation.

So Descartes knows that he is still operating in the shadow of an evil genius and that before he can progress, he must dispose of the demon. There is only one way to do this, according to Descartes, and that is by proving the existence of God, because the concept of God as an all-powerful, all-knowing, all-good creator of the universe is logically incompatible with the concept of an evil genius. Either *one* of them could exist but not both. So if Descartes can prove God's existence, he will have disproved the existence of an evil genius.

Descartes's proof will have to be strictly a priori because no observation can be trusted. It will have to be absolutely certain and rest firmly on the foundation of the "cogito." Perhaps the simplest version of Descartes's first argument (he has a number of them) is this:

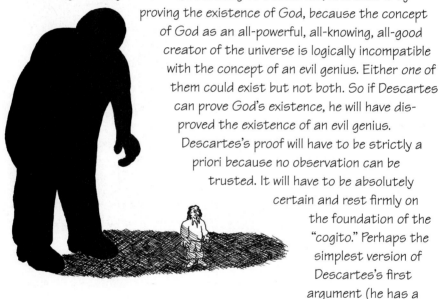

Operating in the Shadow of the Evil Genius

[R]eflecting on the fact that I doubted, and that consequently my existence was not quite perfect (for I saw clearly that it was a greater perfection to know than to doubt), I resolved to inquire whence I had learnt to think of anything more perfect than I myself was; and I recognized very clearly that this conception must proceed from some nature which was really more perfect. . . . [B]ecause it is no less contradictory to say of the more perfect that it is what results from and depends on the less perfect, than to say that there is something which proceeds from nothing, it was equally impossible that I should hold [the idea of a perfect Being] from myself. In this way it could but follow that it had been placed in me by a nature which was really more perfect than mine could be, and which even had within itself all the perfections of which I could form any idea—that is to say, to put it in a word, which was God. (pp. 128–129)

Let's formalize this argument:

1. A being that doubts is an imperfect being (because a perfect being would have full knowledge, hence no room for doubt).
2. I doubt; therefore I am an imperfect being.
3. Yet I could know that I am imperfect only by having the concept of perfection; therefore I do have the concept of perfection.
4. I could not have received the concept of perfection from something imperfect; therefore my concept was not derived from myself.
5. Therefore my concept of perfection was derived from something that is in fact perfect.
6. Only God is in fact perfect, so I derived my concept of perfection from him, and therefore he exists.

Do you find this argument convincing? (If not, perhaps you would be more convinced by Descartes's second argument, to be discussed in Chapter 5. You may want to jump ahead and look at it.) Here Descartes's "proof" will not be criticized. We will let it stand to see what Descartes does with it.

Variation on a Cartesian Theme

If Descartes has really proved the existence of God, then he has, by his reckoning, eliminated the evil genius. If he has eliminated the evil genius, then mathematics is valid (because the only argument against math was derived from the possibility of an evil genius). Also Descartes now knows that his innate ideas were not placed in him by an evil genius so they may be true as well. Still, at this point, Descartes remains in a nearly **solipsistic** universe. That is, with the exception of his knowledge of God, Descartes does not know if anything other than his own mind exists. He does not even know if he has a body. So his next task will be to determine whether an external world exists, and his final epistemological task will be to determine what knowledge we can have of such a world.

How do I know that other people exist? How do I know I have a body? How do I know I didn't make all this up?

Descartes in His Solipsistic Universe

First, Descartes notes that we have two sources for our idea of material objects. One source is a mathematical idea (i.e., one involving measurable objects). This idea is of something extended in three dimensions, having size, shape, part, and location. These are the objects of geometry. The other source, coming from the senses rather than from the innate ideas of corporeality and math in which geometry is grounded, is perhaps a naive idea of a world populated by physical things such as tables, rocks, and trees (and one's own body). But even if this idea is naive (i.e., not philosophically sophisticated), it is nevertheless compelling. It can be doubted "methodologically" but not *really*. Now, *could* I be wrong about these ideas? In spite of the compelling nature of my idea of the existence of an external world, is it possible that there is in fact nothing "out there"? No! Because God

The Idea That One Has a Body Is a *Compelling* Idea

. . . has given me no faculty to recognize that this is the case, but on the other hand, a very great inclination to believe . . . that [my ideas of the corporeal world] are conveyed to me by corporeal objects, [so] I do not see how He could be defended from the accusation of deceit if these ideas were produced by causes other than corporeal objects. Hence we must allow that corporeal things exist. (p. 215)

So we know there is a physical world because if there is not, God is a deceiver, which is impossible. We can now complete the diagram we started on page 60 and continued on pages 63 and 64, and say that Descartes's finished system looks like this:

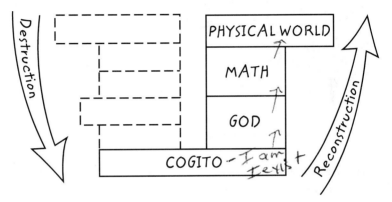

But what is the nature of these corporeal objects that make up the physical world? According to Descartes:

. . . Corporeal things exist. However, they are perhaps not exactly what we perceive by the senses since this comprehension by the senses is in many instances very obscure and confused, but we must at least admit that all things which I conceive in them clearly and distinctly, that is to say, all things which, speaking generally, are comprehended in the object of pure mathematics, are truly to be recognized as in the objects.

As to other things, however, . . . for example, [the fact] that the sun is of such and such a figure, etc., or . . . [perceptions of] light, sound, pain and the like, . . . they are very dubious and uncertain . . . and . . . it may easily happen that these judgments contain some error. Take, for example, the opinion . . . that in a body which is warm there is something entirely similar to the idea of heat which is in me; that in a white or green body there is the same whiteness or greenness that I perceive; that in a bitter or sweet body there is the same taste, and so on in other instances; that the stars, the towers, and all other distant bodies are of the same figure and size as they appear from far off to our eyes, etc. (pp. 215–217)

The upshot of Descartes's conclusion is the following: the physical world that we know as philosopher-scientists is not the world of appearance, the world presented to us by the senses. It is the world as known by mathematical physics. It is, after all, the world as revealed to us by the new sciences—the world of Galileo. The senses continue to be permanent deceivers. They tell us that bodies contain colors, sounds, odors, tastes, and sensations of heat and cold. But in fact what exists "out there" is whatever math can measure: extension, size, shape, part, location, and moveability—mass in motion, conglomerations of atoms, light waves, and sound waves, but no colors, sounds, and tastes. These exist only in our sensations as subjective states and not as objective reality.

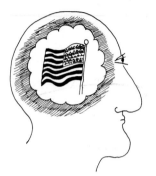

**The Flag's Colors
Exist in Here**

**The Flag's Molecular Structure
Exists out Here**

So the world we lost is *not* the world we regained. But at least there is certain knowledge, and the world has been made manageable again. The center, which seemed to wobble, now holds.

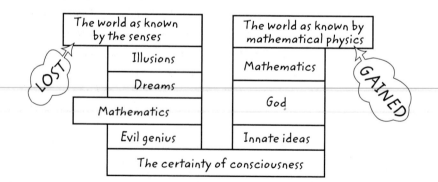

We will speak more about the nature of the Cartesian world in Chapter 4. Here we will take note only of Descartes's success in creating a philosophical-theological compromise. We get both Galileo and God in this system. Not only are Galileo's world and God both *knowable*, but both are also *necessary*. In fact, science rests on a godly foundation. However, the soul (i.e., the self) is not the subject of science because science can know

The Compatibility of God and Galileo

only that which can be measured, and the soul cannot be measured. But it can be known immediately to itself. In truth, the self knows itself before it knows the world. So Descartes leaves our souls to ourselves (perhaps to be shepherded by the Church), and he leaves the physical world (Jupiter's moons included) to the scientists.

Despite their historical differences, the epistemologies of Plato and Descartes are similar. Both repudiate the senses as sources of true knowledge. Both find that there is an intelligible order behind the flux of appearance (the center does hold). Both conclude that true knowledge must be a priori. Both use mathematics as their model of knowledge. Both derive knowledge of the world from knowledge of a higher reality (the Good for Plato, God for Descartes). Both find the source of all knowledge in innate ideas located in the soul. These points sum up the epistemological program of rationalism.

I will defer trying to draw my own conclusions about rationalist epistemology at this point and wait until the end of Chapter 3, when we have viewed rationalism's traditional alternative, empiricism. We will turn to that theory in the next chapter.

Topics for Consideration

1. Pick a general idea (like "gravity" or "justice") and show how it should be analyzed according to Plato's Simile of the Line.

2. Explain Socrates' claim of ignorance (treated in Chapter 1) in terms of Plato's Simile of the Line. If Plato's account of knowledge is right, then are we all ignorant?

3. Write a short story in which a young student discovers that Plato was right—discovers that behind the world of apparent change and flux there is an unchanging world of eternal sameness.

4. State at least three reasons why Descartes thinks that the senses cannot provide certain knowledge. Then compare Descartes's attitude toward the senses with Plato's.

5. Descartes asks, "Am I so dependent on body and senses that I cannot exist without them?" Contrast the answer Descartes gives to his question with the answers given by common sense and science.

6. State as clearly as you can what you take to be Descartes's argument proving that there must be "innate ideas."

7. Some of Descartes's critics have argued that if you start with Descartes's foundation (you are certain only of the contents of your own consciousness) you will never escape from solipsism (the view that there can never be knowledge of anything but one's own mind). Show what those critics might mean by this argument.

8. Write an essay called "Descartes's Flirtation with Madness."

Suggestions for Further Reading: Paperback Editions

Christopher Biffle, *A Guided Tour of René Descartes's "Meditations on First Philosophy,"* 3rd ed., trans. Ronald Rubin (Mountain View, Calif.: Mayfield, 2001). Descartes's own account of the ideas you've read about here, made accessible by an up-to-date translation and by Biffle's marginal notes and questions.

Susan R. Bordo, *The Flight into Objectivity: Essays on Cartesianism and Culture* (Albany: State University of New York Press, 1987). An exciting feminist critique of Descartes's philosophy and the worldview it supports.

Plato, "Meno," in *Great Dialogues of Plato,* ed. Eric H. Warmington and Philip G. Rouse, trans. W. H. D. Rouse (New York: New American Library, 1956). Plato's discussion of knowledge as recovered memory and an excellent example of a Socratic dialogue.

Plato, *Republic,* in *Great Dialogues of Plato.* Books VI and VII contain Plato's account of the Simile of the Line. Difficult reading but manageable after you've come as far as you have now come.

The Rationalists: Descartes, Spinoza, Leibniz, trans. J. Veitch, R. Elwes, G. Montgomery (New York: Doubleday, 1974). The basic works of these philosophers in an inexpensive volume.

Bernard Williams, *Descartes: The Project of Pure Enquiry* (Middlesex, England: Pelican Books, 1978). An insightful analysis by an important contemporary philosopher.

Notes

1. There has been much scholarly debate concerning the best English translation of the Greek terms Plato uses in the Simile of the Line. Here is a transcription of the Greek words in question:

    (1) *noesis*   (2) *eide*

    (3) *dianoia*   (4) *hypothemenoi and ta mathematica*

    (5) *pistis*   (6) *ta horomeva*

    (7) *eikasia*   (8) *eikones*

    In designating (1) *noesis* as "reason" and (3) *dianoia* as "understanding," I am following the translations of both W. H. D. Rouse and Leo Rauch. But it should be mentioned that *noesis* has also been rendered as "understanding" (by G. M. A. Grube), as "knowledge" (by G. L. Abernathy and T. L. Langford), and as "intellection" (by Allan Bloom). *Dianoia* has been translated as "reasoning" (by Grube), as "thinking" (by Abernathy and Langford), and as "thought" (by Bloom). I have opted for Rouse's and Rauch's translation of *noesis* as "reason" because doing so best reveals the continuity between Plato and the later Western metaphysical tradition through Hegel and Kant. I have chosen to call (4) "scientific concepts." Plato gives us two Greek terms for that slot, *hypothemenoi* and *ta mathematica*. Many choose the second, "mathematical objects," as the key phrase here—and it is true that Socrates uses examples from arithmetic and geometry to explain this concept. I have selected "scientific concepts" because this category includes mathematical ideas but in fact encompasses more. I believe Plato did not mean to restrict *hypothemenoi* (literally "assumptions" or "postulates") to mathematical ideas. M. E. Taylor warns us against being misled by Plato's mathematical language here. He says that Plato "had before him no other examples of systematic and organized knowledge" than "the various branches of mathematics as recognized in the fifth century" (M. E. Taylor, *Plato: The Man and His Work* [New York: Meridian Books, 1960], p. 289). Plato is referring to organized conceptual knowledge, that is, roughly what today we would call scientific concepts. According to Plato, they are inferior to Forms both because they are copies (imitations, "shadows," "reflections") of the Forms and because the individual thinkers still depend on visual imagery when they operate at this level. In this sense the Forms and not the concepts are mathematical, because Forms are image-free.

2. Plato, "Meno," in *Great Dialogues of Plato*, ed. Eric H. Warmington and Philip G. Rouse, trans. W. H. D. Rouse (New York: New American Library, 1956), p. 41.

3. Ibid., p. 42.

4. One book challenges the traditional interpretation somewhat. See Pietro Redondi, *Galileo Heretic*, trans. Raymond Rosenthal (Princeton, N.J.: Princeton University Press, 1988).

5. René Descartes, *Essential Works of Descartes*, trans. Lowell Blair (New York: Bantam Books, 1966), p. x.

6. René Descartes, *Meditations on First Philosophy*, in *The Essential Descartes*, ed. Margaret D. Wilson, trans. Elizabeth S. Haldane and G. R. T. Ross (New York: New American Library, 1969), p. 166. Unless otherwise stated, all subsequent quotes from Descartes in this chapter are from this source.

3

What You See Is What You Get
Empiricist Epistemology

The opposite extreme from rationalism is empiricism. According to empiricism, the true foundations of knowledge are found not in "reason" but in observation.

Aristotle as a Precursor to Empiricism

We can find a rudimentary version of empiricism in the philosophy of ARISTOTLE (384–322 B.C.E.), a student of Plato. There are strong Platonic trends in Aristotle's work, but he was much more critical of Plato's views than Plato had been of his teacher, Socrates. This criticism has to do with Aristotle's preference for empiricism over rationalism. We now turn to Aristotle's ideas.

In his Simile of the Line, Plato had placed individual material objects on the second rung of a four-tiered ladder, making them less real than the Forms of which they were mere copies. The only way for the philosopher to arrive at those ultimately real metaphysical objects, the Forms, was to transcend these particular sensible objects and overcome observation—the perceptual act that grasps individual material things.

Aristotle (384–322 B.C.E.)

Aristotle never denied the philosophical significance of the abstractions that Plato called Forms (e.g., Truth, Justice, Beauty, Mammality, Treeness, and so forth), but he denied the rationalistic thesis that these Forms had an independent reality superior to the

Plato's View

physical world, forms which could be grasped only by transcending that world. To the contrary, for Aristotle, the physical world was the *real* world, and sensorial acts that perceived that world were of great epistemological importance. He agreed with his teacher that mere acts of receiving images did not provide knowledge and that the human mind was capable of abstracting from these acts and thereby moving from images to general knowledge. But, unlike Plato, he believed that "universals" or "essences" (i.e., Forms) existed not in some superior realm transcending physical things but in particular objects as their principle of development. (What makes a salamander a salamander is its "salamanderness," which is imbedded in the creature from the moment of its conception.) The human mind is capable of discovering those features that a number of particular objects have in common, but this commonality, that is, this essence, is to be found only *in* those objects through a perceptual act aided by the mind's capacity for abstraction. For example, in observing a multitude of those objects we call "trees," the mind is able to discover those features that all trees have in common by virtue of which we can classify them as "trees" and not, for example, "fish," or "insects," or

even "bushes" or "weeds." For Aristotle, the only intellectual act that needs to transcend observation is the deduction of the existence of an "unmoved mover" or "prime mover"—a godlike entity of pure perfection that all things unconsciously emulate in their striving for self-fulfillment. (When the acorn fulfills its essence by developing into an oak tree, it is unconsciously striving to be god in the way that a runner is striving to reach a goal.) A thing's essence is what the thing is when it is fully actualized. For example, a fully actualized acorn becomes an oak tree. The "things" of the world (such as oak trees) are what Aristotle calls substances. Their essences do not exist in a separate metaphysical sphere, as in Plato's theory; rather, these essences are imbedded in substances as **teleological** goals to be achieved—to be actualized. But substances also have histories—they have pasts, presents, and futures. In striving to achieve their essences, substances endure change. Here, Aristotle, like Plato before him, is trying to solve the Heraclitian-Parmenidean dilemma. He shows how change and permanence are both possible of the same reality—the same substance. What does not change is the essence—what a thing is. What does change is the substance's substratum or matter, which undergoes transformation (it "morphs") as it strives to become what it truly is.

Bringing Plato Back Down to Earth

Along with the unmoved mover, the totality of substances and their histories compose the totality of reality. And most of reality could be discovered by individual acts of perception informed by reason. In short, Aristotle rejected Plato's "other-worldliness." He wanted to bring Plato's philosophy back down to earth. It was this desire that made Aristotle a protoempiricist.

The Empiricism of John Locke

In the same way that rationalism found its first modern expression in the work of René Descartes, the first modern statement of empiricism appears in the work of the English physician JOHN LOCKE (1632–1704). Locke's main thesis is set forth in the following passage:

John Locke (1632–1704)

> Let us suppose the mind to be, as we say, a blank slate (**tabula rasa**) of white paper, void of all characters, without any ideas; how comes it to be furnished? Whence comes it by that vast store, which the busy and boundless fancy of man has painted on it with almost endless variety? Whence has it all the materials of reason and knowledge? To this I answer in one word, from **experience:** in that all our knowledge is founded, and from that it ultimately derives itself.[1]

Locke had read Descartes's work, and he knew that in order to establish the theory of the mind as a "blank slate," he would have to refute the rationalists' contention that knowledge is based on innate ideas. About this Locke says:

> The way shown how we come by any knowledge, sufficient to prove it not innate.—It is an established opinion among some men that there are in the understanding certain innate principles; some primary notions, . . . characters, as it were, stamped upon the mind of man which the soul receives in its very first being and brings into the world with it. It would be sufficient to convince unprejudiced readers of the falseness of this supposition, if I should only show (as I hope I shall in the following parts of this discourse) how men, barely by the use of their natural faculties, may attain to all the knowledge they have, without the help of any innate impressions, and may arrive at certainty, without any such original notions or principles. (bk. I, chap. II, sec. 1)

Locke is here appealing to a principle that would become dear to empiricism, what is known as **Ockham's Razor.** William of Ockham (or Occam), a fourteenth-century philosopher, set forth as a principle of economy the following thesis: "What can be done with fewer [terms] is done in vain with more." This simple principle sounds like something your English instructor might write in the margin of your essay, but William meant it as more than just a stylistic recommendation. (And indeed, William's principle got him into trouble with the ecclesiastical authorities, who suspected that Ockham was trying to shave off the doctrine of the trinity on the grounds that *one* divine entity is simpler than *three*.) William's point has been restated in modern terms in the following way: "Do not multiply entities beyond necessity." That is to say, given two theories, both of which are compatible with all the observable data and both of which purport to explain the same phenomena, the preferable theory is the one with the fewer theoretical entities.

Ockham Wielding Razor

Let's consider a historical example. Even before telescopes were first trained on the sky in the seventeenth century, it was noticed that certain heavenly bodies seemed not simply to be travelling in a consistent orbit but to stop suddenly, back up, and then lurch forward. This discovery was startling—even embarrassing—because people were used to thinking of the movements of the heavenly bodies as exemplars of God's geometrical genius. Some scientific account was needed to "save the appearances." It came about in the theory of epicycles. According to this hypothesis, some heavenly bodies moved around the earth like this:

In this case, from the perspective of the earth, these bodies would *appear* to be stopping, moving backward, then moving ahead. So, indeed, the appearances had been saved along with God's geometrical genius. (Now Heaven's architect was still a mathematical wizard—even though his tastes did run a bit to the baroque.) But then, as telescopes got better, a new embarrassment came to light. Not only did these epicycling bodies seem to stop, move backward, then start forward again, but they also appeared to stop, *wiggle* backward, then *wiggle* forward again. This problem was solved by putting epicycles on the epicycles. Now the Great Architect had become positively rococo. Appearances had been

saved but at what cost? This whole structure had now become so top-heavy that, obviously, it would soon come crashing down. The explanation was crying out for Ockham's razor to come along and shave off the extra weight.

The razor appeared in the form of Johann Kepler's theory of planetary motion. Kepler asked, What if the heliocentric theory is true: the earth travels around the sun but not in a circle, rather in an ellipse and in such a way that "equal areas are swept in equal times"? Then the *apparent* retrograde motion of some heavenly bodies would be explained by the speeding up and slowing down of the earth in its elliptical orbit. And what if the little wiggly movements are the result of the aberration caused by looking back through our own atmosphere? So much for the epicycles and epicycles on the epicycles. Kepler's theory is simpler. It has fewer entities. It represents a triumph of Ockham's razor.

The System of Epicycles Comes Crashing Down

Now perhaps you can see what Locke hoped to accomplish. He hoped to do to "innate ideas" what Kepler had done to epicycles. He also wanted to do the same to Platonic Forms. A theory in which *only particulars exist* would be simpler than one in which there existed particulars *and* abstractions. Locke believed that with the simple image of the "blank slate," he could account for all possible knowledge. He began with several sets of distinctions, one between simple and complex ideas, another between particular and general ideas, and a third between primary and secondary qualities.

Simple and Complex Ideas

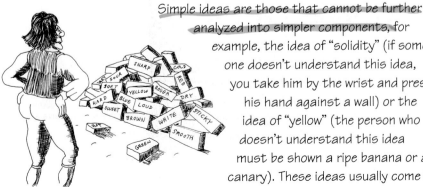

Simple ideas are those that cannot be further analyzed into simpler components, for example, the idea of "solidity" (if someone doesn't understand this idea, you take him by the wrist and press his hand against a wall) or the idea of "yellow" (the person who doesn't understand this idea must be shown a ripe banana or a canary). These ideas usually come in through one sense, though some of them, such as the idea of "motion," can be derived either from the sense of touch or the sense of sight.

Complex ideas are (1) compounds of simple ideas (e.g., "beauty," "gratitude," "a man," "an army," "the universe"), (2) ideas of relations (larger than, smaller than) created by setting two ideas next to each other and comparing or contrasting them, or (3) abstractions, wherein the mind separates out a feature of an idea and generalizes it (e.g., blueness). Abstractions are formed when we recognize a certain characteristic that a group of objects has in common. That characteristic is assigned a name, which is a symbol for that characteristic. This theory has traditionally been called **conceptualism.**

The word ——————→ "FAT"
stands for

the idea, which ——→
is abstracted from

many individual ——→
cases

LARD

Locke's Conceptualism

Locke's view is that the rationalists had confused these "abstract general ideas" with actual existing entities (Platonic Forms) or with innate ideas. (For their part, the rationalists were quick to charge Locke with presupposing the truth of the very thing he thought he was refuting. They asked how the mind can *recognize* a characteristic that a number of objects have in common unless the mind already has the concept of "sameness.")

Primary and Secondary Qualities

Locke's distinction between primary and secondary qualities had been popularized by both Descartes and Galileo. **Primary qualities** were said to be characteristics that necessarily inhered in material bodies. They comprised "solidity, extension, figure, motion or rest, and number." **Secondary qualities** were defined as "such qualities, which in truth are nothing in the objects themselves but powers to produce various sensations in us by their primary qualities, that is, by the bulk, figure, texture, and motion of their insensible parts, as colours, sounds, tastes, etc." (bk. II, chap. VIII, sec. 10).

Now, our *ideas* of primary qualities are, according to Locke, *correct* ideas. That is, these ideas are caused in our minds by those qualities, and these ideas correctly represent those qualities. On the other hand, the ideas we have of secondary qualities do not correctly represent the world. Locke says, "the ideas of primary qualities of bodies are resemblances of them, and their patterns do really exist in the bodies themselves; but the

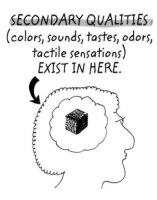

SECONDARY QUALITIES
(colors, sounds, tastes, odors, tactile sensations)
EXIST IN HERE.

PRIMARY QUALITIES
(extension, size, shape, location, motion/rest)
EXIST OUT HERE.

ideas produced in us by these secondary qualities have no resemblance of them at all. There is nothing like our ideas existing in the bodies themselves" (bk. II, chap. VIII, sec. 15). This epistemological view is now known as **representative realism.** It is a version of realism because it holds that there really is a real world "out there." It is representative realism because, according to this view, the mind does not give us direct access to reality; rather it represents reality much in the way that a photograph does. And just as some characteristics of a photo correctly represent the world (e.g., number, shape, relative size, and so on), so do some features of the mind correctly represent the world (these are our ideas of primary

This is a picture of you!

But I'm not flat, glossy, black and white, three inches tall with a white border around my head!!

qualities). And just as some characteristics of a photo are purely features of the photo (e.g., its black and white presentation, its two-dimensionality, its glossiness and portableness, and the like), so do some features of the mind pertain only to the mind and not to the world (these are our ideas of secondary qualities).

Substance

Now, with these tools in hand, Locke believed he had refuted Descartes because he thought he had given a complete account of knowledge using a theory simpler than that of Descartes. But perhaps things aren't that simple, as we see when we turn to Locke's account of the key philosophical category, substance (borrowed, at a distance, from Aristotle).

> *Our Obscure Idea of Substance in general.*—So that if anyone will examine himself concerning his notion of pure substance in general, he will find he has no other idea of it at all, but only a supposition of he knows not what support of such qualities which are capable of producing simple ideas in us. . . . If anyone should be asked, "What is the subject wherein colour or weight inheres?" he would have nothing to say but, "The solid extended parts." And if he were demanded, "What is it that solidity and extension inhere in?" he would not be in much better case than the Indian . . . , who, saying that the world was supported by a great elephant, was asked what the elephant rested on? to which his answer was, "A great tortoise"; but being again pressed to know what gave support to the broad-backed tortoise, replied—something he knew not what. (bk. II, chap. XXIII, sec. 2)

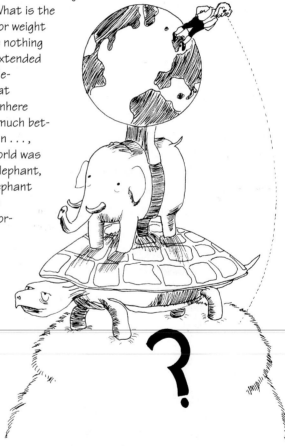

Locke's rather cavalier account of substance is devastating to his own project, though he didn't seem to realize it. Once you buy into the metaphysics of substance, as both he and Descartes had done (that is, once you accept the view that, given anything in the world, it is either a substance or a characteristic of a substance), then you'd better be prepared to render a coherent account of substance. Remember in the wax example it was precisely Descartes's inability to come up with an *empirical* account of "substance" and "identity" that allowed him to posit innate ideas. Now Locke has claimed he can get rid of innate ideas by using Ockham's razor; yet when he turns to that key ontological category, substance, he says it is a "something I know not what." Locke's confusion could be the

The Beginning of the End of Substance

beginning of the end either of empiricism or of the metaphysics of substance. We shall soon see that it is the latter.

Berkeley's Correction of Locke

Locke's empiricist successor, GEORGE BERKELEY (1685–1753), an Irishman who became a bishop in the Church of England, saw Locke's errors clearly and thought they could be corrected simply by a more vigorous application of Ockham's razor—this time, to the notion of material substance itself. Locke had written, "Since the mind, in all its thoughts and reasonings, hath no other immediate object but its own ideas, which it alone does or can contemplate, it is evident that our knowledge is only conversant about them" (bk. IV, chap. I, sec. 1). Berkeley immediately realized that if this statement was literally true, then it is impossible to know something that is not an idea. But Locke, perhaps contradicting himself, had claimed that we *know* that many of these ideas are caused by real things in the physical world (material substances) and particularly by their primary qualities, which have powers to produce the ideas of both primary and secondary qualities in our minds.

George Berkeley (1685–1753)

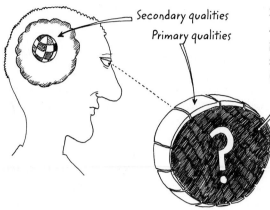

Secondary qualities
Primary qualities

SUBSTANCE (cross-section):
A mysterious support of
primary qualities somehow
standing under them
(sub-stantia)

Locke's View

Sense Data

One of Berkeley's first tasks would be to demonstrate Locke's self-contradiction by undoing the primary-secondary quality distinction. Berkeley argued that primary qualities and secondary qualities really are the same thing. How do I establish the size and shape of a table except by looking at it or feeling it? The first act produces the secondary qualities of color, and the second act produces the secondary qualities of tactile sensation (hard, smooth, etc.).

I know the *size* and *shape* of the brown table by contrasting the brown of the table against the white of the wall and the green of the rug or by running my hand along its surface and noting where the sensations of smoothness and resistance end. In other words, our ideas of primary qualities are really nothing but *interpretations* of secondary qualities. In fact, for Berkeley, all of our ideas (except for our idea of "self," which is known in a Cartesian manner and, as we shall see, our idea of "God") are nothing but our ideas of secondary qualities

The Collapsing of the Primary-Secondary Quality Distinction

or interpretations of them. In *A Treatise Concerning the Principles of Human Knowledge*, Berkeley wrote:

> It is evident to anyone who takes a survey of the *objects of human knowledge*, that they are either *ideas* actually imprinted on the senses, or else such as are perceived by attending to the passions and operations of the mind; or lastly, *ideas* formed by help of memory and imagination, either compounding, dividing, or barely representing those originally perceived in the aforesaid ways. By sight I have the ideas of light and colours with their several degrees and variations. By touch I perceive hard and soft, heat and cold, motion and resistance. . . . smelling furnishes me with odours; the palate with tastes; and hearing conveys sounds to the mind in all their variety of tone and composition. And as several of these are observed to accompany each other, they come to be marked by one name, and so to be reputed as one thing. Thus, for example, a certain colour, taste, smell, figure, and consistence having been observed to go together are accounted one distinct thing, signified by the name "apple"; other collections of ideas constitute a stone, a tree, a book, and the like sensible things; which, as they are pleasing or disagreeable, excite the passions of love, hatred, joy, grief, and so forth.[2]

Almost the whole of Berkeley's theory is encapsulated in this remarkable passage. Let's summarize that theory: like Descartes, Berkeley wants to start with what is certain, with what we can call "the given," and for him, "the given" is what earlier philosophers designated as "ideas of secondary qualities" and what he simply calls "ideas" or "sensations." (We will call them **sense data** from now on.) Babies come into the world, and they are "given" sense data: colors, sounds, tastes, odors, and "feelies" (tactile sensations).

The Newborn Infant Confronts "the Given"

These data do not constitute a world for the baby; rather, they comprise a chaos of fluctuating sensations. (Actually, they constitute five chaotic worlds.) But slowly the child learns to "read" these data, very much the way we learn to read script as children. The baby does this by beginning to notice patterns in the appearance of these data (the rationalist, of course, asks how the baby *recognizes* these patterns without knowing the principle

of identity) and by having parents teach the child a language (". . . a certain colour, taste, smell, figure, and consistence having been observed to go together, are accounted one distinct thing, signified by the name 'apple'; . . ."). Now, to see how very radical Berkeley's theory is, we have to understand that (a) any given "physical object" in the world is just the totality of its sense data, and that (b) sense data are exclusively mental—they exist only in minds. In other words, all so-called physical objects exist only as possible or actual perceptions in consciousness. Berkeley's Latinized motto is "esse is percipi"—to be is to be perceived. His philosophy is a version of **idealism**, the prioritizing of the mental world over the physical world, or in his more radical version, the view that only the mental world exists. There is no physical world, if that term is meant to denote some unperceived matter that exists independently of consciousness. It is important to recognize, however, that Berkeley is not denying that things like tables, cherries, and mountains exist. Rather, he is trying to prove that the correct analysis of such notions as "the table in the next room" or "the cherry on the tree" or "the mountain beyond the horizon" is carried out exclusively in terms of sense data. Do you get it?

If you *do* get it, then at this point you may feel that Berkeley's view, reducing everything to mental states (sense data), is far out of touch with common sense. Indeed, you may begin to feel that in this theory, the center of the world does not hold. Certainly Berkeley's contemporary, Dr. Johnson, thought so when he tried to refute Berkeley by simply kicking a stone. But this act of Johnson's shows a failure to understand Berkeley's theory. He never denied the truth of the sentence "Kicking rocks hurts." His argument was that the sentence could be analyzed totally in terms of sense data.

Dr. Johnson Refutes Bishop Berkeley

Notice that there are two features here in Berkeley's account of how we interpret our sense data, transforming them into a picture of a *world*. First, there is the objective fact that sense data appear in recognizable patterns (". . . having been observed to go together . . ."). This is nature's role in making interpretation possible because these are natural patterns—bright red, yellow, and orange flamelike sense data are associated with heat and pain. Second, there is the fact that language is used to unify these ideas in our minds (". . . signified by the name 'apple' . . ."). This is convention's role in making interpretation possible.

What makes Berkeley's theory so modern is the large part he assigns to language in his epistemology. Doing so allows him to account for a fact that modernity had discovered and traditional rationalism could not explain, namely that different peoples cut up the world so differently (all those stories that you've learned in your anthropology classes). If human conventions—primarily linguistic conventions—can determine which ideas are associated with each other, then this finding can explain quite nicely why Eskimos have no word for "snow" in their language but have a number of nouns designating different substances, all of which look like "snow" to us and to the Caucasian Yukon neighbors of the Eskimos; and why Spanish speakers think that there are two kinds of "being" (*ser* and *estar*), although English speakers find only one kind. If Descartes's theories of substance and of innate ideas were true, we should all see the world identically. Keep in mind, however, that Berkeley's theory is not primarily one about language; it is one about sense data. Esse is *percipi*; there are only sense data and interpretations of sense data. Some interpretations are "natural," that is, there is pretty much universal agreement on them (like "pain" and "water"), and some are conventional (perhaps like color words—"purple" and "chartreuse"). Different languages will express these conventional differences differently.

Snow? No. There's no snow here. Tiqsiq we've got, and Tuva, or Pukajaq, or Piqsirpoq, or Gana or Aput. But snow there isn't any of. Lots of Qimuqsuq!

But language does play a big role in Berkeley's epistemology as a bridge of intersubjectivity. This role can be seen in the following consideration: No two people have exactly the same sense data because no two people can share exactly the same geometrical perspective on any object. If thirty people in a room look at a book on a table, each has a slightly different datum in consciousness.

No Two People See Exactly the Same Thing

In fact, it is logically possible that no two people have the same experience when they use such basic terms as the word "red." But none of this matters practically because even if I see what you call "green" when I look at something "red," we both describe it as being red because we were taught to associate that particular noise ("rĕd") with that particular experience. So the upshot is that each of us dwells in his or her little solipsistic world of sensorial consciousness, but language allows us to build bridges between those solitary islands.

Language Forms the Bridge of Intersubjectivity

Also, there is a kind of "democratic" element in Berkeley's theory. Our picture of the world (that is, our interpretation of sense data) is built up, not only conventionally, but also partly by consensus. All sense data are in some ways qualitatively identical. The sense data that lead the delirious person to say, "There's a pink elephant in this room," are as real as mine are when mine lead me to say, "No, the room is empty." The visual sense data involved in claiming to see a pink elephant should allow us to predict certain tactile sense data from them. The sentence "There's a pink elephant in the room," entails the prediction, "If you walk twelve steps in that direction, you will be blocked by something whose skin feels hard and rough." Of course, the delirious person may say that she feels that she *is* blocked by something hard and rough. Or if not, she may reinterpret her sense data, saying, "There's an *intangible* pink elephant in the room." In either of those cases, we call in other perceivers at this point. If thirty-nine people look into the room and all say that the room is empty, and if the fortieth person says that there's a pink elephant there, then the majority wins. Even though all sense data are individually equally existent, what we mean by "reality" are those sense data from which we can consensually predict with success the greatest number of other sense data. If there were only one person in the world, then her sense data would be "reality." It turns out, however, that there are more than one. This analysis constitutes Berkeley's solution to the famous problem of the distinction between reality and appearance.

The Source of Sense Data

Now, a typical objection to Berkeley's theory at this point will be If there exist only sense data (ideas, sensations), where do these sense data come from? Normally (or at least in the Cartesian-Lockean picture of normality) we would say that they come from material things "out there." But Berkeley has eliminated those "things" with Ockham's razor, so where *do* these sense data come from? Before we make Berkeley answer that question, let's ask Descartes and Locke where *material substances* come from. Sense data are caused by substance, they would say, but what causes substance? Both Descartes and Locke answer, "from God." (In fact, the only other obvious answer would seem to be that it comes "from an infinite series of causes"—the table comes from atoms,

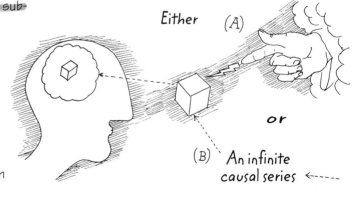

Either (A)

or

(B) An infinite causal series ←-----

Locke's Version of Causality

the atoms come from the "atomic bake" that took place in the "Big Bang." But where does the stuff that was baked into atoms by the Big Bang come from? Presumably from something yet earlier and so on to infinity.) Now back to Berkeley. By eliminating material substance from this chain of events, he has simply eliminated "the middle person" (formerly "the middleman"). Consequently, he can give exactly the same answer to the question, "Where do sense data come from?"

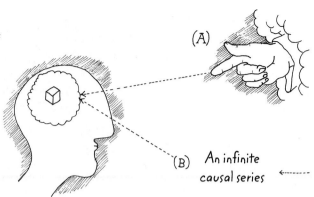

(A)

(B) An infinite causal series

Berkeley's Version of Causality

that everybody else gives to the question of where matter comes from: either from God or from an infinite causal series.

Berkeley preferred the first alternative, of course. He was a bishop, after all. In fact, God plays a key role in Berkeley's theory, just as it did in Descartes's. Without God, the center would not hold. The center does hold, therefore, God exists. God is the guarantor of the orderliness of the universe (i.e., the orderliness of sense data). He is the "eternal perceiver" who guarantees by his perpetual vigilance that the room we are in does not flash out of existence when we all leave it. (And if it did flash out of existence, who knows if it would flash back on?) Ronald Knox wrote a lovely limerick to express this point:

POOF

There was a young man who said, "God
  Must think it exceedingly odd,
If he finds that this tree
Continues to be
When there's no one about
      in the Quad."

Dear Sir:
Your astonishment's odd.
I am always about in the
      Quad.
And that's why the tree
Will continue to be
Since observed by me,
      Yours faithfully,
      GOD

There does seem to be a big problem here, however. How can a god exist in a system whose main claim is that *esse* is *percipi* (*to be is to be perceived*)? In such a system, it would seem that either God can be perceived (which he can't) or he doesn't exist. Berkeley was obviously troubled by this dilemma and hoped he could escape it by call-ing our thought of God a "notion" rather than an "idea." But very few critics have accepted Berkeley's semantical solution.

Hume's Radicalization of Berkeley's Empiricism

The third of the three classical empiricists was DAVID HUME (1711–1776), who became a librarian at the University of Edinburgh in his native Scotland but who, despite his early brilliance, was never offered the professorial chair for which he hoped. (He had figured out many of his best ideas by the time he was nineteen years old.)

Hume was committed to the general tenets of empiricism ("blank slate" theory, adoption of Ockham's razor, denial of innate ideas, and the view that all knowledge derives from sense data), but he thought that neither Locke nor Berkeley had been consistent in applying them.

Perhaps the best way of scrutinizing Hume's view is to begin with his distinc-tion between two kinds of sentences: those that express "relations of ideas," and those that express "matters of fact." (Later philosophers have fol-lowed the terminology invented in the next century by Immanuel Kant and

David Hume (1711–1776)

called these two categories "analytic" and "synthetic," respectively. We will follow that custom here.)

Analytic propositions ("relations of ideas") have the following characteristics:

A. Their negation leads to a self-contradiction.
B. They are a priori.
C. They are true by definition.
D. They are necessarily true.

Take, for example, the sentence, "All triangles have three angles."

A. If you deny it ["*Not all triangles have three angles*"], you say something not merely false but something self-contradictory, because any figure that does not have three angles is *not* a triangle.

B. The sentence is a priori. You don't discover its truth by looking anywhere or by counting angles. You understand its truth by contemplating its meaning.

C. The sentence is true by definition. That is, given the definition of a triangle as "a three-sided closed figure," it follows that a triangle must have three [and only three] angles. (Another way of saying that a sentence is true by definition is to say that it expresses a **conceptual truth,** because the concept of triangularity logically entails the idea of three angles.)

D. The sentence is *necessarily* true. It can't be false given the current conventions of the English language.

So far all these characteristics sound like a rationalist's delight. But . . . Hume adds one other characteristic of analytic sentences:

A Delighted Rationalist

E. They are all **tautologies.** That is, they are redundant and repetitious. The predicate (e.g., "has three angles") only repeats what was already in the subject (e.g., "A triangle.")

A Disillusioned Rationalist

So even though there is a priori knowledge, it is never about anything but itself. A priori truths can never tell us about reality, so the rationalistic dream of a deductive system of knowledge composed of purely a priori truths is a phantom. (Basically, analytic truths comprise definitions, parts of definitions, mathematics, and logic. They are all true but only show how we can relate ideas to each other: "A = A," "2 + 3 = 5," "brothers are males.")

Synthetic propositions ("matters of fact") are the opposites of analytic propositions on all counts. They must be derived from sense data (Locke's "secondary qualities," Berkeley's "ideas" and "sensations"). To find out whether a sentence like "Jill has a brown dog" is meaningful, we have to ask ourselves whether the key ideas could be traced back to simple perceptions. In fact, our sentence can be traced back to sense perceptions. At least we know what it would be like to do so. (It may turn out that Jill's dog is green or that she has no dog at all [one of the features of synthetic propositions is that they are not necessarily true], but we know what it would be like to find out.)

Now, according to Hume, analytic and synthetic propositions are the only possible kinds of meaning in a truly empiricist program. Any sentence that is neither analytic (not a tautology) nor synthetic (its ideas can't be traced to sense perceptions) is nonsense—period!

A Priori Thought Misplaced

Finding Out the Hard Way That Jill Has a Dog (A Posteriori Proof)

So much for Berkeley's God! The sentence "God exists" when negated ("God does not exist") does not produce a self-contradiction. (See Chapter 5 for St. Anselm's view to the contrary.) And the *idea* of God cannot be traced back to sense data. It is literally *non-sense*. Ockham's razor slashes again!

But Berkeley had argued that without the idea (or "notion") of God, we could not explain what makes the center hold—how could there be any consistency in reality (i.e., in the appearance of sense data)? Well, Hume had to admit that on purely empirical grounds it would be hard to answer that question. This difficulty is because Hume assumed that it is not God but universal causality that holds things together, and there is no sense datum to which we can trace the idea of a cause. That is, no perceptual difference exists between causality and repeated seriality. (The sentences "X causes Y" and "First X happens, then Y happens" are confirmed by exactly the same sense data, yet they seem to have very different meanings.) Hume does not seem to have seriously doubted that there are causal relations among objects in the world (that is, using Hume's terminology, that there are "necessary connections" between events in the world), but he admits that he is unable to provide a rational justification of his commonsense belief in causality. Even this much of a concession is bad news for his empiricism. There are hints of a suspicion that, after all, the center does not hold, or at least that the belief that it *does* hold is irrational. (Søren Kierkegaard, the founder of **existentialism,** was a close reader of Hume, and it has been said that Friedrich Nietzsche, another early existentialist, was the first to feel in his bones what Hume only experienced intellectually. We will run into Kierkegaard and Nietzsche later.)

What about Descartes's absolutely certain idea of the self—an idea that neither Locke nor Berkeley felt the need to criticize? Hume was as skeptical of that idea as he was of the ideas of "innate knowledge" and of "God" and of "causality." In his *Treatise of Human Nature* (1735) he wrote:

> There are some philosophers who imagine we are every moment intimately conscious of what we call our *self;* that we feel its existence and its continuance in existence; and are certain, beyond the evidence of a demonstration, both of its perfect identity and simplicity. . . . For my part, when I enter most intimately into what I call *myself,* I always stumble on some particular perception or other, of heat or cold, light or shade, love or hatred, pain or pleasure. I never can catch *myself* at any time without a perception, and never can observe anything but the perception. . . . But setting aside some metaphysicians of this kind, I may venture to affirm of the rest of mankind that they are nothing but a bundle or collection of different perceptions, which succeed each other with an inconceivable rapidity and are in a perpetual flux and movement. Our eyes cannot turn in their sockets without varying our perceptions. Our thought is still more variable than our sight; and all our other senses and faculties contribute to this change; nor is there any single power of the soul which remains unalterably the same, perhaps for one moment.[3]

Nooo. Not the self! Don't take that too!

Hume Discovers the Self—Such As It Is

This is an amazing passage. The self—the foundation of certainty and the centerpiece of Cartesian rationalism—is an empty idea (". . . consequently, there is no such idea" [p. 252]). There is no experiential continuity of selfhood. In fact, there is no experience of selfhood at all. According to Hume, this discovery is so repugnant to us mortals that "we feign [its] continued existence . . . and run into the notion of a soul, and self, and substance, to disguise the variation" (p. 254). This discovery cuts to the heart of, not only the philosophy of rationalism, but also Western religion and of common sense itself.

So Hume's radical empiricism could find no justification for the concepts of "God," "Causality," or "selfhood." In fact, his view led to a **skepticism** so deep that it seemed to be untenable. Upon reading Hume, it is as if we feel the ground begin to slide beneath our feet. The center begins to give. Yet in the twentieth century, a group of influential philosophers adopted his views with only minor modifications. Their ideas came to be known as **logical empiricism,** or **logical positivism.**

Logical Positivism: The Further Radicalization of Empiricism

The logical positivists were a bunch of hard-nosed, scientific-minded philosophers who formulated their original position at the University of Vienna in the early 1920s. There, a small group of philosophers calling themselves "the Vienna Circle" was led by Professor Moritz Schlick. The positivists agreed with Hume that math and logic are tautological but appreciated the analytic power of math and logic more deeply than did Hume, and in fact most of their work was in the logical analysis of the propositions of science and common sense. They agreed roughly with Hume about causality but solved his problem by redefining the idea. "Causality" no longer named some mysterious necessary connection between events; instead they suggested "X causes Y" simply predicts the occurrence of Y after the occurrence of X. That is, they decided that "causality" is after all nothing but "repeated seriality." They solved Locke's problem of "substance"

Hume Hanging Out in a Pool Hall Studying Causality

("thingness") in a similar way. To say "There is a table in room 506" is a way of making predictions about future sense data. It means "*If you went into room 506, then* you would have the following sense data: brown, rectangular, resistant, etc., etc.*" By claiming that the meaning of a declarative sentence can be correctly analyzed by translating it into an if-then hypothesis— where the *if* clause contains an action ("If you went into room 506, . . .") and the *then* clause contains a prediction of sense data ("then you would have the following sense data . . .")—the positivists totally bypass the problem of the table that flashes on and off. A table just is, to use the phrase of John Stuart Mill, "a permanent possibility of sensation."

The positivists had a great difficulty with the *idealistic* implications of Berkeley's and Hume's versions of empiricism. (Idealism is the view that the only things we can know to exist are ideas.) Because both Berkeley and Hume thought that only sense data can be known and believed that sense data were mental, they seemed to be idealists. The logical positivists believed that idealism was both too metaphysical and not scientific enough. Their solution was to adopt a version of *neutral* **monism,** the view that reality (in this case, sense data) is neither mental nor physical; rather, it is some third kind of unanalyzable, neutral "stuff." According to the positivists, the categories "mental" and "physical" are simply **logical constructs** that are interpretations of sense data from different perspectives. We call "material" those sense data that we can categorize in terms of concepts like dimensionality, size, and shape; and we call "mental" those that somehow escape those categories. If the empirical facts about sense data were slightly different, perhaps we would draw the boundaries of these categories differently. For example, if every time people entered room 506 they immediately got a headache, we might talk about headaches differently, warning folks to avoid that room because it contained a headache. We would thereby be placing headaches in the category of the physical instead of the mental. So headaches, tables, mountains, rainbows, sandstorms, and acts of revenge are "logical constructs"; that is, they are conceptual organizations of sense data in ways that allow

Oh-Oh! There's a headache in room 506.

for objective analysis of them and communication about them. This view is not so far from Berkeley's, after all, but it robs him of both his idealism and his theism.

The positivists were impressed by Hume's empiricist critique of the concept of selfhood, and they took the heroic step of declaring that other people are also merely "logical constructs." In other words, you are my sense data. (Sounds like the title of a positivistic country-and-western song, though perhaps not a very romantic one.) Or at least you are constructed out of my sense data. The technique of reducing selfhood to categories of observable data bypasses the need for any theory of consciousness and, indeed, for any psychology at all. In other words, the positivists became radical **behaviorists** about everyone but themselves, and they even attempted a behavioristic account of themselves, that is, of the self in the first person. (We'll study behaviorism in Chapter 4.)

You are my sense data, my only sense data. You make me happy when other logical constructs are blue . . .

Sung to the Tune of "You Are My Sunshine"

Finally, the logical empiricists introduced a category called theoretical entities. This notion was meant to account for such items as atoms and electrons, whose *esse* is clearly not *percipi* because they can't be perceived at all. Theoretical entities are entities that are neither sense data nor logical constructs composed of sense data. Rather, they exist solely as entities in *theories*, and these entities are included in theories in order to facilitate more precise predictions of sense data. For example, consider the notion of "the average American housewife." Obviously, it

The Average American Housewife Has 1.78 Children

would be a big mistake to suppose that she actually exists, and it would be ludicrous to imagine trying to find her (perhaps in Akron, Ohio?) in order to interview her. The mistake becomes obvious once we remember that she has 1.78 children! Nevertheless, the notion of the average American housewife can be very useful in fields such as economics and sociology because it allows us to articulate information about consumer habits and demography in America and make accurate predictions concerning them. Now, the positivists were forced to treat atoms and electrons in the same way as they treated the average American housewife. These entities did not exist except in theories whose function it was to structure information in such a way as to facilitate predictions about the world that could be tested in terms of sense data. If talking "electron-talk" leads to more accurate predictions, then electron-talk is justified. (Philosophers

and scientists who were not positivists did not find this notion to be a very convincing bit of theorizing, but they did have to admit that whatever status electrons, photons, and the like had, they did not exist in the same way that tables and chairs do. So any theory about their status probably would seem a bit odd.) So logical positivism is yet another radical application of Ockham's notorious razor. One begins to get the feeling that it is perhaps an *abuse* of that razor, and one is reminded of Einstein's felicitous version of that principle: "Say everything as simply as possible but not more so."

William of Ockham and Albert Einstein

Attacks on Logical Positivism's Notion of Sense Data

Despite the flourish of interest in radical empiricism among philosophers from Britain, America, and Austria in the 1930s and 1940s, it has fallen on hard times more recently. A number of attacks on it originated from a variety of camps. A common denominator in these attacks (whether from **gestalt psychology,** linguistic philosophy, **structuralism,** or poststructuralist positions such as **deconstruction**) is one that goes right for the jugular vein of classical empiricism—a denial of the existence of such a thing as a sense datum (or an "idea" in Locke's and Berkeley's sense of the term). Logical positivism (and, with it, most empiricism) stands or falls with "psychological atomism"—the view that our knowledge of the world is built up from discrete, sensorial impressions such as "yellow," "sharp," and "hot." According to this hypothesis, we construct the whole from the assemblage of parts. But recent developments in philosophical theory and psychological investigation have brought this hypothesis into doubt. The gestalt psychologists, for example, claim that we move in the other direction, from whole to part, and that what creates the "whole" is not the bricks of ineffable, absolutely certain sensation (raw feels, sense data) but a complicated and probably inextricably fused combination of neurological and social facts about perception. The neurological facts—expressed psychologically—have to do with the discovery that perception always takes place in a field where a foreground is contrasted with a background. A sensation becomes a perception in a field of meaning, in which that sensation is given a specific meaning by being distinguished from its background. The background, in turn, also has a meaning, though perhaps a vaguer, more inarticulate one than the "something" that upstages it in the foreground. The social fact (i.e., conventional fact) here is the fact that what bestows meaning on the field is a combination of knowledge and expectation that can be traced ultimately to a specific social structure.

This is a difficult point. Let me illustrate it with an example from my own experience. I was once sitting at my breakfast table, awaiting the arrival of a colleague who would drive me to work. I kept lifting my eyes from the morning paper, looking through the window down to the street in anticipation of seeing his bright red Volkswagen "bug." Finally I heard the unmistakable whining of a VW engine. Once again I looked to the road, where I saw, through the shrubs in the front yard, my friend's red car stationed in the driveway. I gulped down my coffee, grabbed my briefcase, and ran down the stairs to the road. Once in the driveway, I was surprised to see nothing there. Puzzled, I waited a moment, thinking that my colleague might have driven up the street to turn around. After several minutes, I returned sheepishly to the house and sat down again at the table.

The Case of the Missing Volkswagen

I looked down at the driveway and suddenly realized that what I had taken to be the bright red paint of my friend's VW was in fact the dull orange of some poison oak leaves in the shrubbery between me and the driveway. My anticipation of his arrival, my knowledge of his car's color, and the recognition of the sound of a Volkswagen automobile (which had probably driven past my house) conspired to create a "sense datum" of bright red. My picture of the world at that moment had moved (fallaciously, in this case) from whole to part, not the other way around, as "psychological atomism" would have it.

Let me relate one more episode whose "moral" also undermines psychological atomism. I was sitting at that same kitchen table, reading and drinking a dark ale. My ten-year-old son was sitting across the table from me having a cola drink. Without moving my eyes from the page of my book, I reached for my ale and mistakenly grabbed his glass of cola. I took a big swig of what I expected to be ale and immediately suffered the shock of what psychologists call **cognitive dissonance.** I knew that the taste was not that of ale, but for a brief moment, I had no idea what taste it was. It was only upon realizing my mistake that the distinctive taste of cola came flooding into my consciousness. Again, the part had been created by the whole, by the gestalt, and the "whole" was composed not just of purely perceptual facts but of anticipations and expectations drawn from my personal psychological history and the history of my culture.

Cognitive Dissonance

Attacks on Logical Positivism's Language

Yet another major flaw occurs in the empiricist program, according to contemporary wisdom. It has to do with the role of language in empiricism. Because of his Lockean suspicion about innate ideas, Berkeley ingeniously displaced the role of innate ideas (particularly the role of generating our concepts of "identity" and "thingness") onto language. For that move to work, however, it would have to be demonstrated that a consistent empiricistic theory of language is possible, one compatible with the "blank slate" hypothesis. This task was taken up in our own time by the behavioristic psychologist (or "behavioral engineer," as he preferred to be called) B. F. SKINNER (1904–1990). In his book characteristically named *Verbal Behavior*, he used his notion of **operant conditioning** (involving the repetition of noises, reinforced or discouraged by a system of rewards and punishments) to show how we learn the language we speak. His idea has a certain natural plausibility. We've all watched the linguistic exchange when a parent teaches a small child the "color words" or the parts of the body. But Skinner's book was soundly trounced in a review of it by NOAM CHOMSKY (1928–), then a relatively unknown young linguist, now perhaps the best-known living linguist in the world. Chomsky demonstrated that if all that were involved in language learning were the "blank slate" and operant conditioning, no one would ever learn a language. Among other things, Chomsky pointed out that Skinner's theory could not account for the linguistic novelty of which any competent native speaker is capable. Any such speaker can produce a completely new sentence that every other competent speaker can understand even though none of them has heard it before. In fact, I shall produce such a sentence now: "It is not a good idea

Skinnerian Linguistics

Noam Chomsky (b. 1928)

Uncle Elmo's Martini

to freeze small woolly mammoths into tinted ice cubes that will be served in the dry martini of Uncle Elmo (whose grandmother fought in the Crimean War)." I am reasonably certain that no one has ever uttered just that sentence before (and for good reason!). Yet, according to Chomsky, Skinner cannot account for the fact that all of us understand it perfectly well.

Furthermore, Chomsky reminded us of the kinds of grammatical mistakes children make. The little boy comes crying to his mother, saying, "Johnny hitted me!" This sentence is, of course, incorrect; yet it is incorrect in an interesting way. What the little boy had to "know" in order to make that error is that the way to make the preterite in English is to add "ed" to the infinitive. It's not *his* fault that this particular verb is irregular. Where did he learn to say "hitted"? Not from imitating his parents or even from other kids, according to Chomsky, but from his *native ability* to generate rules. This ability, which Chomsky calls the capacity for "deep grammar," results from the structuring of the human brain. It is something we bring to the phonetic system we learn and not something we derive from it. All this sounds suspiciously like the function of Descartes's *innate ideas*, and, indeed, Chomsky has no qualms about making the connection between himself and the classical rationalists. He went as far as to title one of his books *Cartesian Linguistics*, and he has this to say:

> On the basis of the best information now available, it seems reasonable to suppose that a

**Chomskian Linguistics
(Followed by a Skinnerian Attempt
at Negative Conditioning)**

child cannot help constructing a particular kind of **transformational grammar** to account for the data presented to him, any more than he can control his perception of solid objects or his attention to line and angle. Thus it may well be that the general features of language structure reflect, not so much the course of one's experience, but rather the general character of one's capacity to acquire knowledge—in the traditional sense, one's innate ideas and innate principles.[4]

Je pense, donc je suis.

CARTESIAN LINGUISTICS
noam chomsky

Kant's Compromise

So we have seen problems with each of the two traditional Western epistemologies, rationalism and empiricism. (Briefly, one ignores Ockham's razor and the other takes it too far.) Is it possible to construct any compromise that salvages the best of each view while eliminating the worst? The first serious attempt came from IMMANUEL KANT (1724–1804), whose *Critique of Pure Reason* was written as a direct response to David Hume's radical empiricism. Kant rejected the empiricists' "blank slate" hypothesis on the grounds that the mind was not simply a passive receptacle of neutral sense data. However, Kant also rejected the rationalistic notion of "innate ideas" on the grounds that claiming babies are born with ideas is just too far-fetched. He replaced these innate ideas with innate *structures*, which he called "categories of the understanding." These structures were formal and active features of the mind that imposed a kind of order on the raw data of the senses. Kant detected as innate structures of the mind a spatial-temporal perceptual gridwork (space and time) and twelve categories of the understanding, including the following:

unity
plurality
totality
relations of substance and
    characteristics of substance
relations of cause and effect
relations of reciprocity

Immanuel Kant (1724–1804)

Again, these categories are not derived passively by the mind from sensorial data but rather are actively brought by the mind to the world and imposed upon the raw data. But raw data themselves are never perceived; we perceive only data that have already been "processed" by the categories of the understanding and the spatial-temporal gridwork. This idea is the meaning of Kant's famous dictum: "Thoughts without content are empty, intuitions without concepts are blind." This conclusion grants to the empiricists that there can be no knowledge in the absence of sensorial contribution and grants to the rationalists that sense data alone cannot provide knowledge. It also squares with the gestaltist insight about the relation between part and whole in our understanding of the world.

Conclusion

So where do these discussions leave us? In the last two chapters, we have seen strengths in both the rationalists' and the empiricists' camps, but we have also seen weaknesses. If we accept the rationalists' notion of innate ideas, we are able to explain how the human mind receiving data translates individual data into a representation of a full and continuous world of things and facts. The rationalists also thereby manage to give a satisfactory account of mathematical knowledge. But rationalism does not fare well against Ockham's razor, and the notion of (God-given?) innate ideas is still somehow mysterious and easily abused. (E.g., imagine someone saying, "It is well known that men are inferior to women, and if there is no empirical evidence of this fact, that just goes to show that this knowledge is derived from an innate idea.") On the other hand, the empiricists do fare well with Ockham's razor, and there are few mysterious entities in their theories because everything is open to observation. Their ingenious move to make language carry the burden of the rationalists' "innate ideas" almost works because language is more open to investigation than are innate ideas and because such a move accounts for epistemological variation from culture to culture in a way not open to Descartes's kind of **nativism.** However, as we've seen, apparently no viable empiricist theory of language has been forthcoming, and the latest data from the field of psychology indicate that "psychological atomism," the backbone of empiricism, is in deep trouble.

Kant's view, though definitely a compromise between rationalism and empiricism, sides more with the former than with the latter. As such, it still suffers from a few of the old Cartesian problems. Like Descartes's doctrine of innate ideas, Kant's theory is still incapable of explaining why some cultures conceive differently than others such categories as space, time, unity, plurality, thingness, and causality. To bring Kant up to date, we might make Berkeley's move of supposing that these categories are more related to conventionality than Kant realized, particularly to language. But then we could preserve some rationalism by asserting Chomsky's thesis that these categories may be culturally relative because they are partially bound to "surface grammar." Then, in turn, this surface grammar itself is bound to "deep grammar," which is derived from innate neurological facts.

Recent developments in philosophy may persuade us to make other adjustments as well. We may have to consider abandoning the search, shared by both rationalists and empiricists, for the *foundations* of knowledge. Descartes and all his epistemological followers as well as his detractors latched onto the architectural metaphor of "a house of knowledge," believing that knowledge could exist only if it were based on something absolutely certain. For the rationalists, this certainty was to be found in the a priori truths derived from innate ideas. For the empiricists, it was derived from the privileged experience of sense data. But it is beginning to look as though there is something wrong with the metaphor. Perhaps (as the contemporary American philosophers W. V. O. Quine and Richard Rorty suggest) rather than being like a house, knowledge is more like a net or spiderweb. If some segments prove weak or worn out, we repair them while hanging on to the relatively stable parts, which still offer support.

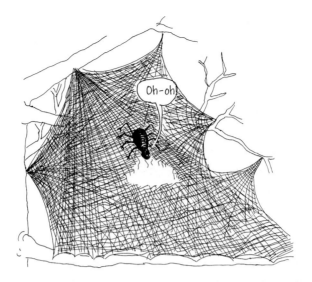

Speech bubble: Oh-oh!

Is Our System of Knowledge More Like a Spiderweb Than a House?

Besides objecting to the knowledge-house metaphor, Rorty suspects that the main error in epistemology was that of accepting Plato's simile that *knowing* is like a kind of *mental seeing*, in which case knowledge is always a relationship between a belief and its object. In Rorty's influential book *Philosophy and the Mirror of Nature*, he accepts the Platonic view that knowledge is justified belief, but he tries to show that "justification" is constituted by establishing a relation not between a belief and an object of belief but between a belief and *arguments*. He says, "If . . . we think of 'rational certainty' as a matter of victory in argument rather than of relation to an object known, . . . we shall be looking for an airtight case rather than an unshakeable foundation."[5] We will then realize that there is no natural end to justification. Rather, the defense *could* go on forever. Perhaps, as in a court of law, the defense is usually terminated somewhat arbitrarily. Certainly, no claim to knowledge is ever immune to revision. Furthermore, according to Rorty, we have to realize that justification is a *social*—hence a *historical*—phenomenon. (Not every form of argument will be convincing at all historical moments.) Rorty holds that traditional epistemology is an attempt to escape from history by claiming to establish extrahistorical and extrasocial criteria of rationality and objectivity. Rorty distinguishes between "normal discourse" (any form of discourse—whether scientific, moral, theological, or political—governed by agreed-upon criteria for reaching consensus) and "abnormal discourse" (any form of discourse that lacks such criteria). And he claims that traditional epistemology has been

"a self-deceptive effort to eternalize the normal discourse of the day."[6] Nevertheless, innovation has always been the result of struggles between "normal" and "abnormal" discourse. There's something exciting about this relativistic, pragmatic message but also something slightly disconcerting because Rorty admits that his view brings us back to the position of the Greek Sophists—those relativists who, according to Socrates and Plato, championed a world with no center.

Topics for Consideration

1. Write a short essay stating how you think Plato would analyze an idea like "justice" or "mammal" (see Chapter 2) and compare it with the way you suppose Aristotle would treat the same topic.
2. Why does Locke think that his "blank slate" theory of the mind is superior to Descartes's theory of the mind based on "innate ideas" (see Chapter 1)? How does Locke go about establishing his proof? Why, according to the presentation of Locke's theory in this chapter, does his argument falter?
3. Locke says, "Since the mind . . . hath no other immediate object but its own ideas, which it alone can contemplate, it is evident that our knowledge is only conversant about them." Show how this view, taken very literally, "deconstructs" Locke's own general theory and leads directly to Berkeley's theory that "*esse is percipi.*"
4. State the main principles of empiricism, then show how Hume applies them more consistently than either Locke or Berkeley and how his radical empiricism leads to skepticism.

5. Take these three propositions and show how the logical empiricists would analyze them:

   a. No unicorn has more than one horn.

   b. Removing support from weighted objects causes them to fall.

   c. God is love.

6. Try to clarify the difference between Descartes's theory of "innate ideas" (Chapter 2) and Kant's theory of "innate structures."

7. Berkeley thought he could apply Ockham's razor to the rationalists' notion of "innate ideas" by showing that we learn the concepts of "sameness" (= identity) and "thingness" (= substance) when, as children, we acquire a language. Show how Chomsky's critique of this empiricistic view takes us right back to the rationalists.

Suggestions for Further Reading:
Paperback Editions

Alfred Jules Ayer, *Language, Truth, and Logic* (New York: Dover, n.d.) A short, well-written presentation of the main tenets of logical positivism by one of its most able practitioners.

George Berkeley, *Three Dialogues between Hylas and Philonous* (New York: Bobbs-Merrill Library of the Liberal Arts, 1954; also in *The Empiricists*). Berkeley's theory presented for the general reader in the form of a humorous Platonic dialogue. "Hylas" is John Locke, and "Philonous" is Berkeley himself.

The Empiricists: Locke, Berkeley and Hume (New York: Doubleday Anchor Books, 1974). A good anthology of the most important epistemological works of the three major empiricists.

John Lyons, *Noam Chomsky* (New York: The Viking Press, 1970). A short, comprehensive overview of Chomsky's main arguments. In the "Modern Masters" series.

Steven Pinker, *The Language Instinct: How the Mind Creates Language* (New York: HarperPerennial, 1995). A readable, spirited defense of a Chomskian picture of language, written by a very bright, annoyingly opinionated guy.

Roger Scruton, *Kant* (Oxford: Oxford University Press, 1982). A nice overview of the work of a very difficult philosopher. In the "Past Masters" series.

Notes

1. John Locke, *An Essay Concerning Human Understanding*, ed. A. C. Fraser (Oxford: Clarendon Press, 1894), bk. II, chap. I, sec. 2. Unless otherwise stated, all subsequent quotes from Locke in this chapter are from this source.

2. George Berkeley, *A Treatise Concerning the Principles of Human Knowledge*, ed. G. J. Warnock (Cleveland: World Publishing, 1963), part I, sec. 1.

3. David Hume, *A Treatise of Human Nature*, ed. L. A. Selby-Bigge (Oxford: Clarendon Press, 1941), bk. 1, part IV, sec. 6, pp. 251–253. All subsequent quotes from Hume in this chapter are from this source.

4. Noam Chomsky, *Aspects of the Theory of Syntax* (Cambridge, Mass.: M. I. T. Press, 1965), p. 59.

5. Richard Rorty, *Philosophy and the Mirror of Nature* (Princeton, N.J.: Princeton University Press, 1980), pp. 156–157.

6. Ibid., p. 11.

4

Who's on First,
What's on Second?
Ontology

Ontology is theory of reality or theory of being. The big questions in ontology are these:

- What is real and what is merely appearance?
- Can there be a theory that draws the distinction between reality and appearance and accounts for everything that exists, or must these distinctions always remain contextual, *ad hoc*, and informal?

The historical framework for ontological discussions has been in terms of the following categories:

What Is Real and What Is Merely Appearance

Monism: the view that there is only one reality or only one kind of ~~body~~ thing that is real. 1) materialism - no minds, only atoms

Dualism: the view that there are two forms of reality or two kinds of real things. physical substance & mental substance

Pluralism: the view that reality is composed of many different kinds of real things.

Nihilism: the view that nothing is real (or sometimes, as a moral doctrine, that nothing *deserves* to exist).

We have inadvertently witnessed quite a bit of ontological discussion in Chapters 1 through 3 because most of the traditional epistemologists defined knowledge in terms of its *object*, which was always some real entity (e.g., Forms for Plato and sense data for Berkeley). We have seen that Plato, Descartes, and Locke should all be categorized as dualists. Berkeley's idealism is a form of monism.

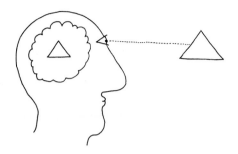

Knowledge Defined in Terms of Its Object—Which Is Some Real Thing

Dualism

Descartes's version is the most radical form of dualism, and even though it is an extreme version, its very exaggeration throws light on the problems of dualism in general. We saw in Chapter 2 that Descartes circumscribed two distinct spheres of being: the mental (mind, or as Descartes sometimes calls it, "spiritual substance") and the physical (body, or "material substance"). The subtitle of Descartes's *Meditations on First Philosophy* includes this line, ". . . in which . . . the Distinction between Mind and Body [is] Demonstrated." (In fact, in his first draft, the subtitle had been ". . . in Which the Immortality of the Soul Is Demonstrated," but when a critic pointed out that Descartes had nowhere even *mentioned* the immortality of the soul, much less proved its existence, Descartes changed the subtitle wording to refer to the absolute distinction between mind and body, which to Descartes's way of thinking at least made *possible* the immortality of the soul.) According to Descartes, a body is "an extended thing" (res extensa) whose characteristics are these: extension, size, shape, location, divisibility, motion, and rest. At the other extreme is mind (or soul or self), which is "a thing which thinks" (res cogitans). Descartes asks, "What is a thing which thinks? It is a thing which doubts, understands, conceives, affirms, denies, wills, refuses, which also imagines and feels."[1] These two "things" are completely different from each other and can exist independently of each other.

Descartes says:

Substance	MIND	BODY
Essence	Thought	Extension
Modes	affirmation denial doubt volition hope	size shape location part mobility

Descartes's Ontology of Finite Things

I rightly conclude that my essence consists solely in the fact that I am a thinking thing (or a substance whose whole essence or nature is to think). And although possibly (or rather certainly, as I shall say in a moment) I possess a body with which I am very intimately conjoined, yet because, on the one side, I have a clear and distinct idea of myself inasmuch as I am only a thinking and unextended thing, and as, on the other, I possess a distinct idea of body, inasmuch as it is only an extended and unthinking thing, it is certain that this I (that is to say, my soul by which I am what I am), is entirely and absolutely distinct from my body, and can exist without it. ("Meditation IV," pp. 213–214)

Well and good! Descartes has established that, given his definitions of mind and body, they can exist without each other. But the real question is how they can exist with each other. How can a nonextended spiritual substance located nowhere have any effect on something so different from itself as inert matter? How can the human being be some strange combination of mind and body? (This issue is what

"I Am Absolutely Distinct from My Body and Can Exist without It."

the British philosopher Gilbert Ryle called the problem of "the ghost in the machine.") Now, we know that there is interaction between mind and body. (If I stomp on your foot, you will be conscious of a sensation of pain [body influencing mind], and if you remember that you left your car lights on, you will rush to the parking lot to extinguish them [mind influencing body].) The question is, on Descartes's account, how is this possible? Descartes addressed the issue in the following way:

The Ghost in the Machine

> I am not only lodged in my body as a pilot in a vessel, but . . . I am very closely united to it, and so to speak so intermingled with it that I seem to compose with it one whole. For if that were not the case, when my body is hurt, I, who am merely a thinking thing, should not feel pain, for I should perceive this wound by understanding only, just as the sailor perceives by sight when something is damaged in his vessel. ("Meditation VI," p. 216)

This is good! Imagine a ship's pilot on his bridge trying to maneuver his vessel between two rocky promontories. It is a narrow passageway, but he thinks he can make it. He keeps looking from left to right. As he is looking port side, suddenly there is a sickening "cruuunch" on his right. He looks starboard and sees that he has scraped a rock, and a yawning tear is gouged in the ship's hull. "Oh criminey," he thinks, "now I'm in trouble!" What if our relation to our body were like that of the captain to his ship? You are standing in the kitchen talking to a friend, resting your hand on the stove. After a while you smell the odor of burning flesh. You look to the stove and see your skin smoking. You pull your burning hand from the stove and say, "Oh criminey, now I'm in trouble!" Or what if you were walking along, heard a sharp "snap," felt a loss of support, looked down, and *noticed* that you'd broken your leg. Descartes is right. This is *not* the relation that exists between our mind and our body. We do not observe that our body is damaged, then deduce that we are in pain. As Descartes says, our consciousness and our body are "so intermingled" as to "compose . . . one whole." Yet, once again, on his account, how is this possible? Here is what Descartes has to say about this problem when he addresses it specifically:

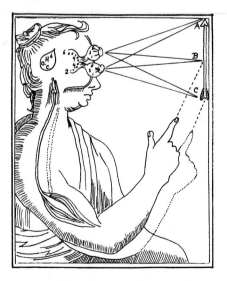

The Smell of Burned Flesh

I had clearly ascertained that the part of the body in which the soul exercises its functions immediately is in nowise the heart, nor the whole of the brain, but merely the most inward of all its parts, to wit, a certain very small gland which is situated in the middle of its substance and so suspended above the duct whereby the animal spirits in its anterior cavities have communication with those in the posterior, that the slightest movements which take place in it may alter very greatly the course of these spirits; and reciprocally that the smallest changes which occur in the course of the spirits may do much to change the movements of this gland.[2]

Copy of a Seventeenth-Century Wood Engraving Demonstrating Descartes's Theory of the Pineal Gland

Descartes has selected what is now called the *pineal gland* as the locus of interaction between body and soul. Perhaps his logic was this: that gland doesn't seem to do anything else—probably it serves this function. Using this logic, he could as easily have decided in favor of the tonsils or the appendix. (Besides, although some debate continues about the pineal gland's function, apparently it has something to do with controlling the size of the gonads. If so, his conclusion makes Descartes much more of a Freudian than he'd like to be.) But the real problem with selecting the pineal gland as the place where mind and body meet is that in doing so, Descartes has *located* mind, and as you will recall, "location" is a characteristic of body, not of mind. If Descartes locates the mind *anywhere*, he thereby transforms it into body, and then he becomes a materialist. This conclusion, of course, would be exactly the opposite of the one Descartes set out to prove, and his whole ontology seems to unravel right here. At this point, Descartes conveniently died of the common cold and left the paradox to be sorted out by later generations.

Herr Professor Doktor Freud and Monsieur Descartes

His soul just departed from the pineal gland.

Did!

Didn't!

Didn't!

Materialistic Monism

Materialism

Descartes had made the relation between mind and body so mysterious that it is no surprise to find later philosophers turning away from his dualism to monism. We have seen how Berkeley tries to apply Ockham's razor to dualism by eliminating the whole material side of it. But idealism has never been very popular in the West. Berkeley and G. W. F. Hegel (the other famous European idealist) each had followers, but even these disciples tried to rewrite their mentors' works to avoid their idealistic conclusions. A much more popular form of monism in the West is that of **materialism,** particularly in current times, because many people, both philosophers and nonphilosophers, feel that the authority of modern science is on the side of materialism. We will look at several versions of this doctrine: behaviorism, the **mind-brain identity theory, eliminative materialism,** and **functionalism.**

Behaviorism

Though this doctrine is primarily promulgated by psychologists, it has philosophical import and philosophical disciples. It is the creature of the American psychologist JOHN WATSON (1878–1958), and its most articulate contemporary spokesman was B. F. Skinner, whom we have already encountered. One reason that this doctrine is a bit difficult to get ahold of is that several variations exist, and sometimes its defenders slide from one version to another (perhaps so as not to get cornered). I will try to reduce these variations to a manageable handful, namely, to what I will call **hard behaviorism, soft behaviorism,** and **logical behaviorism.**

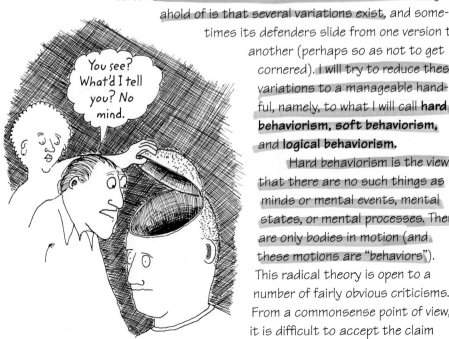

You see? What'd I tell you? No mind.

Hard behaviorism is the view that there are no such things as minds or mental events, mental states, or mental processes. There are only bodies in motion (and these motions are "behaviors"). This radical theory is open to a number of fairly obvious criticisms. From a commonsense point of view, it is difficult to accept the claim

that the sentence "Mary is in pain" is either always false or always meaningless, or that the word "pain" merely designates a grouping of various
behaviors (grimacing, groaning, grasping the "painful" limb, etc.). One objection to this view is that we can feign pain or sometimes suppress the
behavior associated with pain. Another objection points out that some
mental activities have no particular outward behavior associated with them
(for example, wondering). Soft behaviorism avoids some of the problems
faced by hard behaviorism. It is the view that there may be minds and mental events, states, and processes but that methodologically scientists can
provide adequate explanations and predictions of activity in general, human
or otherwise, without ever referring to anything mental.

   This second view is not really a philosophical (i.e., ontological) one, and
it is much less controversial than the first—though not without difficulties
of its own. The problem is that behaviorists who seem to be asserting the
"hard" version sometimes slip into the "soft" version when cornered. But
when left alone again, they return to the "hard" position.

   What both versions of behaviorism assert is something like this: all
statements about human activity, including statements about people's
so-called mental life, can be translated into statements about observable
"behaviors" and, if not, can be shown to be either false or nonsense. So if
I say, "Mary thinks it's going to rain," I should be able to show that making
this statement is really shorthand for a whole bunch of other assertions, like:

> "Mary utters the sentence, 'I think it's going to rain'."
> "Mary has worn her raincoat and taken her
>   umbrella."
> "Mary is wearing her boots, not her
>   sandals."
> "Mary canceled her reservation at
>   the outdoor restaurant."

And if I say, "Bill is angry at Sam,"
I should be able to show that some or
all of the following assertions are true:

> "Bill utters the sentence, 'I am
>   angry at Sam'."
> "Bill raises his voice—he says rude
>   things whenever Sam's name is
>   mentioned."
> "Bill's face is red; his knuckles are white."

I know it doesn't seem like it, but they are absolutely furious with each other.

Behaviorism has some plausibility. In a certain sense, we are all behaviorists vis-à-vis other people. Whatever you know about anybody, including your best friends, you know by observing their *behavior* (which includes listening to what they have to say, of course). None of us has an antenna to pick up the thoughts of others. The only access to other people's mind is in fact through observation of these people's activity, which I suppose is in some sense observation of their body. Furthermore, behaviorism becomes philosophically plausible because we were led to it through certain problems with dualism. It was, after all, Descartes who unwittingly opened the floodgates for behaviorism: first, by failing to show how mind-body interaction was possible, and, second, by never dealing satisfactorily with "the problem of other minds." (How do I know that anyone besides myself has a mind?) Shortly after discussing the famous "wax example," Descartes addressed this problem, writing:

> when looking from a window and saying I see men who pass in the street, I really *do* not see them but infer that what I see is men, . . . And yet what do I see from the window but hats and coats which may cover automatic machines? Yet I judge these to be men. And similarly, solely by the faculty of judgment, which rests in my mind, I comprehend that which I believed I saw with my eyes. ("Meditation II," p. 177)

Most critics find this conclusion very unsatisfactory. Descartes may have proved that *he* has a mind (or, as he says, that he *is* a mind), but he certainly hasn't proved that anyone else does. The observable data are quite compatible with the view that "everyone else" is really just a complicated robot (perhaps a *meaty* robot, but a robot just the same). Furthermore, the mind that Descartes proved to exist—that is, his own mind—is *not located;* it is nowhere. The behaviorist asks how much better is a mind that's nowhere than no mind at all.

Hats, Coats, and Automatic Machines

All these problems with dualism support the behaviorist's claims. But nevertheless problems exist for the behaviorist, and some are quite Cartesian in nature. For example, it may well be that I know that you have a stomachache because I see you grimace, hold your tummy, go to the medicine cabinet, and prepare yourself a "fizzy." But that is certainly not the way that I discover that I have a stomachache. I find out that I have a stomachache just the way Descartes says I do—I am immediately conscious of my pain. The soft behaviorist (but not the hard behaviorist) can retort that the scientist doesn't study herself; rather, she is studying others. Even so, a theory that is true for everyone but oneself is an odd one. (What if Newton had claimed that bodies on the earth's surface fall at thirty-two feet per second squared . . . except for his own body, which was exempt from that law!)

I am popping aspirin; therefore I am in pain.

Sir Isaac Newton Discovers the Law of Gravity, Which Applies to Everything but Himself

The second objection to behaviorism is also Cartesian in nature. Descartes had claimed that no account of human existence could be given without allowing a key role to a vocabulary designating mental acts: to affirm, to deny, to conceive, to know, to hope, to expect, to will, and so forth. Now, this is the very kind of list that Skinner wishes to get rid of on the grounds that these terms name mental events that in fact do not exist. Yet his own publications are rampant with these very verbs. Perhaps he thinks (thinks!?) that he is justified in using this "prescientific" language because he has to convert an unsophisticated public to his cause and doing so requires speaking street language with them (in Berkeley's phrase, to speak with the vulgar but think

with the refined).
And every now
and then, Skinner
catches himself
using the hated
vocabulary and
offsets it by
putting the ques-
tionable terms
within quotation
marks. (E.g.,
"Science . . . has
extended our

'understanding' [whatever that may be] . . .")[3] Whenever Skinner does this,
the implication is that if he wanted to, he *could* translate these offending
terms into truly scientific categories (i.e., into descriptions of behaviors
brought about by conditioning).

But *is* it really possible to make this translation? And would there
really be an advance in scientific clarity if we were able to do so? I have a
behaviorist colleague who, when asked at a symposium on love whether he
loved his wife, responded by saying, "I react positively to her behavioral con-
figurations, and she to mine." (!!!) Once when describing panicked people at
the scene of a fire, this
same chap said, "They
jumped from the win-
dows and engaged in
fleeing behavior"
instead of saying,
"They ran away." I
suppose people can
learn to talk this way,
but why would anyone
want to?

The view called "logi-
cal behaviorism" is an
important philosophical
theory. In one sense, how-

**Some People Engaged in Fleeing
Behavior; Others Running Away**

ever, perhaps a treatment of it doesn't belong precisely at this point of our
discussion, because logical behaviorists are not necessarily materialists—
some are and some aren't. We will inspect the version of logical behaviorism

set forth by GILBERT RYLE (1900–1976), the British **ordinary language philosopher** who in fact considered himself not a materialist but a pluralist. Indeed, Ryle never even used the term "logical behaviorism" to describe his own view. But because Ryle's theory came to be the most widely discussed version of logical behaviorism, I will include it here, even if it fits a little awkwardly.

Ryle's influential book of 1949, *The Concept of Mind*, constitutes a sustained attack on Cartesian dualism (though it also provides a critique of Skinner's hard behaviorism, to be discussed shortly). In the first chapter of his book, Ryle wrote:

> The official doctrine, which hails chiefly from Descartes, is something like this. With the doubtful exceptions of idiots and infants in arms, every human being has both a body and a mind. Some would prefer to say that every human being is both a body and a mind. His body and his mind are ordinarily harnessed together, but after the death of the body, his mind may continue to exist and function.
>
> Human bodies are in space and are subject to the mechanical laws which govern all other bodies in space. Bodily processes and states can be inspected by external observers. So a man's bodily life is as much a public affair as are the lives of animals and reptiles and even as the careers of trees, crystals, and planets.
>
> But minds are not in space, nor are their operations subject to mechanical laws. The workings of one mind are not witnessable by other observers; its career is private. Only I can take direct cognizance of the states and processes of my own mind. A person therefore lives through two collateral histories, one consisting of what happens in and to his body, the other consisting of what happens in and to his mind. The first is public, the second private. The events in the first history are events in the physical world, those in the second are events in the mental world.
>
> . . . .
>
> Underlying this partly metaphorical representation of the bifurcation of a person's two lives there is a seemingly more profound and philosophical assumption. It is assumed that there are two different kinds of existence or status. What exists or happens may have the status of physical existence, or it may have the status of mental existence. Somewhat as the faces of coins are either heads or tails, or somewhat as living creatures are either male or female, so it is supposed, some existing is physical existing, other existing is mental existing.
>
> . . . .
>
> Such in outline is the official theory. I shall often speak of it, with deliberate abusiveness, as "the dogma of the Ghost in the Machine." I hope to prove that it is entirely false and false not in detail but in principle. It is not merely an assemblage of particular mistakes. It is one big mistake and a mistake of a particular kind. It is, namely, a category-mistake. It represents the facts of

mental life as if they belonged to one logical type or category (or range of types or categories) when they actually belong to another.[4]

A **category-mistake** is the mistake of taking a term or phrase that belongs in one logical or grammatical category and erroneously placing it in another category and then drawing absurd conclusions from that miscategorization.

In fact, the whole of Lewis Carroll's books *Alice's Adventures in Wonderland* and *Through the Looking Glass* are great repositories of category-mistakes. Consider the discussion between Alice and the White King. The King is concerned about two messengers he is awaiting and says to Alice:

"Just look along the road, and tell me if you can see either of them."

"I see nobody on the road," said Alice.

"I only wish *I* had such eyes," the King remarked in a fretful tone. "To be able to see Nobody! And at that distance too! Why, it's as much as *I* can to do to see real people, by this light!"[5]

I only wish *I* had such eyes!

(After Sir John Tenniel)

The source of the joke here is obvious. The sentences "I see somebody" and "I see nobody" *look* similar. Grammatically, they each have a subject, a verb, and an object. But the category-mistake is that of believing that therefore the terms "somebody" and "nobody" are both names of existing entities.

Ryle, of course, gives us a couple of his own examples of category-mistakes. His first is of a foreigner who visits a university, where he is shown the library, classroom, quad, students, professors, sports fields, and administrative offices. Thanking his guide, he then says, "But where is the university?" He fails to see that the university is not something else *besides* all those things—it just *is* the totality of those items.

Ryle's second example is of another foreigner visiting his first cricket game. Having been shown all the features of the playing field and hearing all the functions of the players, he says, "But no one is left on the field to contribute to the famous element of team spirit. I see who does the bowling, the batting, and the wicket-keeping, but I do not see whose role it is to exercise *esprit de corps*."

This second example is especially instructive. Let's change the sport in the example from cricket to baseball because, if you're like me, you are a foreigner at a cricket game. Imagine that you are attending a baseball game with an interested but ignorant visitor from another culture who, after seeing you point out the bats, mitts, pitcher's mound, bleachers, pitchers, infielders, outfielders, base runners, umpire, and after hearing you explain base hits, home runs, and balls, then asks, "Where is the team spirit?" Obviously, you are not going to respond by saying, "Oh, terribly sorry to have left it out. It's right there between second and third base." It's not a thing you could point out at all. What *would* you say in respose to the question? Let's suppose you were René Descartes. In that case, you might say something like this:

TEAM SPIRIT

Team spirit (like *all* spirit) is a mental phenomenon, hence not a physical one. It is not located at all and cannot be shown. It can only be experienced. Therefore, strictly speaking, there is nothing to see—period.

Now let's suppose you were B. F. Skinner. You might say something like this:

Neither of these answers would be very satisfactory to the foreigner who wished to know what team spirit is, and, according to Ryle, they would both be based on a category-mistake. They would also be based on the same category-mistake

"Team spirit" is supposed to be the name of some mysterious spiritual entity. In fact, there are no such things as spiritual entities, hence no such thing as "team spirit." Frankly, we'd be better off abandoning the term and replacing it with a description of what's really there—namely, behaviors!

in each case—the mistake of thinking that terms like "team spirit" are names of ghostly episodes, then deducing the absurd conclusions that either (1) they can only be experienced in the first person (Descartes's view) or (2) they don't exist at all (Skinner's view). In fact, to say that ball players have "team spirit" is to refer to a certain way of playing. (They hustle; they "talk it up" [say "hey babe!" a lot]; they pat each other on the rear end; they throw the ball from player to player between plays; they run rapidly on and off the field at inning changes.)

Now, what Ryle would say about "team spirit" (which he thinks is what you and I would say about it in our "nonphilosophical" moments, and this is why he is called an ordinary language philosopher) is approximately what he says about other mentalistic terms like "intelligent," "stupid," "hopeful," and "intentional." He would say that these terms are not names of ghostly events that may or may not exist; rather, they are references to ways people do things.

To clarify this view, imagine the following scenario: I am your philosophy teacher. I am lecturing to you about Descartes.

When Team Spirit Departs

Suddenly the classroom door flies open and in strides a young man with a particularly intense look on his face. Before I can prevent it, he reaches into his pocket, pulls out a bottle of ink, uncaps it, and pours it on my head. With a malicious grin on his face, he turns to you and says, "Palmer flunked me last semester." Then he strides out. I yell, "He did that on purpose!" Naturally, I sue! You are my witnesses at the trial. In the state of California, in order to find a person guilty of a criminal act in the first degree, it must be established that he had *mens rea*, criminal intent. Suppose the young man's lawyer is Descartes. He addresses the jury,

An Intentional Act

saying, "My client is accused of intentionally injuring Professor Palmer, but in fact no one can know anyone's intention except his own because intentions are purely private phenomena. Therefore, in the absence of a confession by my client, there can be no evidence whatsoever that he had such an intention. Therefore, he must be found 'not guilty'."

Or suppose the young man's lawyer is Skinner, who might say, "My client is accused of intentionally injuring Professor Palmer. But what in fact is an intention? Can it be observed? Weighed? Passed around? Measured? Can samples be taken from it? No! There are no such things as intentions; therefore my client could not possibly have done anything 'intentionally'; hence he must be found to be innocent."

Neither defense would stand up in court for a minute. In order to establish that the act

Ladies and gentlemen of the jury, ...

was done intentionally, all the prosecuting attorney would have to do is call you as witnesses, and you would describe the *manner* in which the young man performed his act. According to Ryle, when we say that someone did something intentionally, all we mean is that the person did it in a certain manner. What manner? What is the function of saying that someone did something intentionally? It is to distinguish that action from something done accidentally. There is a big difference between running down the stairs to get the mail (intentionally) and falling down the stairs because you stepped on your son's skateboard (accidentally). Skinner's attempt to get

Just Going Downstairs to Check the Mail

rid of intentions has the consequence of abolishing that important distinction. Would the loss of this distinction really be a scientific advance? It's difficult to think so.

    The upshot of this discussion is that Ryle falls somewhere between Descartes and Skinner. He is in agreement with Descartes that it not only makes sense to use mentalistic terminology to describe human activity but it is absolutely necessary. But, despite his agreement with Descartes that mental terms are appropriate for describing features of human activity, Ryle is still closer to Skinner's behaviorism than to Descartes's dualism because Ryle thinks that the meaning of mental terms must ultimately be linked to observable behavior. To say that the young man intentionally poured ink on Professor Palmer is to describe a way of doing something; it is not to describe a ghostly event. This distinction is why Ryle is called a "logical behaviorist." The *logic* of a term like "intentional" must link that term up with some observable behavior.

I think it would be fair to say that Ryle has gone a long way toward dispelling the myth of the ghost in the machine. Yet problems remain. Ryle thinks that mental terms generally refer to *dispositions to behave* in certain ways. In the same way that

A Ghostly Event

we can talk about a pane of glass being disposed to break if struck by a stone, or sugar being disposed to dissolve if placed in liquid, so, according to Ryle, we can discuss human characteristics: "John is courageous."—He is disposed to stand his ground. "John knows long division."—He is disposed to be able to solve certain kinds of problems. "John is thoughtful."—He is disposed to pause in efficacious ways and not act precipitously. So far, so good. But it is certainly possible to be generally courageous yet uncharacteristically do a cowardly thing. And it is certainly possible to think deeply about long division without being disposed to *do* anything. Despite Ryle's efforts, the ghost in the machine has not been completely exorcized. It still haunts us in philosophy.

Either some one-eyed, striped, paranoid cannibal anteaters are diaphanous, or they are not. . . .

Not All Thoughts Can Be Acted Upon

The Mind-Brain Identity Theory

The version of materialism referred to as the mind-brain identity theory does not deny the existence of mental events (as does hard behaviorism) or claim that mental terminology is really a reference to ways of doing things (as does logical behaviorism). Rather, as the name indicates, it claims that mental terms do name real entities but what they name are in fact neurological events. This theory has the advantage over most forms of behaviorism of not needing to deny the Cartesian and commonsensical claim that mental states exist that are experienced as essentially private. (Only I can experience my thought, my headache.) Yet it avoids all the pitfalls of dualism and seems to have the authority of science behind it. In an influential article in 1959, the Australian philosopher J. J. C. SMART wrote:

> It seems to me that science is increasingly giving us a viewpoint whereby organisms are able to be seen as psychochemical mechanisms: it seems that even the behavior of man himself will one day be explicable in mechanistic terms. There does seem to be, so far as science is concerned, nothing in the world but increasingly complex arrangements of physical constituents. All except for one place: in consciousness. . . . So sensations, states of consciousness, do seem to be the one sort of thing left outside the physical picture, and for various reasons I just cannot believe that this can be so. That everything should be explicable in terms of physics (together of course with descriptions of the ways in which the parts are put together—roughly, biology is to physics as radio-engineering is to electromagnetism) except the occurrence of sensations seems to me to be frankly unbelievable.[6]

Smart's thesis is simply that "sensations are nothing over and above brain processes." He admits that his thesis cannot be proven to be true today, but he expects that someday it will be proven, and he is trying to pave the way for the development by establishing that there are no a priori (i.e., conceptual) objections to it. That is to say, he is trying to establish that there is nothing incoherent in the

Darling, I have a wonderful idea! Let's go out for dinner.

Shh. Don't bother me. Can't you see that I'm having a neurological event?

idea (as its critics claim). Smart thinks that the forthcoming discovery that mental states and processes are just brain states and processes will be very much like the earlier discoveries that:

- Lightning is an electrical discharge from cloud to cloud or cloud to surface.
- Water is H_2O.
- The morning star is the evening star.

It is important to see that Smart is not claiming that the terms on the left side of the verb "is" mean the same things as the terms on the right side. People used the words "lightning" and "water" long before the physical composition of lightning and water were discovered. So Smart's equation is not just a linguistic one but a scientific one. It can be proved not by looking at words but by looking at facts.

Yet a number of philosophers (including Jerome Shaffer, Norman Malcolm, and Richard Taylor) have registered objections to the identity theory's claim to be scientific by asking exactly what facts would have to be discovered to prove the **identity theory** true.[7] Keep in mind the nature of a strict identity of the type that holds between the morning star and the evening star (and between mental events and brain events, according to Smart). In terms of spatial and temporal features, everything that is true of the one side of the equation must be true of the other. If the morning star is the evening star, and if the morning star is X miles from the sun at time T¹, then the evening star must also be X miles from the sun at time T¹. If the evening star has a mass of Y, then the morning star must have a mass of Y. If there is any difference in these characteristics, then the morning star is *not* the evening star. What about thoughts and brain events? Do they have the same spatial and temporal features? But here's the rub. Does it make any sense at all to attribute spatial features to thoughts? Shaffer says:

> However, so far as thoughts are concerned, it makes no sense to talk about a thought's being located in some place or places in the body. If I report having suddenly thought something, the question *where* in my body that thought occurred would be utterly senseless. It would be as absurd to wonder whether that thought might have been cubical or a micron in diameter.[8]

We seem to have a rapidly fading, erratic, incoherent, possibly psychotic neuron firing here.

Shaffer's point is not that it is impossible to prove that thoughts have location, nor that the view that they are located may turn out to be false, but that that view is *absurd*. You can say all sorts of things about the physical properties of neurons—you can talk about their size, shape, color, weight. But what sense would there be in asking whether the realization that you left your lunch at home was a triangular or tubular realization, a yellow or a gray one, a light or a heavy one? According to Shaffer, if there are things that make perfect sense to say about brain states but are nonsense when said about mental states, then mental states are not brain states, and the identity theory is false (in the same way that if there were things that made perfect sense when said about the morning star but were nonsense when said about the evening star, then the morning star could not be the evening star). In other words, Shaffer is accusing Smart of committing a category-mistake.

It is difficult to evaluate Shaffer's view. His argument has some weight because it certainly does seem odd to talk about thoughts, feelings,

Talking Nonsense about the Evening Star

hopes, expectations, beliefs, and intentions using the vocabulary of three-dimensional physical objects. Yet perhaps Shaffer is open to the criticism that his argument "begs the question" (i.e., *presupposes* to be true the very thing it ought to *prove* to be true). Is it really impossible that someday linguistic conventions will develop that will allow the association of mental phenomena with physical models? Probably it would have once seemed absurd to associate the experience of warmth or cold with a numerical value, but after the invention of the thermometer, we find that association perfectly normal. Who's to say that a future scientific discovery or invention won't result in the normalization of sentences like "My C-fibers, section M12-0332, just fired at intensity" instead of "I just realized I left my lunch at home"? But even so, Shaffer would ask how could C-fibers firing be *false* or *misleading* in the way that thoughts and sensations can be?

Another argument arises against the identity theory that is easier to understand and evaluate. This criticism does not intend to show the identity theory to be nonsense but to demonstrate it as nonempirical, as not scientific. Suppose that neurophysiology advances so far that someday a kind of brain scanner will exist capable of showing that every time any conscious activity takes place (thoughts, sensations, emotions), certain neurological activities are identified with exactitude. Every time, for example, María reports that she realizes she left her lunch at home, the scanner demonstrates that her C-fibers, section M12-0332, fired at intensity n and vice versa. Would this demonstration prove that mental states are brain states? No. The most it would prove is that mental states are correlated with brain states; that is, that every time one happens, the other happens simultaneously. But correlation—even strict correlation—is not identity.

Even with the most advanced technological equipment, it would be impossible to establish that just because thoughts are always correlated with events in the brain, they are identical with those events. Therefore, even if the mind-brain identity theory were true, it could never be known to be true. It could not, as the philosophers of science say, be "falsified." That is, no evidence could possibly exist that would tend to establish its truth or falsity. This fact certainly detracts from the identity theory's claim to be scientific.

Eliminative Materialism

Some materialists have come to the conclusion that these arguments against the identity theory are cogent, so they have modified the theory to what is called eliminative materialism, or **eliminativism.** According to this version, the identity "Mental events are brain events" should no longer be thought of as being like "The morning star is the evening star" but as being more like the following:

"'Zeus's thunder-bolts' are discharges of static electricity."

"'Demonical possession' is a form of hallucinatory psychosis."

"The 'quantity of caloric fluid' is the mean kinetic energy of molecules."

"'Unicorn horns' are narwhals horns."[9]

In other words, the correct formula is no longer "X = Y." Rather, it is "What people used to call X is now known to be Y." Richard Rorty suggests that future scientific discoveries may so upstage our currently ordinary way of talking about "mental

Ben Is About to Learn Something Important

phenomena" that we may someday say, "My C-fibers are stimulated," instead of, "I am in pain." Rorty is not actually claiming that a sentence like "I am in pain" is *false* but that there might someday prove to be a better way of making this report. (By "better," he means better in terms of explanation and predictability.) In fact, Rorty seems loath to say that even sentences like "Zeus's thunderbolts are lighting up the evening sky" or "Dora is possessed by demons" are false. (This reluctance is because he apparently thinks that terms get their meaning and their truth value from being part of a theoretical or quasi-theoretical system and not from some permanent and ahistorical thing called "meaning.") It is just that we have now eliminated these language games for "better" ones.

Nevertheless, Rorty admits that the claim that there might turn out to be no such things as sensations of pain (in the way that there turned out to be no such things as demons) seems scandalous, but he thinks that the scandal alone does not constitute a refutation of his theory. Not surprisingly, a goodly number of philosophers do think that the scandal is enough to refute eliminative materialism. However, even though eliminative materialism is no longer the most popular theory among materialistically inclined **philosophers of mind,** eliminativism still has some distinguished defenders today, most notably Patricia and Paul Churchland, philosophers at the University of California at San Diego. For the Churchlands, mentalistic talk is simply part of "folk psychology"—the common, prescientific way of speaking about feelings, motivation, and conscious phenomena. For them, folk psychology has approximately the same status as folk physics, a quasi-theoretical system we still use when we say things like "The sun is setting in the West," even though we now know better. According to the Churchlands, some of the components of folk psychology will eventually be shown to be reducible to components of neurobiology, and the rest will be shown to refer to nothing at all (like the "it" in "it is raining") and therefore will prove to be expendable. In this latter category we may find such items as mental images, beliefs, feelings, and desires.

The likelihood of your becoming converted to eliminative materialism may depend a lot on whether you accept the claim of the Churchlands that our normal way of thinking and talking about images, beliefs, feelings, and desires constitutes acceptance of a primitive theory (folk psychology) that, in this scientific day and age, requires replacement with a more sophisticated theory. Indeed, does our normal way of speaking of mental phenomena constitute a theory at all? The sentence "Dora is possessed by demons" is a *theoretical* sentence. It is based on a *theory* of demons. Not every culture has shared that theory, and some that once held that theory during stages of their history have abandoned it at later stages. But "I am in pain" is not a *theoretical* statement at all. One could know that one was in pain whether or not one believed any theory about pain. No doubt members of every culture have had such experiences as pain and have had linguistic ways of reporting those experiences that were independent of any theory and therefore incapable of being upstaged by a later theory. Philosophers like Richard Bernstein think that this fact alone is enough to show that what eliminative materialism wants to eliminate (viz., references to mental phenomena) cannot be eliminated.[10]

Functionalism and Its Discontents

Despite the problems that have plagued behaviorism and the mind-brain identity theory and eliminativism, most philosophers of mind seem to agree that some form of materialism (or physicalism, as it is also sometimes called) must be true. Most recently, the theory that has had the most appeal is functionalism. A great number of philosophers subscribe to it, but it is associated primarily with Jerry Fodor and Hilary Putnam, who are the pioneers, along with David Armstrong, David Lewis, and William Lycan. It emerged from the concerns expressed by **cognitive science**, a synthesis of philosophy, computer science, and neurology. Functionalism attempts, therefore, to develop a theory of mind that takes advantage of the insights of all three fields of study. According to functionalism, the mind must be thought of not as a *thing* (such as a Cartesian substance or a brain) but as a *system*. A system is an ensemble of related components with a function. This function can be described as the job that the system accomplishes—what it gets done. Or, to put it differently, it is the way that the collection of components interacts with the environment. In defining functions it is as if we were giving job descriptions. Think of a nurse or a welder. To qualify for either position you must possess certain knowledge and skills and you must be able to perform certain actions. Such requirements are also true of artifacts like knives and engines. But two different knives or two different engines can be composed of very different materials. They remain knives or engines just so long as they are able to perform their functions— to cut and to produce power, respectively.

Now, what function do minds perform? According to the functionalist model, minds primarily carry out computations. The process of computation can be characterized as the manipulation of symbols in accordance with formal rules. So far, it sounds as if the functionalists are defining minds as computers, and, indeed, most of them do not hesitate to say that computers think. But it is not only humans and computers that have minds, according to functionalism. Lower animals such as jellyfish, or aliens such as Martians have minds if they can carry out computations. Functionalists want to avoid what they call "human chauvinism"—the error of defining minds so that, a priori, they could be attributed *only* to humans. (This error, by the way, may be one fallacy of the mind-brain identity theory. If we equate individual thoughts, intentions, or feelings with individual states or processes of the human brain, then we might be artificially committed to the view that, by definition, beings without brains exactly like our own could not have minds.) Functionalists like to say that mental phenomena are "multiply realizable." The same function, or "job description," might be realized in physical systems that are very different from each other. In fact, if it could be demonstrated that a row of tin cans, or a row of tin cans and jellyfish, could pro-

Functionalism in Action

duce computations, then the functionalists would assert that that "system" had a mind. And if it could be empirically established that there exist angels or gods that can engage in computation, then the functionalist would be committed to agreeing that they too had minds.

This last example shows that functionalism is not *necessarily* a form of materialism. However, it will tend to remain materialistic until empirical evidence of the existence of computational angels or gods becomes overwhelming. Then in what sense can we call functionalism a form of materialism? Well, for example, in human beings thoughts and intentions are caused by events in the brain. Events in the brain are material events, but thoughts and intentions are not material events. The brain relates to its products (mental events) in the same way that a computer relates to its computations. The solution to a mathematical problem—say, the square root of nine—whether reached by a human or a computer, is not itself a material state or event. Mental events are realized in parts of brains but are not themselves identical to parts of brains. If we speak of minds or mental capacities we are abstracting from the brains that realize them and speaking about a higher level—the actions that the brains realize. These mental events enter into causal networks. A decision or an intention can produce something in the world, so decisions and intentions have causal power. We do not have to choose between the language of the programmer and the language of the engineer who builds the computer. They are both right; they are talking about different levels of reality. Similarly, we do not have to choose between the language of the neurologist and the language of common sense. Ordinary language is right. There are mental events (I do intend to go to the movies tonight), and they are real (my intention will produce some action). Materialism is also correct. All mental events are realized in material systems (as far as we know). As philosopher of mind John Heil says:

> Functionalism is staunchly anti-reductionist, firmly committed to a conception of the world as containing distinct and irreducible levels of properties. Although higher levels are thought to be "autonomous" with respect to lower levels—higher levels are not reducible to, identifiable with, or collapsible into lower levels—higher levels are typically said to "supervene" on (to "depend on" and/or be "determined by") lower levels.[11]

Well, then, is functionalism the definitive answer to the mind-body problem? I am sure that you will not be surprised when I tell you that, despite its general popularity among professional philosophers, it has suffered some criticism. Professor John Searle at the University of California at Berkeley has argued against the adequacy of any computer-based model of the mind. First, no successful concept of mind can be generated that avoids explaining how symbols gain meaning (that is, lacks a semantics), and no system involving merely the manipulation of uninterpreted symbols can produce such a theory; it can only produce a syntax—a set of formal rules for maneuvering meaningless cyphers. As Searle says, "a computer has a syntax, but no semantics."[12] To repeat, a set of purely formal rules (syntax) cannot produce meaning (semantics). If I teach a parrot to utter the sounds "fĭn thăŋks" whenever it hears the sounds "hou är yōō?" I will not have bestowed a mind on it. Furthermore, according to Searle, all too much emphasis is placed by functionalists on the idea that computer programs follow rules. Following rules, too, requires a semantics. He says, "In order that a rule be followed, the meaning of the rule has to play some causal role in the behavior. . . . In the sense in which human beings follow rules . . . , in that sense computers don't follow rules at all. They only act in accord with certain formal procedures" (p. 47). He calls this point a metaphorical sense of rule following and claims that functionalism trades on the confusion between the literal and metaphorical senses of the term.

Another kind of argument against functionalism has to do not with the semantic components of mental experience but rather with its qualitative features, an area that functionalism almost totally ignores. You will recall that in his *Meditations*, Descartes asked how it was possible to be certain that the people who surrounded him were not in fact merely well-functioning "automatic machines" that duplicated human behavior and language (see page 121).

Although these machines could manipulate symbols and carry out calculations, they would have no thoughts and no feelings. They could simulate smiles and frowns and produce the sounds equivalent to saying that they had forgotten their umbrellas, but they would feel no pain, no joy, no dread, no excitement, could taste no sweetness

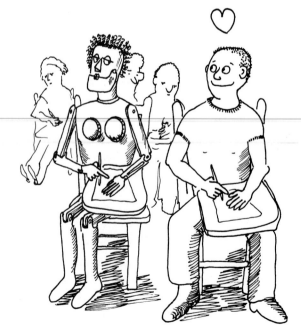

nor feel no breeze caress their "skin." They could distinguish between a fine burgundy and a cheap jug wine (perhaps by molecular analysis), but they could not taste the difference. The sensations that these machines lack have come to be known in the literature as **qualia,** from the Latin word for "qualities." Descartes's automatic machines would experience no qualia. They would be, for all intents and purposes, zombies. Now, the question we must ask is, How do you know that your functionalist philosophy professor is not a zombie? Functionalism seems perfectly compatible with the possibility that no minds experience qualia. So, the next question is, How do you know that *you* experience qualia? And if you think that you *do* experience them (and you probably do think so), how do you know that they are real? Is the last question I posed absurd, as some of the critics of functionalism believe? If so, we seem to be plunged right back into Descartes's world, and it appears that not much progress has been made since his time.

Because of considerations like these, a number of philosophers have once again turned their attention to the problem of the *experience* of mental states. As one of them has recently written, "Consciousness is back. [Despite] becoming a taboo topic for much of the last fifty years, consciousness currently enjoys the status of a 'hot' topic in both psychology and the philosophy of mind."[13] The contemporary version of the problem of consciousness was first dramatically raised by Thomas Nagel in his influential article of 1974, "What Is It Like to Be a Bat?" Nagel points out that "anyone who has spent some time in an enclosed space with an excited bat knows what it is to encounter a fundamentally *alien* form of life."[14] This is because bats

> perceive the external world primarily by sonar, or echolocation, detecting the reflections, from objects within range, of their own rapid, subtly modulated, high-frequency shrieks. Their brains are designed to correlate the outgoing impulses with the subsequent echoes, and the information thus acquired enables bats to make precise discriminations of distance, size, shape, motion and texture comparable to those we make by vision.

Now, as scientists we might someday learn everything there is to know about how the brains and nervous systems of bats work, but we still would have no idea what it is like to be a bat—what "bat experience" is like. Nagel reminds us that he is not asking what it would be like if *you* were a bat (eating insects, hanging from the rafters by your feet, etc.). Rather, he is asking what's it like for a *bat* to be a bat. Nagel and his followers conclude from this failed thought experiment that exhaustive studies of the human brain and nervous system may be able to explain what causes human mental

experience, but not what that experience is. The only way to answer the question, What is it like to be a human being (to have human experiences)? is to be a human being. Luckily, we are human beings, so we know what it is like, but we still have no idea how to give any scientific or philosophical account of mental experience.

We will look at three responses to this new concern about the problem of consciousness. Keep in mind (no pun intended) that each of these responses is well known among contemporary philosophers, but each is a minority report. It seems that most philosophers of mind have opted to stick with one version or another of functionalism.

John Searle, whom we have already met, believes that the mind-body problem is easy to solve. Conscious states are perfectly real and they are material in nature. That is, they are biological states of the brain. He writes:

> Mental phenomena, all mental phenomena whether conscious or unconscious, visual or auditory, pains, tickles, itches, thoughts, indeed, all of our mental life, are caused by processes going on in the brain. (p. 18)

Mental phenomena are not just caused by brain processes. They "just are features of the brain (and perhaps the rest of the central nervous system)" (p. 19). In the same way that microproperties in physics (such as molecules, atoms, and subatomic particles) can be said to produce or constitute macroproperties (such as liquidity or hardness), so the microproperties of the human brain (neurons) produce macroproperties of consciousness (thought, emotions, etc.). In the same way that no individual molecules are wet or hard, no individual neurons are subjective, or **intentional** (that is, neurons are not *about* other things; they do not refer to other things). But in certain dynamic combinations oxygen and hydrogen molecules manifest liquidity, and the lattice structure occupied by the molecules of which the table is composed manifest solidity. Similarly, the firing of neurons at the microlevel produces consciousness at the macrolevel. Such neurological activity manifests itself as the desires that make me *want* liquid or tables. That is, some biological states are intentional. This is simply a scientific fact, according to Searle. Furthermore, the reason that mental events can be the cause of physical events is that mental events *are* physical events. (Remember, Descartes declared the mind to be an independent substance because mental states seemed to him to be so completely different from physical states; but because of these gross differences, he could not explain how mental events could cause physical events. This was the modern beginning of the mind-body problem.)

According to Searle, the reason many philosophers reject his simple solution to the mind-body problem is that they fail to see how the same micro-macro relationship that applies in physics also applies in neurology. Furthermore, they misguidedly assume that the scientific world-picture entails that every fact must be an objective fact, that is, that every fact can be described from a third-person point of view. But according to Searle, it is

> a mistake to suppose that the definition of reality should exclude subjec-
> tivity. If 'science' is the name of the collection of objective and systematic
> truths we can state about the world, then the existence of subjectivity is an
> objective scientific fact like any other. . . [I]t is just a plain fact about biologi-
> cal evolution that it has produced certain sorts of biological systems, namely
> human and certain animal brains, that have subjective features. (p. 25)

Another, more radical response to the question of the relation between the mind and the world comes from David Chalmers. It too is a minority report, but his 1996 book, *The Conscious Mind: In Search of a Fundamental Theory*, published by the Oxford University Press, made a big splash.
Chalmers doesn't deny that functionalism does a pretty good job of dealing
with certain cognitive computational skills, such as cataloguing similarities,
discriminating among stimuli, and responding to challenges, but he chides
the materialistic philosophers of mind for avoiding the "hard" questions
about consciousness. They never did give a theory of consciousness; rather,
they gave theories of everything else. What is missing for Chalmers is
exactly what was missing for Nagel, namely an account of the fact that

there is something it is like to be conscious (as in Nagel's question, "What is it like to be a bat?"), that there is something called *conscious experience* that is rich, deep, and undeniable.

According to Chalmers, a successful theory must deal with consciousness as a fundamental property in the way that physicists deal with fundamental properties in their own fields. Similarly, just as physicists show that these properties behave in accord with basic laws that relate them to other fundamental properties, so must the philosophy of mind face up to the fact that there must be basic laws that relate conscious life to the rest of reality. Chalmers is committed, therefore, to a blatant form of dualism, though it should be called property dualism rather than substance dualism, as in Descartes's ontology. Mental properties, for example, intentionality, are real features of the world, just as are physical properties like three-dimensionality. But the fact that these properties are real does not entail that there are real substances (like "minds") to which these properties belong. It is enough that these are real properties of the real world. According to Chalmers, once we have stated those laws, there will be no mysterious gaps between the physical and the mental features of the world. This dualistic picture will become part of the scientific understanding of reality.

Though Chalmers has impressed many of his opponents with his refutations of some of the standard arguments of functionalism and has gained sympathizers with his demonstration that functionalism as it now exists can never produce a real theory of consciousness, what appear to be the weakest links in his own theory are the psychophysical bridging laws that his theory requires. Critics say that these laws have yet to be clearly conceived.

The last of the antifunctionalists we will look at is Colin McGinn, who is not only a minority voice in the discussion of the mind-brain problem, but is more like a voice crying in the wilderness. But like Saint John the Baptist himself—the first such voice—McGinn is heard by many and has baptized a few converts. His several books on the topic are well known, and his articles appear in many anthologies of the philosophy of mind.

In his latest book, *The Mysterious Flame: Conscious Minds in a Material World,* McGinn starts with a very Cartesian idea.

> We are aware of consciousness inwardly, while we are aware of the brain outwardly. . . . You can look into your mind until you burst, and you will not discover neurons and synapses and all the rest; and you can stare at someone's brain from dawn to dusk and you will not perceive the consciousness that is so apparent to the person whose brain you are so rudely eyeballing.[15]

Yet there must be a unity, McGinn argues. (He is, after all, a materialist.) He agrees with Searle, whom he does not mention in this book, that consciousness must arise from neural states in accordance with a "principle of emergence," the way ice emerges from the properties of liquid. But unlike Searle, McGinn does not believe that anyone—philosopher or neurologist—has come anywhere near explaining what those neurological

Colin McGinn

properties are or "how the brain contrives to generate consciousness to begin with" (p. 69). Furthermore, we "have no idea what an explanation of consciousness would even look like" (p. 61). Because our ignorance is so abysmal, McGinn concludes that the sciences of physics and neurophysiology are radically incomplete—given their current formulations, they cannot solve the problem—and he begins to suspect that they are incompletable. We have stumbled on to such an intractable problem that it shows that science cannot answer all questions about material reality. This barrier does not stop McGinn from speculating that perhaps what we have failed to grasp is something about space itself, because, as Descartes pointed out, it is impossible to understand mental states spatially. Yet, says McGinn, being physical events, they must in some sense be spatial. McGinn wonders "whether the cognitive abilities with which evolution has equipped us are adequate to developing the radically new conception of space that [may be] required for understanding consciousness" (p. 130). After briefly surveying the history of evolution and the kinds of tools for survival that it has provided us, McGinn pessimistically concludes that there is no good reason to suppose that Mother Nature installed in us the necessary conceptual apparata. He says, "We are facing a problem that points to an enormous hole in our conceptual resources, a theoretical blindspot of epic proportions. This is why I refer to the problem as a mystery" (p. 62). He seems to delight in the fact that his enemies have called him a "hard-core mysterian" (p. 134), and he thinks that the mystery is not completely a bad thing. Perhaps it will humble us humans a bit and return us to the awe with which the original Greek philosophers faced being.

So, the purple haze descends,[16] the mysterious flame burns, and the ghost still haunts the machine.

Pluralism

So far we have looked at dualism and materialistic monism. Another alternative exists and that is pluralism. Ontological pluralism is the view that there is a plurality of real things and that this plurality cannot be reduced either to a duality or to a oneness. Historically, Aristotle is the most famous defender of this view. We have already seen in Chapter 3 that he believed reality was composed of individual "substances," which to him were,

The oak tree's "whatness" is its "oakness." It shares this with all other oak trees.

Its "thisness" is what is unique about it—what distinguishes it from all other oak trees.

in almost all cases, material objects with an essence. The essence (or "form," as he called it, borrowing Plato's term but deflating its other-worldliness) is the thing's "whatness" and its materiality is its "thisness." That is, an oak tree's whatness, its essence or form, is the combination of characteristics that make it an oak tree rather than, say, a pussycat; and its thisness is its individuality—what distinguishes this oak tree from all other oak trees (especially its spatial materiality—the fact that this oak tree is here, now, and none other is). Aristotle would have disagreed with the contemporary scientific view that "oakness" itself could be further analyzed into chemical, then molecular, then atomic, then subatomic combinations; so anyone who chose Aristotle's pluralism today would have to rewrite and update it.

Something like a revision of Aristotle's views took place during the twenty-year period after World War II at the hands of a group of British philosophers to whom we have already referred as ordinary language philosophers. Under the influence of Cambridge philosopher G. E. MOORE's (1873–1958) influential paper "A Defense of Common Sense" and the philosophy of Ludwig Wittgenstein (see more about him in Chapter 10), these philosophers defended a version of **naive realism** according to which reality is pretty much what it seems to be. Neither the categories of dualism or monism nor Kant's "Categories of the understanding" but the categories of ordinary language correctly account for the real world. Members of this school, such as Gilbert Ryle (whose logical behaviorism we just inspected) ask why we should accept the dualists' claim that everything in the world

The Argument between the Monist and the Dualist

must fit in either of two boxes (mind or matter) or the materialists' view that everything must fit in *one* box. There are *hundreds* of boxes. There are humans, rocks, clouds, newts, prime numbers, plans, leopards, carrots, square roots, political parties, corporations, marriages, and birthday parties (just for starters). There are also symphonies. Take Beethoven's Fifth. Is it physical, is it mental, or is it a combination of a physical thing and a mental thing? Nobody (but a philosopher) would ever ask such a question. Very little of interest can be said about Beethoven's Fifth in terms of these categories, and people who do have interesting things to say about it hardly ever deliver that information in terms of its being a physical thing or a mental thing.

Ludwig van Beethoven Contemplating the Fifth Symphony, Trying to Decide Whether It Is a Mental or a Physical Thing

What's true of Beethoven's Fifth is true of the U.S. Constitution. Is it a physical thing? No. Even if the parchment in Washington, D.C., burned, we would still have a Constitution. Nor does it make much sense to say that it is a mental thing (in which case, if for a moment everyone stopped thinking about it, would it cease to exist?). If it is a thing at all, it is a *social* thing, which is not at all the same as being a physical and a mental thing.

Ryle and the ordinary language philosophers did not deny that some things that exist in reality could be analyzed in terms of physics and chemistry. But they insisted that those things cannot be reduced to the categories of physics and chemistry. There is a fallacy involved in saying that because a table can be analyzed in terms of its molecular structure, therefore the table itself is unreal (or even less real than the molecules). A colleague of mine, a physics professor, tells his students that tables are not really solid. Then he explains that this is so because there is more space taken up by the distance between the atoms in the table than by the atoms themselves. As Ryle would say, this argument is absurd (another category-mistake). Here the scientist is wrong, and ordinary language is right. Tables

The Table Is Not Solid

are solid (or at least *good* tables are solid) even though the space between the atoms is greater than the space taken up by the atoms. As Ryle points out, the so-called world of science is not a more *real* world than the world of tables and chairs, any more than "the poultry world" (the name of a magazine for chicken farmers) is a more real world than the everyday world.

Conclusion

What conclusion should we draw from the various ontological alternatives presented and the welter of arguments for and against them? First, it seems to me that there is no good reason to believe radical dualism and lots of reasons to disbelieve it. In my opinion, the claim that there are two kinds of substances, a physical one and a spiritual one, has very little, if any, scientific evidence to back it up; and the philosophical problems generated by this view are so great as to overshadow any advantage the theory may have.

What about materialism? My own view is that in some sense, materialism must be true. That is, it must be true that our small corner of the universe is composed of the same "stuff" that the rest of the universe is composed of, and at this point in the history of science, this truth means that the universe is apparently composed of subatomic particles that are themselves composed of bundles or quanta of energy. But the sense in which material-

Dualism, If True, Does Have One Distinct Advantage

ism is true may turn out to be fairly trivial because I don't think there's much reason to expect that the accounts of human activity given by anthropologists, sociologists, psychologists, and by ourselves as ordinary individuals describing our own and other people's thoughts, actions, hopes, fears, and suspicions will ever be given in a more accurate form in terms of molecules, atoms, electrons, and quanta of energy. As the important American philosopher Saul Kripke puts it:

> Materialism, I think, must hold that a physical description of the world is a complete description of it, that any mental facts are "ontologically dependent" on physical facts in the straightforward sense of following from them by necessity. No identity theorist seems to me to have made a convincing argument against the intuitive view that this is not the case.[17]

It isn't just with "mental facts" that materialism seems inadequate but perhaps even more so with "institutional facts." Consider three examples. The first one is, "Bill sees Mary." Is it possible that someday there may exist a purely physical description—a description in terms of the laws and entities of physics and chemistry—that logically entails this statement? I'm not sure what that description would look like, but I think it is plausibly the case so we'll concede victory to the materialist here.

The second example is, "Bill loves Mary." Is it possible that someday there may exist a purely physical description—a description in terms of the laws and entities of physics and chemistry—that logically entails the second statement? Can we imagine some kind of brain scanner, biopsy, or blood test that would definitely answer the question, "Does Bill love Mary?" I don't think this scenario is likely, but it may be *possible* so I'll grant this possibility to the materialist too.

The third example is, "Bill is married to Mary." Can we antici-pate a purely physical description that replaces this statement? I think not. There will be no brain scanner, biopsy, or blood test that can determine that this third statement is true or false for the simple reason that being married is not a *physical* state at all, nor is it merely an emotional or mental state. It is a *legal* state, a social state. If Bill is an unmarried, eligible male, and he stands before an ordained clergyman alongside Mary, who is an unmarried, eligible female, and if they both respond to certain questions the clergyman poses to them by saying, "I will," then they are married, and no brain scanner, biopsy, blood

Fraggely daggely doop?

I will.

I will.

Then I pronounce you frizzlydap and lazltap.

or urine test will be pertinent to determine or refute that fact. Of course, it must be true that in some sense all of Bill's and Mary's molecules had to be in a certain condition for this marriage to take place, but this is the trivial sense in which materialism is true.

Sociology and anthropology are the sciences of human conventions, and there is no reason to expect that their descriptions of those conventions, along with our ordinary discourse about them, will someday be replaced by descriptions of molecules. The error of materialism is that of accepting J. J. C. Smart's claim, "everything should be explicable in terms of physics." Why should everything be explicable in terms of physics? Why, for example, should a description of the historical significance of Velázquez's painting *The Surrender of Breda* and of its aesthetic qualities be "explicable in terms of physics"? There are, as Ludwig Wittgenstein said, many forms of life, and it is a philosophical error to assume that there must be one model to account for all of them.

So in rejecting dualism and in rejecting materialism in any but a trivial sense, I seem to be making a pitch for a Rylean kind of pluralism, and in some ways, I am. I find some loose combination of the categories of discourse of ordinary language, philosophy, literature, and the physical and social sciences to be adequate, or at least very helpful, in trying to make my way about in the world. But what about myself as an *ontologist*? Remember the big questions we asked at the beginning of this chapter: What is real and what is merely appearance? Can there be a *theory* that draws the distinction between reality and appearance and accounts for everything that exists, or must these distinctions always remain contextual, ad hoc, and informal? I think at this point in our intellectual development the latter option seems to be the correct one. But what does this option mean for ontology? Can there not be a *theory* of reality? Maybe not. JOHN AUSTIN (1911–1960), perhaps the best practitioner of ordinary language philosophy, had this to say about the word "real":

[. . . the word "real" is] highly exceptional; exceptional in this respect that, unlike "yellow" or "horse" or "walk," it does not have one single, specifiable, always-the-same meaning. (Even Aristotle saw through this idea.) Nor does it have a large number of different meanings. . . .

"A real duck" differs from the simple "a duck" only in that it is used to exclude various ways of being not a real duck—but a dummy, a toy, a picture, a decoy, etc.; and moreover I don't know *just* how to take the assertion that it's a real duck unless I know *just* what, on that particular occasion, the speaker has it in mind to exclude.

. . . .

It should be quite clear, that there are no criteria to be laid down *in general* for distinguishing the real from the not real. How this is to be done must depend on *what* it is with respect to which the problem arises in particular cases.[18]

What if Austin is right, and there is no such *thing* as "reality," hence no such study as "the study of reality"? Does that mean that the center does not hold and that our only function as ontologists is to communicate that dizzying truth? No. We can still philosophically scrutinize the various "forms of life" (political, religious, artistic, moral, scientific) and try to see how they hang together, if in fact they do hang together. And we must be vigilant for new breakthroughs in some of these areas—for new **paradigm shifts,** as they are now called, because a major shift in science, art, or politics may well call for a shift both in our "ordinary" way of looking at the world and in the content of our philosophy. So the ontological task, like most philosophical tasks, is ongoing.

Topics for Consideration

1. Take the following sentences from ordinary English and relate them to Descartes's mind-body problem:
   She has a good mind.
   He has a good body.
   She almost lost her mind.
   Unfortunately, he is senile. He is no longer the uncle I once knew.
2. Descartes believed that we dream all night and that even when we have been knocked "unconscious," we must still have thoughts moving through our minds. Explain why he is committed to this view.
3. Discuss "the problem of other minds." How do you know that the person sitting next to you in class is not just a (very well made and perhaps attractively constructed) robot?
4. Descartes says that to have a mind is to be able "to affirm, to deny, to conceive, to know, to hope, to expect, to will," and so forth. He denies that animals have this capacity. Do you think *your* dog can perform all or some of these mental acts? On what evidence do you base your conclusion? Are you convinced that the evidence really supports your conclusion? (In other words, do we really need psychological categories to explain animal behavior? What about plant behavior?)
5. In reference to question 4, Skinner says that if we don't need psychological categories for plants and animals, we don't need them for humans either. Explain that view and criticize or defend it.
6. State the difference between the mind-brain identity theory set forth by J. J. C. Smart and the theory of eliminative materialism as defended by Richard Rorty.

Suggestions for Further Reading: Paperback Editions

Brian Cooney, ed., *The Place of Mind* (Belmont, Calif.: Wadsworth, 2000.) An excellent anthology that includes selections from almost all the philosophers mentioned in this chapter: Descartes, Ryle, Smart, the Churchlands, Kripke, Rorty, Fodor, Putnam, Searle, Nagel, and McGinn.

René Descartes, *Meditations on First Philosophy.* You should read Descartes firsthand. His short book is quite manageable, particularly in a contemporary translation like Ronald Rubin's in *A Guided Tour of René Descartes's "Meditations on First Philosophy,"* 3rd ed., Christopher Biffle (Mountain View, Calif.: Mayfield, 2001.) For Descartes's ontology, concentrate on Meditations I, II, and VI.

Colin McGinn, *The Mysterious Flame: Conscious Minds in a Material World* (New York: Basic Books, 1999.) A statement of McGinn's reasons for believing that the mind-body problem may never be solved. Written in a spirited fashion for a general audience.

Thomas Nagel, *The View from Nowhere* (New York: Oxford University Press, 1986). A book by an important American philosopher showing, among other things, why we are probably not in a position to solve the mind-body problem.

Thomas Nagel, "What's It Like to Be a Bat?" *Philosophical Review* 83, No. 4 (Oct., 1974), pp. 435–450. Also available in a number of philosophical anthologies including the Cooney text listed here. A strong, readable argument explaining why consciousness cannot be eliminated in the way the hard-core materialist wants to do.

Gilbert Ryle, *The Concept of Mind* (Chicago: University of Chicago Press, 1984). A classic of linguistic philosophy. Concentrate particularly on Chapter 1, "Descartes's Myth."

John Searle, *Minds, Brains, and Science* (Cambridge, Mass.: Harvard University Press, 1984). One of America's most interesting philosophers tackles the mind-body problem and claims to solve it.

John Searle, *The Rediscovery of the Mind* (Cambridge, Mass.: The M.I.T. Press, 1992). Another readable book by Professor Searle, showing why the mind has not been eliminated yet from philosophy and why it's not likely to be.

B. F. Skinner, *Beyond Freedom and Dignity* (New York: Bantam Books, 1972). A readable firsthand account of behaviorism by its most famous architect.

Notes

1. René Descartes, *Meditations on First Philosophy*, in *The Essential Descartes*, ed. Margaret D. Wilson, trans. Elizabeth S. Haldane and G. R. T. Ross (New York: New American Library, 1969), "Meditation II," p. 174. Unless otherwise stated, all subsequent quotes from Descartes in this chapter are from this source.

2. René Descartes, *The Passions of the Soul*, in Wilson, *The Essential Descartes*, p. 362.

3. Carl Rogers and B. F. Skinner, "Some Issues Concerning the Control of Human Behavior: A Symposium," *Science*, Vol. 124 (Nov. 30, 1956), pp. 1057–1066.

4. Gilbert Ryle, *The Concept of Mind* (Chicago: University of Chicago Press, 1984), pp. 11–13, 15–16.

5. Lewis Carroll, *Alice's Adventures in Wonderland and Through the Looking Glass* (New York: New American Library, 1960), p. 194.

6. J. J. C. Smart, "Sensations and Brain Processes, " *Philosophical Review,* Vol. 68 (1959), pp. 141–156.

7. See Norman Malcolm, *Problems of Mind: Descartes to Wittgenstein* (New York: Harper and Row, 1971); Jerome Shaffer, "Recent Work on the Mind-Body Problem," *American Philosophical Quarterly,* Vol. 2, No. 2 (1965), pp. 81–104; Richard Taylor, *Metaphysics,* 2d ed. (Englewood Cliffs, N.J.: Prentice-Hall, 1974), pp. 11–37.

8. Shaffer, "Recent Work on the Mind-Body Problem," p. 97.

9. All these examples are from Richard Rorty, "Mind-Body Identity, Privacy and Categories," *The Review of Metaphysics,* Vol. 19, No. 1 (Sept., 1965), pp. 24–54.

10. Richard Bernstein, "The Challenge of Scientific Materialism," *International Philosophical Quarterly,* Vol. 8, No. 2 (June, 1968), pp. 252–275.

11. John Heil, *Philosophy of Mind: A Contemporary Introduction* (London and New York: Routledge, 1998), p. 99.

12. John Searle, *Minds, Brains, and Science* (Cambridge, Mass.: Harvard University Press, 1984), p. 33. Subsequent quotes from Searle are from this source.

13. Henry Jackman, review of *The Nature of Consciousness,* ed. Ned Block, Owen Flanagan, and Güven Güzeldere (Cambridge, Mass.: MIT Press, 1997), in *Teaching Philosophy,* Vol. 23, No. 1 (March, 2000), p. 100.

14. Thomas Nagel, "What Is It Like to Be a Bat?" *The Philosophical Review,* 83 (Oct., 1974), pp. 435–450. Reprinted in *The Place of Mind,* ed. Brian Cooney (Belmont, Calif.: Wadsworth, 2000), pp. 321–330. Reference is to page 324 of Cooney. All subsequent quotes from Nagel are from this source.

15. Colin McGinn, *The Mysterious Flame: Conscious Minds in a Material World* (New York: Basic Books, 1999), p. 47. Subsequent quotes from McGinn are from this source.

16. A recent book on the philosophy of mind is Joseph Levine's *Purple Haze: The Puzzle of Consciousness* (New York and Oxford: Oxford University Press, 2001).

17. Saul Kripke, quoted in *The New York Times Magazine* (Aug. 14, 1977), sec. 6, p. 14.

18. John L. Austin, *Sense and Sensibilia,* ed. G. J. Warnock (New York: Oxford University Press, 1964), pp. 64–76.

5

Mount Olympus, Mount Moriah, and Other Godly Places
Philosophy of Religion

The big questions here are: Are there any good reasons for believing in God's existence or nonexistence? What kind of God exists or does not exist? What are the implications of God's existence or nonexistence for humans?

It looks as though every culture that has ever flourished has had some concept of divinity. Of course, it doesn't follow from that fact that therefore there is a divinity (any more than the fact that every culture believes itself to be superior to its neighbors means that every culture is superior to its neighbors). Still, the mere cultural universality of religious belief is an impressive fact. The question "Why do so many people believe in gods?" is a very complicated one because it entangles us in a thicket of psychological,

What Are the Implications of God's Existence . . . or Nonexistence?

sociological, anthropological, and philosophical—not to mention purely religious— issues. In this chapter, we shall be primarily interested in the philosophical issues, which means that we will attend to the kinds of arguments to consider when asking whether there are any good reasons to believe or disbelieve in the existence of god(s).

Every Culture Has Had a Conception of Divinity

Presenting the discussion this way, however, may make us sound unduly rational, as if on issues like religion we all start with Locke's famous "blank slate," then fill it with different arguments for different positions, and then choose the most reasonable one and discard the others. But such an approach is not likely. On the issue of religious belief, very few of us are this antiseptically objective. Bertrand Russell was perhaps an exception. In his autobiography, he tells us that he became an atheist at eighteen when he decided that the "first cause" argument was invalid. But he became a theist again in his fourth year at Cambridge when he concluded that an alternative proof of God's existence was valid. Russell wrote:

> I had gone out to buy a tin of tobacco and was going back with it along Trinity Lane when suddenly I threw it up in the air and exclaimed: "Great God in boots!—the ontological argument is sound!"[1]

The Young Bertrand Russell Discovers That God Exists

Later, however, he discovered what he took to be a flaw in the argument and reverted to **atheism.**

I suspect that most of us have views on God's existence that are less obviously determined by the mere validity of arguments than Russell claimed to be the case for himself. (Keep in mind, however, that this is the man who wrote about his sixteenth year, "There was a footpath leading across the fields to New Southgate, and I used to go there alone to watch the sunset and contemplate suicide. I did not, however, commit suicide because I wished to know more of mathematics.")[2] Then perhaps those of us who are not as dispassionate about religion are merely rationalizing when we give our "reasons" for believing or disbelieving in God (rationalizing in the pejorative sense, the sense of using reason and

logic illegitimately to support biases and opinions that we dearly want to believe). Not necessarily. Probably no such thing as the pure and blind pursuit of reason exists. Russell himself once said that the way the mind works on such things is like this: First you decide where you want to go. (At this point, will, passion, bias, and wishful thinking are a legitimate part of the

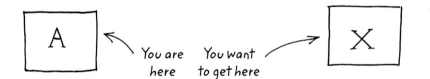

process of rationality.) Then you must ask yourself, "What arguments will I need to get me from [A] to [X]?"

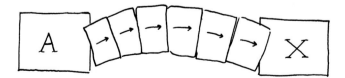

Next you need to ask, "Can such arguments be constructed, and are these good arguments?" (At this point, we need to be most vigilant against rationalization, wishful thinking, and other forms of self-deception.) If the arguments withstand criticism and link up well with each other, then you have good reason to hold belief X. If not, then you should abandon X.

Theism

Well, what kinds of arguments have been set forth to get us to X, where X is a belief in the existence of God or gods? That is, what kinds of arguments have been generated to justify **theism?** The best ones in the Western tradition stem from the late medieval period, a time that has been called "God-intoxicated." This period was one in which, astonishingly, there does not seem to have been any atheism (though there was much heresy). If this is true, then it isn't quite accurate to say that the "proofs" of the Middle Ages provided reasons for believing in God because apparently no alternative existed. Rather, it's as if the medievals were giving an account to themselves of the rational status of their belief—or their knowledge—of God.

God-Intoxicated

The Ontological Proof

Such an attitude is reflected in the curious introduction to one of the most famous medieval arguments and in the fact that this argument proving God's existence is not addressed to the atheist but to God himself! It's hard to believe that God needed proof of his own existence, but its author, ANSELM of Canterbury (1033–1109), was probably offering his meditation as a form of worship or a gift that could not possibly add anything to God's store (nothing could!) but one that nevertheless would be pleasing

I will now prove that I exist.

in God's sight. Here is Anselm's introduction: "I do not seek to understand that I may believe, but I believe in order to understand. For this also I believe, that unless I believed, I should not understand." Anselm goes on to refer to the "fool" of Psalms 53:1, who "says in his heart, 'There is no God.'" Even this fool – atheist

is convinced that something exists in the understanding, at least, than which nothing greater can be conceived. For when he hears of this he understands it. And whatever is understood exists in the understanding. And assuredly that than which nothing greater can be conceived, cannot exist in the understanding alone. For suppose it exists in the understanding alone: then it can be conceived to exist in reality, which is greater.

Therefore, if that than – God which nothing greater can be conceived (God) exists in the understanding alone, the very being than which nothing can be conceived, is one than which a greater can be conceived. But obviously this is impossible. Hence, there is no doubt that there exists a being than which nothing greater can be conceived, and it exists both in the understanding and in reality.

Psalm 53:1

And it assuredly exists so truly that it cannot be conceived not to exist. For it is possible to conceive of a being which cannot be conceived not to exist. Hence, if that than which nothing greater can be conceived, can be conceived not to exist, it is not that than which nothing greater can be conceived. But this is an irreconcilable contradiction. There is, then, so truly a being than which nothing greater can be conceived to exist, that it cannot even be conceived not to exist; and this being thou art, O Lord our God.[3]

Let's try to simplify this argument a bit.

1. It is possible to conceive of a being "than which nothing greater can be conceived." (By "greatest," Anselm does not mean "biggest," but "most perfect.")

2. If that being than which nothing greater can be conceived exists only in the mind, then it is *not* the greatest being that can be conceived (because it is always possible to conceive of a greater one, viz., one that exists not only in the mind but outside the mind as well).

3. Therefore the possibility of conceiving a being than which nothing greater can be conceived entails the logical necessity of the real existence of such a being.

4. This being than which nothing greater can be conceived is the being we call God.

One that exists only here is less perfect than one . . .

that exists out here.

This argument looks suspicious. It appears as though it should be pretty easy to knock over, but it is a slippery argument and more resistant to criticism than you might think. Maybe we can get a little clearer about the structure of the argument if we paraphrase a simpler version of it, one expounded by René Descartes some five hundred years after Anselm's version. It goes something like this:

1. God, by definition, is that being that is absolutely perfect.
2. It is more perfect to exist than not to exist.
3. Therefore, to conceive of God (i.e., to conceive of a being that is absolutely perfect) it is necessarily to conceive of him as existing (because to conceive of God as not existing is self-canceling).
4. Therefore, to say, "God does not exist" is to contradict oneself.
5. Therefore, the sentence "God exists" is necessarily true.

It Is More Perfect to Exist Than Not to Exist. (A Hamburger That Is Perfect in Every Respect Except That It Does Not Exist)

If Descartes's or Anselm's version of this argument (which has come to be known as "the ontological proof") bothers you, it is probably because you think there is some illegitimate move in it from a mere *definition* (an a priori claim) to a statement of fact (an a posteriori claim). In that case, you might want to challenge Descartes's version of the argument, perhaps at step 2, by saying that the assertion "It is more perfect to exist than not to exist" is a debatable value judgment, not a necessary truth of logic. But Descartes could retort that if it is a value judgment, it is one you obviously accept because if you had thought that nonexistence was better than existence, you would have shot yourself this morning. The fact that you are here proves that you accept the

Refuting Descartes (Again)

value of existence. So you can only reject step 2 hypocritically. Furthermore, Descartes might offer an example like this: Suppose you ordered a truckload of bricks from the local brickyard, and the truck driver came to deliver your order, saying, "These are excellent bricks in most respects, but they have one little flaw, namely, they don't exist." If he tried to charge you for these nonexistent bricks, you would certainly refuse to pay—or perhaps you would pay with an equally "flawed" hundred-dollar bill (one that doesn't exist). "All this shows that you agree with me" (Descartes might say) "that existence is more perfect (i.e., better) than nonexistence."

(You might ask Descartes what if, instead of bricks, the driver were delivering an unsolicited load of horse manure. Then [because you don't want any manure], nonexistent manure is *better* than existent manure. But wouldn't Descartes be right to say that in terms of *manure*, real manure is better than unreal manure?)

In spite of this defense, one may well feel that some sleight of hand is involved in the **ontological argument.** Indeed, even Thomas Aquinas, that most religious of philosophers,

It's very good horse manure.

But I don't *want* any manure!

thought the argument was invalid. One of the most famous critiques of the proof was written by David Hume. The following passage is taken from his posthumously published *Dialogues Concerning Natural Religion*:

> I shall begin with observing that there is an evident absurdity in pretending to demonstrate a matter of fact, or to prove it by any arguments a priori. Nothing is demonstrable unless the contrary implies a contradiction. Nothing that is distinctly conceivable implies a contradiction. Whatever we conceive as existent, we can also conceive as non-existent. There is no being, there-fore, whose non-existence implies a contradiction. Consequently there is no being whose existence is demonstrable. I propose this argument as entirely decisive and am willing to rest the whole controversy upon it.[4]

Hume's point boils down to this: it is always illegitimate to move from a pure definition to a statement of fact about reality. Definitions are only about the relation between meanings and as such are purely representations of logic and of linguistic conventions. Statements of fact about reality are always based on observation. Because Anselm's proof moves from the purely ideational sphere to the factual sphere without any reference to observation, its argument must be invalid.

Hume is certainly correct in thinking that if there is a problem with the proof, it has to do with the illegitimate transition from the realm of pure ideas to the realm of factual reality. But is Hume correct in saying that we can never move from the realm of definition to statements about existence? Consider the definition of a "square circle" (four-sided equilateral figure any point of which is equidistant from its center).

We can deduce the following: "no square circles exist."[5] If even once we can go from a definition to a statement of fact about reality, then Hume's argument loses much of its force.

Hume's criticism implied that there must be something wrong with the *logic* of Anselm's argu-ment. Another well-known

The Hunt for the Elusive Square Circle

and more modern criticism is that there is something wrong with its *gram-mar.* Look at this famous passage from the *Critique of Pure Reason* by Immanuel Kant:

Being is evidently not a real predicate, or a concept of something that can be added to the concept of a thing. It is merely the admission of a thing and of certain determinations in it. Logically, it is merely the copula of a judgment. The proposition, *God is almighty,* contains two concepts, each having its object, namely, God and almightiness. The small word *is,* is not an additional predicate, but only serves to put the predicate *in relation* to the subject. If, then, I take the subject (God) with all its predicates (including that of almightiness) and say, *God is,* or there is a God, I do not ascribe a new predicate to the concept of God, but I only posit the subject by itself, with all its predicates, in relation to my concept, as its object. Both must contain exactly the same kind of thing, and nothing can have been added to the concept, which expresses possibility only, by my thinking its object as simply given and saying, it is. And thus the real does not contain more than the possible. A hundred real dollars do not contain a penny more than a hundred possible dollars.[6]

The central points of Kant's criticism are contained in the first line and the last line of the passage: "Being [existence] is evidently not a real predicate" and "A hundred real dollars do not contain a penny more than a hundred possible dollars."

These points can be clarified by returning to Descartes's version of the argument. Descartes saw "perfection" as a predicate of God in exactly the same way that he saw "three-sidedness" as a predicate (or attribute or characteristic) of any triangle. Then he saw "existence" as following from perfection, so "existence" becomes a predicate of God. Now, Kant's claim that existence is not a predicate at all, hence not a predicate of God, might be demonstrated by imagining the following game called "Guess the Predicate." Suppose I take something from my pocket and hide it in my hand behind my back and allow you to ask questions concerning its characteristics, to which I will answer either yes or no. You may ask, "Is it green?" "Is it round?" "Is it heavy?" But could the question "Does it exist?" be a move in this game? The rules of the game already presuppose the existence of the object. If the object does not exist (i.e., if I have nothing in my hand), then

See if you can guess what I have behind my back.

The Predicate Game

I am not playing the game at all. I am simply deceiving you. Or try another game. This one is called "Imagine the Rose." First imagine a rose. Now imagine a *yellow* rose. Now imagine a yellow rose *with thorns*. Now imagine a yellow rose with thorns and *dew on the petals.* Now imagine a yellow, thorned rose with dew on the petals *that exists.* Notice the point. Nothing was added to the concept in the last instance. To imagine a rose and to imagine a rose that exists is to imagine the same thing. In the cases of the yellow color, the thorns, and the dew, we added something to the concept, so those were examples of real predicates. But in the case of existence, nothing was added, so existence "is not a real predicate."

Oooh. They're all thorny and covered with dew!

Imagine they're not.

Kant's criticism certainly does seem to have identified a linguistic weakness, if not a logical error, in the ontological proof. Is that the end of the story? Probably not. I mentioned earlier the fact that Anselm's argument has proved to be tremendously versatile and elastic, able to bounce back from apparently deadly assaults. For example, the twentieth-century American philosopher Norman Malcolm has claimed to have discovered in Anselm's writings a version of the ontological proof that is immune to Kant's criticism. The argument, paraphrased, runs something like this:

1. If God does not exist, his existence is logically impossible (because by definition God is eternal and independent so he cannot come into being or be caused to come into being).
2. If God does exist, his existence is logically necessary (because he cannot have come into existence [for the reasons given above] or cease to exist, for if he did, he would be limited, and by definition God is unlimited).
3. Hence, either God's existence is logically impossible or it is logically necessary.
4. If God's existence is logically impossible, then the concept of God is self-contradictory.
5. The concept of God is not self-contradictory.

6. Therefore, God's existence is logically necessary.
7. Therefore, God exists.[7]

Here we will not try to analyze Malcolm's argument (though it has attracted a number of critics).[8] Rather, we will attend to the somewhat amazing conclusion that Malcolm draws from this argument:

> What is the relation of Anselm's ontological argument to religious belief? This is a difficult question. I can imagine an atheist going through the argument, becoming convinced of its validity, acutely defending it against objections, yet remaining an atheist. The only effect it could have on the fool of the Psalm would be that he stopped saying in his heart "There is no God" because he would now realize that this is something he cannot meaningfully say or think. It is hardly to be expected that a demonstrative argument should, in addition, produce in him a living faith. Surely there is a level at which one can view the argument as a piece of logic, following the deductive moves but not being touched religiously? I think so. But even at this level the argument may not be without religious value, for it may help to remove some philosophical scruples that stand in the way of faith. . . . It would be unreasonable to require that the recognition of Anselm's demonstration as valid must produce a conversion.[9]

Atheist Muzzled

It was Immanuel Kant who gave the name "ontological proof" to the kind of argument invented by St. Anselm. As we've seen, "ontological" means "having to do with the study of Being," and Kant noticed that Anselm's argument was derived purely from the logical analysis of the concept of a "most real Being" or a "most perfect Being," hence the name "the ontological argument." Notice that, unlike the argument we shall now examine, Anselm's argument is a very Platonic one. It is derived from "pure reason." In it, "most perfect" and "most real" turn out to be identical (as on the top of Plato's Line). And it is an exclusively a priori argument. Nowhere did Anselm or Descartes ask you to *look* anyplace or *touch* anything or perform any physical experiments. All they asked you to do was to *think*. Anselm derived God's existence from pure thought. (That fact is probably what, in the final analysis, is wrong with the ontological proof, but one must also admit that the genius of the argument is its purely a priori nature.)

The Cosmological Proof

There is another kind of argument for God's existence, which Kant called **cosmological.** It's called cosmological because the first premise of such an argument makes reference to some observable fact in the world ("cosmos") and is therefore an argument with an a posteriori first premise. Surely the most famous versions of cosmological arguments were formulated by THOMAS AQUINAS (1225–1274), whose thought has inspired most Catholic philosophy ever since his time.

Take a look at one of the arguments from Thomas's *Summa Theologica:*

> In the world of sense we find there is an order of efficient causes. There is no case known (neither is it, indeed, possible) in which a thing is found to be the

Thomas Aquinas
(1225–1274)

efficient cause of itself; for so it would be prior to itself, which is impossible. Now in efficient causes it is not possible to go on to infinity, because in all efficient causes following in order, the first is the cause of the intermediate cause, and the intermediate cause is the cause of the ultimate cause, whether the intermediate cause be several or one only. Now, to take away the cause is to take away the effect. Therefore, if there be no first cause among efficient causes, there will be no ultimate, nor any intermediate cause. But if in efficient causes it is possible to go to infinity, there will be no first efficient cause, neither will there be an ultimate effect, nor any intermediate efficient causes; all of which is plainly false. Therefore it is necessary to admit a first efficient cause to which everyone gives the name of God.[10]

THE BUCK STOPS HERE

The term **efficient cause** is one St. Thomas borrowed from Aristotle, and it is roughly equivalent to what we mean today by the word "cause." Therefore, Thomas's argument seems to boil down to this:

1. Every event in the observable world is caused by some event prior to it.
2. Either (a) the series of causes is infinite, or (b) the series of causes goes back to a first cause, which is itself uncaused.
3. But an infinite series of causes is impossible.
4. Therefore, a first cause exists outside the observable world; this first cause is God.

Hume's Criticism of the Cosmological Proof

Philosophers like Hume and Kant who rejected this argument attacked the first and third premises and also questioned the conclusion. Hume is probably most famous for his critical analysis of the concept of "causality." We looked at a bit of Hume's controversial analysis in Chapter 3, but not in enough detail to evaluate its application to Thomas's argument. Suffice it to say that Hume asserts that no good reason at all exists to claim to know the first premise because it cannot be proven a priori that every event is caused, and no set of observations can establish it a posteriori either. Also, Hume thought that the third premise was false. Why is an infinite series of causes impossible? Unlike Thomas, Hume believed that nothing in the concept of a series of causes required that there be a beginning other than the need arbitrarily imposed by the human mind. Hume thought that no matter what event you imagine, you can always imagine an earlier event preceding it, regardless of how far back into time the imagination goes, just as an infinite series of numbers is possible in mathematics.

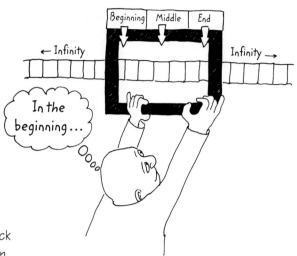

The Need of the Human Mind to Impose a "Beginning" on Things

Therefore, there is no *logical contradiction* in the notion of an "infinite series of causes." And because there are no observable data with which to prove the third premise, Hume concluded that we must remain at least skeptical concerning its claim.

Finally, even if the argument were valid from steps 1 through 3, would it prove the existence of the Christian God in whom St. Thomas believed? Aristotle himself, from whom Thomas borrowed elements of his cosmological proof, believed in a narcissistic God who was so "into himself" that he did not even know that human beings existed. Surely Thomas would not have wanted to prove the existence of that God.

Narcissus

Lest we think that Hume has soundly refuted the cosmological argument once and for all, I should mention that recent Thomistic scholars have warned that Thomas's argument is more complicated than it appears, involving both a horizontal system of causes (in which an infinite series of causes cannot be ruled out) and a hierarchical system of dependencies (which, according to Thomas, cannot

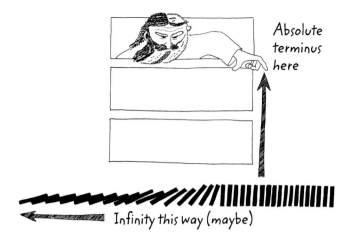

Absolute terminus here

Infinity this way (maybe)

admit of an infinite regress).[11] This version of the argument, with its "hierarchy of dependencies," is much more Platonic than the earlier one, reminding us as it does of Plato's Simile of the Line. A refutation of this interpretation of the proof would involve a rejection of Platonic metaphysics.

The Teleological Proof

A third kind of argument for God's existence goes by several names, the "teleological proof," the "argument from design," and the "argument from analogy." Though this proof was particularly popular in the eighteenth century, we find a thirteenth-century version once again in the *Summa Theologica* of Thomas Aquinas:

> The fifth way is taken from the governance of the world. We see that things which lack intelligence, such as natural bodies, act for an end, and this is evident from their acting always, or nearly always, in the same way, so as to obtain the best result. Hence it is plain that not fortuitously, but designedly, do they achieve their end. Now whatever lacks intelligence cannot move toward an end, unless it be directed by some being endowed with knowledge and intelligence; as the arrow is shot to its mark by the archer. Therefore some intelligent being exists by whom all natural things are directed to their end; and this being we call God.[12]

A **teleological** explanation is one that operates in terms of goals, purposes, and intentions (from the Greek *telos*, "goal" or "end"). We are familiar with teleological explanations because we use them every day to explain our own actions and those of people surrounding us: "Why did John go to the other room?" "In order to phone Jill." This explanation of John's behavior in terms of his purposes and goals makes his behavior intelligible to us.

Notice how different this teleological explanation of John's behavior is from a strictly causal explanation of the type we often employ to make intelligible to us the behavior of natural nonhuman objects: "Why did the tree fall?" "The roots were shallow and could not support the tree's weight in last night's windstorm."

We also use causal, nonteleological accounts in the case of *accidental* human events: "What's John doing on the floor?" "He tripped on his shoelace." Notice that here there were no references to goals, intentions, or purposes, so these explanations were not teleological. Now it might seem that the use of the two distinct forms of explanation is very clear; we use teleological accounts for certain kinds of human behavior (i.e., purposeful as opposed to accidental) and causal explanations for natural phenomena. But consider such exchanges as these:

"Why do ospreys have such good eyesight?"
"In order to see fish from high in the air."

"Why does that moth have brown spots on its wings?"
"In order to blend in with its environment to protect itself from natural enemies."

"Why do we faint when not enough blood gets to the brain?"
"So that the heart can pump blood horizontally."

Each of these explanations is teleological. They explain in terms of goals and purposes. It may turn out that something is wrong with these accounts, as Darwin would claim, but it can't be denied that people (usually parents talking to their children) say things like this all the time.

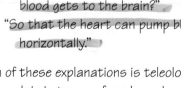

Myopic Osprey

To many people, these kinds of explanations seem perfectly natural. Now it is precisely the "naturalness" of these accounts from which the teleological proof gets its mileage. This proof says that natural phenomena are such that they demand a teleological explanation or at least that the totality of natural phenomena taken as a system demands such an explanation; no other kind proves satisfactory.

A common version of the argument runs like this: If you found a watch on a mountain path, you would deduce from the functioning of the watch that it was designed to serve a purpose and that there had to be an intelligent watchmaker who created the artifact. It would be unreasonable to explain the watch in terms of natural accidents and coincidences. But nature is even more marvelous in the intricacies of its workings than a watch is. The human heart pumps blood at exactly the right pressure to sustain human life; the planets move in their orbits with absolute mathematical precision; each plant is in nearly perfect harmony with its environment. In summary, the universe is such an intricate system of balanced mechanisms that it can be explained only in terms of the purposes and intentions of an intelligent creator, as in the case of the watch. In the case of the universe, that intelligent creator is God.

The Not-So-Intelligent Watchmaker

Darwin's and Hume's Criticisms of the Teleological Proof

The most famous critics of the teleological argument are Charles Darwin and (once again) David Hume. Darwin's criticism, stated simply, runs like this: A difference occurs between the concept of "design" and the concept of "order." It is true that whatever has been designed must have been designed by somebody, but not everything that exhibits order was designed. Take the example of a gravel beach. There we find a distinct order. The smallest grains of sand compose the top layers of the beach, the grains of the second layer are a bit larger, and the largest compose the bottom layer. But no "designer" is needed to explain this order; much less is there any mystery. It is perfectly obvious why the larger pebbles are on the bottom. They are the heaviest, hence were deposited by the surf first. The smallest are the lightest and were deposited last.

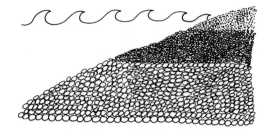

Similarly, the order throughout nature, though often more complex than the gravel beach example, can be explained in the same kind of naturalistic terms. The perfect harmony between the heart and body is explained by the fact that the heart could sustain only a body that could survive with exactly as much blood pressure as that size heart could produce. All other bodies would not survive (and indeed did not survive). The coincidental combination of that particular heart size and this particularly structured body produced the organism that would survive (and did survive). The heart does not pump X pounds of blood pressure in order to sustain the body; rather, the body flourishes because the heart does pump X pounds of blood pressure. Similarly, ospreys do not have excellent vision in order to spy fish; rather, they spy fish because they have excellent vision. The moth does not have spots in order to avoid its enemies; it avoids its enemies because it has spots—and so it goes on and on. If Darwin's argument is successful, it shows that the teleological terminology ("in order to") can be replaced with purely causal terminology, thereby destroying the force of the teleological proof.

Smog breathing, styrofoam eating, radiation powered

Evolutionary Future of the Human

David Hume, in his *Dialogues Concerning Natural Religion*, had at least a pair of arguments against the teleological proof. First, he challenged the validity of the analogy "Watch is to watchmaker as world is to world creator." Hume claimed that the relation between the watch and the watchmaker that allows us to infer the existence of the latter when we find the former is an *empirical* relation. We are able to infer the existence of the watchmaker from the existence of the watch because we have seen watchmakers make watches. Any successful analogy based on the relationship between a watch and a watchmaker will also have to contain the empirical element of that relationship. But because the purported relation between the world and the world creator is not and cannot be empirical, the analogy fails. Besides, says Hume, the aspect of the world that excites the need for a theological explanation is very often the *organic* aspect of the world. The organic world is more like a plant than a watch. Because we know (empirically) where plants come from, Hume states rather mischievously that the argument from analogy should lead us to conclude that the world creator is more like a kind of superturnip than like a watchmaker! Another of Hume's criticisms of the argument from design can be stated in terms of these diagrams. Notice how orderly the three dots are in fig. 1. They form a perfect triangle. Fig. 2 contains even more order. The addition of only three dots created four triangles within the triangle, and an even more complex system of order appears in figs. 3 and 4. Then we get to fig. 5, and we realize what we are actually looking at is a pile of sand, hardly what we think of as an orderly system, rather, a purely random kind of hap-

Superturnip

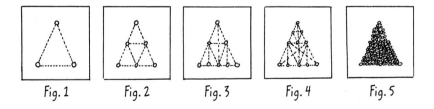

hazardness. Hume is suggesting that order is in the eye of the beholder. The human mind imposes order on the chaos of nature, then infers a divine orderer to account for it. Notice that Hume's point is much more radical than Darwin's. Darwin questioned the notion of "design in nature" but never doubted whether there was "order" in nature. Hume questions the very notion of order.

There is a sandpile; therefore God exists.

Certainly this section has not been a complete catalogue of the philosophical attempts to prove God's existence, and it does not even pretend to have exhausted the richness or variations of the three arguments we've inspected. But it is a fair sampling of this kind of attempt to demonstrate that there are rational arguments that give us good reasons to believe that God exists.

Atheism

We have seen that each of the arguments for God's existence is problematic, but perhaps no more so than the arguments attempting to prove that God does not exist. Such proofs are arguments for atheism. Here we will catalogue a few such arguments, but we will not delay long to inspect them. These kinds of discussions could go on forever. (Indeed, after several hundred years of debate during the medieval period, it began to seem as if they *would* go on forever.) Notice that some of these arguments will be kinds of reverse ontological proofs, trying to show that the very concept of God as Western culture has conceived it is self-contradictory. Other arguments here will be kinds of reverse cosmological proofs, trying to show that certain facts in the world are incompatible with the concept of God. Here are the truncated versions of a few.

1. God's omniscience is incompatible with the freedom he gave his creatures. (If God is omniscient, he knows the future. If God knows what humans will do in the future, then they *must* do what God knows they will do [or else God is wrong]. If God does not know what they will do, then he is not omniscient.)

2. God is defined as omnipotent, but nothing can be defined as omnipotent because the concept of omnipotence is incoherent. (Can God create a rock that is too large for him to move? If he cannot, then he is not all-powerful. If he can, then he is not all-powerful.)

3. God's omnibenevolence is incompatible with his creation of the devil and of eternal punishment. (If God is all-good, how can he let loose such a potent evil force like Satan to tempt weak creatures as humans are and then punish with eternal damnation those poor souls who succumb, even momentarily, to the devil's superior wiles?)

4. God's omnipotence, omniscience, omnibenevolence, and omnicreativity are not compatible with the presence of evil in the world. (There is evil in the world—natural disasters, disease, crime, starvation, phlegm. If God did not create them, then he is not the creator of the universe. If he could not prevent them in his creation, then he is not all-powerful. If he

didn't foresee them, he is not all-knowing. On the other hand, if he did willfully create them, then he is not all-good.)

Most of these arguments had already appeared in the medieval world, not as real attempts to raise doubts about God's existence—atheism was never a serious threat in the Middle Ages—but as a pretext for theologians to flex their philosophical muscles while clarifying to themselves their understanding of God's nature. Yet it is obvious that one of these problems—the problem of evil—is more powerful than the others. I have framed that problem here in its logical form, but to common believers it is not at all like a mere logical puzzle because the evidence supporting it is discovered not primarily through philosophizing but in one's daily journey through life, and unfortunately that evidence is sometimes experienced personally and painfully, by both theologians and nontheologians. The medieval world was so full of suffering at all levels that the argument from evil daily crossed the minds of many of the faithful. We know about this preoccupation from the great number of sermons and theological tracts whose goal was to counteract the thoughts and emotions caused by the suffering, either by explaining away the appearance of evil, or by showing why evil was compatible with God's grace, or even by demonstrating it as a necessary part of God's grace.

Indeed, in the Middle Ages, even at the intellectual level, the arguments for God's existence may have been trying to hold in abeyance the unthinkable, that is, that the world was as it appeared—chaos and horror. During great periods of the Middle Ages famine and plague were interrupted only by violence and death at the hands of marauding troops undisciplined by any rulers or rules. It must have seemed like the visions of the Four Horsemen of the Apocalypse (pestilence, war, famine, and death) depicted in the Book of Revelations, except that in the Bible, the chaos and horror was part of God's plan. That is, for many, the great suffering was seen not as evidence against God's existence, but

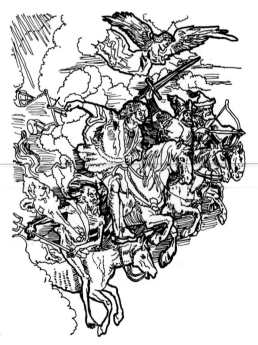

The Four Horsemen of the Apocalypse
(After Albrecht Dürer)

evidence for it. Yet, there must have been moments when the question crept across the minds of suffering individuals and of observers of such suffering—What if this is all there is? What if there is no God? What if the center does not hold? Part of medieval piety involved the silent acceptance of an idea that had been articulated by the ancient Greek playwright Aristophanes: "When Zeus is toppled, chaos succeeds him, and whirlwind rules"—an idea that would later be expressed by Ivan Karamazov, a character in a novel by Fyodor Dostoyevski: "If there is no God, everything is permitted."

After a thousand years, the medieval period did come to an end, and when it did, the totalizing obsession with God ended. There are many historical reasons for this loosening of the viselike grip religion had on the Western mind during the medieval period, and most of these reasons are historical and sociological rather than purely philosophical (for example, the great schisms in Christianity that detracted from the appearance of uniformity and universality of religious persuasion; the revelations of corruption within certain religious institutions, which detracted from the moral authority of religion; and the advent of scientific discoveries that seemed to contradict biblical explanations of the world). Since the eighteenth century, most philosophical arguments for atheism have not taken the form of a proof attesting to the incoherence of the concept of God nor of the incompatibility between that concept and the empirical facts. Rather, these arguments have had as their goal the undermining of religious faith by claiming to reveal that our motives for religious belief are fallacious and illusory, including the fear that the center does not hold. Typical of such arguments in the nineteenth century are those of LUDWIG FEUERBACH (1804–1872) and his erstwhile disciple, KARL MARX (1818–1883).

Feuerbach's "Religion of Man"

In his book *The Essence of Christianity* (1841), Feuerbach tried to show that religious beliefs were basically the result of confusion about human potentiality and that this confusion and the resultant beliefs prevented any serious solution of human problems. Feuerbach's theory went something like this: The human being is fundamentally good and as a species has certain legitimate aspirations that have been present more or less from the beginning of the race. These aspirations are the will to achieve love, truth, beauty, happiness, wisdom, purity, and strength, among others. That is, every human community has aspired, consciously or unconsciously, to achieve and express these values (fig. 1) (shades of Plato!). But life was hard, individually and collectively, and these ideals were rarely realized. Natural disasters,

Fig. 1   Fig. 2   Fig. 3

wars, social chaos, and plagues resulted in these ideals receding, as it were, through the clouds into the sky (fig. 2). Then suddenly a strange thing happened. (Unfortunately, Feuerbach does not give us much detail on *how* it was supposed to have happened.) The clouds opened up, and those same ideals returned in a new, powerful form, as the voice of God (fig. 3). And the great **dialectical** irony of history is that those same beautiful ideals that were expressions of true human nature now returned to earth in the form of religion and crushed the human being to the ground (fig. 4). According to Feuerbach, the "and don't you ever forget it" line is "the essence of Christianity" and, in fact, the essence of all organized religion. He believed that religious history and scriptures are replete with illustrations of this thesis. Consider specifically the Old Testament story of Job from Feuerbach's point of view.

And if **I** am all these things, then you are nothing! (and don't you ever forget it!)

Fig. 4

In a discussion with Satan and other angels, God points out his servant Job, complimenting him before the devil as being a perfect, upright man. Satan retorts that Job is perfect only because God has protected him and blessed him. However, should God allow evil to befall Job, Satan wagers that Job would curse God. In order to prove the devil wrong, God delivers Job to Satan, giving him a free rein to torment Job, though the devil may not kill Job. ("Behold, he is in thine hand; but save his life" [Job 2:6].) The first day of the torment begins with a slave running to tell him that all his oxen and asses have been stolen and all his herdsmen murdered. Before the first slave is done relating his story, a second comes to inform Job that a fire has fallen from heaven and burned all his sheep and shepherds. Before this servant finishes his tale, a third runs up and announces that the Chaldeans have stolen all Job's camels and killed the camel keepers. While Job is reeling from this news, yet another slave approaches, telling Job that a great wind has toppled the home of his eldest son, killing all ten of Job's children. Job rends his robe, shaves his head, and mourns, only to awaken on the second day of the torment to find himself smitten with painful boils from the soles of his feet to the crown of his head. Job's wife, seeing Job sitting among the ashes with his shaven head, his

running sores, and his misery, says to Job, "Curse God and die" (Job 2:9). Though Job does not curse God, he does curse the day he was born, and he talks bitterly of the impossibility of fathoming God's ways. He says to God, "Show me wherefore thou contendest with me"; "Thou knowest that I am not wicked." (This version of the question "Why me?" seems like a perfectly reasonable question under the circumstances.) When God, speaking from the whirlwind, does answer Job, he asks a series of intimidating questions: "Who is this that darkeneth counsel by words without knowledge?" (It's only Job.) "Where wast thou when I laid the foundations of the earth?" (Job doesn't know.) "Hast thou an arm like God?" (Job doesn't.) "Canst thou thunder with a voice like him?" (Job can't.) Finally Job understands. One does not question the ways of God. In God's case, might is right. When Job understands, then he recovers all that was lost and more—new livestock, new lands, new slaves, and new children.

You can see how I have told this story in a Feuerbachian light (though of course there are many other possible interpretations as well).[13] One must be resigned to the misery inflicted upon one, never questioning the system that perpetrated it and never fighting it. Again, if God is everything, the human is nothing.

Feuerbach, like Marx after him, was a socialist, and he believed that a truly human society (i.e., a socialist society) would in fact finally be able to achieve those ideals of love, truth, beauty, happiness, wisdom, purity, and strength that are our legitimate aspirations. It seems as though Feuerbach, recognizing the tremendously important role religion has played in the history of human culture, thought that the only thing standing in the way of such an ideal human world was religion. If humans could only see that they had alienated their subjective essence, objectifying in it a foreign, artificial being, "God," then they could reclaim that essence and build a heaven on earth. It is as though Feuerbach believed that, upon perusing *The Essence of Christianity*, the reader would suddenly see

**A Moment of
Feuerbachian Illumination**

that human alienation was in fact religious alienation. One would strike oneself on the forehead and exclaim, "Of course! Now I see it!" and at that point be delivered from religious alienation and dedicate oneself to the new "Religion of Man" and the building of the new Jerusalem.

Marx's Response to Feuerbach

Karl Marx was tremendously impressed by Feuerbach's book, and at one point early in his career, Marx claimed that the only correct way to philosophize was to "pass through the fiery brook." (In German, *Feuerbach* means "fiery brook.") But he soon began to turn against his mentor, basically on the grounds that Feuerbach was a crypto- (or "hidden") idealist, despite the fact that Feuerbach thought of himself as a materialist. (The nastiest thing that Feuerbach and Marx could call someone was "idealist.") Inspect these passages on religion written by Marx against Feuerbach:

Karl Marx Crosses the Fiery Brook

Feuerbach starts out from the fact of religious self-alienation, the duplication of the world into a religious, imaginary world and a real one. His work consists in the dissolution of the religious world into its secular basis. He overlooks the fact that after completing this work, the chief thing still remains to be done. For the fact that the secular foundation detaches itself from itself and establishes itself in the clouds as an independent realm is really to be explained only by the self-cleavage and self-contradictoriness of this secular basis. The latter must itself, therefore, first be understood in its contradiction and then, by removal of the contradiction, revolutionized in practice. Thus, for instance, once the earthly family is discovered to be the secret of the holy family, the former must then itself be criticized in theory and revolutionized in practice.

. . . .

Religious distress is at the same time the expression of real distress and the protest against real distress. Religion is the sigh of the oppressed creature, the heart of a heartless world, just as it is the spirit of an unspiritual situation. It is the opium of the people.[14]

The language that Marx uses in these passages is a bit difficult, but it is fairly easy to see Marx's objection to Feuerbach's theory. According to Marx, Feuerbach correctly sees that religion is a form of alienation but falsely believes that the solution to the problem is the critique of religion. Marx claims that religion is not the cause of the disease; rather it is the symptom. The disease is the world's social organization. When Marx says that the earthly family must be "criticized in theory and revolutionized in practice," he means that the holy family (Mary, Jesus, and Joseph) is an inverted projection into the skies of a real problem on earth. Marx claimed that marriage in contemporary European society was a form of legalized forced prostitution and that the role of the father as "head of the family" was a form of violent tyranny over mother and child. This view, he thought, gets dialectically reversed in the religious view of the holy family. For Marx, there is no use in outlawing religion. When the tyranny, prostitution, and exploitation of the real family are

The Heavenly Family

The Earthly Family

abolished, religion will simply disappear. This claim is controversial, to say the least, but it ought to be obvious that *if* Marx's theory is true, then Feuerbach's critique of religion is inadequate.

Notice that one of the ironies in the theories of both Feuerbach and Marx is that there is a significant sense in which religion contains the truth—a spiritual truth that should become a social truth. This sense was more clearly visible in Marx's writings even than in Feuerbach's. Remember that, for Marx, religion is "the sigh of the oppressed creature, the heart of a heartless world, . . . the spirit of an unspiritual situation. It is the *opium of the people.*" This view is hardly an absolute indictment of religion. Usually that last line is quoted in isolation from its context, in which case one thinks of opium as a soporific that lulls one into a grinning, drooling, undignified stupor. But Marx had in mind opium's medicinal powers. It kills the pain. And for Marx, the pain is real, so that at least religion is addressing the correct issue, human misery. This view has been understood very well by twentieth-century Marxian philosopher Herbert Marcuse, who wrote in his book *Eros and Civilization*:

> Where religion still preserves the uncompromised aspirations for peace and happiness, its "illusions" still have a higher truth value than science which works for their elimination. The repressed and transfigured content of religion cannot be liberated by surrendering it to the scientific attitude.[15]

Sigmund Freud: The Psychoanalysis of Religion

In spite of their belief in the hidden truth value of religion, both Feuerbach and Marx were atheists who thought religion was ultimately an illusion. One of the most famous atheists of the twentieth century was SIGMUND FREUD (1856–1939). He too thought religious belief was a kind of illusion, and his book on religion is called *The Future of an Illusion*. His view of religion is deeply entwined with the rest of his **psychoanalytic** theory of the mind; however, thankfully, we do not have to recount the whole of Freud's psychology but only a few of its essentials in order to get at the heart of his claim about religion. According to Freud, the human mind preserves all of its earlier stages alongside its final form. This retention is true both ontogenetically and phylogenetically (i.e., true of the history of the individual and also of the history of the human race). Unlike in a city, where some parts must be destroyed for newer parts to be constructed, in the mind, the earliest stages and the latest are contemporaneous. However, the earlier ones are to a great extent submerged or even repressed into the unconscious.

Memory of yesterday's breakfast (fading). } CONSCIOUS MEMORIES

Fallacious and innocuous memories from childhood, screening off more painful and traumatic memories. } CONSCIOUS MEMORIES

Memories of traumatic events and unresolved conflicts in childhood.

Memories of infantile desires.

Memories of the origins of civilization.

Memories of the origin of organic matter. } UNCONSCIOUS MEMORIES

The Human Mind Preserves All of Its Earlier Stages

Therefore, from the point of view of consciousness, the structures and content of the earlier stages seem to have been forgotten forever, but in fact they are present and in some ways active as motives for behavior, as are our conscious thoughts. Now, concerning religion, Freud says:

> The derivation of religious needs from the infant's helplessness and the longing for the father aroused by it seems to me incontrovertible, especially since the feeling is not simply prolonged from childhood days but is permanently sustained by a fear of the superior power of Fate. I cannot think of any need in childhood as strong as the need for the father's protection.[16]

The Bulk of the Mind Is Submerged

The infant comes into the world in some way believing itself to be omnipotent. The slightest or greatest of its needs is attended to upon simple registering of a complaint. It does not take long, however, for the horrible realization to dawn on the infant that she is not only not all-powerful and in command of reality but that she is completely vulnerable and dependent. This discovery (from which she will never recover) produces both fear and resentment. The infant reluctantly recognizes her utter need of a protector to shelter her from the many sources of pain and unhappiness in the world. She comes to see this protector in the guise of the father. This fearful discovery of her vulnerability and dependence on the father,

along with the emotional luggage that accompanies this discovery—fear, need, love, resentment—remain active forces in the unconscious of the adult. As adults,

each one of us behaves in some one respect like a paranoic, corrects some aspect of the world which is unbearable to him by the construction of a wish and introduces this delusion into reality. A special importance attaches to the case in which this attempt to procure a certainty of happiness and protection against suffering through a delusional remoulding of reality is made by a considerable number of people in common. The religions of mankind must be classed among the mass-delusions of this kind. No one, needless to say, who shares a delusion ever recognizes it as such. . . . [Religion's] technique consists in depressing the value of life and distorting the picture of the real world in a delusional manner—which presupposes an intimidation of the intelligence. At this price, by forcibly fixing them in a state of psychical infantilism and by drawing them into a mass-delusion, religion succeeds in sparing many people an individual neurosis. (pp. 30–31, 34)

The Infant Comes into the World Thinking It Is Omnipotent

Although Freud does realize that religion can spare people a neurosis, he nevertheless seems to have contempt for it. He says, "The whole thing is so patently infantile, so foreign to reality, that to anyone with a friendly attitude to humanity it is painful to think that the great majority of mortals will never be able to rise above this view of life" (p. 49).

So according to Freud, religion is for weaklings, for people who need delusions to accompany them into the harshness of the world. In *Civilization* and Its Discontents, Freud deals with alcohol and drugs in the same paragraph in which he deals with religion. For him, too, religion is truly "the opium of the people." Religion can be escaped only by those who can develop the courage to face the harshness of life without delusions and substitute them with scientific truth or by those who can create a different kind of paranoidlike illusion in the production of art. (See Chapter 10 for a development of this idea.)

Volitional Justifications of Religious Belief

Friedrich Nietzsche Makes an Important Discovery

Earlier we looked at a number of arguments claiming to demonstrate the rationality of a belief in God's existence. These arguments stressed reason and evidence. There have been other kinds of arguments for God's existence, appealing not so much to the rational and intellectual side of our nature as to its passional side. (There have also been passional arguments against God's existence. Nietzsche's probably takes the cake: "If there were gods, how could I stand not being one? Therefore there are no gods.") One of the most famous of such heartfelt arguments for God's existence is that of the American pragmatist, WILLIAM JAMES (1842–1910).

First, a bit about **pragmatism.** The term was coined by another American philosopher, CHARLES PEIRCE (1839–1914), and for him, it was essentially the name of a *method* whose goal was to clarify our thought processes by tracing out the practical consequences of beliefs in various ideas.

James's version of pragmatism (which so repelled Peirce that he changed the name of his own view from "pragmatism" to "pragmaticism"—a name he said was "ugly enough to be safe from kidnappers") ultimately became a justification of a certain kind of religious belief. Before developing that justification, we must distinguish between the pragmatic theory of *meaning* and its theory of *truth.* Concerning the former, James wrote:

Ugly Enough to Be Safe from Kidnappers

> Is the world one or many?—fated or free?—material or spiritual?—here are notions either of which may or may not hold good of the world; and disputes over such notions are unending. The pragmatic method in such cases is to try to interpret each notion by tracing its respective practical consequences. What difference would it practically make to any one if this notion rather than that notion were true? If no practical difference whatever can be traced, then the alternatives mean practically the same thing, and all dispute is idle.[17]

In other words, a sentence is *meaningful* only if believing it would make a practical difference in your life as opposed to believing some alternative to it. For example, take the sentence "There is a table in the middle of this room." If you wanted to travel from one end of the room to the other, then believing that sentence to be true (as opposed to believing its opposite) would make a practical difference because your path across the room would be different in one case as opposed to the other. Now consider a slightly more complicated case: "Jupiter has four moons." Whether you believe that sentence or an alternative (such as "Jupiter has no moons"),

it probably won't make much difference in your life either way unless you are an astronomer or an astronaut. But if you *were* an astronomer or an astronaut, we could certainly imagine conditions in which believing the one alternative as opposed to the other would have definite practical consequences. (You won't try to land a rocket on Jupiter's fourth moon unless you believe that Jupiter has a fourth moon.)

So the examples about tables and moons that we have considered are meaningful because believing any of them could make a difference. Contrast those examples with this: "There are many diaphanous, unknowable, invisible, intangible beings hovering over such items as daisies and hamburgers." Believing this sentence or believing its opposite will produce exactly the same practice; hence each belief is *practically* identical.

Now what about *truth?* First of all, notice that only meaningful sentences can be either true or false. (From this, it seems to follow rather curiously that my last example about diaphanous beings is neither true nor false.)

Having said that, let me create a more general context for a philosophical discussion of truth by contrasting James's **pragmatic theory of truth** with the other two theories of truth that have competed with each other throughout the history of Western philosophy: the **correspondence theory** and the **coherence theory.** The correspondence theory has been the dominant one and has been especially favored by empiricists. It simply says that a proposition is true if it corresponds with the facts. The sentence "The cat is

Only Meaningful Sentences Can Be True or False

on the mat" is true if and only if the cat is in fact on the mat. The main attractions of this theory are its simplicity and its appeal to common sense. The main weaknesses are (1) the difficulties in explaining how linguistic entities (words, sentences) can *correspond* to things that are nothing like language; (2) the difficulty in providing a noncircular explanation of exactly *what* it is that sentences are supposed to correspond to (facts? What is a "fact" if not that which a true sentence asserts?); and (3) a particular awkwardness in its application to mathematics (What is it to which the proposition "5 + 2 = 7" corresponds?). The coherence theory of truth asserts that a proposition is true if it coheres with all the other propositions taken to be true. This theory has been preferred by many rationalists. Its greatest strength is that it makes sense out of the idea of mathematical truth ("5 + 2 = 7" is true because it is entailed by "7 = 7", and by "1 + 6 = 7," and by "21 ÷ 3 = (2 x 3) + 1," etc.). Its greatest weakness is its vicious circularity. Proposition A is true by virtue of its coherence with propositions B, C, and D. Proposition C is true by virtue of its coherence with propositions A, B, and D, and so forth. (Think of the belief system of a paranoid. All his beliefs cohere perfectly with one another. Everything that happens to him is evidence that everybody is out to get him.)

Now, the pragmatist says that the test of correspondence and the test of coherence are not competing theories but simply different tools to be applied to beliefs to see if those beliefs "work." James had this to say about truth: "Ideas (which themselves are but parts of our experience) become true just insofar as they help us to get into satisfactory relations with other parts of our experience, . . . truth in our ideas means their power to 'work'" (p. 49). So the key notion here is that of an idea "working," which James defines as "help[ing] us to get into satisfactory relations with other parts of our experience." James also calls this notion the "cash value" of ideas. Now, if believing that there is a table in the middle of the room prevents you from

Church of the Immaculate Visual Image

GIVE TOLLFREE CALL 800-441-BIBL

00000000

bruising your legs and making a fool out of yourself, then that belief *works*. That is, it is true.

Let us, finally, turn to the pragmatists' thoughts about believing in God. James's discussion of this topic was a response to the scientific view that we have no right to hold any beliefs for which we do not have adequate evidence. This view (held by Hume in the eighteenth century and Bertrand Russell in the twentieth) had been popularized in James's own time by the British mathematician W. K. CLIFFORD (1845–1879), who had said, "Belief is desecrated when given to unproved and unquestioned statements for the solace and private pleasure of the believer. . . . It is wrong always, everywhere, and for everyone, to believe anything upon insufficient evidence."[18] To this, James responded by saying:

> Our passional nature not only lawfully may, but must, decide an option between propositions, whenever it is a genuine option that cannot by its nature be decided on intellectual grounds; for to say, under such circum- stances, 'Do not decide, but leave the question open,' is itself a passional decision—just like deciding yes or no—and it is attended with the same risk of losing the truth.[19]

Now, for James, the issue of God's existence is one that the intel- lect by itself definitely cannot resolve. So if it is a "genuine option" (that is, a meaningful belief), it may be entertained on purely volitional grounds. Is the proposition "God exists" prag- matically meaningful? Does believing it make a practical dif- ference in one's life? These questions are problematical. I take it that for some people it does, but for some others it doesn't. Some people would behave exactly the same whether they believed in God's existence or not. But others would behave very differently if they believed in the existence of the God of the Judeo-Christian tradition from the way they would behave if they did *not* believe in him. (If they believe, perhaps they will be nicer to their neighbor than if they do not believe.)

But not everybody for whom a belief in God makes a difference would behave in exactly the same way. Some might become monks or nuns; in the

I am dressed up; therefore God exists.

A Pragmatic Proof of God's Existence

case of others, the only difference their belief makes is that on Sundays they dress up and go to church. This point shows the *subjective* side of James's theory of meaning because the meaning of a proposition is just the difference in behavior resulting from belief in the proposition. So for some, there is no *practical* difference between the sentences "God exists" and "God does not exist." For others, belief, as opposed to nonbelief, would make a radical difference. For yet others, belief would result in very minor differences (e.g., putting on a dark suit on Sundays).

Now, what about the *truth* of the claim "God exists"? According to James, a proposition is true if believing it *works*—that is, if the belief puts the believer in a more satisfactory relationship with the rest of her or his experience. Concerning this, James says:

> On pragmatic principles, if the hypothesis of God works satisfactorily in the widest sense of the word, it is true. Now whatever its residual difficulties may be, experience shows that it certainly does work, and that the problem is to build it out and determine it so that it will combine satisfactorily with all the other working truths. (p. 192)

So we see that for James, both meaning and truth are relative. To some people, the sentence "God exists" is true; for others, it is false. Most philosophers rejected James's solution to the problem of religious belief because they balked at his relativism concerning meaning and truth. Others felt that James left untouched the real question, which they took to be Regardless of the personal satisfaction or lack of it found in a belief in God's existence, does God really exist?

Religious Mysticism

Religious belief is sometimes grounded in certain kinds of extraordinary personal experiences. These experiences can be felt as events lasting only seconds ("We shall all be changed, in a moment, in the twinkling of an eye" [1 Cor. 15:52]), or they can be experienced as lasting minutes, hours, days, or even weeks. They can be experienced as spontaneous implosions upon the

Mysticism: Long-Range Plan

mind. (As apparently was that most famous of conversions—the one that transformed Saul of Tarsus, prosecutor of Christians, into Saint Paul, author of most of the books of the New Testament. On the road to Damascus, he suddenly saw a blinding light that knocked him from his horse, and he heard the voice of Jesus saying, "Saul, Saul, why persecuteth thou me?" Or another example is the experience of the Roman emperor Constantine, who, riding through the Alps with his army, looked into the sky and saw the clouds swirling into the sign of the cross and

How Saul Became Paul

spelling out "In this sign conquer." [Maybe there's some connection between horseback riding and religious experience?]) Or such experiences can be intentionally brought about by engaging in a series of physical and mental preparations of the type outlined by St. Ignatius of Loyola in his book *Spiritual Exercises*. Because these experiences are extra-rational—that is, they seem to transcend logical explanation—

they are often called **mystical** experiences. What they all seem to have in common is the fact that during them, and sometimes after them, everything is seen in a new light— "all things are transformed." Whole conceptions of religion are based on mystical experiences, especially in certain Asian philosophies. In this text we are restricting ourselves to the Western philosophy of religion, where mysticism has never been mainstream, yet there has always been a strong undercurrent of mystical thought in Judaism (the Cabbalistic tradition), in Islam (the Sufi tradition), and in both the Catholic and Protestant variations of Christianity. We can trace each of these Western mystical traditions not only to their own holy texts but also, ironically, to certain neo-Platonic interpretations of Plato's Simile of the Line. In an almost unintelligible passage of the *Republic*, Plato has Socrates say:

Using this assertion as one of their bases, some of the more mystically oriented neo-Platonists interpreted Plato's Line in the following manner:

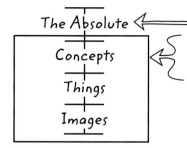

The Absolute

Concepts

Things

Images

Reason and language could apply here, . . .

but because the function of thought and language is to circumscribe and divide, they could not apply here.

The Absolute (ultimate reality, God) is one and indivisible; therefore it is "accessed" not by a rational analysis and understanding (as the traditional Platonists thought) but through an extra-rational mystical experience.

We will use as our example of Western mysticism the stellar case of TERESA of Avila (1515–1582)—later Saint Teresa of Avila. She was born in the ancient and austere walled city of Avila on the stark, arid plateau of Castile in northwestern Spain. As a child, she read the novels of romance and chivalry so popular at that time (the same ones satirized a century later by Cervantes in *Don Quixote*) and biographies of the saints. Motivated by these stories of adventure, when she was seven years old, she

Avila, España

and her brother ran away from home heading for "the land of the Moors," hoping to be beheaded there and become saintly martyrs. Luckily, their uncle ran across them a few blocks from home and brought them back to their worried mother.

As a young woman, Teresa attracted much attention for her

beauty, but she was not interested in the few pleasures that the society of Avila could offer her. She entered the order of the Carmelites when she was twenty. She was always frail and, for much of her first year as a nun, was ill. She heard strange noises in her head and fell into a four-day trance that was so deep the sisters thought she was dead. This trance may have been a precursor to her later mystical visions. She took on as her life's work the reformation of the Carmelite order, which had its roots in twelfth-century Palestine but had lost its original spark and zeal, according to Teresa. She traveled the length and breadth of Spain, living entirely on alms, and established thirty-two convents of the Reform. Her practical acumen in the everyday world contrasts remarkably with the "otherworldliness" of her religious experiences. William James, in his masterful book *The Varieties of Religious Experience*, says of Teresa that she was

> one of the ablest women, in many respects, of whose life we have the record. She had a powerful intellect of the practical order. She wrote admirable descriptive psychology, possessed a will equal to any emergency, great talent for politics and business, a buoyant disposition, and a first-rate literary style.[20]

Teresa was beatified (made eligible for sainthood) only thirty-two years after her death and was canonized (officially declared "saintly") in 1622, along with her Basque counterpart, Ignatius of Loyola. She has always been one of Spanish Catholicism's favorite figures.

We cannot call Teresa a philosopher in any strict sense; nevertheless she is associated with the Platonic tradition through her reading of Augustine's *Confessions* and her conversations and correspondence with contemporary figures in the movement. She lived at a time when the Inquisition suppressed many books—especially for women! This restriction saddened her, but in one of her visions Christ himself said to her, "Be not troubled. I will give thee a living book." That book was Nature, and to nature she paid the closest attention and from nature she drew the images for her mystical philosophy. Even in this respect, she was participating unwittingly in the Platonic tradition, for the neo-Platonic medieval Christian world had left as a legacy the view that everything in nature is a symbol of some higher truth and that therefore each natural object gives analogical—though not literal—knowledge of God. Ironically, this view means that "images" are more highly valued in the neo-Platonic tradition than they were by Plato himself. As we turn to Teresa's mystical thinking, we will see how she uses these images from the natural and human world to describe and perhaps to achieve a mystical state of religious knowledge.

Teresa wrote about her mystical experiences in a number of works. We will briefly concentrate on two, her autobiography, *Book of Her Life*, and *Mansions*, or *Inner Castles* as it was subtitled. In the first book, she distinguishes four stages of religious mentality and explains them using the imagery of gardening. In the second book, she identifies seven stages discussed in the imagery of householding, though the first three "inner castles" seem to be subdivisions of the first "garden" in the autobiography. In the first garden, or "water," as she calls it, one enters into a state of prayer likened to a careful watering of plants that will produce fragrances pleasant to the Master Gardener, God. Here in this first stage, the contemplative soul must perform the difficult work of drawing water up from the well to water the plants. In the second stage of mystical progress,

Saint Teresa of Avila (1515–1582) (After the Sixteenth-Century Statue by Gregorio Fernandez)

she who prays is allowed to use a waterwheel to irrigate the garden. Here the contemplative soul does not need to toil so hard. In the third stage, which Teresa calls "the Prayer of Quiet," the soul is permitted to irrigate the garden with the aid of water running from a stream or a spring. It is as if God himself is doing the gardening now, and the soul is able to benefit from the delicious fragrances of the flourishing plants.

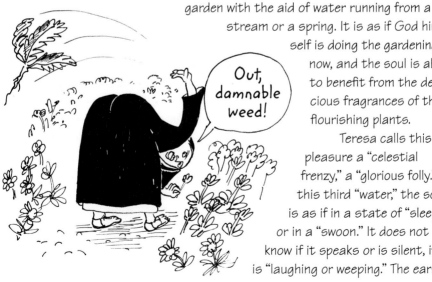

Out, damnable weed!

Teresa calls this pleasure a "celestial frenzy," a "glorious folly." In this third "water," the soul is as if in a state of "sleep," or in a "swoon." It does not know if it speaks or is silent, if it is "laughing or weeping." The ears

Religious Mysticism   **197**

hear, but what they hear is "a torrent of holy nonsense." Eating is
torturous; sleeping produces
anguish. In this Prayer of
Quiet, it is as if a spark has
been ignited that God will now
nurture and lead to the next
stage of progress. This fourth
"water" is like a heavenly
shower that saturates the
whole garden. Then, reverting
to the ignition simile, she says
the fire has burst into full flame,
and the flame rises high above the
fire. This Teresa calls, in *Mansions*,
the "Prayer of Union." Here God
completely possesses the soul.
Mad words escape the soul,
but they are really meaningless,
though meant as praise and

A Torrent of Holy Nonsense

exclamations of almost unen-
durable joy. Teresa also uses
imagery from that most erotic
of all biblical books, *The Song
of Songs*. The soul is
"wounded with love for her
spouse." It experiences the
"kiss of the mouth" from
the Bridegroom. The fire in
the soul causes pain but also
warmth and pleasure. In the
final moment the "self truly
appears not to exist." One
wishes for nothing, neither
life nor death. It is as if,
Teresa says, two candles have
been brought together and now produce a single flame as their wax
melts together.

Associated with Teresa's
mystical "raptures" are always

Saint Teresa in Ecstasy
(After Gianlorenzo Bernini, 1652)

visions. Her most famous vision, the one captured in the statue by Bernini, is called the "Vision of the Transverberation of the Heart." She saw a small angel with a beautiful face holding "a long golden spear," tipped with "a little fire," which he thrust into her heart so that, she says:

> it penetrated into my entrails. When he drew out the spear he seemed to be drawing them out with it, leaving me all on fire with a wonderous love for God. The pain was so great that it caused me to utter several moans; and yet so exceedingly sweet is this greatest of pains that it is impossible to desire to be rid of it, or for the soul to be content with less than God.[21]

Teresa was given this vision many times. It must have been difficult to come down off a "high" like this—very difficult, as she says, to do dishes after you've seen the face of God. Yet, she adds, we must also find God *entre los pucheros*—among the pots and pans.

Trying to Do Dishes after Having Seen the Face of God

The scarcely suppressed sexual imagery of Teresa's vision might suggest a pathology to some. In William James's study of Teresa, he says, "To the medical mind, these ecstasies signify nothing but suggested and imitated hypnoid states, on an intellectual basis of superstition, and a corporeal one of degeneration and hysteria" (p. 450). But, sticking with his pragmatic principles, James goes on to say, "To pass a spiritual judgment upon these states, we must not content ourselves with superficial medical talk but inquire into their fruits for life." (James is here applying the principle that he elsewhere calls "the genetic fallacy"—that of thinking one has refuted the truth of an idea by tracing the idea back to its psychological roots, a charge that could certainly be brought against Feuerbach, Marx, Nietzsche, and Freud.) And James clearly thinks that Teresa's visions indeed produced good "fruits for life," because they motivated her to great activity and a high degree of practical success and happiness.

Teresa admitted that some of her confessors had problems with her descriptions of her visions. Indeed, the brothers of the Inquisition kept a close eye on her. Why? Perhaps because, in the West, religious beliefs have become institutionalized and hence structures of authority and power. But mystical ecstasies are subversive of established power and so are worrisome to the authorities. It is as if the inquisitors would like to

The Brothers of the Inquisition and Sister Teresa Discussing Her Night Out

have asked her, "Sister Teresa, if you have seen the face of God, why hasn't the Pope seen it?" Teresa probably would have answered humbly that she did not know.

Religious Existentialism

One of the most interesting antirationalistic religious stances (I am loath to call it a *theory*) held by any philosopher is that of the nineteenth-century Dane SØREN KIERKEGAARD (1813–1855). Kierkegaard—whom I would call a radical Christian, but who never dared in his writings to call himself a Christian (he was busy attempting to *become* a Christian)—admired Feuerbach's atheism and loathed all attempts to prove God's existence. Indeed, Kierkegaard took as a personal affront all efforts to demonstrate God's being. ("Woe unto all those unfaithful stewards who sat down and wrote false proofs.") Kierkegaard felt that for something to be a truly religious belief, it had to be just that—a *belief*, something that is not knowledge. Indeed, a religious belief would have to be something not only that *is not* knowledge but that *cannot be* knowledge. Rather, it could be accounted for only in terms of what Kierkegaard called "the category of the absurd"—a category he felt Kant had left out of his twelve "categories of the understanding." (This is reminiscent of the view of the early Christian theologian Tertullian [169–220], whose motto was

Søren Kierkegaard (1813–1855)

"I believe that which is absurd.") According to Kierkegaard, knowledge must be something *objective*—in the case of mathematics (e.g., 3 x 3 = 9), science (e.g., f = ma), history (e.g., Caesar crossed the Rubicon in 49 B.C.E.), or common sense (e.g., The cat is on the mat), there are objective criteria for establishing their truth value. But in the case of religious claims (e.g., God is love, whosoever believeth in him shall inherit everlasting life),

Credo Quia Absurdum

there are only subjective criteria, which is to say, *personal* criteria. Arriving at a religious perspective requires a "leap of faith."

Perhaps this notion can be best addressed by taking a look at Kierkegaard's perplexing account of the biblical story of Abraham and Isaac as it is related in his book *Fear and Trembling* (1843), for it is there that we find his most sustained, if convoluted, discussion of religious belief. (Our problem is confounded by the fact that Kierkegaard wrote the book under one of his many pseudonyms, that of "Johannes de Silentio" [an intentional irony worthy of Kierkegaard's hero, Socrates—John the Silent speaks!], and later claimed that he took no responsibility for any views held by his pseudonyms. The curious relation between Kierkegaard and the volumes he wrote under fictitious names has been the topic of more than one book, but here we will ignore Kierkegaard's disclaimer and attribute the views in *Fear and Trembling* to Kierkegaard himself.)

Let us begin by reviewing the pertinent aspects of the biblical text as related in Genesis, chapters 11 through 22. Abraham was a hereditary tribal leader of the Hebrews. Late in life he married his half-sister, Sarah, who was barren. When Abraham was seventy-five years old, God commanded him to take his people and begin a journey to a land that God would show him. God made a covenant with Abraham and promised him that Sarah would become the mother of a son who would be the father of a great nation. The years passed and Sarah did not conceive. Then when Abraham was ninety-nine and Sarah ninety ("and it ceased to be with Sarah after the manner of women" [Genesis 18:11]), God appeared to Abraham again and renewed the promise. Sarah conceived and gave birth to Isaac. The circumcision and weaning of the child were celebrated with great joy by Abraham, who loved his son. Then came that terrible night described in Genesis 22:1–2.

> And it came to pass . . . that God did tempt Abraham, and said unto him, Abraham: and he said, Behold, here I am. And he said, take now thy son, Isaac, whom thou lovest, and get thee into the land of Moriah; and offer him there for a burnt offering upon one of the mountains which I will tell thee of.

Without hesitation and telling no one, Abraham took Isaac, traveled with him three days through that lonely desert, placed him on the appointed altar, lifted the sacrificial knife and was prepared to make the fatal thrust when the Angel of the Lord stopped him, saying that Abraham had passed the test and allowed him to sacrifice in Isaac's stead a ram that was conveniently caught in a nearby thicket. So Abraham got Isaac back, returned to his people, and lived in blessedness the rest of his days.

Now, this story provokes a state of deep perplexity in Johannes de Silentio, the pseudonymous author of *Fear and Trembling*. First of all, Johannes is perplexed because he cannot understand the story; second, he is perplexed because everyone else seems to understand the story perfectly well. (Why else would all the others replace the Bible on the shelf after reading the account, comment, "What a wonderful story of faith!" and then go along on their merry way without being the least bit affected by the story? Yet the story leaves Johannes sleepless in the night and inspires in him the fear and trembling of the book's title.) Johannes cannot understand the story because he cannot understand Abraham himself. He asks:

Johannes de Silentio Reads before Retiring

> Who gave strength to Abraham's arm? Who held his right hand up so that it did not fall limp at his side? He who gazes at this becomes paralyzed. Who gave strength to Abraham's soul, so that his eyes did not grow dim, so that he saw neither Isaac nor the ram? He who gazes at this becomes blind.[22]

Johannes tries to conceive of Abraham as a real human being of flesh and blood, not as a fantastic personality from mythological literature. As an existing human, Abraham is incomprehensible. How could he be so resolute in the face of the horror of his task? "And if . . . the individual was mistaken—what can save him? . . . and if the individual had misunderstood the deity—what can save him? . . . if this man is disordered in his mind, if he had made a mistake!" (pp. 71–72).

Furthermore, Johannes cannot be certain what it is that makes Abraham "the father of faith" and hence the father of us all. Many say that Abraham is great because he was willing to sacrifice to God the best thing he had. Johannes demonstrates the falsity of this view by way of an illustration. He imagines a clerical orator who eloquently presents his flock with just such a misleading interpretation of the story of Abraham. One of his parishioners, taken by the sermon, returns home and executes his son. When the preacher hears of this, he goes to the sinner and thunders down on him in righteous indignation, "O abominable man, offscouring of society, what devil possessed thee to want to murder thy son?" The point, of course, is that this attitude is precisely the one the preacher should have had toward Abraham. Johannes de Silentio asks:

> How is one to explain the contradiction illustrated by that orator? Is it because Abraham had a prescriptive right to be a great man, so that what he did is great, and when another does the same it is sin, a heinous sin? In that case I do not wish to participate in such thoughtless eulogy. If faith does not make it a holy act to be willing to murder one's son, then let the same condemnation be pronounced upon Abraham as upon every other man. (p. 41)

Johannes's conclusion is that "either Abraham was every minute a murderer, or we are here confronted by a paradox which is higher than all mediation." This thought horrifies Johannes, who says, "Abraham enjoys honor and glory as the father of faith, whereas he ought to be prosecuted and convicted of murder." But if Abraham is not to be condemned as a potential murderer (surely *that* cannot make him the father of faith), then he must be condemned as insane. "Humanly speaking, he is crazy and cannot make himself intelligible to anyone. And yet it is the mildest expression to say that he is crazy" (p. 86).

One of the most striking ideas to emerge from Kierkegaard's account of Abraham's madness (and one that is meant to evoke the fear and trembling of the book's title) is that granting the theological premise changes nothing. Abraham is mad whether or not God really did speak to him. If a law-abiding moral man "hears the voice of God" and becomes so inspired as to become socially irresponsible, if he sacrifices his son without criminal intent in order to obey a secret order that God has communicated to him alone, then certainly from the medical-social point of view (i.e., "humanly speaking"), that man is mad.

Jean-Paul Sartre was particularly impressed with this aspect of Kierkegaard's analysis of the plight of Abraham, and he referred to it in order to elucidate his own theory of anguish. Sartre wrote:

> You know the story: an angel[23] has ordered Abraham to sacrifice his son; if it really were an angel who has come and said, "You are Abraham, you shall sacrifice your son," everything would be all right. But everyone must first wonder, "Is it really an angel and am I really Abraham? What proof do I have?"
>
> There was a madwoman who had hallucinations; someone used to speak to her on the telephone and give her orders. Her doctor asked her, "Who is it who talks to you?" She answered, "He says it's God." What proof did she really have it was God? If an angel comes to me, what proof is there that it's an

angel? And if I hear voices, what proof is there that they come from heaven and not from hell, or from the subconscious, or a pathological condition? What proves that they are addressed to me?[24]

Abraham is mad not only in the sense referred to earlier (unable to communicate, prepared to perform an act that goes against his own moral standards and will horrify all) but in the following sense as well: He not only believes his son will die but, at the same moment, he believes his son will *not* die. (Abraham still has faith that God will keep the old covenant.) Abraham believed with certainty two mutually exclusive theses, and he acted on each of them in a single project. (It is as if Columbus believed both that the world was flat and that it was round, and he set out to prove both points by embarking on a single voyage.)

So either Abraham is a murderer, or he is mad, or the story of Abraham is rationally unintelligible. It will probably come as no surprise to you to discover that Kierkegaard (or, at least, Johannes de Silentio) draws the latter conclusion. Faith, he says, is "a paradox which is capable of transforming a murder into a holy act well-pleasing to God." Abraham acted "by virtue of the absurd," and "by virtue of the absurd" he became the father of faith. "Abraham was greater than all, great by reason of his power whose strength is impotence, great by reason of his wisdom whose secret is foolishness, great by reason of the love which is hatred of oneself" (p. 31). Adopting a term from Plato, Kierkegaard calls Abraham's condition "divine madness." For Kierkegaard, of course, the question was not whether Abraham was mad but whether his madness was divinely or demonically inspired. Still, "humanly speaking," it does not matter. In either case, society has an asylum for such heroes.

Earlier I mentioned that, for Kierkegaard, there could be no objective but only subjective, or personal, justification for religious belief. This idea can be clarified if one considers certain features of Kierkegaard's account of

Abraham's story. Notice that Abraham's act is not authorized or justified by God's command; rather, God's command is authorized by Abraham's decision to interpret it in a certain way. When Abraham was awakened on that horrible night by a voice commanding him to kill his child, he could have responded in a number of ways. He might have said, "This is not the voice of God but of the devil. Only the devil tempts men to do evil deeds. Get thee hence, O Satan!" Or he might have said (especially if he had read Freud), "This is not the voice of God but the voice of my own madness. I shall kill myself rather than perform this insane act!" Or he might have said, "This is the voice of God, who is testing me to

Abraham Reads Freud

see if I am willing to perform an immoral act for no good reason. I shall pass the test by refusing to perform the act!" Or he might have said, "If this is the voice of God, then he is not the God I thought he was; rather, he is an evil and cruel monster whose bidding I shall not do!"

Or, . . . he might have said any number of other things. Instead he chose to accept the assignment, and in so choosing, he bestowed his own authority on God's command. Kierkegaard is suggesting that ultimately the individual is the source of all authority and is totally responsible for all his or her decisions and actions. (This belief is the beginning of the school of thought known in the twentieth century as **existentialism,** which puts the existence of the individual human being at the center of the philosophical stage. [See Chapter 10 for a more thorough discussion of existentialism.] Kierkegaard's views greatly influenced such members of that school as Jean-Paul Sartre, Martin Heidegger, Karl Jaspers, Albert Camus, Miguel de Unamuno, and Gabriel Marcel.)

Kierkegaard's complex demonstration of the irreducibility of faith to intellectual categories (which is even more complex than it has been presented here) is indeed profound. Both the traditional proofs of God's existence and the traditional atheistic criticism of the irrationality of religious belief seem lifeless and shallow in the face of Kierkegaard's account. Especially weak vis-à-vis Kierkegaard's explosive treatment of faith are those rationalistic arguments like Freud's, which see religion as a crutch for the frail. Kierkegaard's religious discourse is meant to strengthen, not weaken, the soul. It is not "lemonade-twaddle" for the fainthearted (as he calls most sermonizing); rather, it is only for those who can stand the drama of striving with God and with oneself.

Kierkegaard Driving People from Religion

Yet it must be obvious that this account raises tremendous philosophical problems, not the least of which is the problem of fanaticism (and our poor world has been plagued with plenty of that since Kierkegaard's day). Also, we may ask, *must* we accept Kierkegaard's implication that a truly religious conception of life is ultimately incompatible with a social conception of life? Must one become "divinely mad" to be considered authentically religious? Well, Kierkegaard could at least point to plenty of biblical evidence for his thesis, but it isn't surprising that, as William Barrett says, Kierkegaard's harshness has driven at least as many from religion as it has into religion's embrace.[25]

Conclusion

What conclusion do we draw from these discussions of religion? I must be very careful here, for in talking about religion, everything is controversial. No matter where you walk, you tread on someone's toes. Still, walk we must. Let it be a relatively gentle path!

Concerning the various arguments meant to prove God's existence: it seems to me that no one of them is powerful enough to force rational assent. (The same is true concerning the arguments for atheism.) Yet, taken all together, it is possible to imagine the combination as powerful enough to remove certain philosophical scruples one had against belief. And what is wrong with taking them all together? Usually people have more than one reason for believing what they believe. Our systems of belief and justification are usually multilayered. If I asked you why you enrolled specifically in this class, you would probably answer with a number of reasons: "I needed three units of humanities credit." "This is a good hour for me—it frees my time up for work."

Stepping on Toes

"I heard the professor was good." "I noticed that the course attracts bright people, and I would like to be considered in that category." "There are a number of attractive members of the opposite sex in this class." "My parents said they would cut off my finances if I didn't take some philosophy." Maybe no one of these reasons is a sufficient explanation, but the group together is compelling.

As I said, I can imagine someone finding all the arguments for God's existence similarly compelling as a group. Frankly, I do not find them to be so. (Nor do I find compelling all the arguments for atheism together.) Perhaps more subtle versions of the arguments than I have presented would do the trick, but in their absence, I have to think that there are too many obvious problems with each of them as they stand. So I have to conclude with a negative answer to the question "Is there any good reason for believing in God's existence?"—if by "reason" we mean "logical argument" or "a compelling piece of evidence." However, I have learned enough from Kierkegaard, James, and the mystical poets to know that such a definition of "reason" is too confining and that there are, as Pascal said, "reasons of the heart." These reasons are perplexing and, as are so many things of the heart, very personal and difficult to evaluate, but one scoffs at them at one's risk.

Such a "reason" just may sneak up on one some fine day as a "thought that wounds from behind" (Kierkegaard's phrase).

My own choice has been a kind of impressionable **agnosticism,** asserting a negative answer based on the "evidence" presented so far but open to new evidence or new interpretations of old evidence. I state this opinion knowing full well the disdain with which Kierkegaard would greet my response. He would be quick to point out that the word "agnostic" translates into Latin as *ignoramus.* He was not surprised that there *were* lots of ignoramuses. He was only surprised that they touted their ignorance as an important philosophical position—usually at cocktail parties.

Thoughts That Wound from Behind

Well, I myself am an ignoramus.

Touting an Important Philosophical Position

Topics for Consideration

1. David Hume says, "There is no being whose nonexistence implies a contradiction." State as clearly as you can why Anselm and Descartes disagree. Then comment on the debate between the two sides.
2. Contrast the Platonic (hence rationalistic) features of the ontological proof with the empirical groundings of the cosmological proof. Regardless of your own opinion concerning the existence of God, which of the two approaches do you think would be more fruitful in settling the issue of God's existence or nonexistence?
3. Despite Darwin's and Hume's criticisms of teleological accounts of nature, it is in fact difficult to look at certain natural phenomena (such as the structure of the eyeball and the function of vision) without assuming that there are natural purposes or goals. Is this intuition enough to support the teleological proof of God's existence in your judgment?
4. Explain the sense in which the atheist Marx is more sympathetic to religion than the atheist Feuerbach.
5. Sigmund Freud thinks that religion is for the fainthearted. Contrast his view of religion with that of Søren Kierkegaard.
6. Take a position in the debate between W. K. Clifford and William James concerning the question of whether we have the right to hold beliefs in the absence of sufficient evidence.
7. David Hume would not deny that Teresa of Avila had the experiences she says she had. But he would argue that she was not warranted to describe them as she did (viz., as experiences that justified her belief in God). In your opinion, can an experience of the type Teresa describes be so strong as to authenticate itself?

Suggestions for Further Reading: Paperback Editions

Sigmund Freud, *The Future of an Illusion*, trans. James Strachey (New York: Norton, 1989). An interesting but not terribly compelling introduction to psychoanalytic thought through a critique of the religious mind.

John Hick, *Philosophy of Religion*, 4th ed. (Englewood Cliffs, N.J.: Prentice-Hall, 1978). A short, clear introduction.

David Hume, *Dialogues Concerning Natural Religion* (New York: Hafner, 1960). Hume's famous posthumously published critique of religious reasoning. Short and quite accessible.

William James, *The Varieties of Religious Experience* (New York: Random House, Modern Library, 1994). Lucid and very understandable. A masterpiece by an astute and sympathetic observer of the religious mind.

Søren Kierkegaard, *Fear and Trembling*, trans. Alastair Hannay (New York: Penguin Books, 1985). Kierkegaard's small gem.

Alvin Plantinga, ed., *The Ontological Argument* (Garden City, N.Y.: Doubleday, 1965). A good summary of the arguments for and against Anselm's proof from the eleventh century to our own.

Notes

1. Bertrand Russell, *The Autobiography of Bertrand Russell. The Early Years: 1872–World War I* (Boston: Bantam Books, 1969), p. 43.

2. Ibid., p. 45.

3. Anselm of Canterbury, *Proslogium*, in Anne Fremantle, *The Age of Belief* (New York: New American Library, 1954), pp. 88–89.

4. David Hume, *Dialogues Concerning Natural Religion* (New York: Hafner, 1960), p. 58.

5. The example is taken from Richard Taylor, "Introduction," in *The Ontological Argument*, ed. Alvin Plantinga (Garden City, N.Y.: Doubleday, 1965), p. xv.

6. Immanuel Kant, *Critique of Pure Reason* (Garden City, N.Y.: Doubleday, 1961), p. 358.

7. Norman Malcolm, "Anselm's Ontological Arguments," in Plantinga, *The Ontological Argument*, pp. 141–147.

8. See Alvin Plantinga, "A Valid Ontological Argument?" and Paul Henle, "Uses of the Ontological Argument," in Plantinga, *The Ontological Argument*, pp. 160–171, 172–180.

9. Malcolm, "Anselm's Ontological Arguments," p. 159.

10. Thomas Aquinas, *Summa Theologica*, in Fremantle, *The Age of Belief*, p. 153.

11. Frederick Copleston, *Aquinas* (London: Penguin Books, 1955), pp. 110–122.

12. Aquinas, *Summa Theologica*, pp. 154–155.

13. For example, see Carl G. Jung, *Answer to Job* (Princeton, N.J.: Princeton University Press, 1973).

14. Karl Marx, *Marx and Engels: Basic Writings on Politics and Philosophy*, ed. Lewis Feuer (Garden City, N.Y.: Doubleday, 1959), pp. 244, 262–263.

15. Herbert Marcuse, *Eros and Civilization* (New York: Vintage, 1955), p. 66.

16. Sigmund Freud, *Civilization and Its Discontents* (New York: Norton, 1962), p. 19. Unless otherwise stated, all subsequent quotes from Freud in this chapter are from this source.

17. William James, *Pragmatism* (New York: World Publishing, 1961), p. 42. Unless otherwise stated, all subsequent quotes from *Pragmatism* in this chapter will be cited in the text.

18. Quoted in William James, "The Will to Believe," in *Pragmatism: The Classic Writings*, ed. H. S. Thayer (New York: New American Library, 1970), p. 191.

19. William James, "The Will to Believe," in *Philosophy of Recent Times*, Vol. 2, ed. James B. Hartman (New York: McGraw-Hill, 1967), p. 28.

20. William James, *The Varieties of Religious Experience* (New York: Random House, Modern Library, 1994), p. 379. All subsequent quotations from James in this chapter are from this source.

21. Chapter 21 of Teresa's *Book of Her Life,* quoted in E. Allison Peers, *Studies of the Spanish Mystics,* Vol. I (London: Sheldon Press, 1927), p. 197. All other quotations from St. Teresa are from this source.

22. Søren Kierkegaard, *Fear and Trembling,* trans. Walter Lowrie (Garden City, N.Y.: Doubleday, 1954), p. 36. Unless otherwise stated, all subsequent quotes from Kierkegaard in this chapter are from this source.

23. We know the story, indeed, but Sartre's biblical knowledge fails him here. It was not an angel who spoke to Abraham but God himself.

24. Jean-Paul Sartre, *Existentialism and Human Emotions* (New York: Philosophical Library, 1957), p. 19.

25. William Barrett, *Irrational Man* (Garden City, N.Y.: Doubleday, 1962), p. 262.

6

The Largest Airline
in the Free World
Philosophy of Freedom

Just before the collapse of the Soviet Union, a TV commercial caught my attention. "Blah-Blah Airlines is the largest airline in the Free World." What information was being communicated in that commercial, and what information was being suppressed? The latter question is easy to answer. The suppressed truth in the commercial is this: "The official Soviet airline, Aeroflot, is the largest airline in the world. Blah-Blah is only the second largest." (Can you imagine that as a commercial?) Well, if we weren't supposed to think the hidden thought, what were we supposed to think? I take it that we were supposed to associate in our minds Blah-Blah Airlines/bigness/antitotalitarianism/the Free World (hence **freedom**). These thoughts together were meant to loosen a few dollars from our pockets. Here is the problem. In our culture, freedom is, on the one hand, so cherished that we are taught that it is worth dying for ("Live free or die"—motto on the New Hampshire license plate). Yet, on the other hand, it has been co-opted by the ideo-

Spend your money with us and strike a blow for freedom!

logues and moneymakers to the extent that it has become a meaningless buzzword. Yes, there is indeed a lot of talk in our society about freedom. We hear about it in TV commercials, in political speeches from the left, middle, and right, and not uncommonly see reference to it on bumper stickers.

When philosophers turn to the topic of freedom, they ask the following kinds of big questions:

- What do we mean by "freedom"?
- Does freedom exist, or is there only necessity?
- How is freedom possible in a world governed by natural laws?
- Can we ever know whether there is freedom? *epistémologie guis,*
- If there is freedom, is it an either-or proposition, or are there degrees of it? Can we do anything to maximize it or endanger it?
- Do any of these questions matter practically, or are they only of academic interest?

Determinism: Ancient Greek and Enlightenment Views

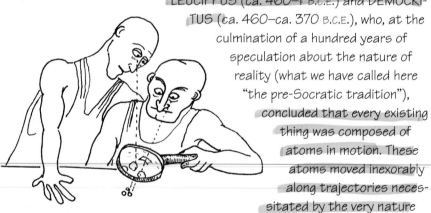

Determinism is the thesis that everything that occurs happens of necessity. This thesis first appears in the history of philosophy in the theories of LEUCIPPUS (ca. 460–? B.C.E.) and DEMOCRITUS (ca. 460–ca. 370 B.C.E.), who, at the culmination of a hundred years of speculation about the nature of reality (what we have called here "the pre-Socratic tradition"), concluded that every existing thing was composed of atoms in motion. These atoms moved inexorably along trajectories necessitated by the very nature of atoms and the nature of motion. The single fragment of Leucippus's book that remains to us today says, "Naught happens for nothing but everything from a ground of necessity."

Imagine the following schema. Each letter in the diagram represents a movement in space. Each number represents a moment in time. Each dot

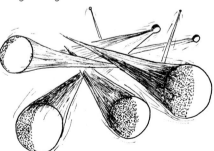

represents an atom. The symbol "⊃" represents a relation of necessity between movements. Let us arbitrarily say that the following relations hold:

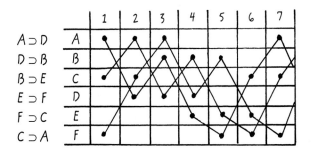

$A \supset D$
$D \supset B$
$B \supset E$
$E \supset F$
$F \supset C$
$C \supset A$

If we let the left column represent the laws of nature, we can see that we could predict the trajectory of each atom in each moment of its career. Given any atom at F, it *must* move to C, and any atom at C *must* move to A, and so on. Of course, Leucippus and Democritus did not claim to know those laws, but they suspected that they existed and therefore everything that happened did so of necessity and that "free will" was an illusion.

Democritus's view did not become the dominant one in his day, mostly because he stood not at the end of the history of science but on its threshold, and he could not appeal to any tradition of scientific authority to support his views. It would take another two thousand years before such a tradition could establish itself as authoritative. But when it did, Democritus's theory came to the fore with a vengeance. In the eighteenth century, armed with the prestigious discoveries of Sir Isaac Newton, a number of **Enlightenment** figures put forth new versions of Democritus's old argument. Foremost among them were the Baron HENRI D'HOLBACH (1723–1789) and PIERRE-SIMON LAPLACE (1749–1827). D'Holbach argued that the same principles that apply to the physical world must necessarily apply to the human brain, which was as much material in nature as were the moon and the stars.

There is a drunken ladybug on this leaf now. Therefore on June 19, 2010, there will be a mudslide in Rangoon.

Pierre-Simon Laplace (1749–1827)

Therefore every thought of every brain followed necessarily from the brain states that preceded those thoughts. Laplace held a similar view and went so far as to say this: if I knew all the laws of nature and had one complete description of the universe at any given moment, then I could predict all future events and retrodict all past events.

Hard Determinism: Modern Views

The key ideas of determinism are those of causality and necessity. According to this theory, every event in the world is caused, where to say that "X causes Y" is to say that if event X takes place, then event Y necessarily happens as well. **Hard determinism** is the view that determinism is true and that its truth rules out the possibility of freedom. If everything is necessary, then nothing is free.

B. F. Skinner

In the contemporary world, hard determinism is perhaps most clearly defended by B. F. Skinner (whom we have already met in Chapter 3). In his book with the telling title, *Beyond Freedom and Dignity*, Skinner says:

> [M]any anthropologists, sociologists, and psychologists have used their expert knowledge to prove that man is free, purposeful, and responsible. This escape route is slowly closed as new evidences of the predictability of human behavior are discovered. Personal exemption from a complete

determinism is revoked as a scientific analysis progresses, particularly in accounting for the behavior of the individual.[1]

As an aside, I might point out what looks to me like a logical fallacy in Skinner's argument. He says, because behavior is predictable, it must be determined. Now, it is certainly true that if (A) behavior is determined, then (B) it is in principle predictable (for Laplace's reasons). But it isn't true that because a behavior is predictable, it is determined.

Beyond Freedom and Dignity

	[A implies B. A. Therefore B.]	[A implies B. B. Therefore A.]
Valid		*invalid*

Assume for the moment that there is such a thing as freedom and that Pierre freely chooses to abide by Christian values. I think in such a case we could correctly predict that Pierre will attend church services and will offer help to his neighbor in distress. Does this mean that he could not do otherwise? Of course not.

Now back to Skinner, who correctly associates the concept of freedom with the teleological model of explanation. You will recall from Chapter 5 that a teleological model is one that explains things in terms of goals, purposes, plans, and intentions. Skinner, an empiricist

**Pierre Attends Church
(He Could Not Do Otherwise)**

and a materialist, is suspicious of nonphysical, unobservable entities, so he wants to get rid of the teleological model of explanation. He has this to say about it:

> Physics did not advance by looking more closely at the jubilance of a falling body or biology by looking at the nature of vital spirits, and we do not need to try to discover what . . . plans, purposes, intentions, or the other prerequisites of autonomous man really are in order to get on with a scientific analysis of behavior.[2]

The Causal Model
(Push from Behind)

The Teleological Model
(Pull from Ahead)

What exactly is at stake here? Well, it's important to remember that normally our explanation of our own behavior is in terms of the teleological model. If you ask me why I'm in such a hurry, I explain that I'm trying to arrive at the grocery store before it closes at 6 P.M. This is an *explanation* of my behavior (it renders it intelligible), and it is an explanation in terms of my *intentions* and *purposes*. Skinner wants to do away with such explanations.

Furthermore, it is important to note that in our moral and legal tradition, we hold people fully responsible only for their intentional acts. If your lawyer can convince the jury that your act was accidental rather than intentional (and we've already seen that the concept of an accident makes sense only against a backdrop of intentionality), the jury will find you not fully responsible for the act. (If you caused someone's death accidentally and not purposefully, you could be convicted of manslaughter due to negligence but not of murder.) Similarly, we hold people responsible only for their *free* acts, not for acts they cannot help (which is why we excuse the mentally ill from responsibility). So if Skinner does away with the teleological model, he also overturns our moral and legal institutions, such as courtrooms and prisons. His theory is a radical one, and he is well aware of that fact.

Skinner wishes to replace the teleological model with a **causal explanation,** namely, with a stimulus-response model based on Pavlov's famous experiment with his drooling dog: when you get ready to feed a steak to a dog, the animal begins to salivate as soon as it sees or

Implementation of Skinner's Theories Would Empty the Prisons

smells the meat. Now, if you repeatedly ring a bell just before you serve the steak, eventually the dog will begin to salivate at the sound of the bell. We need no "dog psychology" to explain this fact and no references to purposes, plans, intentions, and goals. It can be explained in purely mechanical terms. Skinner believed he could extend the Pavlovian model to the human sphere, thereby overturning the traditional teleological model and placing us "beyond freedom and dignity."

Pavlovian Science

Sigmund Freud

Some philosophers have claimed to find in the theory of the mind formulated by Sigmund Freud another version of hard determinism, at least as it concerns any so-called decisions of any weight at all. The deterministic argument runs like this: an individual's personality has crystallized by the age of five years. One has no personal control over the formation of one's own personality, yet everything that happens to an individual after that age will be responded to by that already completed character structure.

Furthermore, the bulk of one's motivational system is unconscious, structured by antisocial biological urges, painful childhood memories, unresolved emotional conflicts, fantastic desires, and fears, all of which have been repressed into the unconscious. The **ego** (more or less the conscious self) is nothing more than a façade masking a ferocious struggle between the **id** (the antisocial, animal self that "wants it all now") and the **superego** (the irrational, nay-saying, guilt-spawning social conscience). According to this deterministic reading of Freud, all significant actions of the so-called normal person, as much as those of the psychotic, are unfree. And, as was the case with Skinner's deterministic scheme, there is no such thing as responsibility here.

John Hospers, a philosopher who interprets Freud pretty much as a hard determinist, says:

> But what is not welcome news is that our very acts of volition, and the entire train of deliberations leading up to them, are but façades for the expression of unconscious wishes, or rather, unconscious compromises and defenses.
>
> . . . .
>
> We may . . . say that a man is free only to the extent that his behavior is *not* unconsciously motivated at all. If this be our criterion, most of our behavior could not be called free: everything, including both impulses and volitions, having to do with

The Standoff between the Id and the Superego

our basic attitudes toward life, the general tenor of our tastes, whether we become philosophers or artists or business men, our whole affective life including our preferences for blondes or brunettes, active or passive, older or younger, has its inevitable basis in the unconscious. Only those comparatively vanilla-flavored aspects of life—such as our behavior toward people who don't really matter to us—are exempted from this rule.[3]

The little twist at the end of this paragraph shows that, in effect, Hospers does not interpret Freud as a strict hard determinist, because Hospers allows that, according to Freud, *some* conscious decisions—namely, those that don't matter at all—may not be caused by unconscious motives. So for Hospers, Freud is a hard determinist only where it matters. Indeed, Freud himself says:

As is known, many persons argue against the assumption of an absolute psychic determinism by referring to an intense feeling of conviction that there is a free will. This feeling of conviction exists, but is not incompatible with the belief in determinism. Like all normal feelings, it must be justified by something. But, so far as I can observe, it does not manifest itself in weighty and important decisions; on these occasions, one has much more the feeling of psychic compulsion and gladly falls back on it. (Compare Luther's "Here I stand, I cannot do anything else.")

On the other hand, it is in trivial and indifferent decisions that one feels sure that he feels he could just as easily have acted differently, that he acted of his own free will, and without any motives. From our analyses we need not contest the right of the feeling of conviction that there is a free will.[4]

So far, Freud seems to be saying that all significant decisions are caused (determined) by unconscious motives. So, by the way, are all "arbitrary choices," such as picking a number between one and one thousand or choosing a pet's name out of the blue. Only indifferent choices (whatever they are!) may escape determination by unconscious motives. However, then Freud finishes the paragraph you were just reading by saying:

If we distinguish conscious from unconscious motivation, we are then informed by the feeling of conviction that the conscious motivation does not extend over all our motor resolutions. . . . What is thus left free from the one side receives its motive from the other side, from the unconscious, and the determinism in the psychic realm is thus carried out uninterruptedly.

In this cryptic passage, Freud seems to take away what he had just given. Now it seems that determinism covers all of psychic life.

Even so, it is possible to interpret Freud as a soft determinist rather than a hard determinist. Remember, the hard determinist denies the possibility of freedom, hence the possibility of personal responsibility. And indeed, as a philosopher and a psychiatrist, Freud does not want to hold people responsible for acts over which they have no control, which seems to be most of them. But Freud does seem to advocate a certain kind of freedom. To the extent that he does so, he is a soft determinist. (As you will soon see, soft determinists believe that freedom, if correctly defined, is compatible with determinism.)

Consider the case of the woman who comes to the psychoanalyst trying to find out why every man she has ever been involved with brutalizes her. "Why do men want to beat me?" (This case may seem on its surface to be a typical example of Freudian sexism, of which there is plenty, but I think a careful scrutiny of it demonstrates that such is not the case here.) Investigation reveals an unconscious childhood memory on the part of the woman, a memory of having observed her father beating her mother. On the typical Freudian model, the woman has chosen her mother as her model of femininity and her father as her model of masculinity, so in choosing herself as a woman, she unconsciously chooses men who will beat her. Yet these are not true choices because she has no control over them. (So far, the model is one of hard determinism.) But what can Freud do for this woman? He cannot "cure" her. Perhaps she will always be in some way attracted to brutal men. But now that she is aware of the motivational forces operating on her, she can gain some control over her life. She will know better than to frequent certain taverns, and she certainly will *not* accept an invitation to the annual Hell's Angels' picnic! Surely this new control restored to her by psycho-analysis is a kind of *freedom* that is incompatible with the theory of hard determinism, which denies the possibility of any meaningful sense of freedom.

**Déjeuner sur l'Herbe sans Marie, Hell's Angels' Style
(With Apologies to Edouard Manet)**

Furthermore, as the British philosopher Richard Peters has pointed out, it is rather far-fetched to read Freud as claiming that *every* act is motivated by the unconscious. Suppose you and I are playing chess, and you see that my queen is unprotected. It's your turn, so you take my piece. We

Why did you take my queen? Is there something unresolved from your childhood?

don't need to seek for an unconscious motive to explain your act. We don't need to know anything about your unhappy childhood or your repressed sexual fantasies. Some of these psychoanalytic topics *might* be pertinent to the question of why you like to play chess in the first place but not to the question of why, while playing chess, you decide to take my unprotected queen. Your ordinary conscious reasons, combined with a knowledge of the rules of chess, are perfectly adequate to explain your action.

In another of Peters's examples, he says that if a person explains why he is crossing the road by asserting that he wants to buy tobacco, this is a perfectly sound explanation under certain circumstances. (The person smokes, he is out of cigarettes, there is a tobacco shop across the street.) No unconscious motive or any psychoanalytic theory is needed here (though an unconscious motive might be useful in explaining why the man smokes in the first place). On the other hand, if the man *rolls* across the street and explains his actions by saying that he's going to get tobacco, *this* explanation needs looking into. In such a case, a psychoanalytic account *might* be needed precisely because our normal account has broken down. Concluding his nondeterministic interpretation of Freud, Peters says,

What are you doing?

Going to get tobacco.

Oh.

> When Freud wants to describe goings-on of which it is appropriate to say that a man is acting, that he has a *reason* for what he does, and so on, he talks about the Ego; when on the other hand, he wants to say that a person suffers something, or is made or driven to do something, he speaks of the Id.[5]

Soft Determinism

There have been philosophers who have affirmed the truth of determinism but who have denied that their deterministic views preclude the existence of freedom. Some of them have been motivated to prove the compatibility of freedom and determinism because they don't like the conclusion, reached by hard determinists like Skinner and Freud (at least, in one interpretation), that no one is ever responsible for anything. Correctly seeing that there can be responsibility only when there is freedom but also believing in the truth of determinism, they have been pressed to demonstrate that freedom can exist even in a world of necessity. This view is called **soft determinism.** This approach has been quite common among some philosophers in the twentieth century, but its roots go back to Roman times. The Stoics (first century C.E.), St. Augustine (fourth century), Thomas Hobbes (seventeenth century), and Baruch Spinoza (seventeenth century), all defended versions of it. Augustine's interpretation is fairly representative, even though his concern about determinism was different from those we've mentioned so far. (Modern determinists derive their conception of necessity from the laws of nature. Augustine derives his from his belief in God's omniscience. If God knows everything, he knows the future; and if he knows the future, the future must unfold in accordance with God's knowledge of it.)

What do we mean by "freedom"? Augustine and other soft determin-

A Soft Determinist

ists ask this not so much as philosophers but as ordinary persons in every-day life. What we mean by freedom is the coincidence of will and capacity; that is, we are free to the extent that we are able to do and get what we want. If you ask me if I am free to go to the movies tonight, and I say that I am not, I am implying that I *want* to, but am *not able* to. This is the sense in which the pris-oners at San Quentin are not free. They are not free to leave if they want to. However, they are free to write their mothers. So, according to this commonsense def-inition, freedom is relative to context. One is both free and not free at the same time. Nevertheless, every-one is free sometimes. (No one has ever been so miserable as *never* to have gotten what he wants.) Some are freer than others or freer at certain periods of their lives than at others. And when one wants to do X and does X, then doing X is a free act, and one is respon-sible for that act.

Dear Mom, I'm FREE! (However, the warden insists that I remain here for another 99 years...)

Furthermore, in this definition, freedom is *compatible* with determin-ism. I sometimes do what I want to do even if my will was determined according to Freudian or Skinnerian principles. So both freedom and neces-sity can exist in the same world.

One of the most curious versions of soft determinism was put forward in the first century C.E. by the *Stoics*, named after the *stoa*, or porch, from which their founder, ZENO of Cyprus (334–262 B.C.E.), preached. (A similar view was held by Spinoza in the seventeenth century.) Having accepted the claim that one is free to the extent that one gets what one wants, the Stoics, such as Seneca and Epictetus, added

that one is happy to the extent that one is free. Then, pointing out that we are all free and happy sometimes they make the astonishing claim that it is possible to be totally free and totally happy *all the time.* How is this feat to be accomplished? *Not by trying to get what one wants but by wanting what one gets*—by identifying your will with the "world will," what Nietzsche called *amor fati,* love of one's fate.

Now, it is easy enough to parody this view ("Just what I wanted, . . ."), but an interesting truth here escapes our mockery, namely, that the unhappiness of many people comes from the fact that they want things they can't have—especially in our material-istic consumer culture where we are constantly bombarded by images of pleasure objects and power that we absolutely must possess if we are to consider our-selves attractive, desirable, inde-pendent, smart, clever, and, mostly,

Don't Try to Get What You Want—Rather, Want What You Get

"cool." So we spend most of our lives burning with frustrated desire for this and that. Happiness and freedom elude us. The stoic wisdom (and I think it is wisdom of an almost Asian type) is that there is happiness in tranquility, and tranquility comes in "flowing with the river." But the stoics knew, as do the Asian philos-ophers, that such peace is not easy to aquire, and sometimes it takes a life-time to achieve. Further-more, its quest presupposes an ideal of passivity, inac-tion, quietism, which for better or worse is not compatible with the main-stream Western ideal of the self. Hence, this stoic form of soft determinism is not a "live option" for most of us.

You Can Either Flow with the River or Swim against the Current

Also, many people are dissatisfied with the soft determinist's definition of freedom as the coincidence of will and ability ("desire to do X" plus "ability to do X" equals "freedom to do X"). A wealthy heroin addict on this account freely engages in his addiction. This interpretation seems to trivialize the idea of freedom. Critics of soft determinism say that a more robust conception of freedom is required. If one sticks with the soft determinist's definition, according to which freedom comprises desire and ability, then it must be demonstrated that the agent's desires themselves are under his or her control. But it is not obvious that such control would be compatible with any form of determinism.

Indeterminism

The opposite of determinism is called **indeterminism.** This is simply the view that determinism is false. There are several versions of this claim. In the twentieth century, a number of scientists and philosophers of science rejected the nineteenth-century conception of causality, according to which, saying that A causes B is to say that A is the sufficient condition of B (given A, B follows of necessity). They urge relacing this one-on-one billiard ball–type model of causality with a looser, more statistical model. For example, according to the newer conception, imagine that A is the sufficient condition of B or C or D or E (but not necessarily of any one of them as opposed to the others). That is, when A happens, one of the members of the series B through E necessarily happens. In the case of the occurrence of (say) E, A caused E, but E is not a *necessary* event. (Given A, there were other possibilities besides E.)

So, an indeterminist can argue either that (1) there are only random events, or (2) there are some random events, or (3) there are some uncaused events, or (4) some caused events are not necessary events. Probably possibility 1 does not find many defenders, if any. (It would be an extreme version of the thesis that the center does not hold.) Possibility 4 is probably the best one for explaining the truth of propositions like "Heavy smoking causes cancer." Not every case of cancer is caused by heavy smoking and not every case of heavy smoking causes cancer, but nevertheless, heavy smoking (statistically) causes cancer. Indeterminists defend possibilities 2, 3, or 4, depending on which model of causality they work with.

Indeterminism has been given a new respectability because of recent developments in physics (which is somewhat ironic because the authority of determinism has usually been associated with its relationship to classical physics). Ever since the work of the Nobel Prize–recipient Werner Heisenberg, it has been suggested that at the subatomic level of physical reality (that is, at the most basic level) the causal model does not work and must be replaced with a statistical model. Let's explain this point by imagining a bird's-eye view of a pool table in a classical Newtonian world. If the ball is propelled here, and we know the exact force applied to it by the cue stick, the exact point of application

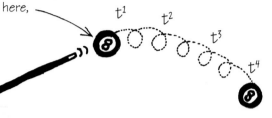

of the force, and exactly the amount of friction provided by the felt tabletop, then in theory we can predict with accuracy the trajectory of the billiard ball and its location at times t^1, t^2, t^3, and t^4. Now, if the Heisenbergian "principle of uncertainty" is true (and apparently most physicists think it is), then the same model will not work at the subatomic level. Imagine an electron instead of an eight ball. Even if we knew its mass, its location, its velocity, and its trajectory at times t^1, t^2, and t^3 (which we can't, by the way), we still could not predict with certainty the location of the electron at time t^4. It might end up at point Y or point X, even though there is a greater statistical probability of it ending up at X. And this failure to be

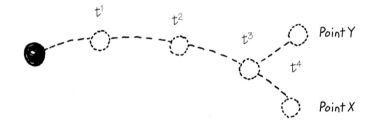

able to predict the fate of the electron is not merely a weakness in our human ability to know but is a fact about the nature of the subatomic world. It follows from this that the movement of our electron from t^3 to t^4 would be either an *uncaused event* or an occurrence that did not happen *of necessity*. If there are such events (as most physicists believe to be the case), then strictly speaking, determinism is false and indeterminism is true.

Libertarianism

Heisenberg himself waxed philosophical at this point and tried to derive a libertarian position from his indeterminism.[6] **Libertarianism** (which has nothing to do with the political movement of the same name) is indeed a version of indeterminism. It is the view that determinism is false and that freedom does exist; that is, some acts do not follow necessarily from their antecedents and in addition are free. Heisenberg hoped that the fact that some events in the brain are uncaused might be the scientific basis for a theory of freedom. But his critics pointed out that uncaused, or nonnecessary, subatomic events can hardly be called free. Rather, they are more correctly called random events.

Similarly, a human act based on such an uncaused brain event would itself be a random and not a free event. If I intend to walk to the window to open it for fresh air, and if, upon arriving there, I have an uncaused brain event and throw myself through the window, we should not call this event a "free act." If a person walking through her living room cannot know whether she will get to the other side of it without kicking the dog or doing a backflip, she would be experiencing the very

A Free Act?

opposite of freedom. Freedom may well be considered the opposite of necessity. Yet there are not just two components of this formula but three.

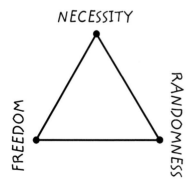

NECESSITY

FREEDOM

RANDOMNESS

Well then, it seems that Heisenberg has not given us theoretical freedom. But at least his principle of uncertainty has broken the backbone of classical determinism by removing the scientific stamp of approval from it. This move should be worth something to the libertarians.

I shall now present what I take to be the mainstream libertarian argument, using ideas from two well-known articles, one by C. A. Campbell and another by Richard Taylor.[7] The first point to make (one that is perhaps a bit surprising) is that the libertarian sides with the hard determinist against the soft determinist on one important topic: the libertarian and the hard determinist agree that if determinism is true, then there is no freedom. Recall that the soft determinist, while accepting determinism in general (the view that every event follows necessarily from its antecedent conditions), did not like the radical conclusions the hard determinists drew from this fact (namely, that there is no freedom, hence no responsibility). The soft determinist, in attempting to salvage responsibility, pointed out that "freedom" means the coincidence of will and capacity ("I can"). Then the soft determinist claimed that, given such a definition of freedom, freedom certainly does exist, even in a deterministic universe. And if freedom exists, says the soft determinist, so does responsibility. Now, libertarians such as Campbell argue that the soft determinist definition of freedom is only half the truth. Freedom entails not only the ability to achieve what one desires ("I can") but also access to genuine alternatives, real choices ("I could have done otherwise"). That is, if I perform act X under conditions A, B, and C, X is a free act for which I *could* be held responsible only if under those identical conditions I could have performed act Y instead of act X. But it is precisely this ability that determinism denies. So the soft determinists are wrong. Their theory does not generate a genuine concept of freedom; hence, it does not generate a legitimate concept of responsibility.

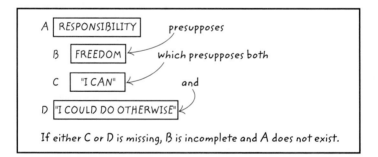

The Libertarian View of Freedom

Well then, is there such a thing as freedom as I have defined it ("I can" and "I could do otherwise")? Libertarians point out that if we appeal to actual experience, our own and that of other humans, we would have to answer that question in the affirmative. Our experience of ourselves in the world certainly seems to tell us that sometimes we are free. But is our experience shown to be illusory by the theory of determinism? The libertarian wants to stress that determinism *is* a theory (that is, it is an intellectual construct); it is not a *better* description of our experience than is ordinary language. In fact, it is not a description of our experience at all. What is the role of a *theory* in general? Normally, a theory's function is to explain some feature of experience. (Newton's theory of gravity is meant to explain features of the physical world as we experience it. Freud's theory of the uncon-

An Alternative to Newton's Theory of Gravity

scious is meant to explain certain impulsive acts as we experience them.) But the puzzling feature of the theory of determinism is that, far from *explaining* the data of our experience, this theory *denies* them.

Given this curious fact about the theory of determinism, the libertarian thinks we should be very skeptical of it. I'll make this point concrete. Let's say that I hold my index finger out and then consider the possible ways I can move it. I can move it up (call this act A), down (B), to the left (C), or to the right (D). And let us say that at times t^1, t^2, and t^3, I have held out my finger but have not yet decided how to move it. Then at time t^4, I move my finger to the left (act C). Now, I experience this act (as trivial as it might be) as a *free* act. I chose to do C, and I could have chosen to do A, B, or D instead. But determinism says that act C was a determined act—that it followed necessarily from the events that preceded it at t^1, t^2, and t^3. Libertarians such as Campbell point out that no one has ever established that such an act is a necessary one. If determinists want to fly in the face of experience and claim that all acts, including act C, are necessary, then the onus is on them to prove that counterintuitional claim. And until they do, the rest of us have every good reason to believe determinism to be false.

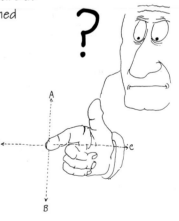

Freedom in Action

Existential Freedom

The foregoing discussion of libertarianism defended a fairly moderate, commonsensical position—"commonsensical" in that it was based on our common experience of ourselves in normal circumstances and "moderate" in that it recognized that determinism *might* be true despite our experience to the contrary and also "moderate" in the sense that it recognized that we are free in only some of our acts, not in all of them. There are, however, more radical versions of the libertarian view, and of them, the existentialist perspective of JEAN-PAUL SARTRE (1905–1980) is perhaps the most interesting.

We shall now look at a few technical terms that need to be

Jean-Paul Sartre (1905–1980)

defined here by way of introduction to Sartre's theory. First is **being-for-itself,** Sartre's term for the human's experience of itself. It is roughly equivalent of "consciousness," but only roughly because it also includes our experience of our own bodies. (Therefore, it is not simply Descartes's *cogito,* which was pure consciousness.) Second is **being-in-itself,** which is nonhuman reality as it exists prior to human intervention in it. Sartre says of being-in-itself, "Being is. Being is in-itself. Being is what it is." It is full, it is inert. It *is.* Nothing more can be said. Now, let the figure below represent the two forms of being.

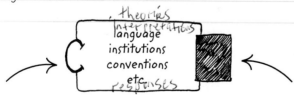

This represents being-for-itself . . .   and this represents being-in-itself

The for-itself is open to being. But the in-itself is closed.

There are certain features of the in-itself about which we humans can do nothing, and those features Sartre calls facticity. Now, the "space"

232   Philosophy of Freedom

between the for-itself and the in-itself constitutes *the world* for human experience. It includes such items as language, institutions, conventions, and theories. It is created by human interpretations of the in-itself and of responses to facticity. Sartre argues that these interpretations, though necessary (we *must* interpret and respond to being; we have no choice about that), are radically *free* at the same time. Therefore, being-for-itself is *open* to the world and, in fact, creates the world freely and is responsible for the world.

Let's explain this claim with a very Sartrean example. Imagine a group of people who set out on a day hike in the Alps. Their goal is to reach a certain mountain peak and return to their camp before dark. After hiking for a number of hours, they find the path suddenly blocked by a large boulder that has recently crashed down upon the trail from above. The path is completely barricaded. There is no hope of getting past the rock. Its presence constitutes facticity. One hiker looks at the boulder and is swept with discouragement. He throws his backpack down in the grass and falls back on it, saying, "Well, that's it! The hike is over." He begins unpacking his lunch as a consolation for his disappointment. For Sartre, this man has chosen the boulder as an "insurmountable

Facticity

obstacle" and has *chosen himself* as "defeated." He sinks back into nature in what Sartre calls a "quasi-pantheistic synthesis of the totality of the in-itself with the for-itself."[8] But there might be another person who responds to this situation by saying, "No! We can get around this! There

must be a way," and begins
scurrying about looking for
an undiscovered bypass.
This person has inter-
preted the facticity of the
boulder as "challenge" and
has chosen herself roman-
tically and heroically as "the
challenged one." Yet another
whips out his camera or
watercolors and says,
"Look how beautifully that
boulder is framed by the pine
trees on either side, and look
at the mountain peak glisten-
ing behind it" (world as photo
opportunity, self as artist).
And another, examining the

Sinking Back into Nature as a Quasi-Pantheistic Synthesis of the Totality of the In-Itself with the For-Itself

boulder closely, says, "Look at these interesting quartz crystals here.
Notice that they aren't found in any of the other rocks around here. This
boulder must have tumbled at least a thousand meters—probably from
that outcropping up above there" (world as specimen, self as scientist).

Sartre argues that each of these hikers has created her or his own
world and has chosen herself or himself in that world. Of course, the determinist will argue that each reaction to the situation is the product not of
freedom but of each individual's past. But Sartre denies this argument
strenuously. He says, "No factual state of affairs whatever it may be (the
political and economic structure of society [attack on Marx's determinism],
the psychological 'state' [attack on Skinner's and Freud's determinism],
and so on) is capable by itself of motivating any act whatsoever" (p. 245).
No matter what interpretation I give to being, I always *could* give others.
There is never a moment when I am robbed of alternative readings.

Sartre's point can be stated in its most radical form by saying that
in the face of any apparent necessity, one could always choose death. Of
course, deciding to throw oneself off the cliff because of the boulder's presence would be a rather extreme and stupid response to the discovery that
one's hike had been interrupted, but doing so *is* an alternative, and as long
as one pursues some other alternative in preference to suicide, one has
chosen that alternative and is responsible for it. If you didn't shoot yourself
this morning, then you chose all of today's projects instead, and they are
your projects.

Sartre is not claiming that choosing an alternative would necessarily always be easy. He says, "I could have done otherwise. Agreed. But *at what price?*" (p. 255). What he means is this: The act of falling back into the grass in defeat is probably not an isolated action but is rather a manifestation of a whole form of life. The person I described as "the defeated one" probably almost always chooses himself passively in the world, and for him, choosing to persevere despite the presence of the boulder would have been tantamount to what Sartre calls

> A boulder? I can't stand it!

a "radical conversion," that is, choosing oneself as a different person. But it is precisely this choice of which we are all capable. Most people, however, prefer to deny this existential truth, but, according to Sartre, they do so in bad faith.

Bad faith (which Sartre sometimes calls "inauthenticity") always takes the form of a flight from freedom, responsibility, subjectivity, anguish (a flight from *anguish* because, according to Sartre, ultimate recognition of one's freedom is experienced as anguish). However, Sartre's concept of bad faith is very subtle, as can be seen in this famous episode from Sartre's *Being and Nothingness:*

Take the example of a woman who has consented to go out with a particular man for the first time. She knows very well the intentions which the man who is speaking to her cherishes regarding her. She knows

Condemned to Be Free *Sartre*

also that it will be necessary sooner or later for her to make a decision. But she does not want to realize the urgency; she concerns herself only with what is respectful and discreet in the attitude of her companion. She does not apprehend this conduct as an attempt to achieve what we call "the first approach": that is, she does not want to see possibilities of temporal development which his conduct presents. She restricts this behavior to what is in the present; she does not wish to read in the phrases which he addresses to her anything other than their explicit meaning. If he says to her, "I find you so attractive!" she disarms this phrase of its sexual background; she attaches to the conversation and to the behavior of the speaker, the immediate meanings, which she imagines as objective qualities. The man who is speaking to her appears to her sincere and respectful as the table is round or square, as the wall coloring is blue or gray. The qualities thus attached to the person she is listening to are in this way fixed in a permanence like that of things, which is no other than the projection of the strict present of the qualities into the temporal flux. This is because she does not quite know what she wants. She is profoundly aware of the desire which she inspires, but the desire cruel and naked would humiliate and horrify her. Yet she would find no charm in a respect which would be only respect. In order to satisfy her, there must be a feeling which is addressed wholly to her *personality*—i.e., to her full freedom—and which would be a recognition of her freedom. But at the same time this feeling must be wholly desire; that is, it must address itself to her body as object. This time then she refuses to apprehend the desire for what it is; she does not even give it a name; she recognizes it only to the extent that it transcends itself toward admiration, esteem, respect, and that it is wholly absorbed in the more refined forms which it produces, to the extent of no longer figuring anymore as a sort of warmth and density. But then suppose he takes her hand. This act of her companion risks changing the situation by calling for an immediate decision. To leave the hand there is to consent in herself to flirt, to engage herself. To withdraw it is to break the troubled and unstable harmony which gives the hour its charm. The aim is to postpone the moment of decision as long as possible. We know what happens next; the young woman leaves her hand there, but she does not *notice* that she is leaving it. She does not notice because it happens by chance that she is at this moment all intellect. She

The Plot Thickens—He Takes Her Hand

draws her companion up to the most lofty regions of sentimental speculation; she speaks of Life, of her life, she shows herself in her essential aspect—a personality, a consciousness. And during this time the divorce of
the body from the soul is accomplished; the hand rests inert between the
warm hands of her companion—neither consenting nor resisting—a thing.
We shall say that this woman is in bad faith. (pp. 146–148)

What would this young woman have to do to be in good faith? Has
Sartre made good faith so difficult that no one can achieve it? He says
that the woman's problem is that "she does not quite know what she
wants." Must we always know exactly what we want? Sartre explains his
objection very technically in the following abstruse paragraph:

We have seen . . . the use which our young woman made of our being-in-the-
midst-of-the-world—i.e., of our inert presence as a passive object among
other objects—in order to relieve herself suddenly from the functions of her
being-in-the-world—that is, from the being which makes there to be a world
by projecting itself beyond the world toward its own possibilities. (p. 150)

Sartre's point is this: we are bodies in the world. This fact is what he calls
our "being-in-the-midst-of-the-world." But we also create the world we
inhabit, and this is our "being-in-the-world." Choosing ourselves at any
moment as exclusively being-
in-the-midst-of-the-world,
that is, as passive, inert being,
is bad faith. Good faith is
choosing ourselves as what we
are, as being-in-the-world, and
accepting responsibility there-
for. (It is still not particularly
clear what the young woman
should have done to be in good
faith.)

**Choosing Oneself as
Being-in-the-Midst-of-the-World**

The extremes to which
Sartre takes his claims about
freedom can be seen here:

Thus there are no accidents in a life; a community event which suddenly
bursts forth and involves me in it does not come from the outside. If I am
mobilized in a war, this war is my war; it is in my image and I deserve it. I
deserve it first because I could always get out of it by suicide or by deser-
tion; these ultimate possibles are those which must always be present for
us when there is a question of envisaging a situation. For lack of getting out
of it, I have chosen it. This can be due to inertia, to cowardice in the face of

public opinion, or because I prefer certain other values to the value of the refusal to join in the war (the good opinion of my relatives, the honor of my family, etc.). Any way you look at it, it is a matter of choice. This choice will be repeated later on again and again without a break until the end of the war. Therefore we must agree with the statement by J. Romains, "In war there are no innocent victims." If therefore I have preferred war to death or to dishonor, everything takes place as if I bore the entire responsibility for this war. Of course others have declared it, and one might be tempted perhaps to consider me as a simple accomplice.

This is your war, kid. You chose it.

But this notion of complicity has only a juridical sense, and it does not hold here. For it depended on me that for me and by me this war should not exist, and I have decided that it does exist. There was no compulsion here, for the compulsion could have got no hold on a freedom. I did not have any excuse; for as we have said repeatedly in this book, the peculiar character of human-reality is that it is without excuse. (pp. 278–279)

Now it seems to me that many people might be prepared to accept Sartre's claim that an adult human being of normal intelligence has options in almost all circumstances and therefore must accept responsibility proportional to the amount of freedom available. But Romain's line, of which Sartre approves ("there are no innocent victims in war") rings hollow when we recall the news photo of the naked little Vietnamese girl running in terror down a country road, her body covered with napalm burns. Perhaps Sartre needed to augment his theory with an account of how children and the mentally handicapped fit into his claim that everyone is always free and responsible for the worlds they create (although it seems that such a distinction would be very un-Sartrean).

Maybe the truth is that Sartre has not *described* an already preexisting human freedom, as he claimed he was doing, but that he opened up new aspects of freedom. Perhaps those who have the good fortune to read and understand Sartre's philosophy thereby acquire a new kind of

awareness that is in fact tantamount to a new kind of freedom, and those who haven't read him (and who have had no other intellectual experience of a similar nature) do not acquire this freedom. The trouble with this assumption is that it makes freedom (or at least this *kind* of freedom) a sort of bourgeois luxury because the ability to study philosophy is in some sense just such a luxury. (Sartre himself seems to have come to a similar conclusion in his last works.)

Existential Freedom as a Bourgeois Luxury

Perverse Freedom

Besides Sartre's existentialist theory, there is yet another radical theory of freedom in the literature, called "perverse freedom."[9] This theory appears not in a philosophical treatise but in a novel, Fyodor Dostoyevsky's *Notes from the Underground.* (Apparently a more literal translation would be *Notes from Under the Floorboards,* implying that the "underground man's" perspective on life is, like that of a rat, looking up at it through the cracks in the floor.) The novel begins with the following curious passage:

> I am a sick man. . . . I am a spiteful man. I am an unattractive man. I believe my liver is diseased. However, I know nothing at all about my disease and do not know for certain what ails me. I don't consult a doctor for it and never have, though I have a

The Man under the Floorboards

respect for medicine and doctors. Besides, I am extremely superstitious, suf-
ficiently so to respect medicine, anyway (I am well-educated enough not to be
superstitious, but I am superstitious). No, I refuse to consult a doctor from
spite. That you probably will not understand. Well, I understand it though. Of
course, I can't explain who it is precisely that I am mortifying in this case by
my spite: I am perfectly well aware that I cannot "pay back" the doctors by
not consulting them; I know better than anyone that by all this I am only
injuring myself and no one else. But still, if I don't consult a doctor it is from
spite. My liver is bad, well—let it get worse![10]

As the "argument" of the novel develops, we discover that the underground man takes deep offense at all the restrictions imposed upon his
freedom by society and reality at large. He takes them as personal insults.
He is offended by the demand that his acts be prudent. He is told that
he is supposed to act in ways that are in his own best interest. If his liver
is ailing, he is supposed to see a physician. If the weather in Moscow is bad
for him, he is supposed to move to St. Petersburg. If his food doesn't agree
with him, he is supposed to change his diet. But in these cases, according
to him, prudence is a determining factor restricting his freedom. Therefore,
he refuses to act for his own advantage, though he admits that there is
one advantage, "the most advantageous advantage," on which he will act:

One's own free unfettered choice, one's own caprice—however wild it may be,
one's own fancy worked up at times to a frenzy—is that very "most advantageous advantage" which we have overlooked, which comes under no classifica-
tion and against which all systems and theories are continually being shat-
tered to atoms. And how do these wiseacres know that man wants a normal,
a virtuous choice? What has made them
conceive that man must want a
rationally advantageous choice?
What man wants is simply
independent choice, what-
ever that independence
may cost and wherever it
may lead. And choice, of
course, the devil only
knows what choice.[11]

Furthermore, the under-
ground man is offended by the
demand that his actions be
reasonable, that whenever he does
anything he is supposed to have a
reason for doing it. In that case, he

Encumbrances on Freedom

believes, reason delimits his freedom. The underground man seeks a mode of action that is *unmotivated*. He seeks to perform acts for which there are no reasons. He says he is a "spiteful man." That is, his acts are motivated by spite, not by reasons. The Russian word is *zlost*, and apparently it means more than "spite"; it also means "whim" and "fancy," "contrariness" and "caprice." If someone points out to the underground man that operating from whim, fancy, or spite is itself to operate with a *reason*, is still to have a *motive*, the underground man will not object because to him, in those cases, the motive for his action is pure freedom. Indeed, we know from experience that children often do things out of spite, and when they do so, they are often trying to establish their independence from their parents.

But it is not only children who operate out of spite. In his book *On Being Free*, Frithjof Bergmann gives us an excellent example of this spiteful freedom.

> Still another parallel to the undergroundman's extreme idea of freedom appears in a scene in the film made after the life of T. E. Lawrence. It occurs in the last third of the film when Lawrence is already in command of a small but formidable Arab army with a long string of brilliant exploits to its credit. After a temporary setback, Lawrence is in the process of preparing a major and well-planned campaign that promises defeat to the Turks and glory and loot to his men. He needs troops, however, and the scene narrates his inter-view with a proud tribal leader. In its course Lawrence tries out reason after reason on the chieftain. "Your fame will spread far if you join me. There will be much money. This is your long-sought chance to get even with the Turks. Together we will lead your people out of their servility. We will lift them up out of their obeisance. You can be the father of a new, proud nation." The Arab sits unmoved and distant. Disdainfully he shakes his massive head to each of these reasons. But he knows full well what force they have, and he feels it. His gesture is a refusal, a fending off; really the sign of his determination not to surrender to their power. Eventually Lawrence's arsenal is exhausted. He has given every reason and all have been parried by the same shaking of the head. So both men sit through a silence, till Lawrence is just at the point of rising and taking his curt leave. Then at last the chief speaks: "I will join you," he says, "but not for fame, nor for money, not even for my people. Not for any of the reasons you have offered. I will do it but only because it is my whim."[12]

As extreme as this version of freedom is, it does capture something of the aboriginal attraction of the idea of freedom. As Bergmann says, "The idea of being totally unbounded, of yielding to no authority whatever (not even to that of reason), of acting without any encumbrances—that image seems close to the root-experience of freedom, ... a distant memory of this expectation still glows behind all talk of liberation."[13]

Conclusion

So what are we to believe? What about determinism? There are some good reasons for taking it seriously, after all. At the macrocosmic level, physical bodies do seem to behave according to laws and to be, in principle, predictable. And because human beings are physical bodies (I do not mean that they are *merely* physical bodies), and because human behavior is to a great extent predictable, we might have a suspicion that determinism is true. Even Heisenberg's attack on determinism at the microcosmic level seems to replace determinism only with a randomness that may exist at the subatomic level but that leaves necessity unchallenged at the level of things the size of human bodies. (Not only that, but random human action might be worse than predetermined action.) Moreover, the belief in human freedom can seem a bit presumptuous because it seems to entail the claim that in one otherwise insignificant minuscule corner of a cosmos so large as to overwhelm the understanding there exists a feature or quality (freedom) that may be nonexistent elsewhere in the cosmos.

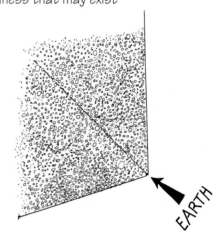

In One Small Corner of the Universe, There Is Freedom

Nevertheless, we do not *know* that determinism is true, even if we do not know that it is false. It may well be that freedom is an emergent characteristic of certain physical systems (in the same way that consciousness might be such an emergent characteristic). By "emergent characteristic," I mean a feature of a system that is not a feature of any its parts, something in the way that "liquidity" is a feature of water but not of either hydrogen or oxygen. Again, we do not *know* that this, or any other, explanation of freedom is true, but there are some good reasons for believing in freedom nevertheless.

First, there is the experiential reason. As the Campbell/Taylor–type argument indicated, we certainly do experience ourselves in the world as free, and we should reject this experience as illusionary only if we are given a very compelling reason to do so. In my opinion, such a reason has not been forthcoming.

Second, there is a practical reason for rejecting determinism. If hard determinism is true, then no one is ever responsible for his or her actions,

I'm sorry I'm doing this to you, but I'm not responsible for my actions.

and there is no moral reason for ever praising or blaming anyone for any act whatsoever. Indeed, in this case, all of our moral and juridical institutions and ideas are wrong and should be dismantled, as Skinner suggested. I would think that the determinist's argument would have to be tremendously convincing for us to be willing to accept such radical consequences. The soft determinist's conception of freedom seems too paltry to bear the weight it must carry—the weight of responsibility.

Furthermore, there is the practical problem of consistency. Is it really possible to make a belief in determinism consistent with our thoughts and actions in the world? Our normal understanding of reality and our discourse about it are loaded with concepts that presuppose notions of freedom and responsibility. As we saw in Chapter 3, when a determinist like Skinner finds it convenient to use these concepts in his more popular works, he likes to put the words denoting them in quotation marks (e.g., he says that a person "can be made to 'choose'"). He seems to be implying that he *could* restate these concepts in more appropriate, scientific language if he wanted to. But *could* he and with what consequences? Even if Skinner taught us to replace the term "chose" with the term "was reinforced by," would it really change our *understanding* of the situation (or as Skinner says, "our 'understanding' [whatever that may be]")? If we outlawed the word "cow" and replaced it with "hide-bound milk machine," would we really have changed our conceptualization of cows? (Moreover, it should be pointed out that Skinner often fails to notice quickly enough his libertarian-laden concepts to put them in quotation marks. In describing his behavioristic utopia in *Walden Two*, he says it is a place "where everyone chooses [sic] his own work." Elsewhere he says, "We must decide [sic] how we are to use

Hide-Bound Milk Machines Refueling

the knowledge which a science of human behavior is now making available." Finally, he says, "we shall, of course, be ready to resist any tyrannical use of science for [sic] immediate or selfish purposes [sic]."[14] If that isn't teleology, I don't know what is.)

All right then, if there are good reasons for rejecting the deterministic claim, can we accept a form of libertarianism? Let us run through a short list of the kinds of freedom that might exist. I will divide these rather arbitrarily into two groups, which I will call "metaphysical freedoms" (denoting their more philosophical nature) and "practical freedoms" (denoting their more pragmatic nature), and I will ask whether we can reasonably believe that any of these freedoms exist. Also, keeping in mind the example with which this chapter began, we will, as an aside, ask to what extent it makes sense to claim that we Americans are members of (nay, leaders of) the Free World.

I. Metaphysical Freedoms

A. Pure Volitional Freedom. We can conceive of something we might call by this name wherein volition and creation are identical. If person P is the possessor of this kind of freedom, and if P wants X to happen, X happens automatically simply because P wants it to do so. This is clearly *God's freedom* (if there is a God). In the Bible, God says, "Let there be light," and there is light. You and I do not possess freedom in this sense, nor can we. (In this sense of "free," we are clearly not members of the Free World. In this sense, our world has at most one member. As Descartes noted, if there were two beings with total freedom in this sense, they would restrict each other's freedom.)

Little Boy Playing God

B. Restricted Volitional Freedom. If person P wants X and, by virtue of her or his desire and effort, gets X, then the act of obtaining X was

244   Philosophy of Freedom

a free act. This is the freedom of soft determinism. It definitely does exist. Some people have more of it than others, and it is quite possible that some societies create conditions that allow more of this freedom than do other societies. (In this sense, are we members of the Free World? That is, is the typical American citizen more likely to get what he or she wants than was the typical Soviet citizen? I really do not know. It is surely the case that there are more opportunities for self-fulfillment here than in the old USSR, but it is also the case that modern capitalism creates more expectations [hence, more desires] than do other social systems. So the question we are posing here, though an empirical one, is nevertheless difficult to answer. I suspect that the answer is yes, and I hope I am not simply being chauvinistic in saying so.)

I wanted vodka. I got vodka. Therefore I am free. (And now I want some more vodka.)

C. Mental Freedom. This is the freedom to assent to or dissent from any assertion or demand. You can hold a sword to my chest and tell me that I must believe that the emperor is divine and perhaps you can force me to say that I believe so, but you can't actually make me believe so. There's an old Spanish Civil War song, sung by the German contingent of the International Brigades: "Die Gedanken sind frei" (thoughts are free). This sense of freedom is what I'm calling "mental freedom," and there is good reason to believe that it does exist universally. In that case, in this sense of freedom, there is no place in the world more free than another, though making this statement overlooks the problem of brainwashing, and the seriousness of that problem should qualify my earlier claim that mental freedom is universal. Then the question about the Free World would have to be posed like this: "Are citizens of our society less brainwashed than those of other societies, such as North Korea?" I don't know the answer to that question. (Determinists cannot say, "Everyone is always brainwashed" because without a significant opposite, the term brainwashing is meaningless.)

(handwritten margin note: agree or disagree)

D. Ontological Freedom. This "libertarian" freedom in its more restricted version (Campbell/Taylor) says that there are almost always alternative possibilities open to us. In its more radical version (Sartre), it says that no matter what course of action we choose, there is always some alternative action we could have chosen. Now, there is probably no way of ever *proving* that such freedom exists. It is true that no matter what act we perform, we usually have a strong feeling that we "could have done otherwise," but in fact it is possible that such a feeling is delusory and that in exactly those circumstances, we could *not* have done otherwise than what we actually did do. That is, there is always the possibility that determinism is true. But *I* say that we should opt for the validity of the experience of freedom rather than for the mere possibility that the experience is deceptive. It is *possible* that my Aunt Minnie will grow antlers, but that possibility is no reason for me to expect her to do so.

Aunt Minnie

However, experience does not bear out Sartre's claim that we *always* have alternatives. On rare occasions, we feel that we have no alternatives, that our acts are compelled. So if we appeal exclusively to experience here, we have to accept the modified thesis of ontological freedom. Some may believe that Sartre's more radical claim is true—that even when we *feel* that our acts are compelled, we still have alternatives. But to accept this view is, as in the case of accepting determinism, to go against, or at least *beyond,* normal experience and intuition. (In terms of this kind of freedom, no particular society can lay more of a claim to the title of "the Free World" than another. In fact, Sartre says, "We were never more free than under the German Occupation."[15] In other words, under conditions of political repression, the presence of our alternatives is clearer, and the need for decision is more obvious than under more standard conditions.)

E. Perverse Freedom. This freedom is the freedom of Dostoyevsky's underground man. It is based on the rejection of rationality and prudence and manifested in an action motivated solely by whim. Such freedom does exist. Of course, the determinist denies that perverse freedom is freedom, saying it is rather a symptom of a deranged mind. But I think that the case of perverse freedom must provoke great anxiety in the determinist. Here is my reason: human nature is such that it can perversely thwart every attempt to make it predictable. If I know that you are trying to predict my behavior, I can incorporate that knowledge into my motivation and behave in ways that will be nearly impossible for you to predict. There may be some deterministic theory that purports to explain this phenomenon. A determinist can argue, for example, that an omniscient observer could factor in an individual's perversity and thereby successfully predict her behavior—the determinist can argue in this manner, but his argument would be purely theoretical. There is no empirical evidence supporting it. It seems to me much more likely that a person could (perversely) train to engage in random acts that no actual observers could predict, as does Dostoyevsky's underground man. The proof that the problem of perverse freedom is of *practical* concern to psychologists is the fact that so many of their experiments with human subjects must involve deception. If the subjects know what questions the psychologists are really trying to answer, the subjects may produce biased responses to please the psychologists, or they may produce perverse responses.

II. Practical Freedoms

A. Freedom to . . .

1. Political Freedom. This term is meant to designate the type of freedom guaranteed by the U.S. Constitution and Bill of Rights (freedom to worship, freedom to associate with people of like interests, freedom to state one's opinion, and so forth). *Constitutional freedoms*

2. Economic Freedom. This term designates the right to buy and sell on the open market without unreasonable governmental interference—what we mean by "free enterprise."

Now, such freedoms as these do exist in certain societies and are often guaranteed by the laws of those societies. In both of these categories, I think it is fair to say that we citizens of the Western democracies live in the Free World. I believe that we have many more of these freedoms than do, for example, the citizens of the former Soviet Union or of today's North Korea.

B. Freedom through. . . This kind of freedom is the result of social agreement and laws of enablement. For example, our laws creating an educational system provide the freedom to learn; our laws creating a highway system provide the freedom to travel; our laws creating a postal service provide the freedom to communicate. (I suspect—but do not know—that we Americans are at least as free in this respect as are the North Koreans, and probably more free.)

C. Freedom from . . . This kind of freedom designates freedom from hunger, medical burden, unemployment, and vulnerability in old age. These are relative freedoms, but we do find some societies more dedicated to guaranteeing these freedoms than other societies are. I am afraid that in this area (which is, after all, not an unimportant one) we do not have a special right to call ourselves the Free World. Let me tell you a story that my friend Al told to me. Al and his wife flew to Moscow on a vacation during the time of the Communist regime. They arrived at the airport late at night and took a cab to their hotel. But before arriving at the hotel, the driver pulled the cab under a dark bridge and stopped, turned off the motor, and asked Al if he had any blue jeans to sell. My friend likes a good argument (even when he's jet-lagged under a bridge in Moscow at midnight, apparently), so he said to the cabby, "Now, this is marvelous. Here I am in the workers' paradise of the world, and you sneak off in the darkness at midnight to ask me to sell you a pair of clandestine jeans. Where I live, I can buy as many jeans as I want, probably twenty-four hours a day, so what kind of paradise is this, anyway?" The cabby (who apparently also liked an argument) said, "All right. You are correct. I can only buy blue jeans illegally on the black market. In that sense, you have more freedom than I do. But on the other hand, I never have to worry about a catastrophic illness ruining me financially or about becoming homeless because of losing my job or about where I will get my meals and lay my head when I'm old. And none of that is true of you. So I am more free than you."

Now, that cab driver was wrong on a number of scores. First, my friend Al has done very well for himself under the capitalist system and will never have to worry about any of the possible disasters mentioned by the cabby. Also, I have read that medical services had deteriorated greatly in the Soviet Union before its collapse, that the quality of apartments was shameful, and that a job was guaranteed to you only if you were willing to "travel." These facts take some of the sheen off the cabby's freedom. Nevertheless, I am embarrassed to say that there is still something to his argument. All in all, in the sense of the freedom we are discussing here, there is a legitimate debate concerning what constitutes the Free World.

So my conclusion is that there is good reason to believe in freedom, but that there is no one thing called "freedom." A number of areas of human life exist where the concept of freedom correctly applies, but that concept is not always identical in each of those areas. Some of these conceptions of freedom are compatible with determinism; some are not. However, I think it's safe to say that you are free to reject determinism.

Topics for Consideration

1. Tie the hard determinism of Leucippus and Democritus to the discussion of the Mythos-Logos debate in Chapter 1.
2. Explain the connection between Skinner's rejection of the teleological model and his commitment to hard determinism.
3. Discuss the disagreement between John Hospers and Richard Peters concerning the correct interpretation of Freud's view of freedom.
4. What is the name of the theory according to which freedom is compatible with determinism? Explain how the compatibility of these apparently mutually exclusive ideas is possible, according to that theory.
5. Show how libertarianism stands in relation to (a) hard determinism, (b) soft determinism, (c) indeterminism.
6. In what sense, according to Sartre, are we always free, and in what sense does "facticity" limit our freedom?
7. Write a critique of Sartre's account of the "bad faith" of the young woman on the dinner date. What would be required of her to be in "good faith"? Is this requirement reasonable?
8. Explain why the ever-present potential of perverse freedom can undermine the possibility of a *science* of human behavior.

Suggestions for Further Reading: Paperback Editions

Frithjof Bergmann, *On Being Free* (Notre Dame, Ind.: University of Notre Dame Press, 1977). A very articulate and carefully argued version of soft determinism.

Fyodor Dostoyevsky, *Notes from the Underground*, trans. Constance Garnett (New York: Dell, 1960). An amazing novelistic presentation of the idea of perverse freedom by one of the greatest fiction writers of all time.

Jean-Paul Sartre, *Existentialism and Human Emotions*, trans. Hazel E. Barnes and Bernard Frechtman (New York: Philosophical Library, 1957). A popularization of the arguments for existentialism by the philosopher who coined the term.

B. F. Skinner, *Beyond Freedom and Dignity* (New York: Knopf, 1971). A popularization of the arguments for behaviorism by its modern architect.

Richard Taylor, *Metaphysics*, 4th ed. (Englewood Cliffs, N.J.: Prentice-Hall, 1992). A provocative and excellent book by a provocative and excellent philosopher. Read Chapter 4 for Taylor's defense of freedom.

Notes

1. B. F. Skinner, *Beyond Freedom and Dignity* (New York: Knopf, 1971), pp. 20–21.
2. Ibid., pp. 12–13.

3. John Hospers, "Meaning and Free Will," *Philosophy and Phenomenological Research*, Vol. 10, No. 3 (March, 1950), pp. 316–330.

4. Sigmund Freud, *Psychopathology of Everyday Life*, in *The Basic Writings of Sigmund Freud*, ed. and trans. A. A. Brill (New York: Modern Library, 1966), pp. 161–162. All subsequent quotes from Freud in this chapter are from this source.

5. Richard S. Peters, *The Concept of Motivation* (New York: Humanities Press, 1969), p. 69.

6. Werner Heisenberg, *Physics and Philosophy: The Revolution in Modern Science* (New York: Harper & Row, 1962).

7. C. A. Campbell, *In Defence of Free Will, An Inaugural Lecture* (Glasgow: Jackson, Son and Co., 1938). Richard Taylor, "I Can," *Philosophical Review*, Vol. 69 (1960), pp. 78–89.

8. Jean-Paul Sartre, *Being and Nothingness*, in *The Philosophy of Jean-Paul Sartre*, ed. Robert Denoon Cumming (New York: Random House, 1972), p. 258. Unless otherwise stated, all subsequent quotes from Sartre in this chapter are from this source.

9. I have borrowed the term "perverse freedom" from Robert C. Solomon, *Introducing Philosophy*, 3rd ed. (New York: Harcourt, Brace, Jovanovich, 1985), p. 457.

10. Fyodor Dostoyevsky, *Notes from the Underground*, trans. Constance Garnett (New York: Dell, 1960), p. 25.

11. Ibid., p. 46.

12. Frithjof Bergmann, *On Being Free* (Notre Dame, Ind.: University of Notre Dame Press, 1977), pp. 21–22.

13. Ibid., p. 18.

14. Carl Rogers and B. F. Skinner, "Some Issues Concerning the Control of Human Behavior: A Symposium," *Science*, Vol. 124 (Nov. 30, 1956), pp. 1057–1066.

15. Jean-Paul Sartre, "Situations III," in Cumming, *The Philosophy of Jean-Paul Sartre*, p. 233.

7

Thou Shalt
Become Perfected
Ethics

Ethics, or moral philosophy, asks the following kinds of "big questions": What is the Good? What is the good life? What ought we to do? Are there such things as moral duties and obligations? Are there absolute moral values, or are moral values relative to time, place, culture, and the individual? Is there any reason to be moral at all? In ethics too we can ask the question, Does the (moral) center hold?

Ancient Greek Moral Philosophers

Like most traditional philosophical problems, those of moral philosophy can be traced back to the Greeks. Nevertheless, ethical concepts have evolved greatly since Greek times, and some modern moral concepts like "duty" do not seem to have had any direct counterpart in Greek thought. We will begin our discussion of ethics where so many philosophical discussions began—in Athens during the fourth century B.C.E.

Justice/Morality

Plato's major work, and one of the masterpieces of world literature, *The Republic*, opens with a discussion of *dikaiosyne*, an umbrella term for all conventions that command respect for the interests of other people. This concept covers much of what we mean in English by the term "morality," though the word *dikaiosyne* is usually translated as "justice." Unfortunately, the English term "justice" designates a much narrower concept than does the original Greek. So when the question is raised in the *Republic*, "Why should I be just?" the ensuing conversation probably makes more sense to us today if we read it as asking, "Why should I be moral?" Knowing what you already

252

Justice!

know about Socrates and Plato, you will not be surprised to find out that they thought this question could not be answered until we knew what *dikaiosyne* was. (Once again, the question "What is X?" is the key theme of the Platonic dialogue.)

Early in the first chapter of the *Republic*, we are shocked by the bald assertion of the Sophist Thrasymachus, one of the protagonists of that dialogue, who informs us that "Justice is the advantage of the stronger." Thrasymachus explains his claim in the following passage:

Don't you know then . . . that some states are under despots, and some are governed by a democracy, and some by an aristocracy? . . . Is not the strong power in each the ruling power? And each power lays down the laws so as to suit itself, a democracy, democratic laws, and a despotism, despotic laws, and so with the rest, and laying them down, they make it clear that this is a just thing for their subjects, I mean their own advantage; one who transgresses these they chastise as a breaker of laws and a doer of injustice. Then this is what I mean, my good friend: that the same thing is just in all states, the advantage of the established government. This I suppose has the power, so if you reason correctly, it follows that everywhere the same thing is just, the advantage of the stronger.[1]

So according to Thrasymachus, "morality" is nothing but a concatenation of rules and conventions imposed upon a gullible community by those who command political power, and these rules and conventions are always contrived to be of advantage to the rulers. So the institutions that enjoin us to behave in ways that are truthful, honest, fair, equitable, open, helpful, and merciful are manipulated by those in power for their own use.

Agent Reginald Smith, Internal Revenue Agency. We're levying a 2000% tax on income. How much did you earn today? (And remember, it would be immoral to lie about it!)

But Socrates gets Thrasymachus to admit that sometimes morality does *not* benefit those in power because sometimes those in power err concerning what is to their own benefit, and that therefore morality cannot be defined in terms of benefit to the strong. Despite his concession, Thrasymachus nevertheless insists that being moral is a great disadvantage to the individual. Thrasymachus says:

Thrasymachus's Best-Seller

> You must consider, my most simple Socrates, that a just man comes off worse than an unjust man everywhere. First of all in contracts with one another, wherever two are in such partnership, and the partnership is dissolved, you would never find the just man getting the better of the unjust, but he always gets the worst of it. Secondly, in public affairs, when there are taxes and contributions, the just man pays more and the unjust less from an equal estate; when there are distributions the one gains nothing and the other much. Again, when these two hold public office, the just man gets his private affairs, by neglecting them, into a bad state, if he has no other loss, and he has no profit from the treasury because he is just; besides, he is unpopular with friends and acquaintances if he will not serve them contrary to justice; but it is quite the opposite with the unjust man. (pp. 142–143)

So for Thrasymachus, being immoral "is to one's profit and advantage." Socrates must prove the opposite—that being moral is profitable and advantageous, and being immoral is unprofitable and disadvantageous. This argument will be difficult to establish in the face of Thrasymachus's examples. The truth of some of those examples grates on us. We all know cases of people who, because of their manipulative lifestyle and shady business practices, drive the cars we would like to drive, maintain great bank accounts, seem especially attractive to people, travel extensively, and in general lead a life we could easily envy. We would like

Actually, he's abysmally miserable. He just doesn't know it.

Socrates to be able to prove that, appearances to the contrary, these people are in fact miserable because of their immorality; but it is hard to imagine what kind of argument could demonstrate a priori that this class of people *must* be unhappy.

At the end of Book I of the *Republic*, Socrates, employing some very questionable rhetorical strategies, manages to befuddle Thrasymachus, who lapses into an angry silence. But the problem Thrasymachus posed does not disappear and is in fact continued and intensified in Book II. The second book begins with a discussion of three kinds of good:

Thrasymachus Feels That Debating Socrates Is Not in His Interest

1. Good in itself (e.g., harmless small pleasures).
2. Good for its consequences (e.g., taking medicine).
3. Combination of number 1 and number 2 (e.g., being healthy).

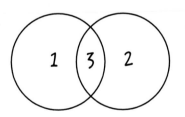

Socrates says that morality ought to be a number 3, but most people take it to be a number 2. We engage in moral behavior because we fear the consequences of not doing so. Glaucon, one of Socrates' companions, paraphrases what he takes to be the standard opinion about justice:

> They say, then, that to be unjust is good, and to suffer injustice is bad, and the excess of evil in suffering injustice is greater than the excess of good in being unjust; so that when people do and suffer injustice in dealing with one another, and taste both, those who cannot both escape the one and take the other think it profitable to make an agreement neither to do nor to suffer injustice; from this they begin to make laws and compacts among themselves, and they name the injunction of the law lawful and just. This, they say, is the origin and nature of justice, which is something between the best,

namely to do wrong and not to pay for it, and the worst, to suffer wrong and not to be able to get vengeance. Justice, they say, is between these two, and they are content with it not as a good, but as honoured in the weakness of injustice; since one who was able to do injustice, if he were truly a man, would never make an agreement neither to wrong nor to be wronged—he would be mad to do so. Then this . . . is the nature of justice, Socrates, and such is its origin, as they say. (p. 156)

Glaucon illustrates his point with the story of the magic ring of Gyges. In the story, the man who possesses the ring is able to become invisible and avoid the normal consequences of his actions. He seduces the queen, kills the king, and takes over the kingdom. The implication of the story is that anybody would do the same and would be a fool not to. If we condemn Gyges, it's because we are envious or don't want to be thought badly of.

Gyges and His Magic Ring

At this point, another companion, Adeimantus, chimes in agreeing with Glaucon. Morality is definitely a number 2. People praise it for the rewards it brings. But the *appearance* of morality gets these rewards as well as the actual morality, so the prudent person will be concerned with *reputation*, not morality. (This view was later defended by Machiavelli in *The Prince*. It is not necessary for the Prince to have piety, faith, honesty, humanity, and integrity. But it is necessary for him to seem to have them.) At this point, Socrates apparently recognizes that he is facing some heavy artillery, and he responds the way many of us do in such situations; he changes the subject . . . or so it seems.

City/Soul

In fact, Socrates concludes that the problem has become so complex and the details so unclear that it can be resolved only by holding a magnifying glass up to it. This metaphor becomes the pretext for Socrates to present a curious theory that will go on to occupy a large part of the *Republic* and will even give the book its title. The theory comes in two parts: first, that

the problem of morality can be resolved only by coming to an understanding of the human soul and, second, that such an understanding can best be achieved by studying the nature of the City (the Polis, the Republic) because, ideally at least, the City is the Soul writ large. The study of the ideal City will reveal to us the ideal soul, and from that picture, we can deduce the nature of justice and an answer to the question of why one should be moral.

Socrates' analysis leads him to the following conclusion (summarized rather cursorily here). The ideal City contains

The City Is the Soul Magnified

three distinct classes. First are the rulers who know philosophy; hence they have beheld the "Platonic" essence of citizenship and, as a class, have the virtue of *wisdom*. Second, there is a military caste called the guardians whose job it is to protect the City from enemies, internal and external. The members of this class know *some* philosophical principles (otherwise they

would not know the difference between friends and enemies of the City). The guardians can eventually be promoted to the ruling class if they prove their philosophical mettle. The collective virtue of this class is *courage*. Finally, there is the class of artisans. This class comprises the numerical majority of the City, but it is incapable of self-governance because it is incapable of philosophy. It must submit to the rule of reason imposed upon it by the ruling class. When it does so, its collective virtue is that of *moderation*.

The Guardian Must Know the Difference between Friends and Enemies of the City

Because the City is the magnification of the Soul, it follows that the Soul, though a unity in fact, can be analyzed into three components—reason, spirit, and appetite. The rational component, reason, finds itself constantly opposed to the appetitive component, which is what we might call the animal part of the psyche. This lower part of the Soul contains all the primitive lusts and irrational desires, which must be constrained if psychic peace is to be achieved. It is very much like the Freudian id, and this similarity is surely no coincidence because Freud was greatly influenced by Platonic philosophy. In fact, in one passage Plato describes (in a most "Freudianly" graphic way) the desires of the appetitive Soul as manifesting themselves in dreams. Discussing "lawless desires" as "those which are aroused in sleep," he says:

> whenever the rest of the Soul, all the reasonable, gentle and ruling part, is asleep, . . . the bestial and savage, replete with food or wine, skips about, and throwing off sleep, tries to go and fulfill its own instincts. You know there is nothing it will not dare to do, thus freed and rid of all shame and reason;

it shrinks not from attempting in fancy to lie with a mother, or with any other man or god or beast, shrinks from no bloodshed, refrains from no food—in a word, leaves no folly or shamelessness untried. (p. 370)

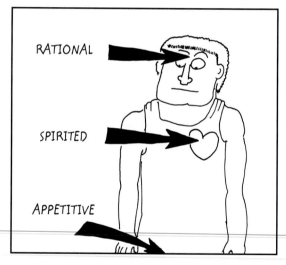

Perhaps not surprisingly, Plato metaphorically locates the appetitive aspect of the Soul "below the midriff" and the rational component of the Soul in the head. The spirited Soul Plato locates in the heart. We can view the battle of the psyche as the struggle between reason and lust for the allegiance of the spirit because spirit is the source of action. If the appetites persuade spirit to join them, then the individual will become lustful and unruly. If reason persuades spirit to side with it, then the individual becomes rational. Each of the components of the Soul has its own virtue (aretê), which manifests itself in the actions of the individual when each component is operating under optimal conditions. The virtue of reason is *wisdom*. The virtue of spirit is *courage*. The virtue of appetite is moderation. When the three parts of the soul operate under the rule of reason, the result is *justice* (*dikaiosyne*), and it would be clear to anybody whose Soul was in order why she or he should behave in a just (i.e., moral) manner. Why is this conclusion so clear?

Because the opposite of justice, injustice, is *confusion*, with the part that naturally should be a slave trying to rebel against rational rule. Confusion is incompatible with *aretê*. The expression of human excellence is possible only where justice triumphs, that is to say, only where the individual takes into consideration the interests of other human beings and not only his own private interests. In other words, the individual discovers that it is in his interest to take others' interests seriously.

Confusion in the Psyche

Plato has Glaucon say, "Virtue [*aretê*] then, it seems, would be a kind of health and beauty and fine fitness of the soul; vice is disease and ugliness and weakness." What about Thrasymachus's question of whether it is more profitable to be just than unjust? Glaucon says, "The inquiry seems to me to become from now absurd." Why? Because Socrates has shown that the question "Why should I be just?" is identical to the question "Why should I be healthy?" This question is absurd, and anyone who asks it does not understand it (with the possible exception of Dostoyevsky's "underground man").

Let us turn once more to Plato's formula, "City equals Soul magnified." We saw that each of the three classes in the City has its

So what's the big deal about being healthy?

cough sputter wheeze

virtue, and when each class sought its virtue, the result was justice in the City. Both in the City and in the Soul, justice follows from certain rational principles that must be obeyed. The individual human behaves morally when he or she grasps these rational principles, seduces the heart to follow its rule, and, with the help of the heart, imposes a regimen on the passions. But there is a grating paradox when this model is applied to the City. Most people in Plato's good City are bad. That is, most of its inhabitants are con-genitally incapable of discovering the rule of reason for themselves and of applying it to their own behavior, so it must be dicta-torially imposed upon them. Ethics must be grounded in reason, but reason itself is not a force—it has no bind-ing power, and it must be enforced. As the contempo-rary British philosopher Bernard Williams puts it, "For Plato, the political problem of making the ethical into a force was the problem of making society embody the rational justification, and that problem could only have an authoritarian solution."[2]

Most People Are Bad

I suppose that today the majority of us in our most negative mo-ments suspect that Plato is right—many people will not behave morally unless coerced to do so. But most people cannot accept Platonism as their own moral doctrine not only because they don't agree with his elitism and its totalitarian implications but also because they are much less certain than he that there is an *absolute Good* and that the only sin is ignorance of it.

Egoism

Plato argued that being moral was in the interest of the individual (though he thought that, unfortunately, most people were too benighted to under-stand that truth). Plato believed that no one would ever knowingly operate in a way that ran counter to her own interests, and if we ever saw someone who was operating in that manner, that would simply be proof that she was *ignorant* of her best interests. We can call this belief the *egoistic assumption* in Plato's thought. I read Plato's egoism as comprising both

psychological egoism (every act is motivated by self-interest) and **moral egoism** (every act ought to be motivated by self-interest). However, according to Plato's spokesman, Socrates, psychological egoism does not amount to the same thing as moral egoism because people are usually wrong about what is truly in their best interest. At this point, philosophical education comes in and bridges the gap between psychological and moral egoism because if people come to know which acts really are in their best interest, they will pursue those acts. For Plato, the claim that one ought to act in one's own interest entails the claim that one ought to act in the interest of others. It is the job of Socrates' philosophical discourse to demonstrate that hidden truth. (By the way, when we talk about self-interest here, notice that the appropriate term is **egoism** and not "egotism." If I call you an egotist, I am intentionally insulting you; I am calling you a name. If I call you an egoist, I am ascribing to you a view about motivation: "ego"—the Latin word for "I.") It is interesting to note that in this important respect, the Socrates of the *Republic* and his antagonist, Thrasymachus, share the same egoistic view. The difference is that Thrasymachus thought that it is *not* in one's best interest to act morally, but Socrates thought that it is. Thrasymachus's egoism, then, creates an opposition between the individual and society (society's interests are not *my* interests), but Socrates' egoism does not. Socrates (like Karl Marx after him) tried to show that the interests of the individual are identical to the interests of the community.

I would be glad to help you, but as far as I can determine, there's nothing in it for me. Make me an offer.

We're all in this together!

And you're for communism, too?

Yes, but only for the elite. The workers are too stupid to get the point.

Karl Marx and Socrates Agree (Sort Of)

Love Thy Neighbor as Thyself

The philosopher who is most famous for his direct commitment to egoism is THOMAS HOBBES (1588–1679). In his book *Leviathan*, Hobbes wrote, "of the voluntary acts of every man, the object is some good to himself."[3] Hobbes's view is what I have identified as psychological egoism. He believes it is simply a psychological fact (which for him as a materialist means a biological fact) that all people always *do* act in ways that they take to be to their personal benefit. He agrees with Socrates that philosophical thinking can clarify what truly is in one's best interest. Hobbes's view, if true, rules out the biological possibility of *altruism* (ego = I, alter = other; egoism = I-ism, altruism = otherism). Altruism as a psychological theory is the claim that people sometimes do sacrifice their own interests for the interests of others, and as a moral theory it is the claim that people sometimes ought to sacrifice their own interests for the interests of others. Altruism, which would be very foreign to the ancient Greek mentality, is a view we often associate with Christianity (though perhaps not correctly because Jesus tells us "Love thy neighbor as thyself" and "Do unto others as you would have them do unto you" [emphases added]. On the other hand, Jesus also said, "If any man cometh unto me and hateth not . . . his own life, . . . he cannot be my disciple" [Luke 14:26]). If altruism is *impossible*, then surely it cannot be a moral duty. (As David Hume said, "ought" implies "can.") Well then, *is* altruism impossible? Is it ever possible to sacrifice one's own interests in order to act in the interest of another? Hobbes says sacrifice is possible only if one perceives it to be in his interest to sacrifice his interests. Certainly most of us are surprised by Hobbes's claim because we tend to draw certain distinctions that he rejects. For example, in the case of a person who, at great risk to his own life, saves a drowning child from the surf, consider the kinds of explanations he might give after the fact:

I saved her because . . .

A. I saw that she would drown if I didn't go in after her. (Somebody had to do it!) (responsibility)

B. I recognized that it was my duty to try and save her. (duty)

C. Only an animal would have stood by and let her drown. (natural sentiment)

D. I know that family, and I love that little girl. (love)

E. Her father helped me once when I was down and out. (debt)

F. Well, I don't know why I did it. I'm as surprised as you are. (?)

G. My conscience would have plagued me for the rest of my life if I hadn't tried. (guilt)

H. I didn't want people to say that I was a coward. (reputation)

I. I hoped I would get some recognition out of all this. (reputation)

J. I wanted to satisfy a need I have to help others. (self-aggrandizement—perhaps out of guilt or feelings of inferiority)

K. I wanted to achieve a benefit for myself. (Hobbesian honesty)

L. I wanted a pleasant sensation. (hedonism)

ALTRUISM ↑ ↓ **EGOISM**

Hobbes says that reasons A through J are really versions of K, and indeed that K is a version of L because he defines "benefit" in terms of pleasure. ("Pleasure . . . or delight, is the appearance or sense of good, and *molestation* or *displeasure*, the appearance, or sense of evil."[4] His definition means that Hobbes's egoism is a form of **hedonism.** More about hedonism in the next section.)

How does Hobbes know that human action is always motivated by self-interest? Surely this claim purports to be an empirical one—one that ought to be the result of a scientific investigation. Yet Hobbes has not only failed to conduct a scientific investigation, he has in fact subverted the possibility of any such investigation. This subversion takes place because truly scientific theories must always be open to possible refutation if new disconfirming data are discovered. This fact is embodied in what has come to be known as the

principle of falsifiability (associated with the British-Austrian philosopher of science, Sir Karl Popper). In other words, for a thesis to be a truly scientific view, its defender must be able to state the conditions under which it would be admitted that the hypothesis had been refuted. For example, obviously, Isaac Newton would admit that his theory of gravity was false if, all other things being equal, repeated instances were reported and confirmed of heavier-than-air objects hovering, floating, or

Things Going Up

rising. Precisely what makes Newton's theory so convincing is the fact that no such events have been confirmed, but what makes his theory scientific is that we know what it would be like for it to be false.

Now, in the face of the principle of falsifiability, what is the status of Hobbes's thesis? What kind of data, if discovered, would refute Hobbes's view? I think the answer to this is: *none*. No matter what possible counterevidence we could imagine, Hobbes would claim that his theory can account for it. For example, let's try to imagine an event that we believe to be paradigmatic of altruism. What about the case of the young soldier who throws himself on the grenade, thereby saving the lives of his comrades at the cost of his own life? Such heroic events are possible (in fact, they have happened). Are these possibilities not evidence of altruism, hence evidence against Hobbes's egoism? Not at all, Hobbes would say. If the soldier sacrificed his life, it was because (whether foolishly or not) he construed it as being in his interest to do so. ("He knew he would be dead either way and preferred to be remembered as a hero," "He was raised in such a way that his concept of self-esteem was intimately tied up with the performance of heroic acts," or "He thought people would like him," and so on.) Hobbes probably believed that it was to his theory's credit that it could be applied to any possible contingency, but we see that the opposite is true. Any theory that accounts for

Wow! A chance to earn a medal!

every possible case in effect accounts for no case. Or, to put it slightly differently, any "theory" that is compatible with every possible state of affairs is no theory at all because real theories must exclude some possibilities. Confucius is supposed to have said, "If the mind is *too* open, everything falls out." The same goes for theories.

Mommy! Flower for you.

Thanks, dear. (What's the hidden agenda here?)

If Hobbes had stated his proposition differently, we might have more sympathy with it. What if Hobbes had said, "There is more self-interest in most motivation than is usually admitted. One should be generally suspicious when estimating an agent's intentions. One should ask, 'What's in it for the agent?'" Then Hobbes would be admitting the possibility, though not the likelihood, of altruistic acts, and the question concerning which acts are egoistic and which altruistic would be an *empirical* one (i.e., one to be determined by *evidence*). As it stands, however, it is hard to take Hobbes's thesis totally seriously when trying to construct a moral picture for oneself.

Hedonism

It was mentioned that Hobbes's egoism is a form of hedonism, which is the view either that human action *is* motivated by the pursuit of pleasure or that it *ought* to be. The first view, which is Hobbes's view, is called *psychological hedonism* because it is a theory of *motivation*. The second is called *moral hedonism* because it is a theory about how we ought to live. (You see that this distinction parallels the distinction between psychological and moral egoism and that between psychological and moral altruism.) Notice that, strictly speaking, psychological hedonism cannot be a form of moral hedonism because the latter, in asserting that one *ought* to pursue one's own pleasure, presupposes that it is possible *not* to do so but that *not* doing so is unwise. There would be no sense in advocating acts that in fact were the only show in town. Because psychological hedonism claims that hedonism *is* the only possibility, psychological hedonism cannot be a thorough-going *moral* view. The most it could do as a moral theory would be to advocate certain kinds of acts as being more wise than others (i.e., as bringing more pleasure than others). Moral hedonism, on the other hand, is logically committed to admit that it is possible to act motivated by interests other than one's own pleasure, but it claims that doing so is a bad idea—indeed, that it is somehow immoral to do so. This distinction, however, has not been drawn by some of the most prominent hedonists, including hedonism's most famous ancient defender, EPICURUS (341–270 B.C.E.), probably because the ancients did not always conceive of ethics the way we do. They were on a Platonic-like quest, looking for the Good. Epicurus thought that this good was *pleasure*. He wrote, "For it is to obtain this end that we always act, namely, to avoid pain and fear. . . . And for this cause we call pleasure the beginning and end of the blessed life."[5] According to Epicurus, no act should be undertaken except for the pleasure in which it results, and no act should be rejected except for the pain it produces. This view provoked Epicurus to analyze the different kinds of pleasure. There are two kinds of desires, hence two kinds of pleasure as a result of gratifying those desires: *natural desire* (which has two sub-classes), and *vain desire*.

1. Natural desire
   A. Necessary (e.g., desire for food and sleep)
   B. Unnecessary (e.g., desire for sex)
2. Vain desire (e.g., desire for decorative clothing or exotic food)

Natural necessary desires must be satisfied and are easy to satisfy. They result in a good deal of pleasure and in very few painful consequences. Vain desires do not need to be satisfied and are not easy to satisfy. Because there are no natural limits to them, they tend to become obsessive and lead to very painful consequences.

The desire for sex is natural but can usually be overcome. When it can be, it should be because satisfaction of the sexual drive gives intense pleasure but involves one in relationships that are usually ultimately more painful than pleasant and are often extremely painful.

The Pursuit of Vain Pleasure

Epicurus actually subscribed to the most traditional Greek values (he advocated the pursuit of beauty, prudence, honor, justice, courage, and honesty) but only because he believed that holding them led to more pleasure than pain. He wrote, "Beauty and virtue and the like are to be honoured, if they give pleasure, but if they do not give pleasure, we must bid them farewell." But he added, "It is not possible to live pleasantly without living prudently and honourably and justly."[6] Apparently, Epicurus thought that rejecting these values would result in tense, hence unpleasant, relations with other people and also

in a guilty con-
science. Epicurus
would probably be
right about the
majority of us, but
isn't it possible to
imagine a sociopath
who, operating on
Adeimantus's and
Machiavelli's advice,
is motivated not by
a desire for virtue
but by the advan-
tages of the appear-
ance of virtue and
who has no guilty
conscience whatso-

ever? Or what about sadists and masochists? Are they *necessarily* more
unhappy than the virtuous? And if they are not more unhappy, are they
really under a kind of moral obligation to pursue the unvirtuous acts that
give them pleasure?

　　We will notice that Epicurus's definition of pleasure is *negative,* that is,
pleasure is the absence of pain. This negative definition prevents Epicurus
from falling into crass sensualism. The trouble with this definition is that,
taken to its logical extremity, the *absence* of life is better than any life at

Beyond the Pleasure Principle

all (as Freud discovered in his
Beyond the Pleasure Principle, where
he claimed that behind the "pleasure principle" is **Thanatos,** the
death instinct). This conclusion is a
bit ironic because Epicurus himself
had claimed that his philosophy
dispelled the fear of death. Epicurus's materialism led him to believe
that death was merely the absence
of sensation and consciousness;
therefore, there could be no sensation or consciousness of death to
fear. "Where death is, we are not.
Where we are, death is not."

Some of Epicurus's Roman followers interpreted "pleasure" quite differently, defining it as positive titillation. It is because of these extremists that today Epicureanism is often associated with sensualistic hedonism. Sickly Epicurus, swinging in his hammock, would have disapproved (though not too harshly because polemics cause agitation, which is painful). Epicurus's theory never constituted a major philosophical movement, but he had disciples in both Greece and Rome for a number of centuries. His most famous follower was the Roman Lucretius, who, in the first century B.C.E. wrote a long poem "On the Nature of Things," expounding the philosophy of his master. It is through Lucretius's poem that many have been introduced to the thought of Epicurus.

Utilitarianism

A historical connection exists between Epicurus's hedonism and a very influential contemporary moral theory called **utilitarianism.** This view was first put forth in the nineteenth century by the British philosopher JEREMY BENTHAM (1748–1832). Then it was criticized and revised by his somewhat wayward disciple, JOHN STUART MILL (1808–1873). The essential difference between Greek hedonism and utilitarianism is that the former was egoistic in nature, and the latter is social.

The Calculus of Felicity

Bentham, who may not have been one of the deepest philosophers in the Western tradition, was certainly one of the most practically oriented and influential. He had an active hand in the reformation of the British legal system of his day. Agreeing with Hobbes, Bentham began his philosophy with the assumption that, like it or not, we humans are all governed by the desire for pleasure and the aversion to pain. Unlike Hobbes, however, he did not conclude that therefore altruism was either impossible or unwise. Again like Hobbes, he believed we are endowed with reason and that therefore it was possible to give moral advice on how one should pursue the goal of the "pleasure principle" (Freud's term).

Bentham formulated his advice in what he called "the calculus of felicity." According to it, pleasure can be catalogued into seven categories, and this catalogue provides a rational analysis of pleasure. The seven categories are:

1. Intensity—how intense?
2. Duration—how long?

3. Certainty—how sure?
4. Propinquity—how soon?
5. Fecundity—how many more?
6. Purity—how free from pain?
7. Extent—how many people are affected?

On a scale of one to ten, this is a "ten" in all categories.

According to Bentham, whenever you consider performing any action, you can analyze its value in terms of these categories and contrast it with its alternatives. For example, say you need to study for tomorrow's chemistry examination, but it turns out that today promises to be the most glorious day of the year. The beach positively beckons. Try out the calculus of felicity on such a decision—between studying for a chemistry midterm and going to the beach with some friends. Obviously, the beach party will be strong in some categories (1, 3, 4, 6) and weaker in others (2, 5). Studying will be weak in most categories but strong in a few (2, and 5 and 7 also, if others have an interest in your succeeding in college). Are the assets of studying strong enough to overcome its deficits in the face of the fun enticing you to the beach? (Of course, the guilt you would experience at the beach has to be taken into consideration too.)

Beach Guilt

We can imagine that if Bentham had lived in today's world of inexpensive calculators, he would have invented a pocket "calculator of felicity." There is something silly about the image of someone punching the values of various acts into a calculator, but Bentham thought that his calculus of felicity was actually the schematization of something we do semiconsciously (hence often poorly) anyway and that once we became experienced in manipulating these figures, we would be able to do it intuitively.

Looking back at the calculus of felicity, take note of category 7, "extent." It is this category that makes utilitarianism a form of *social* hedonism. One must consider the pleasures and pains of others and not only one's own. In fact, what Bentham and Mill call "the principle of utility" stresses precisely this aspect, which allows for the possibility of altruism in utilitarianism— "the greatest amount of happiness for the greatest number of people." If an act I am about to perform will bring about a great amount of happiness for a large number of people, then I should perform it even if it brings mostly misery to me.

Besides this social aspect of utilitarianism, there is also a democratic bias built into it— especially in the case of Bentham. When it comes to evaluating acts in terms of the pleasure they will produce, Bentham firmly believed in the "one person, one vote" principle. Each person's judgment is as important as every other's. No one—be he your parent or the state—has the right to *inform* you that you are or are not having fun. According to Bentham, "Prejudice apart, the game of push-pin is of equal value with the arts and sciences of music and poetry. If the game of push-pin furnishes more pleasure, it is more valuable than either."[7]

Fascistic Hedonism

You are now enjoying yourselves! This is an official proclamation!

The Quality of Pleasure

John Stuart Mill thought of himself as a disciple of Bentham, but he was clearly concerned about the implications of some of Bentham's formulations of utilitarianism. Mill feared that an adherent of the calculus of felicity might conclude that push-pin (or watching football on TV) is better than the arts and sciences, and Mill knew in his heart that such a conclusion is simply not true. Utilitarianism would have to be rewritten in such a way as to be able to demonstrate that the reading of Shakespearean sonnets is better than some of its alternatives. Part of the problem is that the calculus generates a purely quantitative analysis, and Mill was convinced that quality in pleasure was even more important than quantity. Furthermore, he feared that a literal application of the calculus of felicity would, over a number of generations, completely erode culture.

What if you offered the following proposition to the electorate of a particular state: "It has been determined that the teaching of Shakespeare in the schools of this state costs each taxpayer $25 each five years. Now, the state would like to know if you taxpayers would prefer to continue paying $25 a person for the next five years for instruction of Shakespeare or would you prefer a rebate of $25 in the form of two cases of beer per voter?" Mill was afraid that, given the tenuous foothold that culture has among the masses and given Bentham's "one person, one vote" principle, Shakespeare would lose out. In a number of generations, no one would even remember who Shakespeare was. (In fact, a proposition like this was presented to the voters of California in 1978. It was called "Proposition 13." The voters went for the beer.)

Shakespeare or the NFL?

Tough Benthamite Decisions

In order to counteract the possibility of this

"leveling down" of culture, Mill insisted that it was part of our human heritage to have desires higher than those that lent themselves to analysis in terms of the calculus of felicity. He wrote:

> Few human creatures would consent to be changed into any of the lower animals for a promise of the fullest allowance of a beast's pleasures; no intelligent human being would consent to be a fool, no instructed person would be an ignoramus, no person of feeling and conscience would be selfish and base, even though they should be persuaded that the fool, the dunce, or the rascal is better satisfied with his lot than they are with theirs.[8]

Apparently, Mill felt that the "lower" desires (those of animals and perhaps the most biologically basic human desires) could be adequately dealt with in terms of the quantitative analysis provided by the calculus of felicity but that the "higher desires" could be talked about only in terms of quality, something no calculus could evaluate. According to Mill:

> It is quite compatible with the principle of utility to recognize the fact that some kinds of pleasure are more desirable and more valuable than others. It would be absurd that, while in estimating all other things quality is considered as well as quantity, the estimation of pleasure should be supposed to depend on quantity alone.
>
> If I am asked what I mean by difference of quality in pleasures, or what makes one pleasure more valuable than another, merely as a pleasure, except its being greater in amount, there is but one possible answer. Of two pleasures, if there be one to which all or almost all who have experience of both give a decided preference, irrespective of any feeling of moral obligation to prefer it, that is the more desirable pleasure. If one of the two is, by those who are competently acquainted with both, placed so far above the other that they prefer it, even though knowing it to be attended with a greater amount of discontent, and would not resign it for any quantity of the other pleasure which their nature is capable of, we are justified in ascribing to the preferred enjoyment a superiority in quality so far outweighing quantity as to render it, in comparison, of small account.[9]

Mill's objection is perhaps summed up in this famous line: "The uncultivated cannot be competent judges of cultivation."

One can certainly be sympathetic to Mill's concerns. Bentham's calculus does seem to be a bit crass, and in a democracy, there is always the danger of every standard falling to the lowest common denominator. But Mill's solution to these problems brings about problems of its own. Mill can be accused of abandoning democracy for elitism and of abandoning hedonism altogether. The basis of the charge of elitism must be obvious. If one must demonstrate "competence" before one is granted a vote, then on

The Uncultivated Cannot Be
Competent Judges of Cultivation

many issues, only a small minority will have the right to express an opinion. This minority will probably tend to be the best educated, the wealthiest, and most powerful segment of society. (In the United States, we have accepted a compromise version of Mill's solution. We are not a "participatory democracy" but a "representative democracy." Not everybody votes on all issues; rather, we elect representatives who in theory are, by virtue of their excellent education and their paid staff of assistants, competent to decide certain issues concerning which we ourselves have no competence. However, in some states the citizens reserve the right, through the initiative process, to bypass those representatives on certain matters. This is how the system works in theory, though of course not always in practice.)

Let us now look at the charge that Mill has abandoned hedonism. In itself, this charge is perhaps not so devastating, though Mill himself would have been displeased by it. Mill accepts the basic principle of hedonism—the sole criterion of value is pleasure—but he also claims that some pleasures are better (more valuable) than others. We must ask, More valuable according to what criterion? It can't be just "pleasure" because some pleasures are better, and "better" here no longer means "more intense, purer, more lengthy, more certain, more imminent," and so on. Rather, it means "has more quality." But what is this elusive thing called "quality" that only the "competent" can recognize? In an odd way, we seem to have returned to the Platonic doctrine of areté because one of the English translations of that word is "quality." But perhaps this result isn't so bad after all. In fact, most contemporary utilitarians feel no need to defend hedonistic principles. Rather than talking about "pleasure," they prefer to stick to the broader terms like "happiness," "interests," "well-being," and "human flourishing," without trying to "cash them out" in terms of specific ingredients.

Utilitarianism's Problems

On the face of it, utilitarianism is plausible. It does indeed appear that morality must essentially have something to do with promoting happiness and well-being and with minimizing unhappiness and misery. It would be odd to claim that some act was good even though it brought nothing but unhappiness and misery to absolutely everybody. Therefore, there must be something right about the opposite view (that an act is good if it brings happiness and well-being to everyone), which just happens to be utilitarianism's view. Still, some serious problems arise with utilitarianism. One of them has to do with its "consequentialist" nature (I deal with this topic later in this section), and the other has to do with notions of *justice* and *meritoriousness*.

The problem of justice and meritoriousness can be revealed in a fictitious example. Suppose you had to go to court for failing to pay a few parking fines. You are alone in a small courtroom with the judge, the bailiff, and the court reporter. After the bailiff reads the charge ("failure to pay three fines for expired parking meters"), you respond ("Guilty, your Honor"), and she announces her judgment: "I find you guilty on all charges. The punishment will be that you shall suffer death at the hands of a firing squad." "What?!!" you scream. "Death for three lousy parking tickets??" The judge leans forward and whispers, "I know you don't deserve this punishment, but there has been a rash of murders in our community, and a study has just been released demonstrating that immediately after an execution, the crime rate drops substantially. Unfortunately, we don't have any convicted murderers on our hands right now. But we do have you, and there is every reason to believe that if we execute you, the public good will be served. Hence, even though my decision may seem unfair to you personally, it will certainly promote the greatest amount of happiness for the greatest number of people. So it is the only judgment I can really reach in good conscience."

Take another example (one that appears in almost every critical discussion of utilitarianism and that even has a name—"the case of Sam"). Sam, a basically normal, rather nondescript but "nice" human being, goes to the hospital to visit his only living relative, his senile, sick aunt. His visit coincides with five medical emergencies at the hospital. One person needs a liver transplant, another a spleen transplant, another a lung transplant, another a new heart, and a fifth a new pineal gland. Each of the five patients is a tremendously important, much-loved person whose death would bring a great deal of grief and actual physical discomfort to a great number of people. Sam's death, on the other hand, would be mourned by no one (except possibly by his aunt in her lucid moments). The top members of the hospital administration, all strict utilitarians, lure Sam into an operating room, remove all his vital organs, and distribute them to the other needy patients, thereby operating (literally) in accordance with the principle of utility: the greatest amount of happiness for the greatest number of people.

Sam Visiting His Sick Aunt

The reason these fictitious cases are so jarring is that they go so radically against our intuitive sense of justice and meritoriousness. Neither the parking meter violator nor Sam deserves the fate dished out by the executing judge and the hospital staff. Because these cases are compatible with utilitarianism, either something is wrong with our intuitive sense of justice or something is wrong with utilitarianism. Most people are probably more likely to jettison a *theory* than to go against their sense of justice.

Many contemporary utilitarians have recognized this problem and have tried to adjust utilitarian theory to correspond more with our intuitions. To this end, they have drawn a distinction between *act utilitarianism* and *rule utilitarianism*. The term "act utilitarianism" designates the traditional form. According to it, one must perform the specific *act* that will produce the greatest amount of happiness for the greatest number of people. "Rule utilitarianism" says, to the contrary, that in contemplating one of two acts, a person should perform that act governed by a (hypothetical) rule whose general obedience would produce the greatest amount of happiness. According to rule utilitarianism, even if a particular self-serving deceit or lie may go undetected, hence cause no one any unhappiness, nevertheless, I probably should not engage in it because, generally, lying and deceiving cause more unhappiness than happiness. It also means that the executing judge and the hospital administrators cannot proceed as they desire because the rule governing their acts would be something like this: "If the lives of a number of people (or even a few exceptional people) can be saved by sacrificing an innocent bystander, the sacrifice should be performed." But members of a community who knew that they might be set upon by the authorities and arbitrarily killed or disemboweled would be members of a community of fear, one whose citizens would be loath to set foot on the streets in daylight.

A Community of Fear

One critic has argued that rule utilitarianism can lead to unpalatable consequences. He asks, What about the Dutch family during World War II who hid Jews in their attic? According to rule utilitarianism, would they be

required to answer truthfully when the Gestapo comes to their house looking for Jews (on the grounds that lying generally creates more unhappiness
than does honesty and that therefore one may not lie)? But surely the
rule utilitarian can operate according to the general rule: "Lying is wrong,
except when directed to evildoers in order to save the lives of innocent
people." The problem here is that one begins to suspect that the clever,
self-serving rule utilitarian can think of a general rule to rationalize all sorts
of questionable behavior. ("Shoplifting from large department stores is
okay as long as one doesn't get caught and no one ever finds out.") Such
rationalizations would surely begin to unravel rule utilitarianism.

So the modification of traditional utilitarianism (or act utilitarianism)
to rule utilitarianism may allow the utilitarian to meet the objection that
utilitarianism does not square with our sense of justice and meritoriousness, but there was another related objection concerning utilitarianism's
"consequentialist" nature. Notice that according
to the view we are now studying, no act is
good or bad in and of
itself. Rather, an act
is good or bad only
in terms of its
consequences.
Acts that result
in happiness, well-
being, and flour-
ishing are good;
acts that result
in the opposite
are bad. Now, there

is a certain prima facie plausibility to this view, but at some point it too
runs up against the moral intuition of many because a lot of us feel that
certain acts, such as wanton cruelty, are bad in and of themselves regardless of their consequences. We also feel that some acts—those performed
out of moral duty—are right independent of their consequences. The philos-

Consequentialism: The
moral worth of act X depends
on the consequences of X.

Nonconsequentialism: The
moral worth of act X depends
exclusively on act X.

opher who most clearly defended a moral doctrine based on this kind of reasoning was Immanuel Kant.

Duty-Oriented Morality

Immanuel Kant, whose epistemology we inspected briefly in Chapter 3, took a strictly nonconsequentialistic view of ethics. For him, the empirical consequences or results of an act had nothing whatsoever to do with the moral worth of the act. In fact, according to him, any attempt to justify an act by appealing to its consequences immediately removes the act from the ethical sphere. In order to demonstrate this point, Kant distinguishes between two kinds of "oughts" or "shoulds"—a *moral* ought, which he calls a **categorical imperative,** and a merely *practical* ought, which he calls a **hypothetical imperative.** Let's illustrate this distinction. Suppose I say to you, "You know, you really ought not to come to class with your shoes untied, fly open, and eating ice cream that is melting down your arm and dripping off your elbow." You ask, "Why not?" I say, "Because you look like a fool when you do that!" You approach me and whisper in my ear, "That's exactly the impression I want to give. Actually, I'm an undercover agent tailing a suspected terrorist who is in your class." I respond, "Oh! Well, in *that* case, you *ought to* do just as you are doing because you appear to be a *perfect fool*." This conversation contains examples of hypothetical imperatives. The imperative (ought) can be placed in the "then" clause of a hypothetical conditional sentence.

Undercover Agent

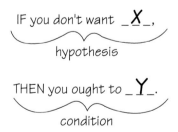

IF you don't want _**X**_,

⏜ hypothesis ⏜

THEN you ought to _**Y**_.

⏜ condition ⏜

In hypothetical imperatives, the ought can be defeated by rejecting the "if" clause of the hypothesis ("Oh, but I *want* to look like a fool. . . ."). This analysis shows what's wrong with the following exchange:

Fran: "You ought not to steal my car."
Jan: "Why not?"
Fran: "Because they'll put you in jail."

Jan can always rejoin, "Oh, but I *want* to go to jail. I've decided that I can't afford life on the outside. I'd like to have the state provide me with room and board, and it seems to me that the most certain way of achieving my goal is to steal your car." Fran now seems to be in the curious position of having to assert, "Oh, in that case, you *ought* to steal my car."

According to Kant, a truly *moral* ought cannot be conditional upon any individual's desires. It must be *absolute*—that is, universal and exceptionless—or as he calls it, "categorical." Are there any such moral demands, and how would we demonstrate their existence? According to Kant, there are indeed such moral

oughts, and once we have discovered them we can discern what our moral duty is. They are rooted in a certain fact about human nature, namely, the fact that we are *rational* beings. (Notice that utilitarianism is rooted in the fact that we are *passionate* beings—that we have desires. Kantianism is rooted in a very different fact about us—that we have reason. Kantianism, like Platonism, contains more than the subtle implication that reason should override desire.)

The principle behind the categorical imperative is a principle that every rational agent must accept. Refusing to do so would be tantamount to abandoning one's rationality, leading to "the obliteration of one's dignity as a human being." Let us state the categorical imperative: "Act only according to that maxim by which you can at the same time will that it should become a universal law." A related version of the categorical imperative (call the first one "version A" and this new one "version B") states, "Act as if the maxim of your action were to become by your will a universal law of nature." These two versions of the categorical imperative presuppose that it is possible to state the general principle behind any act you may consider performing. Before engaging in an act (such as helping your neighbor fix her flat tire), you can ask, "What principle (maxim) governs this act?" In this case, it might be "It is good to help one's fellow human in distress." Now, according to version A of the categorical imperative, we are to universalize our principle to see if any logical contradiction appears in that universalization. In other words, Is the world conceived by the universalization of my principle illogical in the way that a game would be illogical and hence unplayable if its rules contradicted each other? Is there any logical contradiction in the idea of a world in which everyone always helps a fellow human in distress?

A World in Which Everyone Is Fixing Flat Tires

If so, I cannot will such a world without contradiction. Version B of the categorical imperative yields what we might call a material criterion of self-contradiction rather than a logical criterion. It says, Imagine a world in which everyone always helps fellow humans in the same manner that the moon always orbits the earth, that is, out of necessity. Would such a world be materially possible? Again, if so, I can will such a world without contradicting myself. In the case of helping one's neighbor, it appears that there is no contradiction, either logical or material, under either test. So far, then, the conclusion is that there is no moral law preventing me from helping my neighbor. I may help her, but (so far) nothing says that I *must* help her.

Now let's try it in the negative. What if I don't feel like helping out my distressed neighbor? If I'm a Kantian, I must ask these questions in order to find out whether I am duty-bound to assist her:

1. Can I conceive of a logically consistent world in which nobody helps out others in distress? (version A)
2. Can I conceive of a materially consistent world in which nobody helps out others in distress (that is, for psychophysical reasons, they couldn't help each other even if they wanted to)? (version B)

In the first case, there seems to be no logical self-contradiction. It's not like trying to conceive of a world full of square circles. (So far, I'm off the hook. Let her fix her own flat tire!) But according to Kant, in the second case—version B—there is a contradiction. Based on his speculations about human nature, he concluded that human beings are interdependent. Only pathologically are they ever truly solitary individuals. (This view he shares with the ancient Greeks and, as you will see, with Hegel and Marx.) Not only would a maxim denying the duty to help others prevent human babies from surviving, but even "rugged individuals" need support. For Kant, this claim is an empirical one, not a moral one. Because human life cannot flourish without mutual assistance, version B of the categorical imperative says I have a moral duty to help my neighbor. (Darn! There goes my football game.)

Let's try these principles out on some other cases. Let's suppose that you owe a friend five dollars, and to your annoyance, he pressures you to repay. So you say to yourself, "If I kill him, I won't have to repay the debt."
But as a true Kantian, you first check to see if you could universalize the principle governing the proposed action. You ask yourself, What if everyone accomplished his goals by killing some- one? Could there exist a universal law, "Everyone ought to kill someone"? This would be an impossi- ble law because if every- one complied with it,

LAW OF THE LAND
Everyone must kill someone

there would be no one left to comply with it. In this case, it is the material contradiction that kicks in. Therefore we are duty-bound not to kill as a way of solving problems. OK, then, what if you lie to your friend, telling him that you already repaid the debt? Can the principle behind this proposal be uni- versalized? Could there be a general law, "Everyone ought always to lie"? Obviously not, because it would be impossible even to state the law without breaking it. This is a *logical* fact. Therefore we are duty-bound not to lie. Well, what if you repay the five dollars, then steal them back? Can the principle behind this act be universalized? Imagine a general law saying, "Everyone ought always to steal." But this, too, is an impossible law for both logical

and material reasons because the concept of stealing is parasitical upon the concept of property. If everyone always steals, there can be no property; there can only be temporary possession, that is, stuff passing from person to person. So we are also duty-bound to refrain from stealing. (If you are a true Kantian, it's beginning to look as though you will have to pay your debt!)

Where Theft Is the Law of the Land

Kant's Strengths and Weaknesses

Some interesting things are going on in duty-oriented morality. There is some genuine insight and there are some serious problems, too. Let's talk first about the positive features. Kant's moral philosophy recognizes that an essential aspect of morality is the need to view the world, including one's own actions, from the point of view of others. We need to climb out of our own shoes and stand in the shoes of other people. (This view Kant shares with utilitarianism and with Jesus' "golden rule," though the latter two

moral codes are based on the universalizability of desire, and Kant's
is based on the universalizability
of reason. So Kant doesn't ask,
"If everyone behaved like that,
how would you like it?" He
doesn't really care what
you *like*. Rather he asks, "If
everyone behaved like that,
would the standards of reason and dignity still be maintained?" The individual is forced
out of subjectivism and selfishness because he realizes that it
is unreasonable to demand for
himself special exemption from

Standing in Someone Else's Shoes

universal laws.) Kant's principles are fine tools for revealing hypocrisy—that
of others or oneself. If it is wrong for someone to take my property without
my permission, then it is wrong when I take the property of another person
without permission. I am a hypocrite if I claim that it is theft when you take
my stereo but that it is simply redistribution of wealth when I take your
stereo. Kant is correct. If it is wrong for you to take mine, then, in circumstances that are identical in all relevant respects, it is wrong for me to take
yours.

But the problems with Kant's theory lie in the same area as do its
strengths. There is something too absolutistic about his view. If a heavily
armed madman, frothing at the mouth, asks me if I know where Sue Smith
is, and I realize that he intends to kill her if he finds her, my moral intuition
tells me that I *ought* to lie—and in fact
that it would be immoral to tell the truth.
Yet Kant says that I must tell the truth
even to a murderous madman, on the
grounds that the principle behind
lying cannot be universalized without
contradiction.

Critics of Kant have pointed
out something that was mentioned in connection with rule utilitarianism, namely, that it is possible to generate modified rules
that can be universalized, such as

I cannot
tell a lie. She's
over there.

this one: "One ought to lie when doing so will save the life of an innocent person." Kant argued against such modifications on the grounds that they destroy the universalizability of the rule by making it more context bound, but many critics find this argument unpersuasive and point out that Kant believed in capital punishment for capital crimes; hence Kant himself was modifying his injunction against killing. It does seem that only by accepting in principle the possibility of modifying Kant's general rules can we save his moral philosophy from absurdity.

Kant thought that acts whose principle cannot be universalized cannot in any way commit us to moral obligation. This belief seems correct for reasons mentioned previously. (Reminder: if an act is declared to be bad when *you* perform it, then an act that is the same in all relevant respects must be bad when *I* perform it, in exactly the same way that if this figure → △ is a triangle when you draw it, then it must also be a triangle when *I* draw it.) But from this principle, how can we generate the concept of duty, which is so close to Kant's heart? Surely we don't have a moral obligation to perform every act whose maxim can be generalized. (I like to smile when I see birds. The maxim behind that act might be *It is good to express joy in*

The Moral Obligation to Smile at Birds

the presence of pretty things. This maxim *can* be generalized without contradiction, but it's hard to believe that therefore we all have a moral obligation to smile at birds, to whistle in the dark, or to clear our throat before scratching our nose.)

Kant agrees. He does not argue that we have a duty to perform every act whose maxim can be universalized, only that such acts are morally permissible. What gives an act *moral* worth is not simply the fact that it *can* be universalized but the fact that it was chosen as a moral act. Our duty is not that of performing any specific acts but to choose only acts that can be universalized; and what makes them *moral* is that we chose them in order to be performing our duty. In the first sentence of his *Foundations of the Metaphysics of Morality* (1785), Kant says, "Nothing in the world—indeed nothing even beyond the world—can possibly be conceived which could be called good without qualification except a good will." What he means by "good will" is the will to do one's duty. The same act—let's again say the act of helping your neighbor fix her flat tire—may be either moral, morally neutral, or even immoral, depending on its motivation. (Here we see the big difference between utilitarianism, which is *consequentialist* in nature, and Kantianism, which is *nonconsequentialist*. That is, for Kant, the act's moral worth is not determined by its *results*, but by its *intention*.) The act is immoral if my motivation is to deceive her into thinking that I'm a nice guy so she will bestow favors on me. It is morally neutral if the reason I helped her is because I felt sorry for her. (Mere *feelings* can never be the basis of morality, according to Kant.) The act is moral only if my motive for performing it is the desire to do my duty. Kant is surely right to think that the agent's intention must be considered when assigning moral worth (an act motivated by pure greed is not morally worthy even if it happens to benefit many).

Expectation of Reward

Pity

Duty

Three Different Motives for Helping Your Neighbor Fix Her Flat

But there is something disturbing going on here. Kant thought that the Good Samaritan who helped the wounded stranger because the Samaritan's heart went out to the suffering human being had not performed a peculiarly moral act; yet he thought that a Good Samaritan who *loathes* people, including the man he helps, yet helps him nevertheless out of a sense of duty, is a *moral* man. A coldness lurks in the heart of this doctrine. Perhaps feelings cannot be the sole criterion of moral worth, but they certainly enter into the picture in a big way. A truly good person must have

I find you disgusting. But I'm going to help you anyway.

A Kantian Hero

sympathy and empathy for a fellow human being. Thank goodness this icy side of Kant's moral philosophy can be ignored without damaging his insights about universalizability.

Kant's Third Formulation

Kant presented his categorical imperative in several forms. His third formulation runs like this: "Act so that you treat humanity, whether in your own person or in that of another, always as an end and never as a means only." Apparently Kant thought that this formulation was simply another way of stating his first version, which itself was an expression of the principle of universalizability. Whether such an identity between the two versions exists is certainly debatable. A recent book by Yale University philosopher Allen Wood argues that the first two versions (A and B) of the categorical imperative are not meant to be the equivalent of the third version but rather steps leading to it, and that this third version is the essence of Kant's moral philosophy. Because Wood believes that this third version holds good on its own, he minimizes the problems in the first two versions on which critics dwell.[10] In any case, it ap-

Using People as Pawns

pears to be true that the principle of universalizability prohibits one from *using* other people for one's own ends. At any rate, Kant is suggesting that anyone who is committed to rationality is also committed to treating other people as "ends in themselves," and not as pawns in one's own game of personal advantage. To verify Kant's suggestion, we will have to summarize in a very cursory manner some complicated arguments that he presents in his *Foundations of the Metaphysics of Morals.*

Kant believed that, if there were no *persons* in the world, only *things,* there would be no *values.* Nothing would be worth anything more or less than anything else. There are values in the world only because there are persons—that is, individual entities that have not only desires (animals, too, have desires) but also rationality and freedom. Something is valuable only relative to a human goal. Then, as the source of values, humans have *dignity,* which Kant defines as something so valuable that nothing could transcend it in worth. Therefore, to claim one's status as a human—that is, to claim one's dignity—one must value above all else that which bestows dignity and humanness on one, that is, rationality, freedom, and autonomy. One must value absolutely the rationality, freedom, and autonomy not only of oneself but also of individuals other than oneself. Or, in Kant's words, one must treat them as ends in themselves.

There are some striking features of Kant's position here. Despite his argument's highly abstract nature, its conclusion squares with the very widespread moral intuition that it is wrong to use (exploit) people for one's own purposes. Furthermore, if that conclusion is accepted, it can be the basis of taking positions on such morally loaded topics as euthanasia, abortion, racism, equal rights, and feminism. But, of course, some difficulties remain. First, it seems to me that the ecological crisis we humans have provoked must force us to realize that any adequate moral code today will have to be one that demonstrates some responsibility to the natural world. A doctrine like Kant's, which says that nature has value only as a means to human ends must seem to us today to be not just a bit arrogant but perhaps ironically even dangerous—ironic because that doctrine is itself not conducive to human ends. Second, arguments as abstract as Kant's are hard to evaluate and are not always very compelling. (Pointing this out, of course, does not refute Kant's argument.) Third, the difference between using people as a means and treating them as ends-in-themselves is not always clear. Kant says we may not treat people "as a means only." How about as a means *mostly?* For example, I must admit that one of my main motivations in teaching philosophy is to earn a living for myself. Does that prove that I am using my students as means to satisfy my own ends? What if I am deeply committed to teaching my students philosophy, but try along the way to extort money and sex from them? Fourth, real-life situations often present us with dilemmas in which no matter what we do, our act can be interpreted as using someone. For example, the existentialist

philosopher Jean-Paul Sartre cites the case of one of his students who, during the German occupation of France, approached him for advice. The young man came to Sartre under the following circumstances:

> . . . his father was on bad terms with his mother, and, moreover, was inclined to be a collaborationist; his older brother had been killed in the German offensive of 1940, and the young man, with somewhat immature but generous feelings, wanted to avenge him. His mother lived alone with him, very much upset by the half-treason of her husband and the death of her older son; the boy was her only consolation.
>
> The boy was faced with the choice of leaving for England and joining the Free French Forces—that is, leaving his mother behind—or remaining with his mother and helping her to carry on. . . . Who could help him choose? Christian doctrine? No. Christian doctrine says, "Be charitable, love your neighbor, take the more rugged path, etc., etc." But which is the more rugged path? Whom should he love as a brother? The fighting man or his mother? Which does the greater good, the vague act of fighting in a group, or the concrete one of helping a particular human being to go on living? Who can decide a priori? Nobody. No book of ethics can tell him. The Kantian ethics says, "Never treat a person as a means, but as an end." Very well, if I stay with my mother I'll treat her as an end and not as a means; but by virtue of this very fact, I'm running the risk of treating the people around me who are fighting, as means; and, conversely, if I go to join those who are fighting, I'll be treating them as an end, and, by doing that, I run the risk of treating my mother as a means. . . . You will say, "At least, he did go to a teacher for advice." But if you seek advice from a priest, for example, you have chosen this priest; you already knew, more or less, just about what advice he was going to give you. In other words, choosing your adviser is involving yourself. The proof of this is that if you are Christian, you will say, "Consult a priest." But some priests are collaborating, some are just marking time, some are resisting. Which to choose? If the young man chooses a priest who is resisting or collaborating, he has already decided on the kind of advice he's going to get. Therefore, in coming to see me he knew the answer I was going to give him, and I had one answer to give: "You're free, choose, that is, invent." No general ethics can show you what is to be done; there are no omens in the world.[11]

From this story we see that, even accepting Kant's categorical imperative in any of its forms, we still might be confronted with real moral situations in which Kant's philosophy is of little help to us. In fact, Sartre himself accepted Kant's view that to claim our status as human beings we must recognize ourselves and others as autonomous, free, and rational, but Sartre obviously held that ultimately our freedom overrides our rationality. Ultimately, our freedom, not our rationality, generates values. Kant would surely see this Sartrean view as a form of subjective irrationalism (more on Sartre in the next chapter).

Conclusion

I shall not attempt to reach any conclusion concerning ethical theory until we have examined some attacks on its foundation in the next chapter.

Topics for Consideration

1. Socrates does not deny that the immoral person is able to take advantage of the moral person in matters of money and business, yet ultimately, according to Socrates, the moral person wins out over the immoral one. Why?

2. What psychological and sociological presuppositions are there behind Socrates' simile, "The soul is like the city"? How successful is that simile in your view?

3. In this chapter, it is argued that the truth of Hobbes's egoism can never be established empirically (i.e., by appealing to evidence). Defend or attack that view.

4. Explain the details of Epicurus's apparently contradictory theory that (a) the best life is one that engages in nothing but the pursuit of pleasure and (b) the best life is one of relative inaction, of calm and repose.

5. Can you reconcile John Stuart Mill's apparently contradictory views that (a) pleasure is the sole criterion of value and (b) some pleasures are better than other pleasures?

6. Can rule utilitarianism resolve the dilemma presented to the principle of utility ("greatest amount of happiness for the greatest number of people") in "the case of Sam"?

7. Why does Kant think that the only morally right actions are those whose "maxim" can be universalized?

8. Explain how utilitarianism and Kantianism respectively would treat each of these cases:
   A. The case of a physician assisting the suicide of a terminally ill patient.
   B. The case of a person of modest means stealing money from a careless millionaire who will never know he's been robbed.
   C. The case of a woman lying to her dying father who urges her to promise that she will not marry anyone of a religion different from the father's.
   D. The case of a person offered a large sum of money to execute another person whom everyone detests.

9. Defend or attack Kant's view that it is always wrong to use other people for one's own purposes.

Suggestions for Further Reading:
Paperback Editions

Christopher Biffle, ed., *A Guided Tour of John Stuart Mill's "Utilitarianism"* (Mountain View, Calif.: Mayfield, 1993). Utilitarian ethics in Mill's own words but with annotations and questions designed to help the reader. Also contains a section on Kant's ethics with similar aids to facilitate the comparative analysis of Mill and Kant.

Richard M. Hare, *The Language of Morals* (New York: Oxford University Press, 1964). A British ordinary language philosopher whose theory is a bit technical but readable. He employs Kant's universalizability principle in a compelling manner.

Gilbert Harman, *The Nature of Morality* (New York: Oxford University Press, 1977). A book on the topic of this chapter by an important American philosopher.

Plato, *Republic*, in *Great Dialogues of Plato*, trans. W. H. D. Rouse (New York: New American Library, 1956). Particularly Book I, where Plato presents the moral debate between Socrates and the Sophists, and Books II, III, IV, and V, where he develops the analogy between "the soul" and "the city."

Allen W. Wood, *Kant's Ethical Thought* (Cambridge: Cambridge University Press, 1999). A readable but detailed and technical attempt to correct errors that the author thinks most interpreters of Kant (including people like me) have made.

Notes

1. Plato, *Republic*, in *Great Dialogues of Plato*, trans. W. H. D. Rouse (New York: New American Library, 1956), p. 137. Unless otherwise stated, all subsequent quotes from the *Republic* in this chapter are from this edition.

2. Bernard Williams, *Ethics and the Limits of Philosophy* (Cambridge, Mass.: Harvard University Press, 1985), p. 27.

3. Thomas Hobbes, *Leviathan: Or the Matter, Forme and Power of a Commonwealth Ecclesiasticall and Civil* (New York: Collier Books, 1962), p. 105.

4. Ibid., pp. 49–50.

5. Epicurus, *Epicurus: The Extant Remains*, trans. C. Bailey (Oxford: Clarendon Press, 1926), p. 87.

6. Ibid., p. 99.

7. Jeremy Bentham, *The Rationale of Reward*, in *The Works of Jeremy Bentham* (Edinburgh: Tait, 1838–1843), vol. II, sec. i, p. 253.

8. John Stuart Mill, *Utilitarianism* (New York: E. P. Dutton, 1951), p. 10.

9. Ibid.

10. Allen W. Wood, *Kant's Ethical Thought* (Cambridge: Cambridge University Press, 1999).

11. Jean-Paul Sartre, *Existentialism and Human Emotions* (New York: Philosophical Library, 1957), pp. 24–28.

8

Different Strokes
for Different Folks
Critiques of Traditional
Ethical Theories

Existentialism

At the end of the previous chapter, we saw that in a certain sense, Jean-Paul Sartre's existentialism challenges the possibility of any moral code or system. Sartre's philosophy makes this challenge despite the fact that at one level, Sartre accepts Kant's moral views, as we see in passages like these:

> I am responsible for myself and for everyone else. I am creating a certain image of man of my own choosing. In choosing myself, I choose man. . . . Certainly, many people believe that when they do something, they themselves are the only ones involved, and when someone says to them "What if everyone acted that way?" they shrug their shoulders and answer, "Everyone doesn't act that way." But really, one should always ask himself, "What would happen if everybody looked at things that way?" There is no escaping this disturbing thought except by a kind of double-dealing. A man who lies and makes excuses for himself by saying "not everybody does that," is someone with an uneasy conscience because the act of lying implies that a universal value is conferred upon the lie.

This reference to the universalizability of acts is the Kantian side of Sartre's moral views. He goes on to say, "Therefore though the content of ethics is variable, a certain form of it is universal. Kant says that freedom desires both itself and the freedom of others. Granted."[1]

In spite of granting the Kantian premise, Sartre has demonstrated very convincingly, in the example of the young man who came to Sartre for advice, that when moral values conflict, no moral formula can resolve the opposition. The young man simply had to invent, that is to say, choose. Sartre has radicalized Kant's view that the source of value is always the human being, and he has prioritized freedom over rationality. If Sartre is right, then reason cannot compel anyone to behave in one way as opposed to another because reason can be an authority only if one *chooses* to authorize reason. Once I decide that reason has value, then reason can force me to behave only in ways for which I can give cogent reasons. But what if rather than valuing reasons, I—like Dostoyevsky's underground man (see Perverse Freedom in Chap-

Reason Tries to Compel Sartre to Do the Right Thing

ter 6)—choose unreason to guide me? Then I do not need to, nor can I, give reasons for my choice. So we see that even though Sartre accepts many of the same facts about

humans that Kant does (that humans are free and autonomous), he draws exactly the opposite conclusion from Kant's. Because we are free and autonomous, we cannot be *naturally* rational. We are rational only by choice. Or, to put it another way, if we are free, then no moral code can be binding on us.

Hume and the Naturalistic Fallacy

Sartre was certainly not the first philosopher to challenge the foundations of morality. Already in the eighteenth century, David Hume had exploded a bombshell whose reverberations are still heard up through our time. This explosive device had the form of a simple five-worded phrase: "No 'is' implies an 'ought'." What Hume meant by this phrase is that no moral claims what-soever could be derived from any merely *factual* claims. Let's clarify this point by choosing a moral principle with which almost everyone would agree: "It is morally wrong to torture innocent children just for the pleasure of doing so." Now, Hume's point is this: If someone challenges this claim and says, "How do you know this principle to be true?" what demonstration can we give him? The utilitarian will say that the act is wrong because it goes against the principle of utility ("the greatest amount of happiness for the greatest number of people"). But what if the utilitarian is asked why we should accept the principle of utility? Bentham answered that we should do so because "Nature has placed mankind under the governance of two sovereign masters, *pain* and *pleasure*. It is for them alone to point out what we ought to do."[2]

But even if Bentham's factual claim is true and we are all motivated by the desire for pleasure, does it follow logically that we *ought* to be? What if most people, or even all people, derived great pleasure from cruelty? Would it follow in some moral sense that people *ought* to be cruel? Of course not. So the utilitarians' claim that we *ought* to adopt the principle of utility because we all *do* desire happiness simply doesn't work, and left unanswered is our question as to why we ought not to torture innocent children.

Faulty Logic

Kant would answer that we ought not to do so because such behavior conflicts with the categorical imperative. But why should we follow that principle? Kant says we must do so because we are rational. But Hume's point is that even if we *are* rational, it does not follow that we *ought* to be. Hence, from his point of view, the question of why we ought not torture children is still unanswered.

In the twentieth century, Hume's moral skepticism influenced the important Cambridge moral philosopher GEORGE EDWARD MOORE (1873–1958), usually called G. E. Moore. Moore pointed out that the concept of good cannot be *defined* in terms of any "natural" quality, such as "pleasure," "happiness," or "survival value." (What Moore called a "natural quality" is more or less the same as Hume's "factual claims," his "is"). In a true definition, such as "a sister is a female sibling," it would be nonsense to question the predicate of the subject—to ask, for example, "Yes, but *is* a sister a female sibling?" Of course she is—that's what "sister" means. (Or try these: "Is a bachelor an unmarried male?" "Is a triangle a three-sided figure?")

Yet when we turn to attempted definitions of the word "good," curious things happen. For example, the hedonist tries to define "good" in terms of pleasure. Yet the question "*Is* pleasure good?" is not nonsense in the way that the question "*Is* a square four-sided?" is nonsense. (For example, what about Hitler's pleasure? Is it necessarily good?) A similar result is obtained when social Darwinists try to define good in terms of survival value. The question "Yes, but *is* survival always good?" is not nonsense. (Being willing to betray one's friends may have survival value in some situations, but that doesn't necessarily make treachery good.) The

The Good as a Nonnatural, Unanalyzable, Simple Quality

same thing is true of religious attempts to define "good" in terms of obedience to God's will. The question "But *is* it always good to obey God?" at least makes sense, even if we don't know the answer. (Think of God's instruction to Abraham to kill his innocent son.) So the result is that all attempts to define "good" in terms of any existing facts whatever result in a fallacy. Moore called it "the naturalistic fallacy." Pointing it out was his way of affirming Hume's dictum "No *is* implies an *ought*." (Moore's own view in his *Principia Ethica* was that the good is some "nonnatural" simple quality that cannot be analyzed but that can be recognized. Hardly any moral philosophers have agreed with Moore's mysterious claim or even been able to make much sense out of it.) So the question remains: if we cannot derive our moral values from any facts in the world, from where can we derive them? This question threatens any attempt to ground morality in objectivity.

Logical Positivism

In Chapter 3, we saw that Hume had influenced a group of twentieth-century philosophers who came to be known as the logical positivists. Their views are no longer fashionable, but in their day, they were tremendously influential, and ghosts of their ideas still abound. They are worth studying for this reason and also, more pertinent to the point of this chapter, because they mounted one of the most powerful attacks on the possibility of moral philosophy to be carried out by any group of philosophers.

In Chapter 3, we saw that many of the positivists accepted the epistemological view inspired by Hume. As we saw, their attack on ethics derived from their theory of meaning, according to which there are only two kinds of genuine propositions: analytic and synthetic propositions. Remember, analytic propositions are true by definition, mere tautologies, telling us nothing about reality, only something about how concepts are related (e.g., "All circles are round"). Synthetic (or empirical) propositions can be confirmed or refuted only by some actual or possible observation. Only these proposi-

The Three Possibilities		
ANALYTIC True by definition "Unicorns have one horn."	SYNTHETIC Established by observation "Pickles are sour."	NONSENSE . . . . . . "Twas brillig." "God loves you."

tions are truly about reality. Any putative proposition that is neither analytic nor synthetic is cognitively empty, or nonsense. A sentence like "Torturing innocent children is immoral" is not analytic; that is, it is not true simply by virtue of the meaning of its words (as is proved by negating the sentence and seeing that the negation, "Torturing innocent children is *not* immoral," is not a self-contradiction in the way that the sentence "A sister is not female" *is* self-contradictory).

On the other hand, neither is our sentence empirical. That is, there

Find the Immoral Part

is no observation, actual or possible, that could confirm or refute the sentence. If we watched a brute torturing a small child, we would feel horror, revulsion, and fury, but there would be nothing we could point at and say, "There it is! *That's the immoral part*" (in the way that we *can* say, "That's the yellow part" or "That's the heavy part"). So what *is* the status of our moral claim, according to the positivists? Because it is cognitively empty, it is merely expressive. A British member of the school of logical positivism, philosopher A. J. Ayer, who as a young man went to Vienna to study positivism, claimed that

Sir Alfred Jules Ayer (1910–1989)

moral language was simply a disguised display of emotion, often coupled with "commands in a misleading grammatical form." So the sentence "Torturing is immoral" really means something like this:

Only the third part of this division could have truth value; therefore, the whole sentence "Torturing is immoral" can be neither true nor false. It expresses what Ayer called "a pseudoconcept."

TORTURING!
DON'T DO IT!
I DON"T LIKE IT!!

Logical positivism inspired many in its day, and we still see its influence here and there (e.g., in B. F. Skinner's conception of science and in W. V. O. Quine's conception of philosophy; Quine is recognized as one of the two or three most important **analytic philosophers** in that tradition), but positivism's rather shocking views about morality need not distress us too much. The consensus today is that we do not have to take logical positivism all that seriously. It offers some good tools for analysis, but it is fairly obvious that its theory of meaning is much too restrictive. Furthermore, it suffers from a deadly internal defect. If every proposition is analytic, synthetic, or nonsense, what is the status of the proposition that asserts that every proposition is analytic, synthetic, or nonsense? It is not analytic because its negation does not lead to a self-contradiction. It is not synthetic because no observation would tend to confirm it or refute it. What status is left for it except that of nonsense according to its own criterion? Perhaps Professor Jon Wheatley was writing an obituary when he said, "Logical positivism is one of the very few philosophical positions which can be easily shown to be dead wrong, and that is its principal claim to fame."[3]

So what is the ultimate impact of these various philosophical assaults on the foundations of morality? Notice that, each in its own way, the Sartrean, Humean, and positivistic critiques are indeed just that—assaults on the *foundations* of morality. Sartre tries to show that the

The Assault on the Foundations of Morality

foundations of morality must be subjective and unstable. Hume and the positivists try to show that morality cannot have its foundation in any true facts about the world. But what if talk about the *foundations* of morality turns out to be misconceived? At the end of Chapter 3, we saw that the attempt to discover the foundations of knowledge might have been completely wrongheaded. It was suggested there that knowledge may prove to be more like a net or a spiderweb than like a house. The same is true in ethics. As the influential British moral philosopher Bernard Williams says:

> . . . the foundationalist enterprise, [that] of resting the structure of knowledge on some favored class of statements, has now generally been displaced in favor of a holistic type of model, in which some beliefs can be questioned, justified, or adjusted while others are kept constant, but there is no process by which they can all be questioned at once, or all justified in terms

of (almost) nothing. In Neurath's famous image we repair the ship while we are on the sea.[4]

According to Williams, the same is true of ethics. "The aim of ethical thought," he says, "is to help us to construct a world that will be our world, one in which we have a social, cultural, and personal life."[5] Now, for *that* activity, no foundation is needed. By virtue of being human, we find ourselves engaged in it willy-nilly. That is why Williams prefers a version of Aristotle's moral question over that of Socrates. Williams takes it that Socrates' ethical question is "How should *one* live?" This theoretical question is abstract in nature. It tends toward foundationalism. Aristotle's question is more concrete. He asks, "How should *we* live?" Socrates' question presupposes some abstract human nature in universal conditions; Aristotle's presupposes a concrete psychological and communal social situation in which *we* actually find ourselves engaged on a daily basis.

But before we can accept this pragmatic solution to the problem of ethics, we must address another objection to morality, an objection that seems to threaten even a pragmatic solution: the problem of cultural relativism.

Cultural Relativism

Here we must talk about another kind of twentieth-century assault on the possibility of ethics, one that has come not from the field of philosophy but from the social sciences. Associated with some important names in anthropology and psychology, cultural relativism denies that there can be any absolute or objective moral values on the grounds that moral values are the products of individual cultures, which differ from one another in such a fashion that the values central to each society differ from one another. In a famous article of 1934, the anthropologist Ruth Benedict wrote:

> Every society, beginning with some slight inclination in one direction or another, carries its preference farther and farther, integrating itself more and more completely upon its chosen basis, and discarding those types of behavior that are uncongenial. Most of these organizations of personality

that seem to us most incontrovertibly abnormal have been used by different civilizations in the very foundations of their institutional life. Conversely the most valued traits of our normal individuals have been looked on in differently organized cultures as aberrant: Normality, in short, within a very wide range, is culturally defined. It is primarily a term for the socially elaborated segment of human behavior in any culture; and abnormality, a term for the segment that

**Anthropologists Attacking
Moral Philosopher**

that particular civilization does not use. The very eyes with which we see the problem are conditioned by the long traditional habits of our own society.

. . . .

We recognize that morality differs in every society and is a convenient term for socially approved habits. Mankind has always preferred to say, "It is morally good," rather than "It is habitual," and the fact of this preference is matter enough for a critical science of ethics. But historically the two phrases are synonymous.

The concept of the normal is properly a variant of the concept of the good. It is that which society has approved. A normal action is one which falls well within the limits of expected behavior for a particular society.

. . . .

Each of these traits, in proportion as it reinforces the chosen behavior patterns of that culture, is for that culture normal. Those individuals to whom it is congenial either congenitally, or as the result of childhood sets, are accorded prestige in that culture and are not visited with the social contempt or disapproval which their traits would call down upon them in a society that was differently organized. On the other hand, those individuals whose characteristics are not congenial to the selected type of human behavior in that community are the deviants, no matter how valued their personality traits may be in a contrasted civilization.[6]

Benedict's views were echoed a generation later by the psychologist B. F. Skinner, who said:

What a given group of people calls good is a fact: it is what members of the group find reinforcing as the result of their genetic endowment and the natural and social contingencies to which they have been exposed. Each culture has its own set of goods, and what is good in one culture may not be good in another. To recognize this is to take the position of "cultural relativism." What is good for the Trobriand Islander is good for the Trobriand Islander, and that is that. Anthropologists have often emphasized relativism as a tolerant alternative to missionary zeal in converting all cultures to a single set of ethical, governmental, religious, or economic values.[7]

The views of Benedict and Skinner resonate with ideas we have all heard about and that to many people (especially to many college students) seem quite correct—namely, that "good" must always mean "good for her" or "good for them" or "good for me," but never just good. What is good for one person or culture is not necessarily good for another, and therefore there can really never be any genuine moral *reasoning*, only "acknowledgment" of others' "good." ("I hear what you're saying.") And the data from the social sciences sometimes do seem to support such a relativism. (It is not "good" for me to worship cows, but it is "good" for Hindus to worship cows because cow manure provides both fertilizer and fuel for Hindu culture.)

It cannot be denied that this kind of relativism is healthy in struggling against puritanical "uptightness" and dangerous ethnocentric arrogance. ("Our values are right, and we'll impose them on you if we have to kill you to do it!") But our relativism runs up against problems when we turn to questions like this: Must we withhold moral judgment about Nazi "brutalities" on the grounds that we are *not* members of a Nazi culture? Exterminating six million people is "good" for Hitler but not for me? This "different strokes for different folks" philosophy seems dangerously hollow here. So let's go back

A Texas Cow Worshipper

and take a closer look at what ethical relativism is saying. Under scrutiny, its thesis becomes less clear. Is the cultural relativist saying, (1) "There are no universally held moral values" or (2) "No value or set of values can justifiably be recommended for all people"? These are very different claims. Let's look at each of them.

No Universally Held Moral Values

Notice that this first claim is an empirical one. In theory at least, it is capable of confirmation or refutation through scientific investigation. Now, there are several things to say about it. If it is meant to be interpreted *individually*, saying that there never has been a moral value accepted by *absolutely everybody*, then, no doubt, the claim is true but not very impressive. (Just because one person—Cronus perhaps—broke the law against eating one's children doesn't mean there is something wrong with the law.) Then what about interpreting the relativist's thesis culturally rather than individually? Certainly not *all* social scientists are in agreement concerning the truth of this version of the claim. For example, the eminent anthropologists Alfred Kroeber and Clyde Kluckhohn argued that certain universal values have been accepted by all cultures: No culture tolerates indiscriminate lying, stealing, or violence within the in-group. The incest taboo is virtually universal. No culture

**Cronus Eating His Children
(After Francisco Goya)**

places value on suffering as an end in itself. Every culture ceremonializes death. "All cultures define as abnormal [those] individuals who are permanently inaccessible to communication or who fail to maintain some degree of control over their impulsive life."[8] Kroeber and Kluckhohn do not deny that

All Cultures Define as Abnormal Those
Individuals Who Are Permanently
Inaccessible to Communication

what *counts* as lying, stealing, or violence might be culturally defined, but they think that these values are universals behind the particulars.

The social psychologist Solomon Asch holds a similar view. He claims that every society despises cowardice and honors bravery. In every society, modesty, courage, and hospitality are encouraged. Even in cultures where acts that are horrible to us are routinely performed, it is often possible to find that the disagreement between their culture and ours is really *more* of a debate about apparently empirical facts than it is a debate over values. Ancient Chinese cultures commonly engaged in infanticide (leaving unwanted infants exposed to die in nature). But Asch claims that in that culture, infants were not considered human until their first year. The ancient Chinese and we may actually be seen to agree on the value of human life but to disagree on the facts concerning what constitutes a human being.

At least *those* kinds of disagreements are not just disagreements of taste and hence are debatable and, in principle, resolvable—though perhaps not easily, as is seen in the amount of passion engendered by the debate over abortion. Again, to a great extent, this debate is not over the value of human life—both parties are probably more or less in agreement over that—but over the facts concerning what constitutes a human being. Still, I don't want to be seen as oversimplifying a complicated issue. The question "What is a human being?" *looks* like a straightforward question that could be answered either with a dictionary-type definition or with some empirical research. But, in fact, the concept "human being" is probably one involving a complex concatenation of facts and values and does not admit of a purely scientific determination. In an odd way, it is probably a socially negotiable concept, and we are in the midst of a rather painful, protracted debate over it right now. Perhaps we always have been. For example, it has not always been clear to all cultures whether to treat women, strangers, and minorities as fully human or whether to treat volcanoes and winds as if they were adversarial entrepreneurs.

So then, if the thesis of cultural relativism is that there are no values held by all

OK, OK. I'll tell you what. For six smokeless years and no lava, I'll offer you a firstborn infant, three oxen, and a dozen pastrami sandwiches.

Cutting a Deal with a Volcano

or by most cultures, that thesis is probably false. What about cultural relativism's second formulation?

No Value or Set of Values Recommendable for All People

The thesis that no value or set of values can justifiably be recommended for all people cannot be the conclusion drawn from a legitimate scientific investigation. Even if, contrary to the implication of the foregoing discussion, it did turn out that no values are universally held, it wouldn't follow from that finding that no value is *worthy* of adoption by all. (This is another version of the is/ought problem.) Even if we found out that all people enjoyed inflicting suffering on others, it wouldn't follow that they *ought* to inflict suffering on

All People Enjoy Inflicting Suffering on Others

others. In *this* sense, anthropology has nothing to offer to moral philosophy. In *this* sense, it doesn't matter what people from other cultures do. We can't deduce what they *ought* to do from their current or past practices. But there *is* a sense in which anthropology is helpful to moral philosophy. We've already pointed out that the study of the values of other cultures can have a salutary humbling effect, cutting into our tendency to assume that the values of *our* culture are somehow "natural," hence superior. But also, if we accept Kroeber's and Kluckhohn's claim that the universals they listed obviously have survival value, that they are "necessary conditions to social life," *and* if we accept as a moral principle the view that "human life should prevail and flourish," then anthropology, sociology, and social psychology can help us think clearly on behalf of our own moral reasoning.

Ethics and Feminism

Is there after all a fundamental flaw in traditional Western ethics—that of being inappropriate for more than half of the human race? That is, is moral philosophy as it is traditionally expounded biased toward androcentrism (male-centeredness)? Does it fail to take into account the experience of women and to take advantage of the moral insights derived from female experience? A good number of **feminist** critics of moral philosophy think these questions are true.

...A really great ethics...

Except it's inappropriate for half the human race!

Certainly there is good reason to believe that women's experience is in some significant ways different from men's experience. Novelists, psychologists, and sociologists have confirmed this suspicion. It is difficult to establish to what extent, if any, these differences can be traced to fundamental distinctions between the brains of females and males as opposed to differences in the way females and males are treated from birth forward. In our culture, for instance, each sex is immediately assigned a color (pink, blue) and toys (dolls, trucks) as well as behavioral models (passive, active).

However, regardless of the extent to which the differences in experience between females and males can be traced to biological or social distinctions, the question still remains, Is it possible that the experience of girls and women can provide insight into moral life that has been ignored by traditional ethical discourse? Furthermore, is it possible that the same "patriarchal" moral discourse not only has ignored women but has also participated in their oppression and perpetuated a bias against them? In some ways, it would seem so.

The Assignment of Toys

Patriarchal Discourse

Let us begin with this question: What differences exist in the experience of women that might be morally significant? An important step toward answering that question was provided by Carol Gilligan in 1982 with the publication of her book *In a Different Voice: Psychological Theory and Women's Development*. One of Gilligan's techniques was to interview children using a set of questions developed by the psychologist Lawrence Kohlberg. When Kohlberg performed the tests in the 1960s, it seemed to him that girls did not prove to have as clear a sense of justice as did boys nor the same deductive capacity for deriving moral conclusions. There has been a whole literature based on the claim that women have a lower developed moral sense than men. The German philosopher, ARTHUR SCHOPENHAUER (1788–1860) wrote:

But... she's a girl!

JUSTICE

> women remain children their whole life long. . . . the fundamental fault of the female character is that it has *no sense of justice*. This is mainly due to the fact . . . that women are defective in the powers of reasoning and deliberation.[9]

According to psychologist OTTO WEININGER (1880–1903), "A woman cannot grasp that one must act from principle; as she has no continuity, she does not experience the necessity for logical support of her mental processes."[10] Probably the most egregious case comes from (no surprise!) Freud, who wrote:

> I cannot evade the notion (though I hesitate to give it expression) that for women the level of what is ethically normal is different from what it is in

"Because He Thought So Highly of the Penis, He Thought Women Did Too"
(Germaine Greer on Otto Weininger)

men. Their superego is never so inexorable, so impersonal, so independent of its emotional origins as we require it to be in men. Character-traits which critics of every epoch have brought up against women—that they show less sense of justice than men, that they are less ready to submit to the great exigencies of life, that they are more often influenced in their judgements by their feelings of affection or hostility—all these would be amply accounted for in the modification of the formation of their superego. . . . We must not allow ourselves to be deflected from such conclusions by the denial of the feminists, who are anxious to force us to regard the two sexes as completely equal in position and worth."[11]

I hesitate to give this thought expression!

Gilligan replicated Kohlberg's interviews and reinterpreted the data. In one interview, she posed the following question to a girl and a boy, both eleven years old: Should "Heinz" steal medicine from a pharmacist in order to save the life of his sick wife if the pharmacist refuses to lower the price so Heinz can afford it? The boy, Jake, is sure that Heinz should do so and is able to produce a principle ("life is worth more than money") and a logical argument applying that principle. Amy, on the other hand, is less sure. She thinks it's wrong for Heinz to steal the drugs but insists also that it is wrong for the pharmacist to withhold them. She refuses to apply the rules of logic to the case—in fact, in a way she refuses the hypothesis. She thinks if we could talk with the pharmacist and make him understand the situation, he would freely donate the drugs.

This theft is noble.

STOP THIEF!!

Jake's Solution

Is Amy's answer an example of retarded moral development? Is Amy incapable of understanding the abstract concept of justice, of applying a principle to the case, and of drawing deductive conclusions from it? Gilligan does not believe that these conclusions are the correct lessons being taught here. She sees the girl's account as concentrating, not on "a contest of rights," but on "a network of relationships on whose continuation they all depend."[12] In short, Amy *does* refuse to apply abstract principles in a mathematical fashion to unrealistic scenarios as a solution to a human problem. She contextualizes and concentrates on the pragmatics of relationships between human beings.

Amy's Solution

A number of feminists (I say a *number* because there is no such thing as *the* feminist position. In fact, a few have disagreed with some of Gilligan's views.[13]) think Amy got it right. They think that Amy is right to reject the typical extreme-case scenarios in which moral philosophy is often argued (e.g., "the case of Sam"). She is right to stress relationships over rules, and she is right to demand more information regarding the context. That is, she is correct to see moral judgments as *emergent*, flowing out from an understanding of a real situation.

Why would women have such different moral experiences? Agnes Heller believes that precisely women's historical confinement to the home and exclusion from the broader world of commerce, industry, travel, and war in Western society has made their lives more similar over the generations and

has given them more close-up insight into real human relations. They have had to learn to create and manage small communities involving real people, people with all their virtues and foibles. Because ethics must ultimately be about human relations, women may indeed have special insights into this sphere.[14]

Does this special insight mean that women are morally superior to men? Not necessarily so. (Though in Victorian England they were thought to be morally superior, and this supposed superiority was both used against them—they would have to be confined to the home to protect their purity—and used to try to liberate them—they should be given the vote in order to influence society morally.) Nevertheless, special insight means that women might be afforded a unique perspective from which to criticize male-dominated ethical theory and to develop their insights systematically into a moral view.

There's not a lot of space to move around up here.

PEDESTAL OF MORAL SUPERIORITY

Victorian Virtue

The feminist criticism of patriarchal ethics has two prongs. First, as philosopher Alison Jaggar says, feminist ethics "seeks to identify and challenge all those ways, overt but more often and more perniciously covert, in which Western ethics has excluded women or rationalized their subordination."[15] Second, it seeks to develop an ethics inspired by, or at least consistent with, the actual moral experience and intuition of women.

Concerning the first point, some feminists have worried that a masculine tendency toward abstract thought may allow *theories* to be distanced from actual human *life*. Conceptions of morality derived from such alienated thought may have "permeated human social life and institutions in a way that leads to a distorted and dangerous sense of human priorities; to a morality, in fact, that may be seen as underlying such things as militarism," feminist philosopher Jean Grimshaw says. Women's lives, Grimshaw asserts, may "provide the space for questioning the sorts of priorities that see

human lives as easily dispensable in the service of some abstract idea or great cause; that see care for others or a life devoted to serving others as relatively unimportant."[16] Furthermore, precisely because women have to a great extent been historically excluded from the commercial and industrial world and from "world-historical events," they ironically may be in the best position to criticize the morality of the capitalist market economy. Such social commentators need not be professional philosophers. Long-dead female novelists like George Eliot (a.k.a. Marian Evans) in her *The Mill on the Floss* (1860) can be very instructive on such topics.

The second point, the development of a feminist ethics, is still undergoing formulation. An interesting suggestion for it comes from Mary Raugust and is based not on an "ivory tower" perspective from a professor's chair at a university but on a workplace perspective. Raugust was director of the Kennedy Aging Project; she sets forth her proposal for a feminist ethics in seven tenets.[17]

First Tenet: The central priority of ethics is not the concept of individual rights but of relationships with other human beings. (Here Raugust seems to be agreeing with Amy's intuitions as opposed to Jake's.)

Second Tenet: The principal goal of ethics is not to respect and maximize autonomy and liberty of individual humans (as in Kantian and Sartrean ethics); rather, it is "the giving and receiving of care appropriate to specific persons and their situations." (The feminist philosopher

Moral Edicts from the Ivory Tower

who has pursued this feature of ethics in detail is Nel Noddings, in *Caring: A Feminine Approach to Ethics and Moral Education*.[18] For her, "caring" involves setting aside one's own concerns in order to put oneself into the experience of another person as far as possible. Such a definition of "caring" does seem to get at the very heart of morality.)

Third Tenet: Interdependence over individualism. (Again, this seems to square with Amy's intuition. Gilligan, by the way, admits that this side of female experience has its dangers for women, some of whom have a problem in establishing a clear sense of their own boundaries, identities, interests, and needs from those of others with whom they interact.)

Fourth Tenet: The "other" with whom one deals morally must be distinctly personified and not an impersonal, faceless

Boundary Problems in *Wuthering Heights*

abstraction. (The object of the critique here seems to be particularly Kantianism, in which the moral subject has no particular characteristics at all, but also utilitarianism, wherein the "greatest happiness" is established formulaically.)

Fifth Tenet: Moral judgments emerge from actual situations and are not derived by applying logical formulas to general principles. (Once again in line with Amy's intuition, and anti-Kantian and antiutilitarian.)

Sixth Tenet: Feminist ethics are "accepting rather than transformative." (To this extent, they agree with the biblical precept "Judge not . . ." but disagree with

Immanuel Kant as a Faceless Abstraction

another biblical precept—the one that graces Chapter 7 as its title—"Thou shalt become perfected." This tenet is another anti-Kantian thrust in that Kant saw ethics as an engagement in self-improvement.)

Seventh Tenet: Feminist ethics will be a morality of *virtues* rather than primarily one of *justice*. (This

Amy Triumphant

tenet entails a rejection of the main thrust of Western ethics in the modern period. It also, in a way, involves a return to a Greek idea of ethics, particularly that of Aristotle, who, though no hero to feminists in terms of his actual attitude toward women, did provide an ethics based on social contextualization where moral behavior was analyzed in terms of propensities to act virtuously [courage, self-control, generosity, amiability, truthfulness, wittiness, friendliness, modesty, and so on]. Aristotle wrote, "the characteristic of [virtue] lies in moderation or observance of a mean relatively to the person concerned."[19] This description seems much closer to Amy's way of approaching the "case of Heinz" than to Jake's.)

Ethics and Deep Ecology

A powerful attack on traditional Western moral philosophies has come out of an intensified version of the environmental movement calling itself **deep ecology.** It challenges the *anthropocentrism* of Western ethics, that is, its human-centeredness. We have seen, for example, that both Kant and Sartre find the source of value exclusively in *human characteristics*: Kant in reason, and Sartre in freedom. Utilitarianism advocates "the greatest amount of happiness for the greatest number of *people*." Now, it is true that utilitarianism can be extended to cover other animals that are capable of sensing pain, and in fact it has been so extended by some writers supporting "animal liberation."[20] But such an extension is not sufficient for the loosely knit conglomeration of activists, writers, poets, and philosophers known as "deep ecologists." Nor are they satisfied with the views of those conservationists who argue that it is in the interest of humans to defend nature. To the deep ecologists, even this view is spawned by

a human arrogance that sees all of nature as created exclusively for human use and consumption and, all too often, for human despoliation. Deep ecologists point out that throughout the long existence of the human race (say a million years) only a minority of humanity has held an anthropocentric view of the universe. Most hunter-gatherer societies had "ecocentric" religious views involving a sacred sense of the earth. This sense survived into the historical period in certain pantheistic religions, and echoes of it are found in the pre-Socratic philosophies we looked at briefly in Chapter 1. In the theories of Thales, Anaximan-

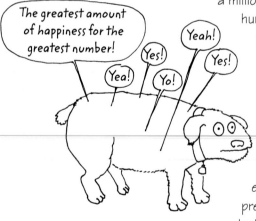

Flea Liberation

der, Pythagoras, Heraclitus, Parmenides, and Democritus, humanity held no special position in reality. Deep ecologists seem to agree with Heidegger that something went wrong in ontological thinking with the advent of the Sophists and Socrates, who abandoned cosmic speculation and introduced the human being as the center of reality and meaning. A similar development took place in the Judeo-Christian tradition when its holy writ intro-

duced the claim that the animal and vegetable world was placed under "man's" dominion for "his" use. (Not every thinker in that tradition has drawn the same anthropocentric conclusions from the Scriptures. The medieval Jewish philosopher, MOSES MAIMONIDES [1135–1204], pointed out that even before God created Adam and Eve, he created nature and saw that it was "good." Also, certain strands of religious mysticism like the medieval cult of divine light seem to be eco-centered. And in seventeenth-century Holland, the Jewish philosopher Baruch Spinoza was a notable exception to the Western anthropocentric tradition. He is revered by a number of the deep ecologists, as we will see.)

The deep ecologists hold a view called "biocentric" or "ecocentric egalitarianism," explained by the Norwegian philosopher Arne Naess (one of the architects

The Fifth Day

Arne Naess

of the movement and the one who named it "deep ecology") with these words:

The earth does not belong to humans. . . . Humans only inhabit the lands, using resources to satisfy vital needs. And if their nonvital needs come in conflict with the vital needs of nonhumans, then humans should defer to the latter.[21]

Naess, along with fellow deep ecologist George Sessions, formulated the principles of the movement while sitting on the desert floor in Death Valley on a camping trip in April of 1984, which they developed into the following eight points:

1. The well-being and flourishing of human and nonhuman life on Earth have value in themselves (synonyms: intrinsic value, inherent worth). These values are independent of the usefulness of the nonhuman world for human purposes.
2. Richness and diversity of life forms contribute to the realization of these values and are also values in themselves.
3. Humans have no right to reduce this richness and diversity except to satisfy vital needs.
4. The flourishing of human life and cultures is compatible with a substantially smaller human population. The flourishing of nonhuman life *requires* a smaller human population.
5. Present human interference with the nonhuman world is excessive, and the situation is rapidly worsening.
6. Policies must therefore be changed. These policies affect basic economic, technological, and ideological structures. The resulting state of affairs will be deeply different from the present.
7. The ideological change will be mainly that of appreciating life quality (dwelling in situations of inherent value) rather than adhering to an increasingly higher standard of living. There will be a profound awareness of the difference between bigness and greatness.
8. Those who subscribe to the foregoing points have an obligation directly or indirectly to try to implement the necessary changes.[22]

Death Valley, 1984

As we see, the first of the eight principles holds that life in all its forms has intrinsic value, as opposed to mere instrumental value. (We can say that X has instrumental value if it leads to value Y. Remember Plato's example: medicine has instrumental value because it leads to good health, and health has intrinsic value.) Now, we might want to ask Naess how he *knows* that all life forms have value in themselves. Why should we believe this assertion, which, if true, puts us under a certain kind of moral obligation to respect all life forms? (And, if we are going to abandon Kantian, Sartrean, and utilitarian anthropocentrism, why stop with *life* forms? Edward Abbey, a radical wilderness defender who has actually influenced both deep ecology and the related activist movement Earth First! once said:

Only rock is real.

—a kind of Platonism in reverse.)

Naess, as a professional philosopher, is well aware of the "naturalistic fallacy" and the need to avoid it. Yet he claims that (living) nature *is good* in and of itself. How does he then avoid the illegitimate logical move from "is" to "ought"? Naess has an answer that we will develop in several stages. First, he rejects the fact/value distinction as an arbitrary philosophical conceit. When we look at certain life forms (and ecological systems of life forms) with the correct form of wonder—the very wonder with which Western philosophy began among the ancient Greeks and one that continues to be found in many strands of nature poetry—we discover a certain *intuition* in us that every living being has the same right to exist and to flourish that we humans have. In this intuition are both rational and extrarational factors—perhaps poetic or even spiritual factors. This intuition seems capable

Animal Rights

of provoking what Freud once referred to as an "oceanic" experience—a feeling of connectedness with the whole of reality—that might be the basis of certain kinds of mysticism. It gives us a new sense of self wherein we realize that we are not simply enclosed within our epidermis (the way potatoes might be held in a sack) but that our skin is a sensuous surface connecting us with the rest of the world, a world that in fact is now realized to be a part of us—part of the self.

Next, given this new broader definition of the self, Naess is satisfied to return to the Aristotelian moral maxim of *self-realization* as the highest goal. "Maximizing self-realization" will then be the moral demand of deep ecology—but now we understand that maxim to mean that we are personally committed to realizing our own undeveloped potentialities and that this realization in turn commits us to letting other life forms realize theirs. (Naess is of course aware of the possible conceptual and factual conflicts that may arise. A good deal of the technical literature of deep ecology is directed toward the practicalities of resolving "disputes" among the conflicting vital needs of different species and ecological spheres.)

Self-Realization

Despite this carefully thought out moral defense, Naess says that he prefers to base deep ecology on ontology rather than on ethics. Morality in the West often seems to demand self-sacrifice, perhaps partly due to the legacy of Christianity and Kant. As we see, Naess wants to emphasize not self-sacrifice but rather self-development once the correct understanding of the self has been grasped. (It is true that for Naess this self-realization will entail an obligation to work for a reduced worldwide human population [point 4 of the eight points] and to oppose individual and national demands for more growth and consumption and higher "standards of living" [point 7]. Therefore, according to the *old conception* of selfhood, this philosophy would involve self-sacrifice.) Apparently, deep ecologists can turn to certain traditional Asian philosophies for inspiration here. Deep ecologists Fritjof Capra and Gary Snyder are influenced by Buddhism, for instance. But Naess and Sessions seem to turn mostly to Spinoza for theirs.

A quick glance at *Ethics*, the main work of BARUCH SPINOZA (1634–1677), might reveal no obvious reason why radical late-twentieth-century ecologists should find inspiration in him. His format is that of Euclid's books on geometry, with definitions, axioms, propositions, corollaries, and con- clusions, each ending in a "Q.E.D." (*quod erat demonstrandum* = "which was to be demonstrated"). His vocabulary is that of Cartesian metaphysics (substances, essences, mind, body, attributes, modes), and his passion is from the medieval phi- losopher Maimonides, who advocated an

Baruch Spinoza (1634–1677)

"intellectual love of God." Where in all this do we find a deep ecology?

We can answer this question by examining an error that Spinoza claims to detect in Descartes's main idea—that of *substance*.

Descartes had said, "By substance we can conceive nothing else than a thing which exists in such a way as to stand in need of nothing beyond itself." Then Descartes had gone on to say, "And in truth, there can be con- ceived but one substance which is absolutely independent, and that is God," which he called "infinite substance." Despite this admission that by definition there could exist only *one* kind of being that was absolutely inde- pendent, Descartes (in a contradictory manner, according to Spinoza) proceeded to distinguish between "infinite substance" and "finite sub- stances"—the latter called corporeal substance (body) and mental sub- stance (mind). This radical dualism led Descartes to his notorious mind- body problem and his universally scorned pineal gland solution.

Spinoza avoided this embarrassment by accepting Descartes's defini- tion of substance (as that which is absolutely independent) and taking seri- ously the inference that there could be only *one* such substance. (If there were two, they would limit each other's independence.) Furthermore, because finiteness would constitute a limitation on God's absolute independence, Spinoza defined God as having infinite attributes. So once again one arrives at the conclusion that there can be but one substance because any substance other than God would have to possess attributes that have already been defined as belonging to God.

Let's look at a schematized comparison of the systems of Descartes and Spinoza:

There ain't room enough in this cosmos for both of us!

FIRST SUBSTANCE

2nd SUBSTANCE

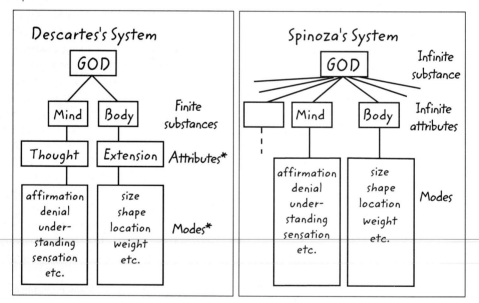

Descartes's System

GOD

Mind · Body — Finite substances

Thought · Extension — Attributes*

affirmation / denial / understanding / sensation / etc.

size / shape / location / weight / etc. — Modes*

Spinoza's System

GOD — Infinite substance

[ ] · Mind · Body — Infinite attributes

affirmation / denial / understanding / sensation / etc.

size / shape / location / weight / etc. — Modes

*An *attribute,* for Descartes, is a characteristic that is the *essence* of a substance (i.e., that which is essential to it). For Spinoza, an attribute is a characteristic that to the human intellect *seems* to be an essence. A **mode** is a specific modification of an attribute (i.e., a characteristic of a characteristic).

Now, you still might be wondering what this discussion has to do with ecology. In fact, to derive deep ecology from Spinoza, its architects had to use Spinoza's principles against some of his own conclusions, because Spinoza personally believed that the human exploitation of the animal world was philosophically justifiable. What principles are these? That secret becomes revealed when we discover that Spinoza equates "infinite substance" not only with God but also with *nature*.

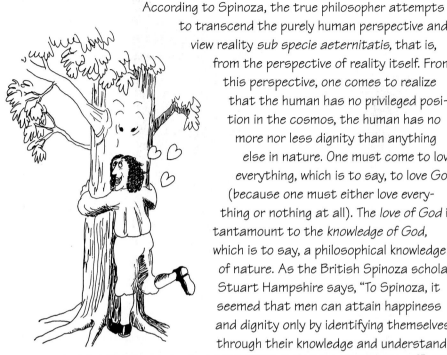

According to Spinoza, the true philosopher attempts to transcend the purely human perspective and view reality *sub specie aeternitatis*, that is, from the perspective of reality itself. From this perspective, one comes to realize that the human has no privileged position in the cosmos, the human has no more nor less dignity than anything else in nature. One must come to love everything, which is to say, to love God (because one must either love everything or nothing at all). The *love of God* is tantamount to the *knowledge of God*, which is to say, a philosophical knowledge of nature. As the British Spinoza scholar Stuart Hampshire says, "To Spinoza, it seemed that men can attain happiness and dignity only by identifying themselves, through their knowledge and understanding, with the whole order of nature."[23]

For Spinoza, it is not easy to achieve this wisdom. He says, "But all

The Unrequited Love of Nature

things excellent are as difficult as they are rare."[24] Yet once one has that wisdom—an understanding of the whole order and of one's connectedness with it—one achieves a state of blessedness and joy. In one of the most marvelous lines in the history of Western philosophy, Spinoza says, "There cannot be too much joy: it is always good;

Can There Be Too Much Joy?

but melancholy is always bad."[25] It is this joy that Naess wishes to tap, and it is this promise, rather than the demand for self-sacrifice, that motivates the ethics of the deep ecology movement.

Conclusion

My own conclusions concerning the topic of moral philosophy are cautiously skeptical. We cannot know what "the Good" is, not for Plato's reasons (that too much ignorance and too many obstacles exist), but because there is no such thing as "the Good"—in about the same sense as there is no such thing as "the Real," according to John Austin. Concerning the question "What is the good life?" we can perhaps be more positive but only if we make some utilitarian-type assumptions about human desires and goals. If we do (and I see no reason not to), then I think that both Aristotle and the utilitarians can be very instructive for us. It should be possible to create a general theory of what is most likely to contribute to a life of happiness—a theory showing in such a life the approximate role of the pursuit of pleasure, the development of potentialities, creative expression, commitment to other persons (including family, friends, and lovers), commitment to causes and a professional life, acceptance of social responsibilities and personal obligations, respect for nature as well as the "virtues" (courage, honesty, temperance, etc.) in one's life.

But it should be understood that though such a theory can be normative (i.e., can guide us in our decision making and in forming our habits), it cannot make anyone either good or happy. Socrates was wrong to think that if one knew the good, one would necessarily become good. Unfortunately, it is possible to know what one ought to do (to know what one's obligations are), to know what would be a good thing or the right thing to do, yet to do the opposite. A moral theory can be part of an argument meant to motivate a certain kind of thinking and acting, but philosophy by itself cannot create right action. (In my view, Plato and Socrates were wrong about that, too.) If one's only reason for behaving in a certain way comes from a philosophical theory, one will probably not find oneself behaving in the desired way very often. And even if one is already motivated by extraphilosophical reasons to engage in a moral form of life, a moral theory can be a guide but

Moral Theory Cannot Make You Good

not a final source of judgment. Sartre is right to say that a theory never makes moral judgments, that only a human being does. He has also shown us that in real life, moral problems are often caused by "conflicts of ideals" (the name of an excellent book on this topic written by Luther Binkley) and not by questions like "Should I be moral?" or "Why should I be moral?"[26] No ethical theory will be able to solve these real conflicts, and we should not expect one to do so.

The moral skeptics (Hume, the logical positivists, the cultural relativists, the existentialists) were right to say that it is impossible to discover the *foundations* of morality, and those philosophers who claimed to do so (Plato, the hedonists, the utilitarians, Kant) were, in my view, wrong to think that they had succeeded. But this admission is not so disastrous after all. It is true that a house without foundations would be in a sorry state, but morality is not a house. Just as many philosophers today have concluded that foundationalism is wrong in epistemology (see Conclusion, Chapter 3), so it is beginning to look as though it is wrong in moral philosophy. As Bernard Williams said, the role of philosophy in this region is not to discover the foundations of morality but "to help us construct a world that will be our world, one in which we have a social, cultural, and personal life." In this quest, I believe (following the legal philosopher Christopher Stone) that a kind of moral pluralism is required.[27] We should not feel that this quest must be guided by only *one* principle (e.g., a hedonistic one, a utilitarian one, or a Kantian one). Rather, we should develop some system of "moral mapping." A Kantian principle of universalizability can be very useful vis-à-vis our relations to other humans yet be fairly useless, and even destructive, vis-à-vis the natural world. A kind of Spinozistic "deep ecology" principle may be needed to reveal the intrinsic value of the natural world, but that same principle might not be as informative concerning my relations to other people as would be the views set forth by the feminist moralists. The decision as to when one moral map should be abandoned and another made to "kick in" would not itself be purely the function of a philosophical theory, though philosophical speculation can guide such a decision. So here, as elsewhere, if we do not expect *too* much of philosophy, she can be an excellent companion.

Topics for Consideration

1. In what way does Sartre agree with Kant, and in what way does he disagree with him?
2. Explain why Hume would have more trouble justifying the claim "Killing people is wrong" than the claim "Murdering people is wrong."
3. How would you argue against a logical positivist who told you that the sentence "Torturing children is immoral" was cognitively empty (i.e., nonsense)?
4. The Nazis claimed to believe that exterminating certain peoples was morally justifiable. From the perspective of a cultural relativist, would it be immoral to invade Nazi Germany to prevent that extermination?
5. What feminist objections do you find to the moral philosophies of Kant and the utilitarians?
6. Combining the ideas of Baruch Spinoza and Arne Naess, explain the deep ecologists' conception of selfhood, and contrast this with the traditional view.

Suggestions for Further Reading: Paperback Editions

Simone de Beauvoir, *The Ethics of Ambiguity*, trans. Bernard Frechtman (New York: Citadel Press, 1970). A careful analysis of existentialistic ethics by one of its best practitioners.

Luther Binkley, *Conflict of Ideals: Changing Values in Western Society* (New York: D. Van Nostrand, 1969). An excellent overview on the moral implications in the writings of Marx, Freud, Jung, Fromm, Sartre, and the ordinary language philosophers, among others.

Jean Grimshaw, *Philosophy and Feminist Thinking* (Minneapolis, University of Minnesota Press, 1991). Well written and forceful.

Alasdair MacIntyre, *After Virtue: A Study in Moral Theory* (Notre Dame, Ind.: University of Notre Dame Press, 1981). The best contemporary presentation available of an ethics based on virtue by one of America's ablest philosophers.

Jean-Paul Sartre, *Existentialism and Human Emotions*, trans. Hazel E. Barnes and Bernard Frechtman (New York: Philosophical Library, 1957). A short, readable account of Sartre's views on morality in about 1946.

George Sessions, ed., *Deep Ecology for the Twenty-First Century* (Boston: Shambhala Publications, 1995). The best access to the works of the deep ecologists.

Bernard Williams, *Ethics and the Limits of Philosophy* (Cambridge, Mass.: Harvard University Press, 1985). A beautifully presented argument against foundationalism in ethics by an important contemporary British philosopher.

Notes

1. Jean-Paul Sartre, *Existentialism and Human Emotions* (New York: Philosophical Library, 1957), pp. 18–19, 47.

2. Jeremy Bentham, *An Introduction to the Principles of Morals and Legislation* (Darien, Conn.: Hafner, 1970), p. 1.

3. Jon Wheatley, *Prolegomena to Philosophy* (Belmont, Calif.: Wadsworth, 1970), p. 103.

4. Bernard Williams, *Ethics and the Limits of Philosophy* (Cambridge, Mass.: Harvard University Press, 1985), p. 113.

5. Ibid., p. 111.

6. Ruth Benedict, "Anthropology and the Abnormal," *Journal of General Psychology*, Vol. 10 (1934), pp. 72–74.

7. B. F. Skinner, *Beyond Freedom and Dignity* (New York: Bantam Books, 1972), p. 122.

8. Alfred Louis Kroeber and Clyde Kluckhohn, "Values and Relativity," in *Culture, a Critical Review of Concepts and Definitions*, Papers of the Peabody Museum, Harvard University, Vol. 47, No. 1 (1952), pp. 174–179.

9. Arthur Schopenhauer, "On Women," in *Self and World: Readings in Philosophy*, ed. James A. Ogilvy (New York: Harcourt, Brace, Jovanovich, 1973), pp. 395–396.

10. Otto Weininger, *Sex and Character* (London: W. Heinemann, 1906), p. 149.

11. Sigmund Freud, "Some Psychic Consequences of the Anatomical Distinction between the Sexes," *The Complete Psychological Works of Sigmund Freud*, Vol. XIX, trans. James Strachey (London: Hogarth Press, 1968), pp. 257–258.

12. Carol Gilligan, *In a Different Voice: Psychological Theory and Women's Development* (Cambridge, Mass.: Harvard University Press, 1982), p. 30.

13. See Judy Auerbach, Linda Blum, Vicki Smith, and Christine Williams, "Commentary on Gilligan's *In a Different Voice*," in *Feminist Studies* 11, No. 1 (Spring 1985).

14. Agnes Heller, "The Emotional Division of Labour between the Sexes," *Social Praxis*, 7 (3/4), 1980.

15. Alison M. Jaggar, "Feminist Ethics: Some Issues for the Nineties," *Journal of Social Philosophy*, XX: 1–2 (Spring/Fall 1989), pp. 91–107.

16. Jean Grimshaw, *Philosophy and Feminist Thinking* (Minneapolis: University of Minnesota Press, 1986), pp. 194, 196.

17. Mary C. Raugust, "Feminist Ethics and Workplace Values," in Robert Paul Wolff, *About Philosophy*, 6th ed. (Englewood Cliffs, N.J.: Prentice-Hall, 1996), pp. 78–82.

18. Nel Noddings, *Caring: A Feminine Approach To Ethics and Moral Education* (Berkeley: University of California Press, 1984).

19. Christopher Biffle, *A Guided Tour of Selections from Aristotle's "Nicomachean Ethics"* (Mountain View, Calif.: Mayfield, 1991), p. 46.

20. See Peter Singer, *Animal Liberation* (New York: Random House, 1990).

21. Arne Naess, "The Deep Ecological Movement: Some Philosophical Aspects," in *Deep Ecology for the Twenty-First Century*, ed. George Sessions (Boston: Shambhala Publications, 1995), p. 74.

22. Ibid., p. 68.

23. Stuart Hampshire, *Spinoza* (London: Faber and Faber, 1951), p. 61.

24. Baruch Spinoza, *Ethics*, part V, prop. XLII. In *The Rationalists: Descartes, Spinoza, Leibniz*, trans. R. H. M. Elwes (New York: Doubleday Anchor, 1974), p. 406.

25. Ibid., part IV, prop. XLII. (Following Hampshire's translation, I have rendered *hilaritas* as "joy" rather than as "mirth.")

26. Luther Binkley, *Conflict of Ideals: Changing Values in Western Society* (New York: D. Van Nostrand, 1969).

27. Christopher D. Stone, *Earth and Other Ethics: The Case for Moral Pluralism* (New York: Harper & Row, 1987).

9

Let Them Eat Cake
Political and Social Philosophy

The distinction between political and social philosophy is fairly arbitrary, one that some philosophers refuse to draw at all. My approach in this chapter is that the key issue in political philosophy is the legitimacy of government and that of social philosophy is the problem of justice—two topics that clearly overlap each other. Political philosophy concerns itself with the proper organization of human beings into groups governed by law or by instinct. It asks questions about legitimate and illegitimate political power: Why are members of political collectives (nations, states, townships, etc.) bound to submit to the laws of these collectives? What legitimately holds the collectives together: blood? land? birth? consent? contract? If consent or contract, must such agreements be formal, or may they be informal? Social philosophy, as I use the term here, already presupposes a state of legitimate authority and asks what role that authority has in the distribution of goods and services to the various citizens of the collective. To what extent may the state determine fair apportionment, and to what extent may it not? What principles are in play to justify these determinations?

Political Philosophy

In a famous passage, Jean-Jacques Rousseau once wrote, "Man is born free; and everywhere he is in chains." This idea is an appropriate one with which to begin a discussion of political philosophy. In a significant sense we, like the beasts of the field and the birds of the sky, are "born free." It was once believed that some people were born to be slaves to others or to be their natural servants,

Everywhere We Are in Chains

RULES

I. CLOTHING
  A. YOU MUST WEAR CLOTHES ON ALL SOCIAL OCCASIONS.
  B. SUCH CLOTHING MUST COVER ALL PRIVATE PARTS (AS DEFINED BELOW)
  C. CLOTHING MUST BE SUCH AS TO AVOID PROVOKING SHOCK OR OUTRAGE.

II. NOISE
  A. NOISE MAY BE MADE, BUT ONLY UNDER CERTAIN CONDITIONS
    1. IT IS SENSIBLE NOISE
    2. IT DOES NOT ANNOY GREAT NUMBERS OF PEOPLE.
    3. IT IS APPROPRIATE NOISE.

III. SNEEZING

but in our culture, we no longer believe that. We are not born with any natural masters (though it is possible, as we saw in Chapter 5, that we are born with a super-natural master—but even most theories that argue for a super-natural lord also hold that he created us as free beings). Yet, Rousseau says, everywhere we are in chains. Well, that view is surely a bit exaggerated, but look at it this way. In civilized society, rules govern almost every aspect of our behavior—rules tell us what we have to wear, how we must behave with other peo-ple, where we can and cannot go, how fast we must do it, and in what cir-cumstances it is all right to say certain things but not others. Further-more, all these rules are enforced by an implied threat of immediate violence and eventual loss of property, freedom, and in some cases, even life. Just breaking a fairly simple rule, such as that against jaywalking—if you persist in breaking the rule numerous times in sequence contrary to the advice of a passing "peace officer"—can produce billy clubs, body searches, and handcuffs. So in a sense, Rousseau is right. We perform all our acts looking up the barrel of a gun. This point raises one of the key questions in political philosophy—*Why should we put up with it?* This is just a rhetorical way of posing some of the big questions in this area, such as these:

- Are we naturally political, or is the politi-cal body a mere artifice? (If the latter, is it a necessary one, or could we do without it?)
- Is there a real distinction between legitimate and illegitimate au-thority? if so, how can we draw that distinction?
- Is revolution ever justified when political legitimacy is challenged, and if so, under what conditions?

Performing Our Acts Looking Up the Barrel of a Gun

Plato

We begin once more with Plato. We started with him in our discussions of epistemology, ontology, and morality; we saw his influence in philosophy of religion; we will begin with him again in Chapter 10 on art. This is because, for better or for worse, Plato determined the course of Western philosophy. In some respects it is true, as A. N. Whitehead said, that the history of Western philosophy is a series of footnotes to Plato. Consciously or unconsciously, philosophers seem to have spent an inordinate amount of time either trying to achieve Plato's ideals or trying to escape from them. But precisely because so much has already been said here about Plato, we will not have to deal with him extensively now. Instead, I will give a cursory sketch of his political views, using them to set the stage for later developments in political philosophy.

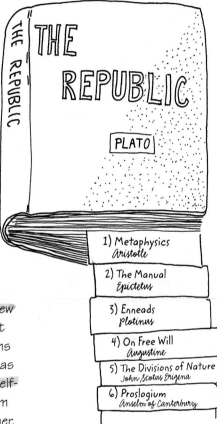

The History of Philosophy as a Series of Footnotes to Plato

Plato shared the typical Greek view that we are naturally social beings. But the "naturalness" of our sociality stems from a natural weakness on our parts as individuals. As individuals, we are not self-sufficient. As we saw in Chapter 6, from our necessary dependence on each other, Plato deduces a kind of natural division of labor along class lines, with skilled laborers and artisans forming one class, a military police caste forming another, and philosophers forming a third, the ruling class, which is created by promoting older members of the military caste. The lower class is incapable of philosophy (though there is no clear explanation in the *Republic* why some people are capable of it and others are not—it seems that these abilities and disabilities must be congenital). He suggests that those unfit from birth or habit for the rule of reason must be forced or tricked into submitting to it. The work and productivity of the laboring class is needed by society, and these workers must be rewarded for their output. Hence, they are allowed to have families, are paid salaries, and are allowed to wear gold and silver decorations. The military caste is capable of philosophy, so its members are able to understand that their virtues of courage and determination are their own rewards. In a remarkable passage, Plato has Socrates describe to Glaucon the conditions in which the two upper classes will live:

Guppies Are Self-Sufficient at Birth. Humans Are Not.

> Then besides this education any sensible man would say that we must provide their lodgings and their other property such as will not prevent them from being themselves as good guardians as they can be, and such as will not excite them to do mischief among the other citizens. . . . First of all, no one must have any private property whatsoever, except what is absolutely necessary. Secondly, no one must have any lodging or storehouse at all which is not open to all comers. Then their provisions must be so much as is needed by athletes of war, temperate and brave men, and there must be fixed allowances for them to be supplied by the other citizens as wages for their guardianship, so much that there shall be plenty for the year but nothing over at the end. They must live in common, attending in messes as if they were in the field. As to gold and silver, we must tell them that they have these from the gods as a divine gift in their souls, and they want in addition no human silver or gold; they must not pollute this treasure by mixing it with a treasure of mortal gold, because many wicked things have been done about the common coinage, but theirs is undefiled. They alone of all in the city dare not have any dealings with gold and silver, or even touch them, or come under the same roof with them, or hang them upon their limbs, or drink from silver or gold. In this way . . . whenever they get land of their own and houses and money, they will be householders and farmers instead of guardians, masters and enemies of the rest of the citizens instead of allies; so hating and hated, plotting and

I've been _very_ courageous!

Congratulations.

You mean, ...that's it? No medals? No glory?

Virtue Is Its Own Reward

plotted against, they will spend all their lives fearing enemies within much more than without, running a course very near to destruction, they and the city together. For all these reasons," I said, "let us agree on this manner of providing our guardians with lodging and all the rest, and let us lay it down by law. What do you say?"

"I agree wholly with you," said Glaucon.[1]

Furthermore, we are told that for the "guardians" (the military and ruling castes), there will be no families as such: "no one must have a private wife of his own, and the children must be common, too, and the parents shall not know the child nor the child its parent" (p. 255). So sexual relations will be by lottery—though there is a hint that the lottery is rigged and that the rulers know who is sleeping with whom. Hence, the upper classes will produce children according to **eugenic** principles.

Plato prescribes a kind of absolute communism but only for the upper classes. This system will protect them from the greed that permeates the lower, more ignorant class; and as we saw, greed is allowed to motivate the workers and the artisans but is always contained and con-

LOVE LOTTERY
Step up and try your luck

And I say the lottery is rigged!

trolled by the philosopher rulers and their military allies. Like Karl Marx some 2,250 years later, Plato saw society as natural but capable of being undermined by greed if not structured in such a way as to contain it. (The difference between Plato and Marx is also striking, of course. For the latter, the destiny of the human race is associated with the **communism** of the working class; for Plato, that class is so benighted that it [and only it] is incapable of communism.)

In the *Republic*, a character named Adeimantus points out that the ideal city Socrates is describing may, through its totalitarian practices, be immune to the dangers of greed, but it can still be corrupted by envy. The lower class will envy the upper classes because of their power and intelligence, and the upper classes will envy the lower class because life at that level just seems more fun.

In order to answer this objection, Plato has Socrates make a very curious suggestion, one that plagues political science to our day. (Indeed, Socrates admits that he is quite embarrassed to have to make the suggestion.) The suggestion is that all members of the City—including the rulers—be told a lie about why they must accept the

Greed and Envy: Two Forces That Can Undermine the Republic

order of things. Plato calls it a "noble lie," and it is introduced in the *Republic* when, with some trepidation, Socrates says:

"Here goes, then, although I don't know how I shall dare, or what words to use. Well, I will try first to convince the rulers themselves and the soldiers, then the rest of the city; and this is the story. The training and education we were giving them was all a dream, and they only imagined all this was happening to them and around them; but in truth they were being moulded and trained down inside the earth, where they and their arms and all their trappings were being fashioned. When they were completely made, the earth their mother delivered them from her womb; and now they must take thought for the land in which they live, as for their mother and nurse, must plan for her and protect her, if anyone attacks her, and they must think of the other citizens as brothers also born from the earth."

Socrates Trying to Get People to Believe the Noble Lie

"I am not surprised," [Glaucon] said, "that you were shy of telling that lie!"

"There was good reason for it," I said, "but never mind, listen to the rest of the fable. 'So you are all brothers in the city,' we shall tell them in our fable, 'but while God moulded you, he mingled gold in the generation of some, and those are the ones fit to rule, who are therefore the most precious; he mingled silver in the assistants; and iron and brass in farmers and the other craftsmen. Then because of being all akin you would beget your likes for the most part, but sometimes a silver child may be born from a golden or a golden from a silvern, and so with all the rest breeding amongst each other. The rulers are commanded by God first and foremost that they be good guardians of no person so much as of their own children, and to watch nothing else so carefully as which of these things is mingled in their souls. If any child of theirs has a touch of brass or iron, they will not be merciful to him on any account, but they will give him the value proper to his nature, and push him away among the craftsmen or the farmers; if again one of them has the gold or silver in his nature, they will honour him and lift him among the guardians or the assistants, since there is an oracle that the city will be destroyed when the brass or the iron shall guard it.' Now have you any device to make them believe this fable?" (pp. 214–215)

This passage is very curious and even quite discouraging. It is curious because, as has been mentioned, part of the job of the *Republic* was to destroy the authority of myth in the Greek world and to replace it with the authority of reason (i.e., philosophy), yet here Plato is required to create a new myth to keep the City cohesive. And it is discouraging because Plato is admitting that reason itself is not strong enough a force to bind the City together. It is especially striking that even the rulers must be lied to, despite the fact that humans are supposed to be naturally social. Plato raises a specter that has haunted some thinkers even in our century: the idea that perhaps a society can remain vibrant and vital only if it has a myth about itself that it can tell itself. And unfortunately, these myths are usually nationalistic and ethnocentric, hence often aggressive, arrogant,

Each Culture Must Have Its Own Myth

xenophobic, racist, and imperialistic. The great twentieth-century sociologist Émile Durkheim thought that when a society lost the capacity to tell itself such a myth, **anomie** (a sense of loss of meaning and direction) set in. Anomie leads to both cultural and individual suicide, according to Durkheim.

Anomie

Thomas Hobbes

In the modern period, a number of important philosophers addressed "the big questions" of political philosophy. Thomas Hobbes's book, *Leviathan* (1651), had as one of its main goals the resolution of the problem of politics, and we shall turn to it now.

It will be recalled from Chapter 7 that Hobbes had a very distinctive view of human motivation, a view called "psychological egoism," according to which all human actions are motivated by self-interest. Hobbes's political views presuppose the truth of psychological egoism, and even though that theory was rather soundly criticized in our earlier discussion as an unsuccessful account of individual human actions, it must be said that it is probably more acceptable as a political model, or perhaps a political metaphor. When we think not of individuals but of foreign policies of various nations, it is difficult to believe that they are *not* motivated by what their framers conceive as the interest of the nation; or when we think of negotiations between labor and management groups, it is hard to imagine them as motivated by pure altruism.

Altruistic Labor Negotiations

So perhaps Hobbes's psychological egoism is a little less offensive here than in a discussion of morality, though here, too, its harshness may taint Hobbes's political views. Like the authors of the American Declaration of Independence, Hobbes begins his essay with the assumption that all people are equal. But his reasons for this assumption are very different from those of the Founding Fathers, who believed that our equality was a kind of moral state into which we were all created by our maker. Hobbes asserted the thesis of equality as a purely physical fact. Even the strongest or smartest among us is not so strong or so smart that two or three weaker, dumber ones could not overcome him or her. One may have some slight advantage over another but not enough to make a difference in the long run. We humans are, after all, more or less the same.

Now, given the fact that human nature is selfish, power-mongering, and equally distributed, Hobbes tries to imagine what human beings would be like in a "state of nature," that is, in a condition prior to any civil state, any rule by law. Concerning such a condition, Hobbes says:

> From this equality of ability, ariseth equality of hope in the attaining of our ends. And therefore if any two men desire the same thing, which nevertheless they cannot both enjoy, they become enemies; and in the way to their end, which is principally their own conservation, and sometimes their delectation only, endeavor to destroy, or subdue one another.
>
> . . . .
>
> Whatsoever therefore is consequent to a time of war, where every man is enemy to every man; the same is consequent to the time, wherein men live without other security, than what their own strength, and their own invention shall furnish them withal. In such condition, there is no place for industry; because the fruit thereof is uncertain: and consequently no culture of the earth; no navigation, nor use of the commodities that may be imported by sea; no commodious building; no instruments of moving, and removing, such things as require much force; no knowledge of the face of the earth; no account of time; no arts; no letters; no society; and which is worst of all, continual fear and danger of violent death; and the life of man, solitary, poor, nasty, brutish, and short.[2]

Hobbes's Five Dwarfs Plus Two

To this bleak and depressing picture, Hobbes now adds:

> To this war of every man, against every man, this also is consequent; that nothing can be unjust. The notions of right and wrong, justice and injustice have there no place. Where there is no common power, there is no law: where no law, no injustice. Force, and fraud, are in war the two cardinal virtues. Justice, and injustice are none of the faculties neither of the body, nor mind. If they were, they might be in a man that were alone in the world, as well as his

senses, and passions. They are qualities, that relate to men in society, not in solitude. It is consequent also to the same condition, that there be no pro-priety, no dominion, no *mine,* and *thine* distinct; but only that to be every man's, that he can get; and for so long, as he can keep it. And thus much for the ill condition, which man by mere nature is actually placed in; though with a possibility to come out of it, consisting partly in the passions, partly in his reason. (pp. 101–102)

So Hobbes's view is this: concepts like right and wrong, justice and injustice, and "mine and thine" (property) are concepts generated by *law,* hence dependent on law. In the absence of law, these concepts cannot be meaningful. Furthermore, the concept of law is itself dependent upon *power.* A law with no power behind it is not authoritative because it cannot be enforced. This view is called **legal positivism,** and according to it, justice is whatever legality *calls* just, and what is legal has been estab-lished as legal by the powers that be and for just as long as they are able to

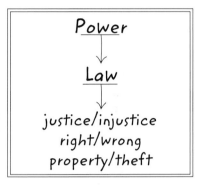

enforce the law. According to this tradition (pretty much the tradition of Thrasymachus and Machiavelli), talk about "unjust laws" simply doesn't make much sense. (In this tradition, calling a law *morally* unjust doesn't carry any weight because the "moral sphere" is just a fantasy, the mental projection of an ideal legal system where the power of the rulers is replaced by the power of an imagined God.)

Notice at the end of the previous anxiously pessimistic passage there was one glimmer of hope. Hobbes said, "And thus much for the ill con-dition, which man by mere nature is actually placed

Legal Positivism

in; though with a possibility to come out of it, consisting partly in the passions, partly in his reason."

The *passionate* part of our self desperately desires to survive. (How else could we acquire power and enjoy pleasure?) And there is a *natural right* to attempt to do so. Hobbes writes:

> The RIGHT OF NATURE . . . is the liberty each man hath, to use his own power, as he will himself, for the preservation of his own nature; that is to say, of his own life; and consequently, of doing anything, which in his own judgment, and reason, he shall conceive to be the aptest means thereunto. (p. 103)

Notice that for Hobbes, there is only *one* natural right, not a great group of them, as we find in our Bill of Rights, Declaration of Independence, and Constitution. Perhaps the best way to state Hobbes's view is to say that everyone naturally values his or her own survival. It is perhaps the only *natural value.*

Now, unfortunately for me, you also have a natural right to try to preserve yourself, with the following consequences:

> And because the condition of man, . . . is a condition of war of every one against every one; in which case every one is governed by his own reason; and there is nothing he can make use of, that may not be a help unto him, in preserving his life against his enemies; it followeth, that in such a condition, every man has a right to every thing; even to one another's body. And therefore, as long as this natural right of every man to every thing endureth, there can be no security to any man, how strong or wise so ever he be, of living out the time, which nature ordinarily alloweth men to live. (p. 103)

Two People Pursuing Their Natural Right

Hobbes assumes that in a state of nature there will be a general scarcity of goods. Because not enough goods exist for everyone's survival and flourishing in such a state of nature, each becomes an enemy of all others. In this condition, even though I have a *right* to try to survive, in fact, there isn't much likelihood of my lasting very long.

So, based on our passions alone, we would not survive long enough to enjoy the goal of the natural right. But at this point our *reason* comes into play. It is associated with what Hobbes calls "natural law."

> A LAW OF NATURE . . . is a precept or general rule, found out by reason, by which a man is forbidden to do that which is destructive of his life, or

taketh away the means of preserving the same; and to omit that by which he thinketh it may be best preserved. (p. 103)

Because none of us has much chance of survival if we each blindly pursue our own natural right, we must appeal to our reason and the "natural law" that reason discovers:

And consequently it is a precept, or general rule of reason, *that every man, ought to endeavor peace, as far as he has hope of obtaining it; and when he cannot obtain it, that he may seek, and use, all helps, and advantages of war.* The first branch of which rule, containeth the first, and fundamental law of nature; which is, *to seek peace, and follow it.* The second, the sum of the right of nature; which is, *by all means we can, to defend ourselves.*

From this fundamental law of nature, by which men are commanded to endeavor peace, is derived this second law; *that a man be willing, when others are so too, as far forth, as for peace, and defence of himself he shall think it necessary, to lay down this right to all things: and be contented with so much liberty against other men, as he would allow other men against himself.* For as long as every man holdeth this right, of doing any thing he liketh; so long are all men in the condition of war. But if other men will not lay down their right, as well as he; then there is no reason for anyone, to divest himself of his: for that were to expose himself to prey, which no man is bound to, rather than to dispose himself to peace. (pp. 103–104)

So the idea of natural right is the foundation of Hobbes's social contract. My natural right justifies my use of violence against you if I perceive the use of such violence as being in the interest of my survival. Unhappily for me, your use of violence against me is equally justified. So I agree to renounce my right to use violence against you if you agree to renounce your right to use violence against me. However, our contract is conditional because each of us will break it the moment we think the other is not going to hold to it. This contract does not provide a very stable peace, especially if Hobbes is correct in attributing to each of us a selfish and power-mongering nature. If I see any advantage to myself in breaking the contract, I will do it. None of us can sleep very easily. In fact, none of us dares sleep at all in this tenuous peace.

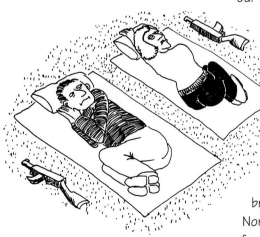

None of Us Can Sleep Easily

The solution to this dilemma requires another step in the contract. All of us must agree to transfer our right to violence and our right to sovereignty over ourselves to a mutually agreed-upon sovereign (a parliament or a monarch), who now has absolute political authority over us. In exchange for absolute power (including an army), this sovereign promises to pass laws that create a state of peace. Basically, the sovereign

The Sovereign

promises to restrain and punish anyone who breaks the initial part of the contract and uses violence against any other member of this newly created artificial body, the state.

Hobbes realizes that there are no guarantees that the sovereign won't abuse its absolute power. In fact, it's almost certain the sovereign will do so, given his, her, or their egoistic propensities. Nevertheless, even abused authority is better than no authority, according to Hobbes. Furthermore, it is hoped that the sovereign will use both its passion (the egoistic side) and its reason (the natural law) and realize that a peaceful state is beneficial to it as well, because otherwise the angry populace may revolt and kill the sovereign. Notice, however, that in Hobbes's political system, revolt is never legitimate unless it succeeds because only power legitimates for Hobbes. However, not even the legitimate absolute tyrant can pass a law that succeeds in taking away my natural right. This is because that right is inalienable except by my uncoerced consent. No law can remove my right to resist law if the law tries to deprive me of my life.

Yoo Hoo! Time to come out and be shot.

Only kicking and screaming!

So, returning to "the big questions" with which we began this chapter, we see that for Hobbes, the state is an artifice (a monster, a "Leviathan") but a necessary one. Legitimate authority is empowered authority. Political bodies themselves determine what counts as just or unjust, so in one sense they cannot be unjust. Yet even when they create a sense of injustice, they are almost always better than their alternative. For this reason we accept the gun constantly aimed at us and the threat of state violence. No matter how brutal the state is, it is the best show in town. Its alternative is chaos, misery, and death, a condition wherein life is "solitary, poor, nasty, brutish, and short." Any state is better than no state. You may not like politics, but according to Hobbes, only because of politics does the social center hold. When the social contract that creates political authority fails, human life is plunged into an abyss.

Leviathan—The Best Show in Town

John Locke

Locke, writing fifty years after Hobbes, used much of the same language as Hobbes did but with very different meanings. For example, Locke too discusses a "state of nature," but for him, this would be the moral state into which all of us are born by virtue of being God's creatures. Hobbes had obviously intentionally kept God out of political theory, not because Hobbes was an atheist (he may or may not have been), but because he thought God belonged no more in political science than he did in physics and because Hobbes was sick of tyrants justifying their power by something called "divine right." But though Locke was also against the so-called divine right of kings, he had no qualms against grounding his political theory in a religious belief. For him, God's power plays a role similar to that of secular power in Hobbes's theory, so for Locke, God created humans and gave them basic rights, the right to "life, health, liberty, and possessions." Each of us is born into a moral "state of nature" in which these rights are ours, along with certain moral obligations that Locke calls the "law of nature," which, as in Hobbes's philosophy, is a law of reason.

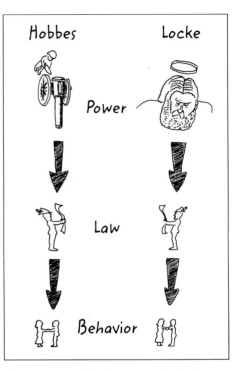

To understand political power right, and derive it from its original, we must consider what state all men are naturally in, and that is a state of perfect freedom to order their actions and dispose of their possessions and persons as they think fit, within the bounds of the law of nature, without asking leave or depending upon the will of any other man. . . .

The state of nature has a law of nature to govern it which obliges every one; and reason which is that law, teaches all mankind who will but consult it that, being all equal and independent, no one ought to harm another in his life, health, liberty, or possessions; for men being all the workmanship of one omnipotent and infinitely wise Maker—all the servants of one sovereign master, sent into the world by his order, and about his business—they are his property whose workmanship they are, made to last during his, not one another's, pleasure; and being furnished with like faculties, sharing all in one community of nature, there cannot be supposed any such subordination among us that may authorize us to destroy another, as if we were made for one another's uses as the inferior ranks of creatures are for ours.[3]

Hobbes had made a particular point of claiming that there is no such thing as "natural property." Property itself could be created only by laws. In the state of nature, there were no laws. Hence, for Hobbes, property is, as Marx was later to call it, a "legal fiction." But, as we have seen, for Locke, God's law creates natural property. Let's look at this curious idea. According to the biblical account, God created the earth and provided it with natural resources for the benefit of humankind. As was indicated earlier, Locke, like Hobbes, was anxious to counter monarchical claims of divine right to property, and he used the biblical account to do so, then added a philosophical touch of his own. In his *Two Treatises on Government*, Locke wrote, "the earth and all that is therein . . . belongs to mankind in common . . . and . . . nobody has originally a private dominion, exclusive of the rest of mankind" (p. 134). Now, the one uniquely natural piece of property we each have is our own body. The property right we have to our bodies can be extended to that which is created by our bodies' labor.

Though the earth and all inferior creatures be common to all men, yet every man has a property in his own person; this nobody has any right to but himself. The labour of his body and the work of his hands, we may say, are properly his. Whatsoever then he removes out of the state that nature hath provided and left it in, he hath mixed his labour with, and joined to it something that is his own, and thereby makes it his property. It being by him removed from the common state nature hath placed it in, it hath by this labour something annexed to it that excludes the common right of other men. For this labour being the unquestionable property of the labourer, no man but he can have a right to what that is once joined to, at least where there is enough and as good left in common for others. . . .

It will perhaps be objected to this that "if gathering the acorns, or other fruits of the earth, etc., makes a right to them, then any one may engross as much as he will." To which I answer: not so. The same law of nature that does by this means give us property does also bound that property, too. "God has given us all things richly" (I Tim. vi. 17), is the voice of reason confirmed by inspiration. But how far has he given it us? To enjoy. As much as any one can make use of to any advantage of life before it spoils, so much he may by his labour fix a property in; whatever is beyond this is more than his share, and belongs to others. . . .

I think it is plain that property in that, too, is acquired as the former. As much land as a man tills, plants, improves, cultivates, and can use the product of, so much is his property. . . .

Nobody could think himself injured by the drinking of another man, though he took a good draught, who had a whole river of the same water left him to quench his thirst; and the case of land and water, where there is enough for both, is perfectly the same. (pp. 134, 136, 137)

Then one may accumulate as much "natural property" as one can use without its spoiling so long as one leaves enough for everyone else. This idea reveals a tremendous attitudinal difference between Locke and Hobbes. Hobbes's political philosophy presupposes a condition of scarcity. Locke's presupposes a condition of *abundance*. Locke's picture of human nature is much more generous than Hobbes's.

The State of Nature
(According to Hobbes)

The State of Nature
(According to Locke)

We might consider the possibility that Locke and Hobbes are both right. Under conditions of abundance, altruism, generosity, and magnanimity might be natural virtues; under conditions of scarcity, stinginess and coldheartedness might be natural. When I was a boy growing up in the fifties, there was a campaign to get people to build backyard A-bomb shelters. At that time, there was a lot of talk concerning a hypothetical postnuclear attack scenario when social order had broken down and the food and water supply had been contaminated with radiation. The typical question was Would you have the right to shoot your neighbor who had foolishly failed to build a shelter for himself and was now trying to get into your already crowded shelter? The consensus was

Protecting Your Backyard A-Bomb Shelter from Covetous Neighbors

that you would be justified in doing so. This was Hobbes's world, not Locke's. And I suppose that if your neighbor tried to get hold of the gallon of uncontaminated water that would keep you and your children alive, you might well defend it with violence.

Back to Locke's concept of "natural property." When he turns to his analysis of money, he says, "And thus came in the use of money—some lasting thing that men might keep without spoiling, and that, by mutual consent, men would take in exchange for the truly useful but perishable supports of life" (p. 144). So there is nothing wrong with hoarding money or passing it along to your sons and daughters so long as you leave enough for others because "gold and silver may be hoarded up without injury to anyone." This doctrine was very convenient for Locke and his well-to-do friends and somewhat counteracted the radicalness of his view that the land belongs to whoever tills it. But it failed to recognize that the excessive accumulation of wealth is a form of power that can be used to undermine the moral state of equality into which we were all supposed to be born. It is well known that Locke's political philosophy was one of the major blueprints for the American Founding Fathers. Some think that Locke's failure to combat the possibility of unjust accumulation of wealth infected our own political system. (Later we will talk again of economic justice in the "good society.")

Locke believed that his theory of our natural moral status (the state of nature) entailed a theory of justifiable punishment. He wrote:

> And thus in the state of nature one man comes by a power over another; but yet no absolute or arbitrary power to use a criminal, when he has got him in his hands, according to the passionate heats or boundless extravagancy of his own will; but only to retribute to him, so far as calm reason and conscience dictate, what is proportionate to his transgression, which is so much as may serve for reparation and restraint; for these two are the only reasons why one man may lawfully do harm to another, which is that we call

punishment. In transgressing the law of nature, the offender declares himself to live by another rule than that of reason and common equity, which is that measure God has set to the actions of men for their mutual security; and so he becomes dangerous to mankind, the tie which is to secure them from injury and violence being slighted and broken by him. Which being a trespass against the whole species and the peace and safety of it provided for by the law of nature. . . . *every man hath a right to punish the offender and be executioner of the law of nature.* (pp. 124–125)

So in the state of nature, each of us has the right to our "life, liberty, health, and property." If any person violates the rights of others, that person alienates himself from the state of nature and thereby forfeits his own natural rights. He has thus earned a punishment, which ought to be meted out. On the principle that "the punishment must fit the crime" (Gilbert and Sullivan), even capital punishment is possible in the state of nature:

By the same reason may a man in the state of nature punish the lesser breaches of that law. It will perhaps be demanded: with death? I answer: Each transgression may be punished to that degree and with so much severity as will suffice to make it an ill bargain to the offender, give him cause to repent, and terrify others from doing the like. Every offence that can be committed in the state of nature may in the state of nature be also punished equally, and as far forth as it may in a commonwealth. (p. 126)

(Those who are against capital punishment today may find Locke's views too harsh, but keep in mind that he was very progressive for his time on this score because in the eighteenth century dozens of crimes could be punished with death. Locke has at least reduced capital punishment to apply to one crime only—murder.) We see here that Locke's theory of justice is *retributive* (the criminal has earned the punishment with his acts and we owe it to him) and *preventative* (he will be restrained from committing similar crimes). In terms of *distributive* justice, Locke's state of nature is a meritocracy.

That is, one may own only as much property as one merits by virtue of one's labor (or inherits from the labor of one's ancestors).

In Thomas Hobbes's political theory, the conditions under which the citizens would probably revolt were pretty predictable, but there could be no such thing as *legitimate* revolt because legitimacy is determined by law, and the sovereign has been given the authority to create law by the social contract. In Locke, however, a very clear doctrine of legitimate revolution exists, once again grounded in our God-given moral condition, the state of nature. Locke wrote:

> There is, therefore, secondly, another way whereby governments are dissolved, and that is when the legislative or the prince, either of them, act contrary to their trust.
>
> . . . The legislative acts against the trust reposed in them when they endeavour to invade the property of the subject and to make themselves or any part of the community masters or arbitrary disposers of the lives, liberties, or fortunes of the people.
>
> . . . Since it can never be supposed to be the will of the society that the legislative should have a power to destroy that which every one designs to secure by entering into society, and for which the people submitted themselves to legislators of their own making. Whenever the legislators endeavour to take away and destroy the property of the people, or to reduce them to slavery under arbitrary power, they put themselves into a state of war with the people who are thereupon absolved from any further obedience. (p. 233)

So the function of the political state is to guarantee our moral state. In this sense, the political state is potentially superior to the state of nature because the latter lacks impartial judges, precise laws, and sufficient power to uphold the moral law. The justification of the political state is the consent of its citizens. The citizens consent to submit to political authority only with the proviso that such political authority will *do whatever is necessary* to protect our natural rights. This proviso is Locke's "social contract." But the citizen is bound to the contract only as long as the government upholds its end of the contract. Locke thought that the populace should not go lightly into a condition of revolt. Because of the seriousness of such a condition, all sorts of attempts should be made to correct the abuses of power before a revolution is declared. But if the state not only fails to uphold the citizens' rights to life, health, liberty, and property, but also becomes the violator of those rights, then revolution is justified.

Locke was writing at a time when King James II tried to impose Catholicism in Britain, which provoked "the Glorious Revolution," a bloodless civil war that ended in a parliamentary victory and the flight of the king. It is

> What? The cost of postage stamps has gone up a penny? That's it! To the barricades!

somewhat ironic that the next use of Locke's doctrine of legitimate revolution was by the American colonists revolting against the British government of King George III. The Founding Fathers wrote in the American Declaration of Independence:

Revolution Should Not Be Entered into Lightly

We hold these truths to be self-evident, that all men are created equal; that they are endowed by their Creator with certain unalienable rights; that among these are life, liberty, and the pursuit of happiness. That, to secure these rights, governments are instituted among men, deriving their just powers from the consent of the governed; that, whenever any form of government becomes destructive of these ends, it is the right of the people to alter or to abolish it, and to institute a new government, laying its foundation on such principles, and organizing its powers in such form, as to them shall seem most likely to effect their safety and happiness.

As I mentioned before, the United States is sometimes thought of as a giant Lockean experiment, containing all the best features of Locke's political theory (government justified by consent of the citizens, basic rights guaranteed by law, recognition of moral and legal equality, and the recognition of the right to revolt if government abrogates its duties) but also suffering from some of the defects of his theory (the contradiction of separating religion and politics, yet grounding political rights in a theological conception of the human being, the lack of a theory of distributive justice based on anything other than merit or inheritance, the failure to recognize that the accumulation of power in the form of wealth can jeopardize the democratic foundations). Attempts have been made to address some of these problems through the passage of laws legalizing labor unions and creating a graduated income tax, among others.

Jean-Jacques Rousseau

JEAN-JACQUES ROUSSEAU (1712–1778) stands approximately to the French Revolution as Locke stands to the American Revolution, though the United States probably continues today to be more a Lockean experiment than France does a Rousseauian one. (And the Soviet Union was probably even less of a Marxian experiment.)

Rousseau, like Locke, believed that all humans are born free and autonomous and that the only legitimate government is one that preserves and maximizes that condition. Again, like Locke, he believed that such legitimacy can come about only through consent to a social contract. However, he believed that such legitimacy in fact existed nowhere in his time and that even the English parliamentarians deceived themselves concerning their own freedom. In fact, we began this chapter with Rousseau's words: "Man is born free, and everywhere he is in chains." Indeed he thought that men were born both free and good but that society had imprisoned them and had corrupted their goodness. Let's take a look at his diagnosis of the political situation of his time and his prescription for it.

Men Are Born Good But Are Corrupted by Society

Consistent with the theories of Hobbes and Locke, Rousseau begins his analysis with an account of the "state of nature." Like Hobbes, and unlike Locke, Rousseau claims that in a condition outside the social order, there would be no morality (no "ought," no "duty"). However, it is possible to talk about *virtues* in the state of nature. For example, Rousseau takes it that *self-love (amour de soi)* is a natural virtue, a natural good. Anyone who lacks it is in some sense perverted and is incapable of truly moral development. (Notice that Jesus' moral teaching—"Love thy neighbor as thyself"—also presupposes self-love as a necessary condition of morality.) Similarly, according to Rousseau, we have (contrary to Hobbes's claim) a natural pity or pain at the misfortune of others. Unfortunately, traditional societies pervert the first of these virtues (self-love) and invert the second (pity). Self-love is turned

Amour de Soi?

into *pride* (amour propre), and pity is transformed into its opposite—delight in others' misery. Pride results from anxious reflection about oneself and the need to feel superior. This need induces one to compare oneself forever with others, to the extent that one finds one's most exquisite pleasure in the misfortune or inferiority of others. Pride and envy are encouraged everywhere by traditional social organization, but in truth, they prevent one from developing into a full person. This speculation leads Rousseau to the view (in *Émile*) that a truly correct education of a child would require the child to be as far from society's corrupting influences as possible. The child should be reared in as nearly a "state of nature" as

Pleasure Derived from the Unhappiness of Others

can be arranged (hence, the understandable but misleading attribution to Rousseau of the philosophy of "back to nature"). In this primary state, the child will be allowed to develop her own natural virtues. Such a child, left to her own devices, learns through *trial and error*, not theories, through *facts*, not words, through *sensations and feelings*, not abstractions. This child is freed from the necessity of holding "opinions" and lives a happy, self-sufficient, timeless existence unaware of artificial needs or worries about the future. The child will be taught to read, but the only book allowed in her education will be *Robinson Crusoe*! Those who have read only *Émile* sometimes think that Rousseau was calling for the abolition or minimalization of the state and demanding a "return to nature" for all. But they have failed to see that, for Rousseau, if one remained at the state of natural virtues, one would fail to develop fully one's humanity. The state of natural virtues must be developed into a moral state, and morality and politics go hand in hand. The move from natural virtuousness to morality involves the development of our social being. Only by filling out the social side of our nature (which was necessarily underdeveloped in childhood) can we find our fullest freedom. But if society is to be a *natural* extension of ourself, it must be consistent with our natural virtues and with our *free* and *rational* status. (A society founded on sheer force would be both unnatural and unjust.) The natural and just society will be constituted by the social contract, which Rousseau describes:

> The clauses of this contract are so determined by the nature of the act that the slightest modification would make them vain and ineffective; so that, although they have perhaps never been formally set forth, they are everywhere the same and everywhere tacitly admitted and recognized. . . .
> These clauses, properly understood, may be reduced to one—the total alienation of each associate, together with all his rights, to the whole community; for, in the first place, as each gives himself absolutely, the conditions

Child Reading Robinson Crusoe (Classic Comics Version)

are the same for all; and, this being so, no one has any interest in making them burdensome to others.

Moreover, the alienation being without reserve, the union is as perfect as it can be, and no associate has anything more to demand: for, if the individuals retained certain rights, as there would be no common superior to decide between them and the public, each, being on one point his own judge, would ask to be so on all; the state of nature would thus continue, and the association would necessarily become inoperative or tyrannical.

Finally, each man, in giving himself to all, gives himself to nobody; and as there is no associate over which he does not acquire the same right as he yields others over himself, he gains an equivalent for everything he loses, and an increase of force for the preservation of what he has.

If then we discard from the social compact what is not of its essence, we shall find that it reduces itself to the following terms:

"Each of us puts his person and all his power in common under the supreme direction of the general will, and, in our corporate capacity, we receive each member as an indivisible part of the whole."

At once, in place of the individual personality of each contracting party, this act of association creates a corporate and collective body, composed of as many members as the assembly contains voters, and receiving from this act its unity, its common identity, its life, and its will.[4]

A number of problems leap out at us from this statement. First, notice that Rousseau completely rejects the notion of representative democracy. According to him, a true democracy must be a participatory democracy; all citizens must vote on all issues of public interest:

Sovereignty, for the same reason as makes it inalienable, cannot be represented; it lies essentially in the general will, and will does not admit of representation: it is either the same or other; there is no intermediate possibility. The deputies of the people, therefore, are not and cannot be its representatives: they are merely its stewards, and can carry through no definitive acts. Every law the people has not ratified in person is null and void—is, in fact, not a law. The people of England regards itself as free; but it is grossly mistaken; it is free only during the election of members of parliament. As soon as they are elected, slavery overtakes it, and it is nothing. The use it makes of the short moments of liberty it enjoys shows indeed that it deserves to lose them. (p. 240)

Also, notice that Rousseau is saying a legitimate political body must be very limited in size because all its members must be capable of convening at regular intervals. Rousseau was from Switzerland, and his model is similar to the democracy of the local Swiss cantons (though they did not completely legalize voting for women on national issues until 1981, and as late as April 29, 1990, the male citizens of the town of Appenzell denied the vote to women in local elections!) or of the town meetings of New England. A country

The Hills Are Alive with the Sound of Democracy

as massive as the United States could not possibly be a true democracy for Rousseau—at least, not in his own day. Ironically, today, with our so phisticated technology, it would be at least theoretically possible to engage

every American on every vote. Imagine that Monday evenings were set aside for politics. For three hours, the TV stations would be dedicated to debating the political issues, followed by a vote in which each legal voter would punch her or his social security number into a computer and would vote on each issue. These votes would be instantly tallied and the results known immediately.

Monday Evening TV

Another problem in Rousseau's political schema is the apparent contradiction between his claim that only in the political body does one find one's true freedom and his assertion that one must transfer all of one's rights to the whole political body and accept as one's own will what he calls "the general will." Rousseau was aware of the problem. He wrote:

> When the State is instituted, residence constitutes consent; to dwell within its territory is to submit to the Sovereign.
>
> Apart from this primitive contract, the vote of the majority always binds all the rest. This follows from the contract itself. But it is asked how a man can be both free and forced to conform to wills that are not his own. How are the opponents at once free and subject to laws they have not agreed to?
>
> I retort that the question is wrongly put. The citizen gives his consent to all the laws, including those which are passed in spite of his opposition, and even those which punish him when he dares to break any of them. The constant will of all the members of the State is the general will; by virtue of it they are citizens and free. When in the popular assembly a law is proposed, what the people is asked is not exactly whether it approves or rejects the proposal, but whether it is in conformity with the general will, which is their will. Each man, in giving his vote, states his opinion on that point; and the general will is found by counting votes. When therefore the opinion that is contrary to my own prevails, this proves neither more nor less than that I was mistaken, and that what I thought to be the general will was not so. If my particular opinion had carried the day I should have achieved the opposite of what was my will; and it is in that case that I should not have been free. (p. 250)

The General Will

In other words, in consenting to live in a state (and tacit consent is given by mere residency ["love it or leave it"]), one is not only consenting to abide by the will of the people, but one is also recognizing that that will *is* the state. Therefore, every vote is a vote for the general will, even if one's vote on any particular issue is overridden. So even if I vote "no" on Proposition P, and Proposition P wins the majority of the votes, then I have actually voted for P in a general sense despite voting against it in fact. Therefore, I can happily follow it as a law even if I thought it was a bad idea when it was first proposed. Or, to put it another way, all legitimate political activity must transcend individual opinion and selfish desire. The only nondespotic way of determining the general will is through a democratic act determined by majority rule. Therefore, I am not only bound by the outcome of such an act, but I also recognize that its outcome is my desire qua social being.

Of course, Rousseau's readers must decide for themselves if this explanation is a real insight or mere sophistry.

John Stuart Mill

We have just seen that according to J.-J. Rousseau, individuals come into their full humanity precisely by alienating their individual wills to the general will (or by submitting it to the general will, thereby identifying their individual wills with the general will). Three-quarters of a century after Rousseau and on the other side of the Channel from him, JOHN STUART MILL (1806–1873), whose utilitarian moral philosophy has already been discussed, had a political agenda that was exactly the opposite from that of Rousseau. Mill saw his goal as that of distinguishing between the public and the private. He believed there was a realm that was genuinely the concern of society (and hence of the body politic). But he also believed there was a realm that was genuinely the concern of the individual, and in that realm, politics had no business. Even if with 100 percent unanimity the "general will" approved of interfering in the legitimately private sphere, it could interfere only by doing violence to the truly human charter. On this, Mill wrote:

The Private versus the Public

> Let us suppose, therefore, that the government is entirely at one with the people, and never thinks of exerting any power of coercion unless in agreement with what it conceives to be their voice. But I deny the right of the people to exercise such coercion, either by themselves or by their government. The power itself is illegitimate. The best government has no more title to it than the worst. It is as noxious, or more noxious, when exerted in accordance with public opinion, than when in opposition to it. If all mankind minus one,

were of one opinion, and only one person were of the contrary opinion, mankind would be no more justified in silencing that one person, than he, if he had the power, would be justified in silencing mankind.[5]

In order to draw the distinction between the public and the private, Mill formulated a principle he called "the principle of liberty." Mill began his essay, *On Liberty*, with this assertion:

> The object of this essay is to assert one very simple principle. . . . That principle is, that the sole end for which mankind are warranted, individually or collectively, in interfering with the liberty of action of any of their number, is self-protection. That the only purpose for which power can be rightfully exercised over any member of a civilized community, against his will, is to prevent harm to others. His own good, either physical or moral, is not a sufficient warrant. He cannot rightfully be compelled to do or forbear because it will be better for him to do so, because it will make him happier, because, in the opinion of others, to do so would be wise, or even right. These are good reasons for remonstrating with him, or reasoning with him, or persuading him, or entreating him, but not for compelling him, or visiting him with any evil in case he do otherwise. [6]

In other words, the body politic, the general will, or whatever one wants to call political authority, can legitimately restrain the action of individual members of the society only if those actions harm other members of the society. What Mill is ruling out here is what is called "state paternalism." Or, to put it another way, he is ruling out "victimless crime." That is, the state has no right to criminalize behavior it deems harmful to the agent but to no one else. This principle means that drunkenness or drug abuse in the privacy of one's home cannot be a crime, nor prostitution, nor the reading of pornography, nor the refusal to wear a helmet while riding one's motorcycle, among other activities.

State Paternalism, or Government as Daddy

Mill's principle strikes an intuitive chord with me. I could do or say or think certain things that I claim are nobody's business but my own and over which society has no legitimate authority. Nevertheless, there seem to me to be serious problems with Mill's principle. First, from a historical perspective, we might detect an ideological component of Mill's principle. It supports a cherished middle-class Victorian dream, the vision of separate spheres—a

**A Drunken Male Prostitute Riding His Motorcycle
without a Helmet in the Privacy of His Own Home**

peaceful private home life isolated from the noisy, combative competition of
the ongoing industrial revolution—hence the English aphorism "A man's
home is his castle." Social critics have recently attempted to burst this
bubble, pointing out the intimate connections between hearth, factory, and
imperial militarism.[7] Second, even granting a possible Victorian domain of
separate spheres, the social world has become much more complicated
since Mill's time. Social welfare schemes and tax schemes have become so
entwined today that the motorcyclist who foolishly opts to forgo a helmet
in the name of "coolness" no longer involves just himself when he enters the
hospital for brain surgery. Rather, the price of his surgery is charged partially to me, the taxpayer.

　　This situation is also somewhat true concerning the abuse of alcohol
and drugs. And some studies conclude that there is a significant connection between the pornography industry and violent crimes. If so, then the
demarcation between the private and the public begins to deteriorate. Furthermore, a conceptual difficulty exists with Mill's notion of "harm to others" that emerges as soon as we try to define "harm." If we construe it as
purely "physical harm," we shall have circumscribed it too narrowly because
it will exclude theft, fraud, and, in rare cases, even rape. As the contemporary American philosopher Richard Taylor says:

> If we say, for example, that harming a man consists not merely of injury to
> his body, but to any of his deepest interests then of course we bring such

> **Officer, that man is parting his hair in the middle. That does irreparable harm to my sense of propriety. Arrest him!**

things as theft and fraud within its meaning. Men do have a deep interest in the security of their property as well as of their persons. But unfortunately, men have other deep interests as well which no believer in freedom supposes for a minute should never be foiled.

Thus, there are men who have a deep interest in such things as religion, patriotism, public manners, the preservation of wildlife, and so on, without end. Now if we say that no one shall be permitted to do anything that would foil, frustrate, or damage any such interest held by anyone, this will be about equivalent to saying that no one may do anything at all. The whole of the criminal law would be summed up in saying that all actions are prohibited. And a principle having that consequence can hardly be called a principle of liberty.[8]

The solution will have to be that actual courts of law must determine exactly what constitutes harm, using the concept of criminal law to make the appropriate distinctions. The problem with that approach is that the principle of liberty was meant by Mill to determine criminal law, not the other way around, or the whole process becomes circular.

Mill extended his principle of liberty to encompass such areas as freedom of thought, expression, and assembly. No government, not even a pure democracy, can legitimately legislate against these rights, according to Mill. He would have

> **All in favor of expropriating the property of people wearing striped socks, raise your hand.**

FIRST NATIONAL BANK

approved of the American idea of a "Bill of Rights" that in fact if not in principle somehow transcends public opinion. It is clear that, for him, democracy was the best form of government. But it was not an end in itself; rather it was the most likely means of guaranteeing the interests of both the public and the private domains. And these, contrary to Rousseau, not even democracy could override.

This is the doctrine of laissez-faire or "hands off" (literally, "leave alone"). There are certain realms where government has no business, except to protect the existence of precisely those realms. Otherwise, government must "butt out" of them. Mill extended this doctrine of laissez-faire throughout his social philosophy. Not only must there be no state interference in the inner life and harmless activities of the citizens, but in general, "Laissez-faire . . . should be the general practice: every departure from it, unless required by some great good, is a certain evil."[9] Among other applications, this doctrine means that, in most respects, the government ought to keep its hands off the marketplace, allowing a system of free enterprise unhampered by state controls. Even though John Stuart Mill is thought of as "the saint of liberalism," the doctrine of laissez-faire is now usually associated with the economic policy of conservatism. Still, despite his enthusiasm for economic laissez-faire policy, he thought that deviations from it were required:

> But if the workman is generally the best selector of means, can it be affirmed with the same universality, that the consumer, or person served, is the most competent judge of the end? Is the buyer always qualified to judge of the commodity? If not, the presumption in favor of the competition of the market does not apply to the case; and if the commodity be one, in the quality of which society has much at stake, the balance of advantages may be in favour of some mode and degree of intervention by the authorized representatives of the collective interest of the state.
>
> Now, the proposition that the consumer is a competent judge of the commodity can be admitted only with numerous abatements and exceptions. He is generally the best judge (though even this is not true universally) of the material objects produced for his use. These are destined to supply some physical want, or gratify some taste or inclination, respecting which wants or inclinations there is no appeal from the person who feels them; or they are the means and appliances of some occupation, for the use of the persons engaged in it, who may be presumed to be judges of the things required in their own habitual employment. But there are other things of the worth of which the demand of the market is by no means a test; things of which the utility does not consist in ministering to inclinations, nor in serving the daily uses of life, and the want of which is least felt where the need is greatest. This is peculiarly true of those things which are chiefly useful as tending to raise the character of human beings. (pp. 952–953)

Such a policy of legitimate state intervention not only justifies for Mill a governmental subsidy of the arts, but it could also be used in today's world to protect citizens from the contamination of dangerous pesticides and to protect the environment from the competition of vicious profiteers who see their short-term profit as necessitating the destruction of the natural world. To quote Mill once more: "The uncultivated cannot be competent judges of cultivation" (p. 953).

Social Philosophy

The problem of justice is the key issue of social philosophy. This problem is usually seen as having to do with fairness and desert (deservedness) in meeting the claims of citizens and in the distribution of goods and services. The big question here is What is the state's legitimate role in these activities? We will look at three views concerning this issue: the communist solution, the **minimal-state** solution, and **liberalism.** I will view liberalism as located between the other two positions, though I do not mean to imply that because communism and minimalism are extremes relative to liberalism, therefore they could not be true. Indeed, these two "extreme" views are not the most extreme possible in any absolute sense. Such extremes would be these: On the one hand is a kind of statism that holds the state and only the state totally responsible for the fair distribution of goods and services to its citizens and says only it can determine the legitimacy of the citizens' claims. On the other hand is an **anarchistic** position, claiming that the state itself is illegitimate, hence can never play a role in fair distribution or in responding to legitimate claims of individuals.

Communism

The political philosophy of KARL MARX (1818–1885) was greatly influenced by his early contact with the metaphysics of G. W. F. HEGEL (1770–1831), whose theory of reality is distinctly organistic. (Organicism is the opposite of atomism: **Atomism** says that reality is composed of individual, simple units—that the individuals are more real than the whole, which is somehow actually only an abstraction. **Organicism** says that the whole is more real than the parts; the whole is an organic unity, and the parts depend completely on the whole. Hence, the parts are somehow less real than the whole.) In Hegel's version of organicism, the so-called individuals are themselves just points of intersecting relations of power within the system, so in a certain sense, each individual is really a microcosmic mirror of the macrocosm—a reflection of the whole system.

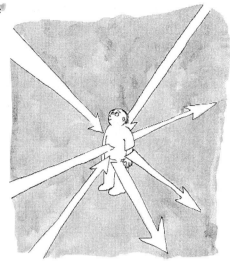

The Individual as a Point of Intersecting Relations of Power

Marx's Materialism   Marx rejected Hegel's grandiose metaphysical schema, but he too tended toward organicism. Not only did he see the human race as ecologically closely related to nature (according to one story, Marx had written to Charles Darwin asking Darwin's permission to let Marx dedicate *Das Kapital* to him, but Darwin declined the honor, saying that his own theory had caused him enough trouble without being blamed for Marx's theory as well), but Marx also saw the individual human as ecologically related to his or her society. Society was not merely the totality of individuals; rather, it was an organic whole that in certain ways created the individual. Therefore for Marx, there could be no question of individual rights that somehow superseded social

Every Product Is the Result of the Efforts of Many People, Living and Dead

rights. Everything that an individual does is a result of the efforts of many people, living and dead. Hence, all products were in that sense social products and belonged to society.

Historical societies have been unjust, according to Marx, almost from the very beginning (even though the most aboriginal social arrangements, hence the most natural ones, were forms of primitive communism). This unjustness is because a minority of individuals managed to wrest power and material wealth from their communal source, thereby setting up systems of privilege and generating social institutions that would guarantee those privileges—protected at first by armed thugs called "police" or "army," eventually by social institutions and internalized guilt. (Marx thought that this grabbing of power and wealth was somehow "unnatural." Some of his Hobbesian critics claim it was all *too* natural.) Ever since the original power grab, the history of the social world has always been the history of the quest for material justice. This quest has taken on the guise of class antagonism and sometimes of class warfare, where the interest of the majority (a dispossessed working class: slaves, serfs, laborers) is pitted against the interests of the privileged minority. Marx's optimistic teleological conception of history tells him that the interests of the majority must finally triumph.

The Interests of the Few versus the Interests of the Many, According to Karl Marx

Marx's materialistic organicism, based as it is on categories from economics and sociology rather than physics, is such that the socioeconomic structure of society is a very powerful determinant of the individual in society. So the problem is not simply that unjust socioeconomic structures of power create unfair conditions for individuals; rather, they create *mutilated individuals*. For example, Marx writes:

> The alienation of the worker in his object is expressed as follows in the laws of political economy: the more the worker produces the less he has to consume; the more value he creates the more worthless he becomes; the more refined his product the more crude and misshapen the worker; the more civilized the product the more barbarous the worker; the more powerful the work the more feeble the worker; the more the work manifests intelligence the more the worker declines in intelligence and becomes a slave of nature. Labor certainly produces marvels for the rich, but it produces privation for the worker. It produces palaces, but hovels for the worker. It produces beauty, but deformity for the worker. It replaces labor by machinery, but it casts some of

the workers back into a barbarous kind of work and turns the others into machines. It produces intelligence, but also stupidity and cretinism for the workers.[10]

According to Marx's positive, optimistic conception of human nature, humans are naturally creative, productive, artistic, aesthetic beings who must express their being in their products. (Humans thus objectify their subjectivity.) Marx prefers the name *Homo faber* (man the maker) over *Homo sapiens* (man the knower)

You Are What You Make

because, for him, all *knowing* follows upon *doing* and *making*. So another effect of unjust socioeconomic systems is that the individual's being is stolen from her. She does not produce as a natural outlet of her creative urge; rather, she is forced to sell her work to another person. Her work is stolen from her and becomes a part of an economic system that is hostile to her own interests. This effect is what Marx calls "alienated labor," and here is what he says about it:

> What constitutes the alienation of labor? First, that the work is *external* to the worker, that it is not part of his nature; and that, consequently, he does not fulfill himself in his work but denies himself, has a feeling of misery rather than well being, does not develop freely his mental and physical energies but is physically exhausted and mentally debased. The worker therefore feels himself at home only during his leisure time, whereas at work he feels homeless. His work is not voluntary but imposed, *forced labor*. It is not the satisfaction of a need, but only a *means* for satisfying other needs. Its alien character is clearly shown by the fact that as soon as there is no physical or other compulsion it is avoided like the plague. External labor, labor in which man alienates himself, is a labor of self-sacrifice, of mortification. Finally, the external character of work for the worker is shown by the fact that it is not his own work but work for someone else, that in work he does not belong to himself but to another person.[11]

Marx's Vision of Society   So what would a just society look like for Marx? (Or what *will* it look like? He thought its advent was inevitable.) First, its social production must be addressed to what he calls *true needs* rather than *false needs*. True needs derive from our real nature as biological and social beings (e.g., the need for food, shelter, clothing, medical care, love, and

Mama! Me need green cereal!!

FLAKEY FLAKES
CEREAL for KIDS

False Needs

education). False needs are any artificial needs of the privileged that are at the expense of the true needs of the majority, any exaggeration of true needs that are instilled in some while others go without (the need for mansions, luxurious clothes, and gourmet excesses) or the instillment of economic needs in the masses whose real goal is not satisfaction but profit for the privileged owning class (planned obsolescence: lightbulbs that burn out in a month, razors that go dull and are to be thrown away, automobiles whose bumpers collapse in collisions at five miles per hour).

Second, the foundations of social production (natural resources, means of production, means of distribution) must not be privately owned but must be socially owned and democratically controlled. Third, social production must be such that individual workers are not forced to enter into streams of specialization that constrain the natural abundance of the creative urge. No one may be objectified in a specific role—become *the* waiter, *the* teacher, *the* janitor, *the* physicist, or even *the* neurosurgeon. Marx does not mean that no one can *specialize*. (Who wants to have one's brain operated upon by one's hairdresser or by one's philosophy teacher?) A person may

TRIPLE-BLADED Disposable Shaving System (formerly "razors")

Karl Marx Inspects a Triumph of Capitalism

spend years training to learn neurosurgery, but still, one does not become *the* neurosurgeon. (In today's America, perhaps one also becomes a golfer?)

In a famous passage in which Marx announces the abolition of "the division of labor," he says:

> in communist society, where nobody has one exclusive sphere of activity but each can become accomplished in any branch he wishes, society regulates the general production and thus makes it possible for me to do one thing today and another tomorrow, to hunt in the morning, fish in the afternoon, rear cattle in the evening, criticize after dinner, just as I have a mind, without ever becoming hunter, fisherman, shepherd or critic.[12]

Under these conditions, the motto of justice will be "from each according to his ability, to each according to his need." Here we will have the recovery of true human nature, the release of the human creative potential, and for the first time, *true* individuality because true individuality requires "true consciousness" (recognition that the needs of the individual and the needs of the society are identical) and unconstrained creativity—which is really where individual differences come into play. Marx has no trouble handing these new humans over to a democracy.

Criticisms of Marx's View   Many of Marx's ideas are impressive. In my view, he is right that much of world history has been characterized by the power and privilege of a few, supported by the misery of many, and I think he is also right that any complete theory of the just society must include the concept of **distributive justice** (the fair distribution of socially produced wealth or the fair distribution of scarcity). But Marx's system is itself fraught with problems.

First, consider Marx's tremendously optimistic picture of human nature. As opposed to pessimists like Freud and Hobbes, Marx thought we are naturally social and naturally workers. (Freud thought we were natural egoists and natural bums, so our true nature would have to be suppressed if civilization was to flourish.) According to Marx, we are naturally cooperative. Competition and selfishness are primarily the result of unhealthy social arrangements. Now, one can hope that Marx was right, but the evidence available to you and me is not always on the side of his argument. His response to this charge is that such evidence comes to us from cultures of alienation and is being evaluated through a fog of alienation (your fog and my fog). But because all cultures have been alienated to one degree or another, according to Marx, what evidence can he point to in order to establish that people are basically "good"?

Doc, I'm a greedy bum.

It's only natural. That will be $100.

A second objection concerns the mystification of the working class. Why should we accept Marx's claim that the destiny of the human race is the destiny of the working class? Why should a particular class of oppressed, alienated, and unhappy people contain the hidden meaning of human history? (And are we sure that human history has a meaning, a telos?)

Trying to See through the Fog of Alienation

A third criticism concerns Marx's essentially Platonic claim that, in the truly human society, the interests of the individual and those of society will be identical. Certainly, Marx is right that every effort must be made to reduce the opposition between these two, but isn't there a suspicion, as critic Alan Brown says, that:

> It's 49 B.C.E. I am Julius Caesar. I have just crossed the Rubicon. But what does it all _mean_? In the long run, what's it all _for_?

> the only way in which the individual interests can be reconciled with collective interests is for those collective interests to _replace_ the individual's own self interests in his own consciousness? . . . Consider the problem of congested traffic in rush hours. There is a collective interest in everyone using public transport, since this would be so much more convenient. The individual has to curtail his own behavior to achieve a second-best solution—he would prefer that he should use his car and everyone else the bus.[13]

> I'm all for public transportation. Let _them_ use it.

Civic-Mindedness

And finally, what about Marx's willingness to accept democracy as valid only "after the revolution"? He would reject as factitious the Western democracies of the contemporary world on the grounds that the voters in them are all alienated ideologues in a state of false consciousness who misunderstand their own interests and those of the human race. Marx will only give the vote to those nonalienated communalists in true consciousness who will be the second or third generation product of the revolution; yet their creation will depend on an interim "dictatorship of the proletariat"—an absolute totalitarianism that will guide the newly revolutionized society for several generations until the "new human" has been fully hatched. Because at that point social classes will be no more, and class struggle, exploitation, and the need for the state as an instrument of exploitation will have disappeared, the dictatorship of the proletariat will simply "dissolve itself," voluntarily stepping down and handing its absolute power over to "the people." Doesn't one have to be a bit *naive* to accept this vision? Is one simply a capitalist lackey if one observes that, unfortunately, Lord Acton was probably more accurate than Marx? (Acton: "Power corrupts; absolute power corrupts absolutely.")

The Newly Hatched True Human Being

These criticisms matter because of Marx's organicism. He believed that no piecemeal corrections of injustice can succeed. If the game is rotten, then every possible move in the game is rotten. The whole thing must be swept away, or there will be injustice forever. So, according to Marx, we must accept his judgment in all these issues or be ourselves condemned eternally as reactionaries, lackeys, and mouthpieces of the forces of injustice.

The Minimal State

At the opposite pole from Marx's communist society (or "communalist" society) is the idea of the minimal state. This state would have the legitimate power to prevent the use of force and fraud and to punish such uses but without the express consent of all adult citizens, could not have the legitimate power to tax or confiscate property in order to perform any actions above and beyond these minimal duties. No public works or systems of aid to the needy would be justified.

Such a minimal state has been defended in a much-read and greatly discussed book by Harvard philosophy professor Robert Nozick called *Anarchy, State, and Utopia*. The starting point for Nozick's defense is Locke's "state of nature," in which, as we have seen, individuals have a natural right to "life, liberty, health, and property." Nozick holds the view that only a minimal state can defend these rights without itself becoming a violator of them. The reason the minimal state is the maximum state allowed is that any more extensive state must finance its projects through taxation, and if this taxation is not consented to by some individuals, it will violate their rights. Of course, the minimal state taxes its citizens for the protective services it offers them, and only those who pay the tax receive the benefits.

I'm protecting you against violators of your rights. That will be $20,000 please.

I'm not really a slave. I'm a citizen of the state.

According to Nozick, beyond this, unconsented taxation is on a par with forced labor. It makes the government part owner of you (because on the Lockean principles from which Nozick's argument proceeds, you own yourself, and your labor is an extension of yourself) and is indistinguishable from semislavery.

Nozick criticizes both socialism (of which communism is a version) and liberalism (which, like socialism, claims that fairness demands some kind of redistribution of wealth) on the grounds that they are what he calls "patterned" theories of justice rather than historical theories. That is, they impose a certain kind of pattern on the distribution of goods (e.g., Marx's "from each according to his ability, to each according to his need") that has nothing to do with the *history* of the goods distributed. This distribution would be fine, says Nozick, if goods fell from heaven like manna. But, in fact, most goods come to us with a history. They are already encumbered, already owned—purchased, traded, earned, or received as a gift. Those goods, or "holdings," are covered by an absolute right to them by their owners—a right whose overriding would be unjust. This right pertains if the initial acquisition was just and if all subsequent transactions with it are just (e.g., if I own an object by virtue of having made it or purchased it with money that is legitimately mine, and the like). Furthermore, people have a right to transfer holdings. I can trade or give away things I own (which means there is a right to inheritance). Finally, people have a right to demand rectification. In an anarchy (the "state of nature"), I have a right to defend myself and my property against those who would injure me, or my holdings, steal from me, or defraud

Goods Falling Like Manna from Heaven

me, and I have the right to punish those who do so. In a minimal state, I give up the right to punish others personally, by my own hand, but I do have the right to demand that the state perform these protective and punitive functions (though there are no other demands I can make on the state).

The implication of the minimal state concept is that *only* an unrestricted capitalism can produce a just society and that any state that prohibits "capitalist acts between consenting adults" is a tyranny. Nozick seems to recognize that one consequence of his view is that some people will amass great wealth and power while others will struggle in poverty. But he believes that this unfortunate side effect of his system is nevertheless consistent with justice. On the first page of his book, Nozick says that he knows many readers will reject his conclusions, which are "so apparently callous toward the needs and sufferings of others." Throughout his argument, he does little to alleviate this concern, though he does make a gesture in its direction by subscribing to Locke's proviso that, in acquiring property, "one must leave enough for others." Says Nozick:

Thus a person may not appropriate the only water hole in a desert and charge what he will. Nor may he charge what he will if he possesses one, and unfortunately it happens that all the water holes in the desert dry up, except for his. This unfortunate circumstance, admittedly no fault of his, brings into operation the Lockean proviso and limits his property rights.[14]

In a footnote, Nozick adds, "The situation would be different if his water hole didn't dry up, due to special precautions he took to prevent this" (p. 180).

Pleased by Nozick's Views

Not surprisingly, Nozick's theory has delighted a number of people whose political posture is decidedly to the right. But most of the literature that his book has inspired has been critical. Still, the sheer volume of this literature is an impressive testimony to the significance of Nozick's book. It's as if political writers see Nozick's arguments as important enough to require a response.

Numerous critics attack the notion of rights on which Nozick's libertarian utopia is based. The first sentence of his book is "Individuals have rights, and there are things no person or group may do to them (without violating their rights)." These rights are the right against coercive interference in one's affairs and the right to property. Where did one get these rights? Nozick does not really tell us; yet for him they are absolute and override any other moral claims. A typical strategy against Nozick is to insist that the existence of such rights cannot be merely presupposed but must be demonstrated. One group of critics simply denies that such absolute rights exist at all. For example, Alasdair MacIntyre, a prominent

Once upon a time in a far distant land there existed witches, unicorns, and natural rights. . . .

British philosopher, says, "belief in them is one with belief in witches and unicorns."[15] Another British philosopher, Alan Brown, says that claiming that I have a *right* to something is just an elliptical way of saying that "all things considered, there is a good moral reason to respect or promote my freedom in this case" (p. 106). Therefore, rights cannot be absolute or foundational; rather, they are derived from other moral deliberations. Other philosophers have agreed with Nozick that there are basic rights but claim that *his* list of them is arbitrary. For instance, Ronald Dworkin says:

> I agree that rights ought not to be violated. But sometimes claims of rights conflict, and I see no reason why Nozick's right to property is exclusive of other rights, or why it is necessarily more important than others.[16]

Another kind of criticism attacks the purely utopian (hence impractical) nature of Nozick's argument. For example, Nozick claims that only a *historical* theory of acquisitions can be truly just and also claims that current entitlement to holdings is just only if original acquisition was just. But what is original acquisition? Adam's and Eve's? Certainly, most current holdings are historically traceable to items that were once the spoils of war or of other forms of removal by force or intimidation. My county was once the territory of the Miwok Indians. I don't know if the Miwoks wrested this land from an earlier prehistoric people, but I do know that the Miwoks did not simply bestow the land on the European settlers who are my ancestors. In today's world, does anybody have just entitlement to her or his property derivable from an original acquisition? Amazingly, Nozick seems to admit that these historical facts undermine his historical theory and force us to accept some form of "patterning." He says, "Although to introduce socialism as the punishment for our sins would be to go too far, past injustices might be so great as to make necessary in the short run a more extensive state in order to rectify them" (p. 231). Critic Alan Brown concludes from Nozick's hedging:

Adam and Eve and the Original Acquisition

So Nozick's theory is essentially Utopian in the worst sense of the term: it has no practical relevance. Like the Garden of Eden before the Fall it can offer no insight into the problems of what we are to do here and now, since we are left ignorant of what principles are to inform our choice. The theory has application nowhere. (p. 99)

Nozick Goes to Hell

Liberalism

Somewhere in the theoretical spectrum between the communistic utopia of Marx and the minimalist utopia of Nozick we can find the idea of "the liberal state." It has been heartily defended by Nozick's colleague at Harvard, John Rawls, in his book *A Theory of Justice*.[17] The liberal state is pretty much what exists today in the Western democracies: a large degree of free enterprise with capital and many of the natural resources in private hands but regulated by the state in order to foster low inflation and high employment. Tax-financed social security tries to control poverty for those who cannot work or for whom no work exists. The presupposition behind liberalism is that society is necessarily much more complex than it is seen to be in either Marxian or Nozickian utopias—that it is necessarily a cooperative enterprise and that therefore its products and wealth are partially the result of cooperation (and that therefore all members of the cooperation—the stakeholders—have a claim to a fair share of the products and the wealth, as in Marx), but also that there will necessarily be competition both in producing and obtaining the goods (and that therefore some members of the cooperative—those who contribute most to it—have a claim to unequal portions of the products, as in Nozick). Any adequate theory of justice will have to balance these legitimate claims and find a formula for dismissing illegitimate claims. Rawls thinks that such a theory, once formulated, could apply to a democratic capitalist society or a

Cooperation But Also Competition

democratic socialist society. In any case, society must have a public school system, must be dedicated to equality of economic opportunity, must have social security, and must define a minimum standard of living below which its citizens will not be forced to exist.

Rawls's conception of justice is "justice as fairness." Besides guaranteeing that all citizens will get a reasonable share of the social goods, the doctrine of fairness consists of a set of constraints on what people may do to each other in the pursuit of those goods. On the one hand, Rawls thinks that no *theory* of justice can be justly forced down people's throats—the correct theory would have to be one that rational people would somehow arrive at by themselves. On the other hand, Rawls is pretty sure he knows what such a theory would look like. Justice would be whatever was chosen by rational, self-interested, unenvious people who knew that they would have to inhabit the society created by their mutual agreement but who did not know what personal characteristics

Justice as Fairness

they would bring to that society (i.e., they wouldn't know their race, their physical and mental abilities, their inheritances, or their social backgrounds). Such people, Rawls says, would choose the following principles in the following order:

1. Equal and maximum liberty (political, intellectual, and religious) for each person consistent with equal liberty for others.

2. Wealth and power to be distributed equally except where inequalities would work to the advantage of all and where there would be equal opportunity to achieve advantageous positions of equality.

A Rawlsian Citizen

If these principles are true, then it follows (unlike in Nozick's theory) that the only society that can be just is a liberal society that partially redistributes wealth and income for the benefit of its most disadvantaged members.

Notice that Rawls's theory, like Plato's, begins with a political myth—a "noble lie." In Plato's myth, people are told that their memories of their past are really only memories of a dream and what they believe of themselves is in fact false. Similarly, Rawls's myth establishes what he calls a "veil of ignorance," in which the facts we know about ourselves are set aside (our psychological, physical, social, and racial characteristics). The myth also supposes that we are not envious and that we rationally pursue our own self-interest. If you tell Rawls that his myth is *only* a myth, that none of it is true, he will respond that it is merely a philosophical device for use as an analytic tool to demonstrate the rationality of a certain kind of society. (In this respect, his "original position" [as he calls the status of his mythical negotiators behind

Students Wearing the Veil of Ignorance (Proudly)

their veil of ignorance] is very much like the "state of nature" in traditional contract theories.) Rawls's veil of ignorance allows the political philosopher to acknowledge the intuitive fact that some inequalities in a naturally evolving society are unjust because they are undeserved. It is unjust that some should have to suffer through life because they were born with less and that others are surrounded by excessive amounts of goods due to the mere accident of birth. The veil allows Rawls to arrive rationally at a conclusion that he intuits to be true, namely, that the society can only be just if it partially redistributes wealth for the benefit of its most disadvantaged. In short, it shows how a just society requires that we all be transformed from Hobbesian egoists into Kantian universalists. The veil purports to show that if we were forced to enter into a society that we would negotiate with others, denuded of all the characteristics that were ours merely by accident of birth, we would choose the liberal society.

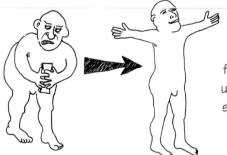

The Transformation from Hobbesian Egoist to Kantian Universalist

Though Rawls's theory strikes a responsive chord in many of its readers, you will not be surprised that it has also found its share of critics. Many are suspicious of any theory that sets out to determine the most rational of all possible societies and concludes that it just happens to be the type inhabited by the theory's author.

A specific criticism says that Rawls ignores our natural gambling nature. Rawls thinks that his liberal society is superior to a utilitarian society because the latter is compatible with slavery (a *few* miserable, hard-working slaves might produce the greatest amount of happiness for the greatest number of people), but slavery is incompatible with liberalism because negotiators in the "original position" would not risk opting for slavery as they themselves might end up as slaves. But, ask the critics, wouldn't some people risk the low odds of being designated a slave if the odds for a great benefit from such a system were high enough?

Yet another criticism is that no contract is legally binding if the signers of it are kept in ignorance of their own real interests; yet *all* signers to Rawls's social contract are ignorant of even their personal identity. So, on this account, Rawls's contract, produced behind the veil of ignorance, is invalid. Finally, we should remind ourselves of Nozick's main criticism of Rawls. Nozick says that it would be okay to divide the goods according to some patterned formula of equality "if goods fell from heaven like manna." But it is unjust to divide up the pie equally when it is known who contributed to it and who in fact owns it. Nozick asks, how do the people in the "original position" get the *right* to divide up the pie as they do? (But of course it could be asserted that *the right to fair treatment* is as basic as Nozick's right to property.)

Conclusion

I began this chapter by noting that much of our behavior is controlled by rules and laws enforced by a not-so-subtle threat of the use of force

The Self as a Selfish Atom

against violators. The question was posed, Why do we put up with it? Well, I think at one level we can accept Hobbes's answer to this question: Putting up with the regulation of our behavior by a threat of force is better than the radical alternative—anarchy, a state of social existence in which the center does not hold. But this conclusion doesn't mean (as it seems to for Hobbes) that we should settle for just any form of government. Exactly what we can reasonably expect from a government depends very much on whether the Hobbesian (and Freudian) picture of the self is true. Is the self essentially a selfish atom, naturally seeking only its own gratification and acting cooperatively only when forced to do so? Or is the self naturally social, cooperative, and sympathetic to the plight of others, as Locke and Marx would have us believe?

If the former picture is true, the political state *is* an artificial creation, and a culture without excessive repression (and also excessive guilt, in the Freudian account) is impossible. Furthermore, some kind of "noble lie" or myth will be required to keep the citizens in line. If the latter, more optimistic picture is true and we are naturally social, then society is not artificial or necessarily excessively repressive, and reason, rather than myth, should be able to represent, explain, and justify social values to its citizens. But which picture is correct?

The Noble Lie Keeping Citizens in Line

This is a tough question. One could spend a lifetime pondering it and testing different hypotheses concerning it (though Freud thought the issue could be settled in twenty minutes of observing children's play in the sandbox). My own view is that no believable account of human nature corresponds to one or the other of these pictures. But in a situation of scarcity, Hobbes is more or less right, and in situations of abundance, Locke is more or less right.

Children at Play

The British anthropologist Colin Turnbull in his book *The Mountain People* has described the effect of virulent scarcity on a particular culture, the Ik. These people seem to have no sympathy for each other, they are selfish and vicious, parents withhold food from their children, children steal from their parents and take advantage of the feebleness of their grandparents. Yet in his later book *The Forest People*, Turnbull describes another culture, the BaMbuti, Pygmies of the Congolese rain forest, who have a fairly easy time filling their basic material needs and whose members are social, cooperative, and sympathetic. Turnbull's data don't *prove* anything, but they can give us hope that when our fundamental material needs are met, a more positive aspect of human nature can be activated. Turnbull's descriptions also lead us to fear that when these basic needs are not met, a more sinister side of human nature may be activated. And if *that* fear is true, then the government's role cannot be simply that of protecting us from each other (following Hobbes) but must also be that of promoting a certain moral or spiritual state (following Locke). On my hypothesis—though not explicitly on Locke's—the government must also promote a certain level of material well-being, but not in an authoritarian mode. Hobbes, Locke, and Rousseau are right to say that the key concept of legitimacy is *consent*, though it is problematical exactly how this concept is to be understood. One of the primary features of political theory must be the development of a theory of consent.

A discussion of consent leads us to the topic of *justice*, which is a key concept of social philosophy. My own conclusions are not offered up as being trouble-free. Any position one takes on this important topic involves its author in serious problems. Still, that difficulty does not excuse us from thinking this problem through to the best of our ability and reaching some tentative conclusions; here are mine. I agree with Marx when he says that a just society cannot be one in which an oppressed majority is constrained to support a system of privileges for a nonproductive minority. Everyone who hopes to benefit from social productivity should contribute to it. But Marx (in contrast to Mill) needs to be criticized for his view that the individual has no legitimate rights vis-à-vis society, and he was wrong to think (if he did think) that society must be founded on one view of human good—that of productivity. Liberalism (Mill and Rawls) is to be applauded for its view that the state must be open to as many views of human good as are compatible with each other. Nozick correctly reminds us that the goods that offer themselves to us for consumption, purchase, or trade do not fall from heaven like manna. We cannot create justice by simply taking away from some to give to others without considering entitlement—that is, without considering that some people have legitimate claims of ownership or control of certain goods by virtue of having legally produced them, purchased them, or inherited them. But "entitlement" is not an absolute category.

I find Rawls convincing when he sides with Marx against Nozick in holding that a just society cannot be based on entitlement alone but that claims of entitlement must be balanced with claims of need or social victimization, and that therefore the just society must be committed to an ongoing partial redistribution of wealth to guarantee that the least advantaged in society are not forced to fall below a certain agreed-upon standard of living and are provided with opportunities to rise above their position of disadvantage—not only because it is morally right to do so but also because otherwise that vicious (Hobbesian) side of human nature may be activated that can make human relations dangerous for all.

Topics for Consideration

1. Most features of Plato's justification for his ideal republic are unappealing or even repulsive to citizens of modern democracies. Why? Do you find anything correct in his account?
2. Do you agree with Plato that no culture can survive without some kind of myth (or "noble lie") justifying its mission?
3. Despite using similar language, Hobbes and Locke have very different justifications of government. Discuss the differences in their respective answers to the question of why we should submit to a rule of law, and take a position one way or the other. (Or hammer out a compromise between them.)
4. Why does Rousseau think that participatory democracy is the only true democracy? What is his critique of representative democracy?
5. Contrast as clearly as you can the difference between Rousseau and Mill on the topic of the private and the public realms.

6. Pick out the feature in Marx's theory of social justice that you like the most and the feature that you like the least. Explain your judgment. How are these two features related in Marx's theory?

7. Contrast the kind of social fairness defended by Nozick in his account of the minimal state with that defended by Rawls in his account of the liberal state. Which view is more in line with your conception of fairness?

Suggestions for Further Reading: Paperback Editions

Alan Brown, *Modern Political Philosophy: Theories of the Just Society* (New York: Penguin, 1986). A clear summary with insightful commentary.

Thomas Hobbes, *Leviathan: Or the Matter, Forme and Power of a Commonwealth Ecclesiasticall and Civil* (New York: Collier Books, 1962). The old cynic's famous treatment of government and humanity—long, often tedious, somewhat difficult in its seventeenth-century English but contains lightning bolts of brilliance. Especially see Part I, Chapter 13 through Part II, Chapter 18 for topics discussed here.

John Locke, *The Second Treatise of Civil Government*, in *Two Treatises of Government* (New York: Hafner, 1964). The "bible" of modern government that inspired the American Declaration of Independence. Surprisingly readable.

David McLellan, *Karl Marx* (New York: Viking Penguin, 1976). Short, excellent account in the Modern Masters series.

John Stuart Mill, *On Liberty* (Chicago: Henry Regnery, 1955). Somewhat difficult reading because of the artificiality of Mill's Victorian style but short and impressive.

Robert Nozick, *Anarchy, State, and Utopia* (New York: Basic Books, 1974). Big and formidable, but Nozick is a good writer.

Karl Popper, *The Open Society and Its Enemies*, 5th ed. (Princeton, N.J.: Princeton University Press, 1971). A heavy-handed but very interesting attack on Plato's politics in Volume I and on Marx's politics in Volume II by one of this century's foremost philosophers of science.

John Rawls, *A Theory of Justice* (Cambridge, Mass.: Harvard University Press, 1971). Sometimes pretty technical for a beginner but a good read.

Richard Taylor, *Freedom, Anarchy, and the Law*, 2nd ed. (Buffalo, N.Y.: Prometheus Books, 1982). A short, highly readable account of the basic issues raised by Hobbes, Locke, Rousseau, and Mill.

Notes

1. Plato, *Republic*, in *Great Dialogues of Plato*, trans. W. H. D. Rouse (New York: New American Library, 1956), pp. 216–217. Unless otherwise stated, all subsequent quotes from the *Republic* in this chapter are from this edition.

2. Thomas Hobbes, *Leviathan: or the Matter, Forme and Power of a Commonwealth Ecclesiasticall and Civil* (New York: Collier Books, 1962), pp. 98–99, 100. Unless

otherwise stated, all subsequent quotes from Hobbes in this chapter are from this source.

3. John Locke, *The Second Treatise of Civil Government*, in *Two Treatises of Government* (New York: Hafner, 1964), pp. 122–124. Unless otherwise stated, all subsequent quotes from Locke in this chapter are from this source.

4. Jean-Jacques Rousseau, *The Social Contract and Discourses*, trans. G. D. H. Cole (London: J. M. Dent and Sons, 1982), pp. 174–175. Unless otherwise stated, all subsequent quotes from Rousseau in this chapter are from this source.

5. John Stuart Mill, *On Liberty* (Chicago: Henry Regnery, 1955), pp. 23–24.

6. Ibid., p. 13.

7. See, for example, Leonore Davidoff and Catherine Hall, *Family Fortunes: Men and Women of the English Middle Class, 1780–1850* (London: Hutchenson, 1987); and Dorothy O. Helly and S. Reverby, *Gendered Domains: Beyond the Public and Private in Women's History* (Ithaca, N.Y: Cornell University Press, 1992).

8. Richard Taylor, *Freedom, Anarchy, and the Law: An Introduction to Political Philosophy* (Englewood Cliffs, N.J.: Prentice-Hall, 1973), p. 58.

9. John Stuart Mill, *Principles of Political Economy* (New York: Longmans, Green, 1929), p. 950. Unless otherwise stated, all subsequent quotes from Mill in this chapter are from this source.

10. Karl Marx, *Economic and Philosophical Manuscripts*, in *Marx's Concept of Man*, ed. Erich Fromm, trans. T. B. Bottomore (New York: Frederick Ungar, 1969), p. 97.

11. Ibid., pp. 98–99.

12. Karl Marx, *German Ideology*, in Fromm, *Marx's Concept of Man*, p. 42.

13. Alan Brown, *Modern Political Philosophy: Theories of the Just Society* (New York: Penguin, 1986), pp. 117–118. All subsequent quotes from Brown in this chapter are from this source.

14. Robert Nozick, *Anarchy, State, and Utopia* (New York: Basic Books, 1974), p. 180. All subsequent quotes from Nozick in this chapter are from this source.

15. Alasdair MacIntyre, *After Virtue* (Notre Dame, Ind.: University of Notre Dame Press, 1981), p. 67.

16. Interview with Ronald Dworkin, in Bryan Magee, *Men of Ideas: Some Creators of Contemporary Philosophy* (London: British Broadcasting Corporation, 1978), p. 254.

17. John Rawls, *A Theory of Justice* (Cambridge, Mass.: Harvard University Press, 1971).

10

But Is It Art?
Philosophy of Art

The urge to produce art seems to be as old as the human race. If you compare the thirty-thousand-year-old representations on the cave walls at Altamira or Lascaux with the images of typical prime-time TV production—or worse, with graffiti on men's room walls in the bus depot (or worse yet, if such is possible, with the drawings in this book)—you may think that there has been a downward spiral since the times of our Cro-Magnon ancestors. But at least there have been some great moments in between!

What are human beings doing when they create "art"? Are their works frivolous or even dangerous distractions, or do they exhibit something deep and essential about human nature? And what is the relationship between art and "reality"? Is art a poor imitation of reality, as some philosophers have held? Or is art a spiritualization and enrichment of nature—an improvement upon the world—as other philosophers have asserted? These are some of the big questions in the philosophy of art. Whatever answers exist to these questions, it is not surprising that for thousands of years people

Early Graffiti

383

have been provoked to philosophize about art because, for better or for worse, art has been such a persuasive part of human experience.

Plato and Freud

You were advised earlier that our discussion of art, like so many of our discussions, would begin with Plato's views. However, you may or may not have anticipated that these views would be decidedly negative. His indictment of art, based on the metaphysics of the Simile of the Line (see Chapter 2), can be stated in three parts. There is an ontological objection, an epistemological objection, and a moral objection. The ontological objection has to do with Plato's view that art is imitation (**mimesis**). This was the standard Greek view, and it went unchallenged by all the greatest Greek thinkers on the subject. But what is art an imitation of? Well, according to to Plato, art must be imitating the world as it *appears*, not the world as it *is*. Artists imitate "particular objects." If so, then art itself must be consigned to the realm of "images" (being a copy of "particular things," which are themselves but copies of higher things). In Book X of the *Republic*, Plato says that art is "thrice removed from the truth." It is a copy of a copy of a copy.

Review of Plato's Simile of the Line

Because most of us today do not approach art under the influence of the Simile of the Line, and because we are no longer satisfied with the view that art is simply imitative, we probably do not feel that Plato's ontological objection is very forceful. Therefore, to be able to understand his point better, consider the following example. Imagine a novel by someone like Charles Dickens that begins with this line: "It was a foggy day in London." Now, precisely *what day* was a foggy day? June 21, 1836? August 7, 1829? Obviously, the sentence does not refer to any real day. Strictly speaking, the sentence is false, or at least, its status has nothing to do with the truth. Such is the case with *every* sentence in the novel, even those that coincidentally could correspond with the facts. (For instance, if Dickens had said,

"September 26, 1782, was a foggy day in London," we might check the records and discover that that day really *was* foggy, but it wouldn't matter to the work of art whether that was so. The work is no better or worse as a work of art if that sentence is true. Similarly, medieval and renaissance paintings of Jesus would be none the worse off as paintings even if it were proved that Jesus never lived.)

It follows that works of art are what they are by virtue of being *illusions*. The success of Dickens's novels depends upon his creating the illusion that he is describing real events and real people, just as the success of a realistic painting depends upon the artist's creating the illusion that these blotches of color are clouds, mountains, houses, people, and the like. So for Plato, the function of art is always to deceive. It always draws attention away from reality (the Forms) and toward illusion (images). Plato did not deny that an art whose function was more noble might be ontologically justifiable, but it seemed to him that almost all art was deceptive in the way just described.

Plato's epistemological objection is directed against both the work of art and the artist. The work of art, being false, does not give us any true knowledge of the world, and the artists do not know what they are doing. They cannot give the Logos.

Art Whose Function Is More Noble

Plato's *moral objection* is multifaceted. First, if Plato has established that the pursuit of knowledge is the pursuit of the Good, and if art produces ignorance, then art is immoral. Second, art seems to concentrate on the flaws in human and divine nature and often depicts great men and gods doing immoral things. Here Plato had in mind Homer and the Greek tragedies. How much respect can you have for a god like Zeus, who cheats on his wife and then lies to her when she asks him where he's been? Or can he be admired when on other occasions he is henpecked and even cuckolded by her? And what about the story of Odysseus in the underworld? When Odysseus meets the ghost of Achilles, Odysseus tells this honored hero of the Trojan War how much he envies him as prince among the dead. Achilles responds despairingly, "I'd rather be a serf or labouring man under some yeoman on a little farm than be king paramount of all the dead." How can you inspire courage in young men so that they will fight to defend their country if a role model like Achilles says it is better to be a live coward than a dead hero? If the people have flawed gods and heroes to imitate (even tragically flawed ones), the people themselves cannot be expected to try to achieve perfection.

Achilles and a Horrified Odysseus

And because we forget that art is an illusion, we do appeal to it for examples of ideal cases. Ask yourself how many times in the past week some of your own teachers have used an example from fiction to make a point. "A perfect example of madness is, of course, Don Quixote," "Hamlet exemplifies the feelings of indecision from which we all suffer," "Picasso's *Guernica* analyzes the horrors

A perfect example of madness is, of course, Don Quixote.

of war." But, in truth, a madman named Don Quixote never existed, nor did Hamlet have any *real* feelings of indecisiveness; not even bombed horses look like Picasso's horse, and real "tygers" do not burn in the forests of the night.

A Real Tyger Burning in the Forests of the Night

This brings us to the third and most important of Plato's moral objections to art. Art does not appeal to the highest faculty of the soul, Pure Reason. (How could it? It must deal with *images*.) Rather, it appeals to the basest part of the soul, the emotions. Plato, like Freud after him, was very suspicious of the irrational passions. Both Plato and Freud believed that in the darkest recesses of the soul is a cauldron of sexuality and violence—unruly emotions. These passions are antisocial and destructive of the individual. One of the most difficult jobs we face is reining these passions under our control instead of surrendering to their control. It is interesting that both Freud and Plato point to dreams as proving the existence of this part of the psyche, which Freud calls "the id" and Plato calls "the appetitive soul." You will remember from Chapter 7 that, in the *Republic*, Plato presents the following exchange between Socrates and his friend Glaucon:

Philosophy appeals here.

Action appeals here.

Art appeals here.

REASON

COURAGE

PASSIONS

The Structure of the Soul

Soc: See here, this is what I want to look into. . . . I feel that some of the unnecessary desires and pleasures are lawless: they are born in everyone. . . .

Glau: What are these, pray?

Soc: Those which are aroused in sleep, whenever the rest of the soul, all the reasonable, gentle and ruling part, is asleep, but the bestial and savage, replete with

Plato and Freud **387**

food or wine, skips about and, throwing off sleep, tries to go and fulfil its own instincts. You know there is nothing it will not dare to do, thus freed and rid of all shame and reason; it shrinks not from attempting in fancy to lie with a mother, or with any other man or god or beast, shrinks from no bloodshed, refrains from no food—in a word, leaves no folly or shamelessness untried.[1]

According to Plato, the way to control this part of the soul and thereby to prevent dreams of violence and sex is to live moderately, eat and drink little before retiring, think philosophical thoughts before sleeping, and above all, avoid art! Precisely the reason we like art is that it titillates the passions and provokes us. Sophisticated people are provoked by Bach, unsophisticated people by martial arts movies; but in some strange sense, the content is identical. We could almost say, in Plato's name, all art is pornographic.

Before you condemn Plato's view, ask yourself where you stand on this controversial claim from a contemporary debate of our own: "Violence on television perpetuates violence in society. Children who spend a great deal of time watching TV

Preventing Violent and Sexual Dreams

are less sensitive to violence and are more prone to solve their own problems by resorting to violence." If you agree with that passage, you are siding with Plato, for television is *the* contemporary art form; and all of Plato's objections—ontological, epistemological, and moral—apply vividly to the bulk of what we see on our screens, including the commercial messages.

Before leaving Plato and his objections to art, let's return for a moment to the comparison between Plato and Freud. You may have noticed earlier a striking similarity between Plato's doctrine of innate ideas and parts of Freud's psychoanalytic theory. For both thinkers, liberation comes when we remember the past, a past buried deep in our unconscious. Also, both men divided the soul into three aspects: for Freud, the id, the ego, and the superego; for Plato, the appetitive, the spirited, and the rational portions. Now, in their suspicion of art, we have found another similarity. Freud's theory of art is interesting in itself, but a brief discussion of it will shed light on Plato's similar theory. It will also prepare you for Herbert Marcuse's twentieth-century attempt to solve the problem of art (which I discuss later in this chapter).

Freud's theory of instincts (*triebe*, better translated as "drives" or "impulses") changed substantially over the forty-year period of his work, but I'll try to present a representative version of it. The sexual and aggressive drives contained in the id are irrational and antisocial. If rationality and society are to survive, these passions must be controlled. The rational com-

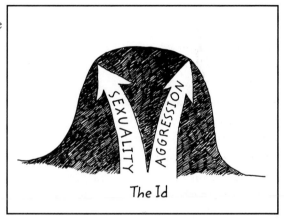

The Id

ponent of the psyche (the ego) is not by itself capable of containing the explosiveness of the id, so it must ally itself with the harsh irrationality of the superego. (For this alliance, the psyche pays a high price in terms of unconscious guilt.) Together they form a barrier that blocks the animal drives and returns them to their source. There they are "deanimalized" and redirected into socially acceptable forms of creativity: art, religion, philosophy, law, science, and morality—"higher culture." Freud calls this process **sublimation**. It produces a cultural product that is a substitute gratification for the primary

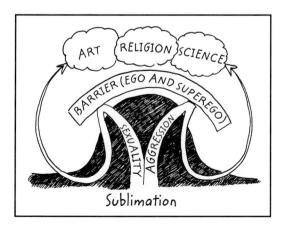

Sublimation

aim from which the drive was deflected. Yet the cultural product never completely loses its original (sexual or violent) nature. For example, imagine a little boy with a particularly strong aggressive drive. His idea of fun is to tear flesh, maim, and make people bleed. We can't afford to let him loose on the streets, so we send him to medical school, where he may sublimate his hostility into science and become a surgeon. He is now able to tear flesh, maim, and make people bleed and thereby receive wealth, prestige, and respectability. Freud believed that one could successfully sublimate one's animality into science (he believed that he and Einstein, at least, had done so), but apparently Freud was suspicious of artistic sublimation, even though he personally had a great reverence for art. His investigation of two of his

favorite artists, Leonardo da Vinci and Michelangelo, did not alleviate his suspicions. Arnold Hauser has summarized Freud's most pessimistic estimation of art in this passage:

> Both neurosis and art are essentially purposive; they are not only the expression of a failure and resignation in the face of reality, but also a kind of escapism. They represent partly an outcome of, partly a means of withdrawal from the real. "Every neurosis," says Freud, "has the result, and therefore probably the purpose, of forcing the patient out of real life, of alienating him from actuality." As far as the work of art is concerned, there can be no doubt about the existence of such a purpose. Neurosis and art equally reject reality, but neurosis does not deny it, only tries to forget it; art, on the other hand, tries both to deny and to replace it. The artist's attitude is, therefore, in this respect at least, more akin to insanity than to neurosis.[2]

Furthermore, the artist's product, unlike the scientist's, doctor's, or lawyer's, is still too close to its source in unconscious fantasies. Fantasies are guided by the infantile pleasure principle and have refused to submit to the reality principle. Therefore, art is not a rational response to the demands of reality but an irrational denial of reality. Freud's approach is just another, more complicated way of stating Plato's objection to art.

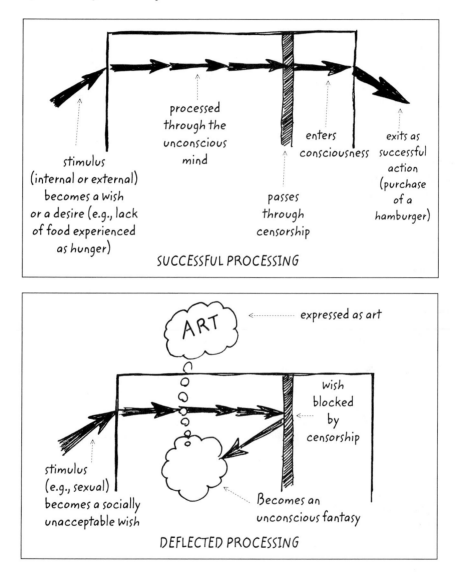

Aristotle

Despite Plato's tremendous influence on Western philosophy, very few of his followers have agreed with his condemnation of art. In fact, the first philosopher after Plato to come to art's defense was Plato's most important student, Aristotle (384–322 B.C.E.). We have already seen in Chapter 3 that Aristotle, though in many respects faithful to his master, ultimately rejected Plato's doctrine of Forms as too "other worldly." Aristotle believed that the world we are born into is the real world and not just a shadow of a more ultimate world. He brought Plato's philosophy down to earth by claiming that

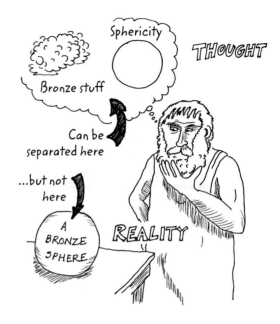

the Forms must be "imbedded in matter." He believed that the distinction between Form and matter was only an *intellectual* distinction, a distinction that could be drawn in theory but not in reality. His theory does not have the bias against "the visible world" that we saw in Plato; thus, Aristotle could accept Plato's claim that art deals in mimetic images without thereby condemning art.

There is another comment about Aristotle's metaphysics that is pertinent here. The late British philosopher Sir Isaiah Berlin liked to apply the story of the fox and the hedgehog to philosophers. The hedgehog has one *big* idea, and the fox has many *small* ideas. (Berlin said that the Russian novelist Tolstoy was a fox who wanted to be a hedgehog.) According to Berlin's criterion, then, Plato is a hedgehog and Aristotle is a fox. That is to say, Aristotle's metaphysics is more

The Hedgehog and the Fox and Their Respective Collection of Ideas

piecemeal than Plato's. This means that his discussion of art was less under the domination of some central, overriding philosophical idea; therefore Aristotle could consider art more as an autonomous activity (though not completely so because no Greek would consider any activity as independent of moral and political implications).

So Aristotle met Plato's ontological objection to art by rejecting Plato's hierarchical ontology. Yet he never denied that art is *mimesis*, imitation. Then what is art an imitation *of*?

Aristotle, who was particularly interested in poetry and drama, tells us that art imitates an *action*. But it does not imitate an *action* in the way that the writing of history imitates actions, simply recounting particular events (the second stage on Plato's line). Art is superior to history because it *theorizes* about actions (the third stage on the line). It does not tell us what *has* happened; rather, it tells us what *can* happen. Art deals with universals and not with particulars, so it is more philosophical than history is. So we see that Aristotle has also answered Plato's epistemological objection to art. Nevertheless, I must point out that, for Aristotle, art is still inferior to philosophy. It is, as it were, on the third level of the line and cannot achieve the fourth level. Aristotle believed, as Plato did, that the fourth level can be achieved only by philosophy.

What about Plato's moral objection to art? Aristotle agreed with Plato's claim that art appeals to the passions, and even though Aristotle was less suspicious of the passions than was Plato, he too believed that they can be wild, unruly, and dangerous. However, rather than holding that art encourages the passions to take control away from reason, Aristotle believed that art *purges* the passions. Let's read Aristotle's famous passage about this purgation (*catharsis*).

> An emotion which strongly affects some souls is present in all to a varying degree, for example pity and fear, and also ecstasy. To this last some people are particularly liable, and we see that under the influence of religious music and songs which drive the soul to frenzy, they calm down as if they had been medically treated and purged. People who are given to pity or fear, and emotional people generally, and others to the extent that they have similar emotions, must be affected in the same way; for all of them must experience a kind of purgation and pleasurable relief. In the same way, cathartic [songs and] music give men harmless delight. We must therefore make those who practice mousikê [poetry and music] in the theater perform these kinds of tunes and songs.[3]

Keep in mind that, unlike the more domesticated audiences of today, when Athenians went to the theater, they laughed, moaned, shrieked, beat

Greek Audience

their chests, and tore their hair as the drama unfolded. It is easy to see why Aristotle claimed catharsis to be the function of art in such a context, but before you decide between him and Plato, ask yourself again whether you think that watching violence on television and in the movies *replaces* real violence or stimulates it. And perhaps you'll be even more confused when you ask yourself the same question concerning sex in films and literature. Does pornography replace sexual activity or encourage it? Does it replace sexual crimes or provoke them?

Regardless of your opinions concerning these topics, I think you may be somewhat disappointed with parts of Aristotle's defense of art when you read the passage that follows his description of catharsis:

> There are two kinds of spectator: the one kind is a free and educated man, the other, the vulgar kind, is made up of mechanics and general laborers and other such people; these too must be provided with contests and spectacles for their recreation. Their souls are perverted from their natural state; so there are perversions of melody and songs that are tense and corrupted. Every man takes pleasure in what is naturally akin to him, and we must therefore allow the performers to use this kind of *mousikê* with this kind of spectator in view.[4]

We see here that the experience of catharsis is most needed by "mechanics and general laborers" and other such "vulgar" people. Plato had worried about the effects of art on the aristocracy as well as on the plebeians. Aristotle seems to see the production of art as a way of pacifying the masses (another "opiate of the masses"?). This view appears to conflict with his claim that art is philosophical.

There is a final point. Despite Aristotle's defense of art against Plato's attack, it is clear to any reader of both authors that Plato has much more feeling for art than does Aristotle. In fact, ironically, Plato is a poet and artist par excellence, but no one will ever accuse Aristotle of being that. Aristotle never felt the stirring of passion produced in the sensitive soul by the confrontation with art. Plato had done so and was fearful of it. When he drummed the artists out of the Republic, he said he did so with tears in his eyes.

The Interlude between Aristotle and the Nineteenth Century

We have treated the Freudian theory of art as a twentieth-century adjunct to Plato's theory. Shortly we will leap from Plato and Aristotle in the fourth century B.C.E. to Karl Marx in the nineteenth century C.E. But I do not want to leave the impression that nothing significant was thought about art in the intervening twenty-two hundred years. During the long medieval period, a number of views were expressed, but the overriding one was that art should only be a form of worship or be conducive to worship. During the renaissance, art theoreticians were mainly neo-Platonic. This term does not mean that they condemned art, as did Plato, but that they were Platonic revisionists, seeing art as expressing higher truths about beauty and sensuality.

The association between art and pleasure came to a head in the eighteenth century with the work of Alexander Baumgarten, who coined the term "aesthetic." He believed that the perception of "forms" (with a small "f") in art and nature produces "changes in the soul" that are experienced as delight or repugnance. This hedonistic "formalism" became a powerful influence in the early nineteenth century through the work of Johann Herbart and Robert Zimmermann. (This school may have reached its point of absurdity with Zimmermann's remark: "The large beside the small pleases, the small beside the large displeases.") Immanuel Kant, in his great *Critique of Judgment*, saw art as a moral symbol. G. W. F. Hegel defined art as "nature passed through spirit." JOHN RUS-

The large beside the small

The small beside the large

KIN (1819–1900) understood art to be the expression of emotion or instincts. Some of the Romantic poets combined Ruskin's view with a return to the medieval idea that art is religious service. LEO TOLSTOY (1828–1910) claimed that art was the communication of feeling and saw its function as the unification of humanity in a universal brotherhood. Nineteenth-century artists like Flaubert, Baudelaire, Poe, and Wilde were members of the school of "art for art's sake," which claimed that art had *no* function; it was valuable in and for itself. These examples demonstrate that, although traditional philosophy of art may have been kicked off by the debate between Plato and Aristotle, it was by no means restricted to their polemic.

Marx

The debate about the relation between art and justice, initiated by Plato, was reopened in the work of Karl Marx. Marx never wrote a treatise on art, but he was obviously fascinated by it and very concerned over it because references to art and art theory are scattered at significant places throughout his philosophical, sociological, and economic works. The attempt to reconstruct his ideas about art is complicated by the fact that two separate strands of thought concerning art run through Marx's writings, and these strands sometimes seem at odds with each other. On the one hand is his claim that the need for artistic expression and aesthetic enjoyment is an *essential* aspect of human nature. On the other hand is his assertion that art and aesthetics are components of ideology and as such are political captives. The first assertion sides with those traditional authors, such as Kant and Tolstoy, who extoll art. The second claim sides with Plato's condemnation of art. We shall examine both strands and see whether they can be made consistent with each other; then we shall briefly look at the theory of Herbert Marcuse, a mid-twentieth-century philosopher in the Marxian tradition who believed that the tension between Marx's

views can be relieved and art restored to its correctly exalted position by, ironically, infusing a bit of Freudian thought into **Marxism.** (The irony has to do with Freud's own ambivalence toward art, which we have just noted, and with the fact that, in general, Freud and Marx seem so incompatible.)

Marx's view is that human beings cannot be studied in a vacuum but must always be studied in their relation to the world. The world of human beings is composed of relations to nature, to fellow humans, and to the products of their hands and minds. Under optimum conditions, these relations are positive. They are productive, artistic, aesthetic, and creative. Wherever those relationships are ruptured, humans are alienated from their world and hence from themselves. (In Chapter 9, we took a look at alienated labor.) Marx wrote that man is independent only "if he affirms his individuality as a total man in each of his relations to the world, seeing, hearing, smelling, tasting, feeling, thinking, willing, loving—in short, if he affirms and expresses all organs of his individuality."[5] For Marx, the fully *human* being is essentially an artist who approaches the world aesthetically and forms things "in accordance with the laws of beauty."[6] From this point of view, we can say that the goal of communism (or at least as envisioned by the young Marx) was the liberation of *Homo artisticus*, the human being as artist. Robert Tucker has characterized this aspect of Marx's conception of communism in the following passage:

> What will remain is the life of art and science in a special and vastly enlarged sense of these two terms. Marx's conception of ultimate communism is fundamentally *aesthetic* in character. His utopia is an aesthetic ideal of the future man-nature relationship, which he sees in terms of artistic creation and the appreciation of the beauty of the man-made environment by its creator. The acquisitive and therefore alienated man of history is to be succeeded by the post-historical aesthetic man who will be "rich" in a new way. . . .
>
> Economic activity will turn into artistic activity, with industry as the supreme avenue of creation, and the planet itself will become the new man's work of art. The alienated world will give way to the aesthetic world.[7]

However, this general theory, which turns all truly human productivity into artistic and aesthetic acts, does not tell us anything about the difference between artistic production and nonartistic production in history up to Marx's own time. When we look not to Marx's future communist society, where all are artists, but to the present and the past, where only some are artists, we run up against Marx's theory of ideology. To understand this theory, we must first draw Marx's distinction between the *foundation* and the *superstructure* of society. Marx says:

> In the social production of their means of existence men enter into definite, necessary relations which are independent of their will, productive relationships which correspond to a definite stage of development of their material productive forces. The aggregate of these productive relationships constitutes the economic structure of society, the real basis on which a juridical and political superstructure arises, and to which definite forms of social consciousness correspond. The mode of production of the material means of existence conditions the whole process of social, political and intellectual life. It is not the consciousness of men that determines their existence, but, on the contrary, it is their social existence that determines their consciousness.
>
>   . . . .
>
> Then an epoch of social revolution opens. With the change in the economic foundation the whole vast superstructure is more or less rapidly transformed. In considering such revolutions it is necessary always to distinguish between the material revolution in the economic conditions of production, which can be determined with scientific accuracy, and the juridical, political, religious, aesthetic or philosophic—in a word, ideological forms wherein men become conscious of this conflict and fight it out.[8]

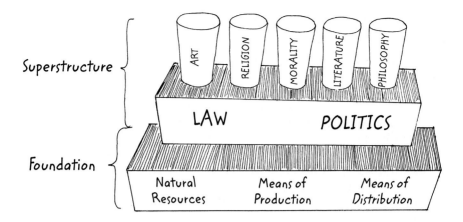

Furthermore, Marx added, "The ideas of the ruling class are in every epoch the ruling ideas."[9]

"Ideology" is Marx's term for the myth of self-aggrandizement that each socioeconomic system necessarily (if unintentionally) creates by monopolizing and controlling the form and content of the spiritual productions of its creative members. These products become a form of unconscious political propaganda. The theory of ideology clearly applies to artistic as well as philosophical and political ideas. That is, artists also express the values of the ruling class that supports them; therefore, artists, intentionally or not, endorse and perpetuate the status quo. Medieval art glorified

"The Ruling Ideas of Each Age . . ."

God and condemned worldliness, thereby reflecting the values of the papal authority that ruled over the Christian world. Renaissance painting depicted religious themes as well but also mythological allegories, the faces of the Medici, and great military victories, thereby affirming the values of the ruling elite who provided the artists' livelihood. The amazing treatment by Vermeer and the northern baroque artists of light and air in Dutch drawing rooms, kitchens, and studies was a celebration of the values of the bourgeoisie who bought those paintings. The lovely nineteenth-century English landscapes of Constable left one with the feeling that all's well with the (bourgeois) world. Constable's beautiful *Dedham Vale* shows the lush English countryside leading down the valley to the peaceful village of Dedham, whose church spire we see glimmering in the sun. We do not see the jute facto-

Portrait of Louis XIV (after Hyacinthe Rigaud)

Laws establishing aristocratic privilege (e.g., antipoaching laws)

Property ownership by the nobility

Art as Ideology

ries in which tubercular children are slaving twelve hours a day in order to be able to add a few pieces of bread to their parents' table and add their "surplus labor" (profit) to the sumptuous table of the capitalist mill owner. Again, art, like religion, is an opiate. Even the most beautiful art, the greatness of the classics, is ideology.

But I must add a further complication. For Marx, the material foundations of society, from which all art emerges, are fractured in terms of antagonistic classes. That is, one class owns the material wealth of the society, and a dispossessed class must sell its labor to this owning class. The interests of the one class are not the interests of the other. The interests of the ruling class will always be expressed as the dominant ideas in any historical period, but the interests of the disadvantaged class may find

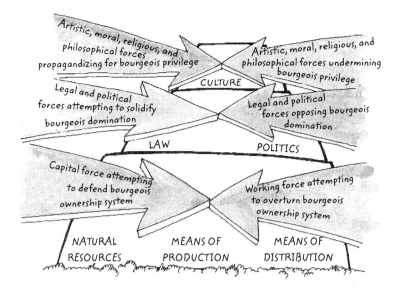

Artistic, moral, religious, and philosophical forces propagandizing for bourgeois privilege

Artistic, moral, religious, and philosophical forces undermining bourgeois privilege

CULTURE

Legal and political forces attempting to solidify bourgeois domination

Legal and political forces opposing bourgeois domination

LAW

POLITICS

Capital force attempting to defend bourgeois ownership system

Working force attempting to overturn bourgeois ownership system

NATURAL RESOURCES

MEANS OF PRODUCTION

MEANS OF DISTRIBUTION

cultural expression too. So for every expression of the socioeconomic foundation in terms of a cultural form, there can be a counterexpression as well. After all, the morality of the aristocrat is not the morality of the serf, nor are their ideas the same, nor their religion, nor their art. Cultured art may be the portrait of the king; counterculture art may be a caricature of him, drawn on a wall accompanied by scatological graffiti or, among the working class imbued with class consciousness, a political poster or a mural by José Orozco or Diego Rivera. But apparently from the perspective of the theory of ideology, it must be admitted that counterculture or revolutionary art, like mainstream art, is propaganda. (Of course, Marx would say that the propaganda of the revolutionary working class is not ideology because ideology is always a form of illusion, and the proletariat is the one class that does not need illusion. But this claim itself seems ideological. Left-wing propaganda can be just as ideological as right-wing propaganda.)

As if his approach to art were not complicated enough, Marx also held that some socioeconomic systems were inherently antagonistic to art, specifically capitalism. Marx says, "Capitalistic production is hostile to certain branches of spiritual production, for example, art and poetry."[10] Capitalism is hostile to art because "the bourgeoisie has stripped of its halo every occupation hitherto honored and looked up to with reverent awe. It has converted the physician, the lawyer, the priest, the poet, the man of science, into its paid wage-labourers."[11] In capitalism, says Marx:

> Only that wage-labour is productive which produces capital. . . . For example, Milton, who wrote *Paradise Lost* for £5 sterling, was an *unproductive labourer*. On the other hand, the writer who turns out stuff for his publisher

in factory style, is a *productive labourer.* Milton produced *Paradise Lost* for the same reason that a silkworm produces silk. It was an activity of his nature. Later he sold the product for £5 sterling.[12]

In capitalism, to be productive is to put out a commodity. But art is not a commodity. It is a necessary expression of true human essence. Therefore, art and capitalism are incompatible.

Another sense in which capitalism is hostile to art has to do with the division of labor. Marx and his collaborator Friedrich Engels say:

> The exclusive concentration of artistic talent in particular individuals, and its suppression in the broad mass which is bound up with this, is a consequence of the division of labor. . . . [The issue is not] that each should do the work of Raphael, but anyone in whom there is a potential Raphael should be able to develop without hindrance. . . . In a communist society there are no painters but at most people who engage in painting among other activities.[13]

John Milton (1608–1674)

So far, Marx's theory seems to be the following: the artistic impulse is a natural and necessary expression of human nature. In a truly human and humane community (i.e., in communism), each individual would find an artistic form of expression "according to the laws of beauty," some reaching great heights of artistic excellence but all achieving a satisfactory expression of the aesthetic urge. However, the artistic impulse has historically been co-opted at times and sometimes suppressed. The artistic urge has also been corrupted and twisted into a conduit of political propaganda. The artistic form of expression will be liberated only in a postrevolutionary communist society where humankind's creative birthright will be restored to it.

But a problem arises with this interpretation (not to mention the problem of deciding whether there is any good reason to think Marx is right). If we look at Marx's actual examples, we see that he extolls the very artists whom, as it would seem, his theory should condemn. Obviously, Milton and Raphael, the two artists referred to in the preceding passages, are not being denigrated by Marx; rather, it is implied that he holds them in high esteem, yet these are two artists whose work is essentially religious. Furthermore, if we look at the

Karl Marx Contemplates Raphael's
Madonna Del Granduca

list of artists Marx admired (Balzac, Dickens, Cervantes, and Heine) and consider the fact that every year Marx reread the complete works of Goethe, Shakespeare, and Aeschylus, we discover that his own taste in art was decidedly traditional.

How does Marx's personal preference in art square with his theory of art as ideology? Marx himself seems to have realized the tension between his general theory of culture as ideology and his personal aesthetic taste. He explained the apparent inconsistency by saying that, in some epochs, art is more in bondage to the economic substructure than in others. Art can have a relative autonomy if the economic system is not highly developed, if it is not especially hostile to art, and if there are a number of intermediary connections between material production and artistic production. Marx uses Greek art and Shakespeare as exemplifying the possibility of uneven development between economy and art. Apparently, Marx felt that neither the form nor the content of the works of Aeschylus and Shakespeare could be explained purely by the structure of the socioeconomic relations in their day. Such an admission seems to amount to a major qualification of the theories of materialism and ideology. Some might even pose the question as to whether it marks a total abandonment of those theories.

Indeed, after Marx's death in 1888, his collaborator, Friedrich Engels, admitted that perhaps he and Marx had overstated the dependence of culture on economics. And Marx himself was so upset by the exaggerations of certain French Marxists that he uttered to Engels, "All I know is that I am not a Marxist."

But perhaps Marx's general theory

Romeo, Juliet, and the Profit Motive

of culture can be maintained if certain corrections are made to the theory of art. So thought the contemporary Marxist philosopher, Herbert Marcuse, to whose work we now turn.

Marcuse

HERBERT MARCUSE (1898–1979), who came to America fleeing Nazi persecution, was a controversial figure in the American left. He was very influential in Europe and the United States during the activist period of the late sixties and early seventies. During one demonstration in Rome in 1968, radical students chanted "M-M-M" (Marx, Mao, Marcuse). Though ultimately a falling-out took place between Marcuse and the student activists because of his refusal to endorse the dismantling of Columbia University in 1972, there can be no question as to his impact on intellectual developments in the West. The work that will chiefly concern us here is *Eros and Civilization* (1955). Despite its subtitle, *A Philosophical Inquiry into Freud*, this book basically deals with the problem of art as raised by Plato and Marx and in fact represents a valiant effort to synthesize Freud and Marx. This attempt is complicated by the fact that these two architects of the modern mind seem to disagree fundamentally on so many important issues (which may partially explain why the modern mind seems so schizoid).

We can begin our discussion of the pertinent themes in Marcuse's book by reminding ourselves of one basic disagreement between Marx and Freud. The anarchistic side of Marx envisions a world in which all restraints and all forms of repression are ultimately removed. In that world, the true artistic nature of the human being will flower in ways that heretofore have been possible in only a handful of unique individuals. Freud, on the other hand, saw art as possible only in a world of repression. The doctrine of sublimation holds that only under repressive conditions established against libidinal energies by the authority of the ego and the superego and by the harshness of reality can those energies be redirected into

**Herbert Marcuse
(1898–1979)**

art. As opposed to Marx, Freud felt that the abolition of repression would not result in a flowering of art but in a reversion to our murderous, rapacious prehistoric past.

How in the world can Marcuse synthesize these extreme opposites? He does so in truly dialectical fashion by finding truth in both views. Freud is right (and Marx is wrong) to say that society without repression is inconceivable. There will always be restraints and requirements backed up with the implied threat of force. (Someone has to plant and reap the corn, slaughter the fowl, and keep the sewers open.) This facet of society Marcuse calls "necessary repression." But Marx is right (and Freud is wrong)

to recognize that the bulk of social repression does not serve the purpose of meeting basic biological and social needs; rather, it serves the purpose of guaranteeing the privileged position of the elite classes. This domination Marcuse calls "surplus repression" In short, we can say that for Marcuse, the goal of philosophy (and of political action) is to eliminate surplus repression and to reduce necessary repression to an absolute minimum.

So far, Marcuse's argument has leaned more heavily on Marx than on Freud, but his "Marxism" is decidedly qualified. For example, Marx thought that the dialectical laws of history would guarantee progress and the ultimate success of socialism, but Marcuse demonstrates that the "dialectic" has broken down. Marx had held that history would resolve itself into the two ultimate classes, the bourgeoisie and the proletariat, and the clash between these two would end the class system as such and result in a classless society, the initial stage of his true communism. But Marcuse believed that, rather than clashing with the proletariat, the "cunning of capitalism" (far more cunning than Marx gave credit) simply opened its jaws, swallowed the proletariat, chewed it up, and spat it back out as its own best representative. In Marcuse's day, especially in America, the best spokesperson for capitalist values was not the executive of the corporation but members of the working class itself, who owned stock in the corporations, who marched in hard hats against the peace movement, and whose most radical demand was that they be given the opportunity to consume even more goods. Today, too, all walks of American life have accepted uncritically the view that they are "the consumers." Even the good guys, the protectors of the people, are called "consumer advocates." We consume movies, lectures, education, and even landscapes. As Erich Fromm, Marcuse's erstwhile ally on the Freudian left, puts it: "He (modern man) is the eternal consumer; he 'takes in' drink, food, cigarettes, lectures, sights, books, movies; all are consumed, swallowed. The world is one great object for his appetite: a big bottle, a big apple, a big breast."[14]

If the Marxian dialectic were in fact operational, we could expect that this "thesis" would spawn a negative "antithesis," which would fundamentally oppose and eventually destroy the prevailing consumer world. But the cunning of capitalism

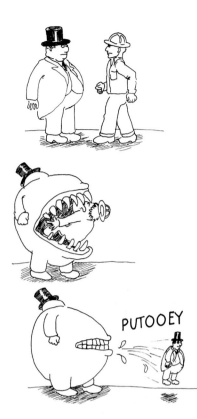

The Confrontation between Capitalism and the Working Class, According to Marcuse

(or really, the cunning of advanced technocracy) has preempted all possible opposition. So argued Marcuse in *One-Dimensional Man* (1964). Nothing counts as opposition to the system. It has become totalitarian, not in the Stalinist or Hitlerian sense, but in that it has totalized itself. Everything is, or becomes, a version of the system. In the sixties, the flower children concocted a kind of antiestablishment, psychedelic art, which soon found its way to billboards and TV commercials, advertising the useless products spewed out by the system. The "V" sign, which was a symbol of the antiestablishment peace movement, became the victory sign of Richard Nixon. The peace symbol itself

The Consumer

was quickly available as a decorative embellishment on the checks of a large national bank whose investments in South Vietnam helped bolster the makeshift government there. The symbol was also found on the packages of one of the largest cigarette companies. The growing of long hair as an antiestablishment gesture was so successful that the establishment itself took it over. Patched jeans and farmers' overalls were similarly quickly co-opted. In fact, soon jeans made entirely of prefaded denim patches were available at all the most fashionable, expensive shops. It became obvious to Marcuse that the enemy was no longer Wall Street, but Madison Avenue. Capitalism had not only become cunning, it had gone "cool."

Capitalism: Old Style, New Style

Other apparently antiestablishment activities met the same fate under Marcuse's scrutiny, sometimes to the annoyance of his would-be followers. Marcuse insisted that smoking marijuana was not a revolutionary activity, nor were the demonstrations to legalize it. Similarly, the so-called sexual revolution came in for criticism. It was no revolution at all but a new form of manipulation orchestrated by Madison Avenue, or at least quickly co-opted by it. "The pill" was not invented by a hippie but by a pharmaceutical company. It was not revolutionary fervor that lowered women's necklines, tightened men's trousers, removed "modesty shields" from the front of desks, put full-frontal nudity in the cinema, steamed up prime-time TV, and created such entities as "sexy floorwalkers." Capitalism was not going to be consumed by the fire from burning brassieres or overturned by young people tumbling in and out of each other's beds. Rather than calling all this activity a sexual revolution, Marcuse called it "repressive desublimation." It is the act of **reifying** ("thingifying") sexuality, turning it into yet another commodity. Marcuse wrote:

> The most telling illustration is provided by the methodological introduction of sexiness in business, politics, propaganda, etc. To the degree to which sexuality obtains a definite sales value or becomes a token of prestige and of playing according to the rules of the game, it is itself transformed into an instrument of social cohesion.[15]

So not only was the sexual freedom of the flower child generation incapable of threatening the foundations of the commodity world, it itself had been transformed into a commodity.

It is finally time to return to our discussion of art. Did Marcuse find any hope in the antiestablishment art that abounded in the sixties and seventies? According to the Marxian theories of the dialectic and ideology, this kind of art ought at least to provide some ideological opposition to the established powers. But the dialectic has been neutralized, and antiestablishment art has also been co-opted and has simply become avant-garde capitalism. The living theater, guerrilla theater, and rock music (or at least *white* rock music) all came in for their share of abuse. (To demonstrate that the goal of rock music is not revolution but "noisy aggression," Marcuse enjoyed quoting Grace Slick of the Jefferson Airplane. "'Our eternal goal in life,' Grace says, absolutely deadpan, 'is to get louder.'"[16]

Where, then, if anywhere, is there any hope? Now comes the surprise (if it is still a surprise): in traditional art—in the art that Marx himself loved but could not easily explain! In order to understand Marcuse's rationale here, we will have to return to Freud. Recall that both Freud and Plato found the source of art in fantasy. It was for precisely this reason that both of them were suspicious of art. For Freud, fantasy, particularly unconscious fantasy, was still guided by the pleasure principle and therefore under the dominion of **Eros.** It was the one realm that had escaped the reality principle. Marcuse accepted the Freudian account of art but not Freud's judgment of it. Art indeed has its source in fantasy, and fantasy, deriving from infantile memories and hopes, indeed escapes the reality principle. But Marcuse came to associate Freud's reality principle with what Marcuse

Marx and Marcuse Contemplate Constable's *Dedham Vale*

called "surplus repression." Fantasy, and the art deriving from it, is the one component of the contemporary psyche that has refused to accept the domination of surplus repression or, for that matter, *any* repression. Art is indeed a hallucinatory realm. It is based on the infantile promise of happiness found, perhaps, at the mother's breast, a promise that was betrayed. Therefore, Marcuse calls art "the promise of happiness"—*la promesse du bonheur*—and he calls its beauty "the sensuous appearance of the idea of freedom." Art, as Freud's "return of the repressed," is the "negation of the commodity world." Marcuse says, "The return of the repressed makes up the tabooed and subterranean history of civilization."[17] It haunts repressive civilization as the memory of happiness that civilization denies us—a memory from our own individual infancy and perhaps from the infancy of the human race. The value of psychoanalysis is that it has elevated memory to a status of supreme importance. Of psychoanalysis, Marcuse says:

> Its truth value lies in the specific function of memory to preserve promises and potentialities which are betrayed and even outlawed by the mature, civilized individual, but which had once been fulfilled in his dim past and which are

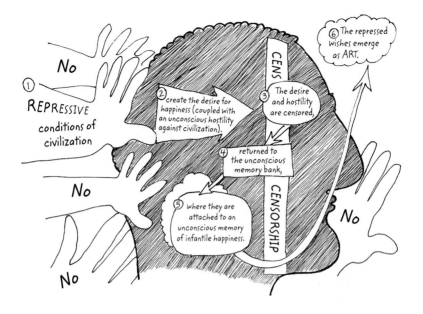

never entirely forgotten. . . . The psychoanalytic liberation of memory explodes the rationality of the repressed individual.[18]

When we look at a work of classical art, such as one of Vermeer's bourgeois drawing rooms or Constable's English countrysides, we enter into the source of utopian thinking. Rather than these works serving ideologically to convince us that all is well with the world (as a perhaps oversimplistic "Marxist" reading would have it), instead they indict the world. When we return from the realm created by Gauguin, whether it be the softness of the Breton countryside or the lushness of Tahitian eroticism, we must again occupy our own hollow world of dreary *things* to be consumed. The person who correctly enters into the spirit of art will be disturbed by the fact that her world is not what it could or should be. She will be moved to do something concrete about this fact. All great art, art that refuses to be co-opted by the prevailing reality, is revolutionary. It is subversive. It reactivates the dialectic. It is what Marcuse calls "the power of the negative."

Notice that Marcuse's solution to the problem of the status of art never really denies one of Plato's main criticisms. Art lies. It promises a happiness that cannot be achieved. We shall never recline among the green, yellow, and purple shadows of Gauguin's tropical world, nor shall we stroll through the sensuous density of Constable's vale of Dedham. A totally nonrepressive world is impossible. Still, if we do not believe in these possibilities, do not believe in the "noble lie" (Plato's term), we shall never be able to overcome that great surfeit of suppression that is irrational and that *can* be overcome.

A final critical note here: I believe that Marcuse's synthesis of Marx and Freud has given us an interesting and plausible account of what is exciting in great art. But his account is problematical, for it seems untestable. What would count as evidence for or against Marcuse's interpretations? This question is difficult to answer. But perhaps Marcuse's theory is no more problematical than other theories about the nature and status of art. Aesthetic theories are often like recommendations concerning the proper way to view art than they are like scientific theories that could be verified or refuted through careful attention to empirical detail.

Existentialism

Existentialism is a twentieth-century philosophical movement that has had a great interest in art. The term "existentialism" was coined by Jean-Paul Sartre (see Chapter 6), but the philosophy itself derives from certain currents in the nineteenth century, especially from the thought of Friedrich Nietzsche and Søren Kierkegaard. The task of defining existentialism is complicated by the great variety of philosophers called existentialists and by the many discrepancies among their views. One can sympathize with those who finally abandon in exasperation the task of defining existentialism as a philosophy, settling for calling it "a shared mood" or "an attitude," but I think the task is really not that hopeless. Sartre himself has tried to define existentialism in a simple, relatively successful manner. I will follow his lead.

Existentialism: A Shared Mood

Sartre says that an existentialist is any philosopher who has as a guiding idea the view that, in the case of human beings at least, "existence precedes essence." Now, traditionally in philosophy, it has been held that the opposite is so, that "essence precedes existence." To sort out this debate between Sartre and the philosophical tradition, we have to return to Plato and Aristotle. In Greek thought, "essence" is associated with "nature" (as when we ask, "What is the nature of the beast?") and with "Form" in the Platonic sense. The Platonic doctrine, with which we are familiar, holds that a natural object or a human being exists only as a copy of a Form, so for Plato, "essence precedes existence." As we saw, Aristotle tried to bring Plato's Forms down to earth, pointing out that "Form" with a capital "F" was really "form" with a small "f." In other words, the Form of a knife is actually related to its shape, which is related to its function. (What would a knife with flabby edges be like? Well, it wouldn't be a knife because it couldn't function as a knife.) So to say that "essence precedes existence" is to say that first the nature and function of a thing exist, then the thing exists.

Sartre agrees that this formula is true of artifacts, such as knives, and he seems to agree that it is true of natural entities too. For instance, in the case of a knife, first the human being conceives of a function (fig. 1). He needs something that will cut the bread. Then he creates an object that fulfills this function (fig. 2). It is perhaps less clear how this analysis applies to natural objects, such as oak trees, mountains, and pussycats, but I suppose we can say that there really is a thing called the species "cat" (i.e., there is a "cat nature") and that, to be a cat, a thing must fulfill certain criteria of "catness." (This all sounds very Platonic.) Now, the old picture of the human being, that is, the preexistential picture, treats the human being the same way as it treats the cat or knife. First, there is God. He conceives of the human being. ("What I need is one like me, only smaller, weaker, and dumber" [fig. 3].) Then, Michelangelo-style, he creates one (fig. 4). The creature is truly human only insofar as it fulfills certain divine criteria. Actions falling outside these criteria will be viewed as "inhuman," or even "insane." Then along comes Friedrich Nietzsche with

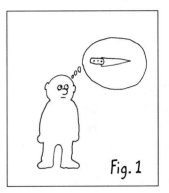

Fig. 1

Fig. 2

Fig. 3

Fig. 4

Fig. 5

his bad news: "God is dead!" If we erase God from the picture, all we get is the scene in fig. 5, which is the human condition according to the existentialists. The human being is, as Kierkegaard said, in "absolute isolation" and, as Sartre says, "abandoned." Sartre asks:

> What is meant here by saying that existence precedes essence? It means that, first of all, man exists, turns up, appears on the scene, and, only afterwards, defines himself. If man, as the existentialist conceives him, is indefinable, it is because at first he is nothing. Only afterwards will he be something, and he himself will have made what he will be. Thus there is no human nature, since there is no God to conceive it.[19]

This account seems to make existentialism atheistic and would appear to rule out Kierkegaard's inclusion in its ranks. And indeed Nietzsche and Sartre, along with many other existentialists, are radically atheistic; but a few pages beyond the passage just quoted, Sartre himself says, somewhat contradictorily perhaps, "even if God did exist, that would change nothing."[20] And, like Kierkegaard, Sartre uses the case of Abraham as an exemplification of the human condition. For Kierkegaard, the human condition is one of absolute isolation. In his despair, the human calls out for God's help, but instead of an answer there is only silence. (The Swedish film director, Ingmar Bergman, deeply influenced by Kierkegaard, titled one of his movies The Silence.) For Kierkegaard, if there were no God, this silence would be bad enough; but in fact it is worse because there is a God. A qualitative abyss gapes open between man and God. As in Sartre's philosophy, the human

is left alone, forlorn, dreading the total freedom that is his, despairing over the immense task of assuming the responsibility for the world he must create. If you agree with this picture, you are an existentialist.

From its first moments in the writings of Kierkegaard and Nietzsche, existentialism has always been fascinated by art. However, contemporary existentialists do not simply philosophize about art in a technical manner; many of them actively produce art. Sartre, Simone de Beauvoir, and Albert Camus produced systematic treatises on philosophy but also wrote novels, short stories, and plays. Nietzsche wrote poetry; Miguel de Unamuno wrote novels, plays, and poetry. And the novelists Franz Kafka and Fyodor Dostoyevsky are often included in the ranks of the existentialists. In order to see how existentialism theorizes about art, we will briefly inspect the work of two twentieth-century American existentialists, Arturo Fallico and Maurice Natanson. I have selected them not because they are well known (they are not), but because their books are readable and at the same time they are good representatives of the technical philosophizing about art that emerges from the **phenomenological**-existential school.

In Arturo Fallico's book *Art and Existentialism* he says, concerning the possibility of an existentialistic aesthetic, "we must try to see what we can learn about the condition of man from the art phenomenon, and about the art phenomenon from the existential condition of man."[21] One of the main themes in his book is that in some sense the world confronts us like a work of art, but there is also a sense in which the world confronts us quite differently from a work of art, and there is something about art and human existence that we can learn from each of these phenomena. The sense in which the world confronts us like a work of art is that our lived-in world is fundamentally aesthetic rather than scientific. The hegemony of science over the modern mind may make us forget this fact, but actually the world

The World Confronts Us Like a Work of Art

presents itself in terms of experienced qualities of the type better described in the language of the art critic than the language of the physicist. To the unjaded eye, the world looks like a spontaneous work of art. Under the impact of this insight, Fallico, with Nietzsche, talks about the possibility of "the aesthetic transformation of our experience" becoming our individual existential project. He approvingly quotes Nietzsche, who said, "To the extent that man is artist, he is already delivered from his ego and has become a medium through which the true subject celebrates his redemption in illusion." In *The Birth of Tragedy*, Nietzsche tells a story, which he calls "an old legend," about King Midas, who:

> hunted a long time in the woods for the wise Silenus, companion of Dionysos, without being able to catch him. When he had finally caught him the king asked him what he considered man's greatest good. The daemon remained sullen and uncommunicative until finally, forced by the king, he broke into a shrill laugh and spoke: "Ephemeral wretch, begotten by accident and toil, why do you force me to tell you what it would be to your greatest boon not to hear? What would be best for you is quite beyond your reach: not to have been born, not to be, to be nothing. But the second best is to die soon."[22]

In the context of Nietzsche's version of existentialism, the moral of this terrible story is that the demon Silenus is correct *unless* an individual does something to prove Silenus wrong. Unless one *creates* something—and, for Nietzsche, creation itself is artistic—then it would be better that one had never been born. For Nietzsche, existence can only be redeemed artistically.

Having asserted the similarity between art and the world and the significance of this similarity for humans, Fallico then turns to the difference between the world and art, which inheres in the fact that in its spontaneity, the world presents itself to us as "not-done-and-having-to-be-attended-to." The artwork, in contrast, presents itself as a totality, a completed unity, a fullness, and a completeness that is unavailable anywhere else in existence. The "still life" is the exemplar of all art. "In art," says Fallico, "everything *is*, nothing is becoming or has need to

OK, I've got you now. What's first best?

You've got to be kidding!

become." Only art conquers time. Like Faust, in Goethe's great drama of the same name, we cry out to time, "Stay!" But time does not stay. In art, time does stay. Art shows that "human existence is a lack rather than a plenitude of being and meaning."[23] It is a testimony of "man's home-

The World as Not-Done-and-Having-to-Be-Attended-To

less condition and his lack of essence." So once again, according to Fallico, art shows us that we must *create*. "Art places on exhibit a way of validating existence."[24] Art shows us what value, in its pure possibility, is.

Another American author in the phenomenological-existential tradition is Maurice Natanson. The title of his book *The Journey-ing Self* also emphasizes our homeless nature. We are told by Natanson that the confrontation with art affords the individual the opportunity of passing from the typical to the symbolic or from the familiar to the transcenden-tal. In artworks, we find repre-sented the great "metaphysical constants of human existence, Birth, Aging, Intersubjectivity, and Death." Of course, in daily life, we continually run up against these

Transient!

Art Reveals Our Homeless Condition

great constants, too, but precisely because they are so enmeshed in our day-to-day existence, we are unable to isolate these themes in terms of their true significance. In art, I confront birth, sociality, and death in a way that is "primordially unlike all my acquaintance with individual births and deaths." Here, "the naive attitude of daily life is forced to the edge of its limits" as "the symbolic cuts a gash in common sense and draws its hot blood."[25] The radical confrontation through art with the ultimate themes of birth, sociality, and death forces the individual to philosophize existentially as she or he struggles to construct the foundations of her or his own world. The existentialistic point might be best expressed by relating an anecdote told of the German poet Rainer Maria Rilke, who, after spending an afternoon contemplating the beauty of the statue of Apollo in an Athenian museum, returned to his hotel and made the following single entry in his journal: "You must change your life."[26] This anecdote demonstrates a common denominator in existentialism and the theory of Herbert Marcuse. According to both, art can and should provoke us into action and creativity.

Wittgenstein

We will now turn to a discussion of art very different from those we've seen so far. It will be less dramatic than some of the material we have reviewed in this chapter, but it is interesting in a different way. This view stems from the work of the Viennese philosopher LUDWIG WITTGENSTEIN (1889–1951), who studied and taught at Cambridge. Wittgenstein is hardly a household name among the general public. We dealt with him briefly in Chapter 1, but you probably had not heard of him before taking a philosophy class. Nevertheless many people believe he will prove to be one of the two or three greatest philosophers of the twentieth century, certainly one of the most influential.

Wittgenstein's work is usually divided into two periods, one centering on his *Tractatus Logico-Philosophicus*, written early in his career, and the other on his *Philosophical Investigations*, a much later work (published posthumously). The first book is a strange combination of a variation on the theme of logical positivism and mysticism. The second book apparently abandons these strains and concentrates on the subtle workings of everyday thought, language, and action.

In the *Tractatus*, only one passage could be construed as dealing with art. Characteristically, it is an obscure passage. Wittgenstein says, "Ethics and aesthetics are one and the same." Because in that book Wittgenstein had put ethics outside the realm of language ("It is clear that ethics cannot be put into words"); it follows that the object of aesthetics (philosophical meditation on beauty) is part

of the mystical and that nothing intelligible can be said about it.[27]

In the *Tractatus*, Wittgenstein followed his own advice and said nothing about art. (His admonishment at the beginning of the book had been "Whereof one cannot speak, thereof should one remain silent!") However, the later Wittgenstein had a number of things to say with implications for art theory, some of which have proved to be quite provocative and have become grist for the mills of later philosophers. We will examine two areas of the later Wittgenstein's thought on art that have proved especially instructive. One has to do with Wittgenstein's discussion of the

**Ludwig Wittgenstein
(1889–1951)**

"open-endedness" of certain concepts; the other concerns his notion of a language as a "form of life." As can be seen, neither of these two topics contains any specific reference to art; yet their application to the problems of the philosophy of art has generated much interest and controversy of late. However, before we can apply Wittgenstein's ideas to art, we will have to spend some time developing the key Wittgensteinian notions.

Open Concepts

Wittgenstein believed that over and over again in the history of philosophy, thinkers had been deceived by taking a particular successful model of clarity and trying to force all of language and thought into the mold of that one model. He called this error linguistic bewitchment of the intellect. A clear example of this kind of error is the attempt to come up with a general theory of meaning based on certain examples from mathematics or logic. For instance, take the definition of a triangle: "A triangle is a three-sided closed figure." Now assuming standard meanings for words like "side" and "closed," this definition is exhaustive. Any candidate for the term "triangle" must meet this criterion. There can be a variety of kinds of triangles (isosceles, right, obtuse), but each one must nevertheless be a three-sided figure. Then this feature, which can be called "the essence of triangularity," is the feature common to all possible triangles. A similar kind of analysis can be performed on such concepts as "brother" (a brother is a male sibling) or "bachelor" (a bachelor is an unmarried, eligible male). Inspired by this kind of clarity, many philosophers—especially philosophers of a Platonic bent who are looking for "essences"—have claimed that a word is meaningful only if it is the name of a certain feature common to all members of a class, and in fact it is possible to view Socrates as spending his whole life trying to force all concepts to behave the way mathematical concepts behave.

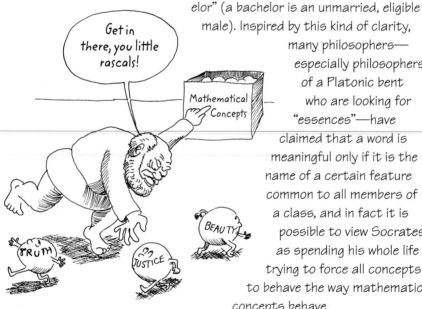

In order to destroy the illusion that a successful theory of meaning can be based on such a model, Wittgenstein asks us to consider the concept of "game." However, he does not ask us to *philosophize* about the concept; rather, he asks us to *look* at all the activities we call "games" in order to see whether we discover anything they all have in common.

> Consider for example the proceedings that we call "games." I mean board-games, card-games, Olympic games, and so on. What is common to them all?—Don't say: "There *must* be something common, or they would not be called 'games'"—but *look and see* whether there is anything common to all.—For if you look at them you will not see something that is common to *all*, but similarities, relationships, and a whole series of them at that. To repeat: don't think, but look!—Look for example at board-games, with their multifarious relationships. Now pass to card-games; here you find many correspondences with the first group, but many common features drop out, and others appear. When we pass next to ball-games, much that is common is retained, but much is lost—Are they all 'amusing'? Compare chess with noughts and crosses. Or is there always winning and losing, or competition between players? Think of patience. In ball games there is winning and losing, but when a child throws his ball at the wall and catches it again, this feature has disappeared. Look at the parts played by *skill and luck*; and at the difference between skill in chess and skill in tennis. Think now of games like ring-a-ring-a-roses; here is the element of amusement, but how many other characteristic features have disappeared! And we can go through the many, many other groups of games in the same way; can see how similarities crop up and disappear.
>
> And the result of this examination is: we see a complicated network of similarities overlapping and criss-crossing: sometimes overall similarities, sometimes similarities of detail.[28]

Notice what Wittgenstein means when he refers to characteristics like "amusing," "winning and losing," "competition," and "skill and luck." Take the term "amusing." Is it the case that everything that is amusing is a game and that all games are amusing (or "fun" or "enjoyable")? Exactly who must be amused? Must the players be amused as well as the spectators, if there are spectators? Imagine a professional baseball game on the last day of the season between the two last-place teams. Only a handful of fans have made the mistake of showing up to see what turns out to be the most sloppily played game of the season in the most miserable weather of the year. It is quite possible that you could interview every person in the stadium and discover that nobody was having any fun. Nevertheless, it certainly would not follow that, because no one was having fun, no game of baseball was being played. (And the fact that the game was a *professional* game doesn't keep it from being a game either.) In fact, I am sure that I have played games of Monopoly that went on so long that, toward the end, no one was enjoying the game. It was just that no one wanted to be the first to admit that the game was not fun. Finally, it is simply absurd to say that the only way of establishing that a particular activity is a game would be to interview people to find out whether anybody was having a good time.

Similar fates await any attempt to define games in terms of "winning and losing" or "skill and luck." Just look at ring-around-the-rosy. There is no winning or losing there, and how much skill or luck do you need just to fall down? (Ring-around-the-rosy, by the way, is one of those games whose origins, at least, are hardly amusing. It probably derives from the period when the Black Plague swept England. The "rosy" is the red ring around the mortal sores or, in some theories, the rosary. Thank goodness, the sinister meaning of the last line, "Ashes to ashes, we all fall down," usually escapes our children.)

What about "competition"? Consider the game my son invented when he was five years old (probably along with every other five-year-old boy) called "hit-the-ball-against-the-wall." With whom was he competing? Perhaps he was competing against himself. But surely there's a difference between the case of the boy who plays to see how many times he can hit the ball without missing and the case of the boy who first pretends he is Tom, then Bill. When "Tom" misses the ball,

it is "Bill's" turn to hit it. In this latter case, the boy really is competing against himself. When I was small, my cousin talked me into playing a game he invented. He called it "push-the-boy-down-the-stairs." There may or may not have been competition involved in that game.

It might be suggested that all games have rules in common by virtue of which they are called games. It is probably true that all games have rules (a possible exception is the Caucus race in *Alice's Adventures in Wonderland*), but so do all sorts of other things that are not games—crossing the street, giving a lecture, attending a movie, and so on. In fact, in a significant sense all recognizable human activities are rule governed. In the face of this fact, some of my students like to say that, after all, everything *is* a game, especially school. (To this, I usually reply that Aztec jai-alai was also a game, and the loser was decapitated; some games are more

Push-the-Boy-Down-the-Stairs

serious than other games.) And in fact, it is curious that almost any activity can be made into a game. (When I was a kid and had to mow the lawn, I used to pretend that the unmowed grass was "the Nazis." I still shave that way sometimes. I knew a man who drove home in the commuter traffic pretending he was a pilot in a bombing squadron. I found this out once when he forgot I was with him; as he pulled into his suburban driveway, he put his fist to his mouth as if he was talking into a microphone and muttered, "Lame Duck, Lame Duck; clear runway number five for a crash landing!") The fact that any

activity can be made into a game proves that not all activities *are* games. Eric Berne wrote a book about how people try to escape responsibility for their actions. He called it *Games People Play*. It was a success precisely because the activities he listed were not really games. My favorite in his list was the "game" he called "see-what-you-made-me-do!" There is a ritualized, game-like quality in the activities of people who scapegoat, but if you buy a book called *Party Games*, you will never find "see-what-you-made-me-do!" in it. If you could find such a game, then Berne could not have included it in *his* book.

Games People Play

As we saw in Chapter 1, Wittgenstein's conclusion concerning the undefinability of the concept "game," despite the many similarities among games, is this:

I can think of no better expression to characterize these similarities than "family resemblances"; for the various resemblances between members of a family: build, features, colour of eyes, gait, temperament, etc. etc. overlap and criss-cross in the same way.—And I shall say: 'games' form a family.[29]

"Game," then, is an "open concept." We cannot state the necessary and sufficient conditions for something's being a game. That is, we could never close the concept with a specific definition in the way that we *can* do with "triangle" because it is always possible, and even likely, that at a later date we will want to include a new activity under the concept "game."

You may have already guessed what this discussion of games has to do with art (or have deduced it from the few comments concerning this issue in Chapter 1). Those who seek an exhaustive definition of the word "art" may be in the same bind as those who seek to define the word "game." Wittgenstein himself only hinted at this conclusion. It has been explicitly drawn by a follower of his, Morris Weitz, in an influential article, "The Role of Theory in Aesthetics." Professor Weitz defines the term "open concept" in the following way:

> A concept is open if its conditions of application are emendable and corrigible; i.e., if a situation or case can be imagined or secured which would call for some sort of *decision* on our part to extend the use of the concept to cover this, or to close the concept and invent a new one to deal with the new case and its new property. If necessary and sufficient conditions for the application of a concept can be stated, the concept is a closed one. But this can happen only in logic or mathematics where concepts are constructed and completely defined. It cannot occur with empirically-descriptive and normative concepts unless we arbitrarily close them by stipulating the ranges of their uses.[30]

According to Weitz, then, questions like "Is Andy Warhol's *Elvis* art?" cannot be answered by appealing to an already established definition; rather, a *decision* is called for: shall we extend the concept "art" to cover this case? Apparently the reasons one can give to justify one's decision to apply or withhold the title "art" must have to do with what Wittgenstein calls "family resemblances." (Is "push-the-boy-down-the-stairs" similar enough to other activities we call games to justify our extending the term "game" to cover this case also?)

If Weitz's Wittgensteinian account of the concept of art is correct, at least he will have explained what is surely one of the most puzzling features of contemporary art. He will have explained why the current crisis in art need not undermine the very concept of art itself. Only in our day could an event like the one described in Chapter 1 take place (a dump truck backs into an art museum and dumps a pile of gravel; the driver places a small embossed card by the pile bearing the title *The Gravel Pile*; people seriously interested in art read the card and slowly circle the pile, gazing studiously at it, arguing among themselves about its artistic merit). Old Socrates would have said that if one could not define art in such a way as to give its essence, and thereby give absolute reasons for calling something "art" or for declaring it not to be art, then one had no right to claim to know anything about art. But Weitz's analysis allows *all* the museum visitors to be certain that Vermeer's *Woman Reading a Letter beside a Window* is art, and it also allows them to argue rationally about the status of *The Gravel Pile*.

A Form of Life

It is perhaps ironic that the most serious challenge to Morris Weitz's Wittgensteinian analysis of the concept of art comes from a group of philosophers who are themselves deeply influenced by Wittgenstein. They base their challenge on an aspect of Wittgenstein's philosophy different from the one that inspired Weitz. The basic position of these philosophers of art was laid down in articles by Arthur Danto and George Dickie. It is called "the institutional theory of art." It was Dickie who actually formulated the theory, but his formulation is based on this line of Danto's: "To see something as art requires something the eye cannot de(s)cry—an atmosphere of artistic theory, a knowledge of the history of art: an artworld."[31] Professor Dickie takes Danto's idea of "an artworld" and interprets it in the light of the following remark of Wittgenstein's: "And to imagine a language means to imagine a form of life."[32] Wittgenstein insisted that we always consider language as a *social* activity. Similarly, Dickie stresses the social context of art and of the discourse about art. He believes that if we *do* place art in its social context, we will be able to define art adequately despite Weitz's assurance of the wrongheadedness of such attempts. Here is Dickie's definition: "A work of art in the classificatory sense is (1) an artifact (2) upon which some person or persons acting on behalf of a certain social institution (the artworld) have conferred the status of candidate for appreciation."[33] Dickie's definition is based on an analogy between the institutional nature of "the artworld" and other social institutions. For example, a particular round, white, hidebound pellet becomes a "strike" when it has that status conferred upon it by an umpire; an adult male human and an adult female human become "married" when they have that status conferred upon them by a member of the clergy or justice of the peace; the author of a particular action becomes "guilty" when that status is conferred upon him by a jury or a judge. Similarly, a particular object becomes "art" when the title is conferred upon it by some member of the artworld, usually the artist who created the artifact, but sometimes the "artist" can confer that status on "ready-mades," as the twentieth-century French **dadaist** artist Marcel Duchamp did in the case of urinals and snow shovels. (In fact, Dickie tells us that it is the work of Duchamp and his followers, Rauschenberg, Warhol, and Oldenburg, that inspired his new definition of art.) Professor Dickie summarizes his argument, saying, "The main point I am trying to make is that something is art because of the place it has in a certain social system."[34]

Dickie's view has been influential among contemporary aestheticians, but not all of them are satisfied that he has refuted Weitz's claim that art is an open concept. For example, B. R. Tilghman implies that Dickie's definition really comes down to claiming that "it's art if the artist says it's art," and he claims that such a definition "is altogether wide of the mark; the real issue of understanding and appreciation is not touched."[35] Nevertheless, Tilghman agrees with Dickie in stressing the social nature of art. Tilghman quotes Wittgenstein's *Lectures and Conversations*, where Wittgenstein says, "The words we call aesthetic judgments play a very complicated role, but a very definite role, in what we call the culture of a period. To describe their use or to describe what you mean by a cultural taste, you have to describe a culture."[36]

Finally, I want to report on a contribution to this discussion of art made by Timothy Binkley, another contemporary philosopher deeply influenced by Wittgenstein. Binkley completely disarms Dickie's definition by making the following stipulation: "I hereby create a prodigious class of pieces of art by specifying everything to be art."[37] If Dickie's definition allows *everything* to be art, what is the point of drawing the distinction? (Compare Binkley's stipulation with the piece of "conceptual art" alluded to in Chapter 1, to which Binkley refers, created by Robert Barry: *All the things I know but of which I am not at the moment thinking—1:36 P.M., 15 June 1969, New York.*) So Binkley wants to return to Weitz's Wittgensteinian claim that art is undefinable. However, he finds that Weitz's specific account makes art seem too tame. Binkley says that the family resemblances of "games" allow us to discriminate clear cases of games from clear cases of nongames, but the recent history of art indicates that this is not the case with art.

He says that art is "radically open, radically indefinable." This conclusion is exciting—but it is also a little scary. A few years ago in an art gallery in London I saw a work that was composed of a large rectangular block of clear plastic with a complete standing cow inside it. The cow's body had been sliced like large crosscuts of sausage, and the slices were separated within their plastic tomb so that all of its internal organs were on exhibit. "Is this art?" I asked myself, and a queasy feeling of repulsion came over me. I felt at that moment that the center—at least, *my* center—might not hold.

Conclusion

Even if we accept the Wittgensteinian view about art—that it is a "radically open concept" and that art is always a part of the social fabric of any culture—we can still appreciate Plato's perplexity about art. We can recognize its seductive and manipulative features. (I am *not* speaking of sliced cows here.) Because art, as Freud and Marcuse point out, is extrarational and grounded in fantasy, it pulls us away from reality and "the reality principle." There is good news and bad news here.

The bad news: the pull is toward phoniness, frivolity, danger, and even madness. All art is, as Arnold Hauser has said, a version of Quixotism.[38]

(You will recall that Don Quixote abandoned real life for the life of romantic novels and went mad in the process. And of course the delicious irony here is that Don Quixote himself is merely a character in a novel [and what a novel!]. We readers are the Don Quixotes who escape our real world for his. Art always offers an alternative reality, hence the possibility of madness or sometimes a substitute for the madness that is the everyday world [the title of Freud's book: *The Psychopathology of Everyday Life*].)

The good news: but art also pulls toward philosophy (as Aristotle and the existentialists have it) and toward joy and the celebration of life (as Nietzsche has it)—the large beside the small pleases!

Plato and the Greeks called art a form of mimesis (imitation). The very term connoted for Plato a kind of simulacrum—a replacement for reality by something not as rich as what it replaced. This Platonic concept is too narrow (what do a painting by Jackson Pollack, a musical composition by John Cage, or James Joyce's *Finnegan's Wake* imitate?) but not so far off after all. Art does not imitate the world, but it *represents* the world. However, what it represents is neither Plato's icy, timeless Forms (though it does formalize and arrest what it represents, and in that sense rescues it from time), nor does it represent mere "things." It represents the world in all its actual and possible aspects. And in doing so, it reveals itself as being a kind of infinite regress, as art represents itself representing itself. (Most paintings are influenced more by other paintings than by the natural world, and most books [including this one] are about other books.) The nature of art, then, is not so different from the nature of the mind, whose nature it also is to represent the world and to represent itself to itself. So if art offers the possibility of madness and degradation, it also offers the possibility of insight, joy, progress, sophistication, and redemption. Once again, in this respect, it is like the human mind itself.

Topics for Consideration

1. Test the competing theories of Plato and Aristotle concerning the moral status of art by applying their views to television or movies, "art forms" that play a similar role in today's world to that of the theater in ancient Athens.
2. Freud is ambivalent about art as a form of sublimation. In some ways it seems successful. (It provides a substitutive satisfaction both for the artist and the audience.) But in other ways it seems too much like a neurotic symptom or even like a psychotic denial of reality and an escape into a self-created world of delusion. Discuss this thesis.

3. Use visual art before the twentieth century to defend the view that art is mimesis, and use visual art in the twentieth century to attack that view.

4. A tension stretches between Marx's view that art is ideological and his view that art expresses the human mind at its most liberated. Show how Marcuse's theory tries to resolve that apparent contradiction.

5. Why do you think that many existential philosophers (e.g., Sartre, de Beauvoir, Nietzsche, Unamuno) have also been artists, novelists, poets, and playwrights and that some novelists (e.g., Dostoyevsky, Kafka) have also been considered existential philosophers?

6. Pick a contemporary work of art that has puzzled or outraged some citizens (Christo's fence? Maplethorpe's "obscene" photos?) and discuss them from the Wittgensteinian/Weitzian perspective.

7. Just how "radically open, radically indefinable" is art? What could not count as art?

Suggestions for Further Reading:
Paperback Editions

Lars Aagaard-Mogensen, ed., *Culture and Art* (Atlantic Highlands, N.J.: Humanities Press, 1976). A good selection of philosophical essays on art, many from theorists influenced by Wittgenstein.

Aristotle, *The Poetics* in *Aristotle: On Poetry and Style*, trans. G. M. A. Grube (New York: Liberal Arts Press, 1958). Aristotle's classical treatise on art in general and poetry and drama in particular.

Sigmund Freud, *Leonardo da Vinci and a Memory of His Childhood*, trans. Alan Tyson (New York: Norton, 1964). A glimpse not only into Leonardo's mind but also into Freud's.

E. H. Gombrich, *Art and Illusion: A Study in the Psychology of Pictorial Representation* (Princeton, N.J.: Princeton University Press, 1972). Not only one of the best books about philosophy, psychology, and art, but one of my favorite books of all time.

Arnold Hauser, *The Philosophy of Art History* (Cleveland, Ohio: Meridian Books, 1963). An excellent work touching on numerous topics discussed in this chapter.

Herbert Marcuse, *Eros and Civilization: A Philosophical Inquiry into Freud* (New York: Vintage Books, 1955). Marcuse's synthesis of Freud and Marx and his statement concerning the revolutionary status of art. Difficult and controversial but worthwhile.

Joseph Margolis, ed., *Philosophy Looks at the Arts: Contemporary Readings in Aesthetics* (New York: Charles Scribner's Sons, 1962). Another good anthology.

Iris Murdoch, *The Fire and the Sun: Why Plato Banished the Artists* (New York: Oxford University Press, 1978). A short, excellent book written by a woman who was both a top-notch philosopher and a first-rate novelist.

Friedrich Nietzsche, *The Birth of Tragedy*, trans. Francis Golffing (Garden City, N.Y.: Doubleday Anchor, 1990). The proto-existentialist statement about the status of art in culture.

Plato, *Republic*, in *Great Dialogues of Plato*, eds. Eric H. Warmington and Philip G. Rouse, trans. W. H. D. Rouse (New York: New American Library, 1956). There are remarks about the relation between art and philosophy throughout the *Republic* but Book X is dedicated to its discussion.

Adolfo Sánchez Vázquez, *Art and Society: Essays on Marxist Aesthetics*, trans. Maro Riofrancos (New York: Monthly Review Press, 1973). A fine collection of essays by a Mexican Marxist philosopher.

Notes

1. Plato, *Republic*, in *Great Dialogues of Plato*, ed. Eric H. Warmington and Philip G. Rouse, trans. W. H. D. Rouse (New York: New American Library, 1956), pp. 369–370.

2. Arnold Hauser, *The Philosophy of Art History* (Cleveland, Ohio: Meridian Books, 1963), p. 56.

3. Aristotle, *Politics*, in *Aristotle: On Poetry and Style*, trans. G. M. A. Grube (New York: Liberal Arts Press, 1958), pp. XV–XVI.

4. Ibid.

5. Quoted in Erich Fromm, ed., T. B. Bottomore, trans., *Marx's Concept of Man* (New York: Friedrich Ungar, 1969), p. 38.

6. Karl Marx, "Alienated Labor," in Fromm, *Marx's Concept of Man*, p. 102.

7. Robert Tucker, *Philosophy and Myth in Karl Marx* (New York: Cambridge University Press, 1965), pp. 157–158.

8. Karl Marx, "Preface to a Contribution to the Critique of Political Economy," in Fromm, *Marx's Concept of Man*, pp. 217–218.

9. Karl Marx, "The German Ideology," in Fromm, *Marx's Concept of Man*, p. 212.

10. Marx, "Theories of Surplus Value," quoted in Adolfo Sánchez Vázquez, *Art and Society: Essays in Marxist Aesthetics*, trans. Maro Riofrancos (New York: Monthly Review Press, 1973), p. 155.

11. Karl Marx and Friedrich Engels, "Manifesto of the Communist Party," in *Marx and Engels: Basic Writings on Politics and Philosophy* (Garden City, N.Y.: Doubleday, 1959), p. 10.

12. Karl Marx, "Theories of Surplus Value," quoted in Sánchez Vázquez, *Art and Society*, pp. 200–201.

13. Karl Marx, "The German Ideology," quoted in Sánchez Vázquez, *Art and Society*, pp. 282, 285, 286.

14. Erich Fromm, *The Dogma of Christ and Other Essays on Religion, Psychology, and Culture* (New York: Holt, Rinehart & Winston, 1963), p. 96.

15. Herbert Marcuse, *Eros and Civilization: A Philosophical Inquiry into Freud* (New York: Vintage Books, 1955), pp. IX–X.

16. Herbert Marcuse, *Counterrevolution and Revolt* (Boston: Beacon Press, 1972), p. 115.

17. Marcuse, *Eros and Civilization*, p. 15.

18. Ibid., p. 18.

19. Jean-Paul Sartre, *Existentialism and Human Emotions* (New York: Philosophical Library, 1957), p. 15.

20. Ibid., p. 51.

21. Arturo B. Fallico, *Art and Existentialism* (Englewood Cliffs, N.J.: Prentice-Hall, 1962), p. 52.

22. Friedrich Nietzsche, *The Birth of Tragedy*, trans. Francis Golffing (Garden City, N.Y.: Doubleday Anchor, 1956), p. 29.

23. Fallico, *Art and Existentialism*, pp. 74–75, 65.

24. Ibid., pp. 66, 81.

25. Maurice Natanson, *The Journeying Self: A Study in Philosophy and Social Role* (Reading, Mass.: Addison-Wesley, 1970), p. 122.

26. Quoted in Arthur Danto, *Mysticism and Morality: Oriental Thought and Moral Philosophy* (New York: Harper & Row, 1972), p. 77.

27. Ludwig Wittgenstein, *Tractatus Logico-Philosophicus*, trans. D. F. Pears and B. F. McGuinness (London: Routledge and Kegan Paul, 1961), sec. 6.421, p. 147.

28. Ludwig Wittgenstein, *Philosophical Investigations*, trans. G. E. M. Anscombe (New York: Macmillan, 1964), pp. 31–32.

29. Ibid., p. 32.

30. Morris Weitz, "The Role of Theory in Aesthetics," in *Philosophy Looks at the Arts: Contemporary Readings in Aesthetics*, ed. Joseph Margolis (New York: Charles Scribner's Sons, 1962), p. 54.

31. Arthur Danto, "The Artworld," in *Culture and Art*, ed. Lars Aagaard-Mogensen (Atlantic Highlands, N.J.: Humanities Press, 1976), p. 16.

32. Wittgenstein, *Philosophical Investigations*, p. 8.

33. George Dickie, "The Institutional Conception of Art," in *Language and Aesthetics*, ed. Benjamin R. Tilghman (Wichita: University Press of Kansas, 1973), p. 23.

34. Ibid., p. 30.

35. Benjamin R. Tilghman, "Artistic Puzzlement," in Aagaard-Mogensen, *Culture and Art*, p. 80.

36. Ibid.

37. Timothy Binkley, "Deciding about Art," in Aagaard-Mogensen, *Culture and Art*, p. 109.

38. Hauser, *The Philosophy of Art History*, p. 55.

Glossary

(Boldface type indicates terms that are cross-referenced within the glossary.)

a posteriori A belief, **proposition,** or argument is said to be a posteriori if its truth or falsity can be established only through observation. Classical **empiricism** was an attempt to show that all significant knowledge about the world is based on a posteriori truths.

a priori A belief, **proposition,** or argument is said to be a priori if its truth or falsity can be established independently of observation. Definitions, the propositions of arithmetic, and the principles of logic are usually held to be a priori. Classical **rationalism** was an attempt to show that all significant knowledge about the world is based on a priori truths, which most of the rationalists associated with **innate ideas.**

aesthetics The branch of philosophy that studies those features of the world that call for qualitative judgments—typically, but not exclusively, the study of the concept of beauty and of judgments about it. Aesthetics tends to be dominated by the **philosophy of art,** but it also concerns itself with beauty and related qualities as they are found in nature. Just as **ethics** asks whether there are such qualities as the good, duty, and right and wrong, and whether objective judgments and arguments about these moral qualities can be legitimately formulated, so does aesthetics ask whether there are such objects as beauty, ugliness, the sublime, and the comic, and whether objective judgments and arguments about these aesthetic objects can legitimately be formulated.

agnosticism A view that holds open the possibility that God exists but that claims we do not know, or cannot know, whether in fact a deity exists.

analytic geometry The branch of mathematics created by René Descartes in which algebraic procedures are applied to geometry.

analytic philosophy The view that, in philosophy, logical analysis and analysis of meaning must be prior to the construction of philosophical theories about the world. Analytical philosophers believe that certain key concepts in ordinary language and in scientific, moral, religious, and **aesthetic** discourse are philosophically vague or misleading. Philosophical problems can be solved and pseudophilosophical problems can be dispelled through the clarification of these concepts. The theories that analytical philosophers do generate tend to be demonstrations of the logical relations among these different realms of discourse rather than grandiose **metaphysical** schemes. Although many of the pioneers of this school were Continental Europeans, the movement has become primarily an Anglo-American one.

analytic proposition A **proposition** is analytic if its negation leads to a self-contradiction. For example, "squares have four sides" is analytic because its negation, "squares do not have four sides," is a self-contradiction. See also **tautology, conceptual truth,** and **a priori.**

anarchism The political doctrine according to which the state is both unnatural and unjustifiable because it necessarily violates the rights of individuals.

anomie A sociological term designating a condition in individuals or societies characterized by a loss of direction, meaning, values, and norms.

apocrypha Works, sayings, or acts misattributed to an important individual or an authoritative tradition when in fact they are inauthentic or fraudulent.

aretê A term in ancient Greek philosophy usually translated as "virtue," though sometimes as "excellence" or "quality."

atheism The view that there is no God.

atomism As an **ontological** theory, the view that the ultimate building blocks of reality are basic, irreducible particles of matter—atoms. (This view is a version of **materialism.**) As an **epistemological** theory, the view that the ultimate building blocks of knowledge are basic, irreducible, perceptual units—**sense data.** (This view, called "psychological atomism," is a version of **empiricism.**)

bad faith A technical term in the philosophy of Jean-Paul Sartre naming a state of human inauthenticity, a flight from responsibility, **freedom,** and anguish. A kind of willful self-deception in which one tries to convince oneself that one is not the sole source of one's being and actions.

behaviorism The theory that only observable, objective features of human or animal activity need be studied to provide an adequate scientific account of that activity. See also **hard behaviorism, soft behaviorism,** and **logical behaviorism.**

being-for-itself A term in the philosophy of Jean-Paul Sartre designating human reality.

being-in-itself A term in the philosophy of Jean-Paul Sartre designating non-human reality—"being" as it is prior to human intervention.

categorical imperative The name given by Immanuel Kant to a purported universal moral law: in one form, "So act that the maxim of your action could be willed as a universal law"; in another form, "So act as to treat humanity . . . always as an end, and never as merely a means."

category-mistake A key philosophical error noted by the British **ordinary language philosopher** Gilbert Ryle wherein a term that belongs to one logical category is mistakenly categorized as belonging to another. Then faulty questions are asked based on the miscategorization. An example would be (according to Ryle) Descartes assuming that the mind is a *thing* in the same way that the body is a *thing* and then asking how these two "things" interact.

causal explanation A mechanical kind of explanation in which the object or event to be accounted for is rendered intelligible by demonstrating how that object or event follows necessarily from antecedent objects or events. Causal explanations are usually represented in terms of natural laws. Contrast with **teleological explanation.**

cognitive dissonance A state of perceptual confusion caused by the experience of sensations that are different from those anticipated.

cognitive science An interdisciplinary study involving philosophy, psychology, linguistics, and computer science, stressing the computational model of the mind. See also **functionalism.**

coherence theory of truth The theory that a **proposition** is true if it coheres with the body of all the other propositions taken to be true; that is, if it follows logically from those propositions, or supports them and is supported by them, or at least does not contradict any of them. This theory, which opposes both the **correspondence theory of truth** and the **pragmatic theory of truth,** has been especially appealing to **rationalists.**

communism The political theory that advocates the abolition of private property and asserts that goods must be held in common and that the ideal social unit is the commune. See also **Marxism.**

conceptual art A development in art during the last forty years of the twentieth century in which it is claimed that the technique, methods, and materials of production rather than the final artistic product are themselves the real work of art. Also, in some cases, the designation of concepts themselves rather than objects as works of art.

conceptual truth A **proposition** expresses a conceptual truth if that truth is based on a merely logical relationship rather than on an empirical fact. For example, "widows are female" is a conceptual truth. See also **analytic proposition, tautology,** and **a priori.**

conceptualism The epistemological view that concepts are generalized ideas existing only in the mind but that they are derived and abstracted by the mind from real similarities and distinctions in nature.

contingent (or **contingency**) A relation between two objects or ideas is contingent if one of the terms of the relationship could exist without the other. For example, Descartes says that the relation between the soul and the body is contingent because the soul can exist without the body, and bodies can exist without souls. Contrast with **necessity.**

correspondence theory of truth The theory that a **proposition** is true if it corresponds with the facts. "Caesar crossed the Rubicon" is true if and only if there was in fact a man called Caesar, and he did in fact cross the Rubicon; otherwise, the proposition is false. This theory, which opposes both the **coherence theory of truth** and the **pragmatic theory of truth,** has been especially appealing to **empiricists.**

cosmological argument An attempt to establish God's existence by deducing it from some observable facts in the world. For example, Thomas Aquinas's claim that from the observation of causal chains in the world we can deduce the necessity of a "first cause," or God.

dada (or **dadaism**) From the French word for "hobbyhorse," a continental art movement conceived as a protest against the mechanized slaughter of World War I. It manifested a **nihilistic** irrationality calculated to inform the public that all established moral and aesthetic values were meaningless after the horrors of the war.

deconstruction The intellectual creation of the contemporary French philosopher Jacques Derrida; based on his eccentric but provocative reading of the linguistic theory of Ferdinand de Saussure, deconstruction is a theory of texts (philosophical, fictional, legal, scientific) according to which, because of the very nature of thought and language, almost all traditional texts can be shown to "deconstruct" themselves, to undermine and refute their own theses. Or, deconstruction is the activity of demonstrating that a particular text undermines and refutes itself.

deep ecology A development within the ecology movement decrying as "shallow" those currents within the movement that justify conservation as being in the interest of human beings. Deep ecologists (like Arne Naess, George Sessions, and Gary Snyder) find an intrinsic value in all living systems, and condemn the human arrogance of anthropocentrism. They are committed to "ecocentric" political action, such as the control of world population and abandonment of the goal of "increased standards of living" in areas where such an increase has already devastated nature.

determinism The view that every event occurs necessarily. Every event follows inevitably from the events that preceded it. There is no randomness in reality; rather, all is law governed. **Freedom** either does not exist (**hard determinism**) or exists in such a way as to be compatible with **necessity** (**soft determinism**).

dialectic In the philosophies of Hegel and Marx, the dialectic is a mechanism of change and progress in which every possible situation exists only in relation to its own opposite. This relationship is one of both antagonism and mutual dependency, but the antagonism (a form of violence) eventually undermines the relationship and overthrows it. (However, sometimes the term "dialectical" is used only to emphasize a relationship of reciprocity between two entities or processes.)

distributive justice The form of justice that is achieved in a society when the opportunities and material goods of the society are fairly distributed in ways that recognize both the contributions and needs of all members of the society.

dualism The **ontological** view that reality is composed of two kinds of beings, usually (as in Descartes) minds and bodies.

efficient cause A term from Aristotelian philosophy designating one of the four kinds of causes in the world—the physical force operating on the object undergoing change (e.g., the sculptor's chiseling of a piece of granite). (The other three Aristotelian causes are "the material cause" [the piece of granite], "the formal cause" [the idea of the statue in the mind of the sculptor], and "the final cause" [the ultimate purpose of the statue].)

ego In **psychoanalysis,** the name of the rational, most conscious, social aspect of the psyche, as contrasted with the **id** and **superego.**

egoism A theory of motivation according to which the motive behind all acts either *is* self-interest (psychological egoism) or *ought to be* self-interest (moral egoism). See also **hedonism.**

eliminative materialism A materialistic theory of mind according to which sentences that seem to refer to nonmaterial conscious states (such as "I have a headache") will be capable of being eliminated in favor of more accurate sentences referring to material states (such as "My C-fibers are firing").

eliminativism See **eliminative materialism.**

empiricism The epistemological view that true knowledge is derived primarily from sense experience (or, in "purer" strains of empiricism, *exclusively* from sense experience). For these philosophers, all significant knowledge is **a posteriori,** and **a priori** knowledge is either nonexistent or tautological. The "classical" empiricists were the seventeenth- and eighteenth-century Britons (Locke, Berkeley, and Hume), all of whom denied the existence of **innate ideas** and conceived of the human mind as a "blank slate" at birth.

Enlightenment, the A philosophical movement of the eighteenth century characterized by the belief in the power of reason to sweep away superstition, ignorance, and injustice.

epistemology The branch of philosophy that answers questions such as: What is knowledge? What, if anything, can we know? What is the difference between opinion and knowledge?

Eros The name of the Greek god of love, which in **psychoanalytic** theory becomes the name of a purported "life instinct" and is opposed to **Thanatos,** the "death instinct."

ethics Moral philosophy: the branch of philosophy that answers questions such as: Is there such a thing as the Good? What is "the good life"? Is there such a thing as absolute duty? Are valid moral arguments possible? Are moral judgments based only on preference?

ethnocentrism The biased belief that one's own ethnic, social, or cultural group holds values that are superior to those of other groups, leading to an attitude that blinds the believer to the values of other cultures or social systems.

eugenics The advocacy of controlled breeding in order to improve the human race.

existentialism A twentieth-century philosophy associated principally with Jean-Paul Sartre but also thought to encompass the work of Karl Jaspers, Simone de Beauvoir, Martin Heidegger, Gabriel Marcel, Albert Camus, and Miguel de Unamuno, among others. More of a shared attitude than a school of thought, it can nevertheless be roughly defined by saying with Sartre that existentialists are those who believe that, in the case of humans, "existence precedes essence." This is the thesis that there is no human nature that precedes our presence in the world. All humans individually create humanity at every moment through their free acts.

experience As a technical term in empiricistic **epistemology,** the term designating the data provided directly by the five senses. See also **sense data.**

experimental A theory or **proposition** is experimental if observable evidence is pertinent to its confirmation or falsification. See also **a posteriori, synthetic proposition,** and **principle of falsifiability.**

feminism The sociopolitical theory and practice defending women's dignity and rights against male chauvinism and male-dominated power structures that have denied legal and social equality to women and have demeaned, marginalized, and constricted women throughout history.

forms Usually associated with the philosophies of Plato or Aristotle. For Plato (in whose philosophy the word "Form" is capitalized in this text), everything that exists in the physical or conceptual world is in some way dependent upon Forms, which exist independently of the world but are the models (essences, universals, archetypes) of all reality. Forms are eternal, unchangeable, and the ultimate object of all true philosophizing. For Aristotle too, forms are the essences of things, but they exist *in* things and are not independent of them. The form of an object and its function are ultimately related.

freedom Freedom exists if there are such things as free acts and free agents, that is, if some acts are performed in such a way that the authors of those acts could legitimately be held responsible for them. Some philosophers (called **libertarians**) say that these acts do exist, that some acts are freely chosen from among genuine alternatives, and that therefore **determinism** is false. ("I did X, but under exactly the same circumstances, I could have done Y instead. Therefore X was a free act.") Other philosophers (called **soft determinists**) also say that free acts exist but define "free acts" not in terms of genuine alternative choices but in terms of voluntary acts. ("I wanted to do X, and I did do X; therefore X was a free act.") Still other philosophers (called **hard determinists**), while agreeing with the definition of "free act" given by libertarians, deny that any such free acts or agents exist.

functionalism A currently popular theory in the **philosophy of mind** according to which minds are not "things"; rather, they are systems capable of interacting with their environment through computational activity. Any computational system capable of manipulating symbols to solve problems can be said to have mental states, according to functionalism, whether those systems be brains, computers, or extraterrestrials. In the case of humans, those mental states (desires, hopes, expectations, etc.) are real (i.e., are causally effective). They are realized in the brain but are not themselves brain states. The computations of computers are not themselves physical states but are realized in physical components of the computer hardware. Functionalists consider themselves to be **materialists,** but they oppose the **mind-brain identity theory** and **eliminative materialism.**

gestalt psychology The theory according to which perception does not occur as the summation of a number of perceptual parts; rather, these perceptual parts themselves are derived from the general perceptual field, which has properties that cannot be derived from any or all of the parts.

hard behaviorism The view that there are no minds and that, therefore, psychology can study only "behaviors"—an **ontological** view as opposed to the merely methodological view of **soft behaviorism.**

hard determinism The view that **determinism** is true and that therefore **freedom** and responsibility do not exist. Contrast with **soft determinism.**

hedonism A theory of motivation according to which the motive behind all acts either *is* pleasure (psychological hedonism) or *ought to be* pleasure (moral hedonism). See also **egoism.**

hypothetical imperative The name given by Immanuel Kant to the nonmoral use of the word "ought." This use of "ought" can always be stated in a hypothetical form (e.g., "You ought to be nice to people *if* you want them to like you").

id In **psychoanalysis,** the name given to one of the three aspects of the psyche. It is the mostly unconscious, antisocial, irrational but cunning "animal" self, containing the primitive sexual and aggressive drives, as contrasted with the **ego** (the rational, mostly conscious social self) and the **superego** (the irrational, authoritarian, mostly unconscious familial and social conscience).

idealism The **ontological** view that, ultimately, every existing thing can be shown to be spiritual or mental (hence, a version of **monism**), usually associated in Western philosophy with Berkeley and Hegel.

identity theory See **mind-brain identity theory.**

indeterminism The view that there are such things as uncaused events and that therefore **determinism** is false.

innate idea An idea present at birth, hence, **a priori.**

intentionality As used in the **philosophy of mind,** the referential feature of mental phenomena; their "aboutness." Mental states refer to objects beyond themselves. One thinks *about* something, looks *at* something, alludes to something, is afraid of something. The term covers intentions in the nontechnical sense ("She intended to drop her philosophy class") but also desires, hopes, expectations, and fears. A major question in **materialist** theories in the **philosophy of mind** is How is it possible for certain material objects (brains or parts of brains) to have intentionality in this sense?

legal positivism The view that justice and legal legitimacy are defined exclusively by the established political powers.

liberalism The political view that advocates a democratic government and asserts that the state has a legitimate right and an obligation to set standards of living below which none of its citizens may be forced to live and to enforce laws providing equal opportunity and **distributive justice.**

libertarianism The view that **freedom** exists.

logic The branch of philosophy that studies the structure of valid inference; a purely *formal* discipline, interested in the structure of argumentation rather than in its content.

logical behaviorism The **epistemological** view that all meaningful mentalistic terms must ultimately be capable of being traced back to some observable behavior and not back to some purely mental facts. For example, the term "intelligent" must ultimately be related to certain observable capacities, not to a mental state called "intelligence."

logical construct A term from twentieth-century **empiricism** naming an entity that can be inferred from **sense data.** For example, the belief that a table exists independently of our perceptions is based on an inference drawn from our perceptions. In this view, only sense data can be known directly. Logical constructs can be known only indirectly.

logical empiricism See **logical positivism.**

logical entailment A relation of logical **necessity** between two concepts or **propositions.** If concept or proposition X necessarily implies concept or proposition Y, then X logically entails Y. The assertion of X with the simultaneous denial of Y would constitute a self-contradiction; for example, the concept "brother" logically entails both the concept "sibling" and the concept "male."

logical positivism (or **logical empiricism**) A school of philosophy that flourished between the two world wars according to which the only cognitively meaningful utterances are those of science. All other utterances can be shown, under analysis, to be merely expressions of emotions or to be nonsense.

logical possibility Something is logically possible if its *idea* contains no self-contradiction (such as the idea of a one-million-sided figure). Conversely, something is logically impossible if its idea does contain a self-contradiction (such as the idea of a four-sided circle).

Logos (1) A Greek term meaning "word" or "study," from which is derived the English term "logic" and the "-logies" of "biology," "sociology," etc. (2) In Plato, a term designating the rational justification of beliefs.

(3) As opposed to **Mythos,** Logos designates a scientific or philosophical account of the world.

Marxism A political or philosophical doctrine based on the writings of Karl Marx: politically a form of **communism,** philosophically a form of **materialism** known as **dialectical** materialism.

materialism The **ontological** view that all reality can be shown to be material in nature (e.g., that "minds" are really brains).

Meno's paradox An **epistemological** paradox set forth by Meno in the Platonic dialogue of the same name: How is it possible to seek knowledge? If one does not know what one is looking for, one will not recognize it if one finds it. If one *does* recognize it, then one already knew it and did not need to seek it. Therefore, the pursuit of knowledge is either impossible or useless.

metaphysics The branch of philosophy that attempts to construct a general, speculative worldview: a complete, systematic account of all reality and experience, usually involving an **epistemology,** an **ontology,** an **ethics,** and an **aesthetics.** (The adjective "metaphysical" is often employed to stress the speculative, as opposed to the scientific or commonsensical, features of the theory or **proposition** it describes.)

methodological doubt (or **radical doubt**) The name of the philosophical method employed by Descartes to discover the absolutely certain foundations of all knowledge. Every belief that can be doubted should be doubted until one arrives at a belief that itself is indubitable.

mimesis Literally, "imitation" or "copy" but in **aesthetics,** the doctrine that art in its main function is imitative—of reality, ideality, or possibility.

mind-brain identity theory The **ontological** view that minds and brains are not two different kinds of things; rather, that all references to minds and mental states are really references to brains and brain states.

minimal state The social ideal of certain theorists such as Robert Nozick according to which the only rights and obligations a government has are those of protecting the persons and property of its citizens, punishing offenses against those citizens, and taxing its citizens to finance these activities. The state has no other legitimate obligations or rights.

mode A property of an essential property. For example, for Descartes, "thought" is an essential property of "mind" and "understanding" is a property, or mode, of thought.

monism The **ontological** view that only one entity exists (e.g., as in Spinoza) or that only one *kind* of entity exists (e.g., as in Hobbes and Berkeley).

moral egoism See **egoism.**

mysticism The view that a special experience can be achieved that transcends ordinary rational procedures and provides a direct intuition of the presence of God or an extrarational insight into ultimate truth.

Mythos The whole body of myths, legends, and folktales that attempts to make sense of the world by placing it in a narrative context tracing things back to their supernatural origins. Sometimes contrasted with **Logos.**

naive realism The prephilosophical **epistemology** attributed to the "person in the street," according to which the perceptual data in the mind accurately duplicate the external world as it actually is.

nativism The psychological or **epistemological** view that there are certain **innate ideas,** principles, or structures in the mind that organize the data of consciousness.

necessary condition X is a necessary condition of Y if Y cannot exist in the absence of X. For example, oxygen is a necessary condition of fire. See also **sufficient condition.**

necessity A relation between two things or ideas is *logically* necessary if the existence of one logically entails the existence of the other. For example, the relation between triangularity and three-sidedness is logically necessary. (Contrast with **contingency.**) A relation between two things is *physically* necessary if the existence of one always results physically in the existence of the other. For example, death is the necessary result of the brain's destruction.

nihilism As an **ontological** view, the theory that nothing exists; as a moral view, the theory that there are no values or that nothing deserves to exist.

Ockham's razor (or **Occam's razor**) A principle of simplification derived from the medieval philosopher William of Ockham, according to which if there are two competing theories, both of which account for all the observable data, the simpler of the two is the preferable theory. "Do not multiply entities beyond necessity."

ontological argument An **a priori** attempt to prove God's existence by showing that, from the very concept of God, his existence can be deduced. This argument has been defended by a number of religious philosophers in the Platonic tradition. It was first formulated by St. Anselm and appears in one form or another in the work of Descartes, Spinoza, Leibniz, and Hegel. It has some able twentieth-century defenders (e.g., Charles Hartshorne and Norman Malcolm). But it has been rejected by some notables, too, including St. Thomas, Hume, Kant, and Kierkegaard.

ontology Theory of being: the branch of philosophy pursuing such questions as: What is real? What is the difference between appearance and reality? What is the relation between minds and bodies? Are numbers and concepts real, or are only physical objects real?

operant conditioning A method of behavioral control in which habits are created by positive reinforcement (reward) or negative reinforcement (punishment) of the responses to certain stimuli.

ordinary language philosophy A strong movement in Anglo-American **analytic philosophy,** especially in the 1960s and 1970s, that saw philosophy's main task as the conceptual and logical analysis of ordinary language as it related to philosophical problems. This school rejected the attack on ordinary language that was engineered by earlier analytic philosophers like Bertrand Russell and the logical positivists. Rather, ordinary language philosophers held that many philosophical errors were the result of disdain for ordinary language and a confusion about the nature of meaning. The confusion would be eliminated, not through the construction of artificial mathematical languages, but only by careful attention to the nuances of ordinary language. Major participants in this school included John Austin, Gilbert Ryle, and Ludwig Wittgenstein.

organicism The **ontological** view that reality is more like an organism than like a machine—that the whole is more real than any of the parts and that the parts are dependent on the whole for their reality.

paradigm shift A moment in intellectual history when the key conceptual apparatus of an age gives way to new ones, as when the essentially theological view of reality in the medieval world gave way to a more secular one involving new standards of judgment and criteria of evidence.

phenomenology A philosophical school created by Edmund Husserl employing a method of analysis that purports to arrive at the pure data of consciousness and thereby provide the foundation for **epistemology** and **ontology.** The method involves "bracketing" certain features of experience, stripping them of all assumptions and presuppositions, and laying bare their essence.

philosophy of art The branch of philosophy that studies the **aesthetic** features of art, and the judgments about those features.

philosophy of mind That branch of philosophy that deals with such **ontological** problems as the relation between minds and brains, minds and computers, and minds and behavior.

pluralism The **ontological** view that reality is composed of a multiplicity of things or different kinds of things and that this multiplicity cannot be reduced to one or two categories.

political philosophy The branch of philosophy that explores questions concerning the justification of political entities and political relationships.

pragmatism An American philosophy that claims that the meaning of an idea can be established by determining what practical difference would be produced by believing the idea to be true and that the truth of an idea can be established by determining the idea's ability to "work."

pragmatic theory of truth This theory asserts that to talk about the truth of a proposition is to talk about its power to "work," that is, its ability to put the individual who considers the proposition into a more satisfactory and effective relationship with the rest of the world. This theory employs the **correspondence theory of truth** and the **coherence theory of truth** not as criteria of truth but as two of several tests of efficacy. According to the pragmatic theory, the truth is relative and not absolute.

primary qualities A term from seventeenth- and eighteenth-century **epistemology** and **ontology** designating properties that inhere in material bodies independently of our perception of them (e.g., size, shape, location, and divisibility). Contrast with **secondary qualities.**

principle of falsifiability A criterion of scientific meaning set forth by Sir Karl Popper according to which a **proposition** or theory is scientific only if it is framed in such a way that it would be possible to state what kind of evidence would refute or falsify the theory, if such evidence existed.

proposition As employed in this text, a proposition is whatever is asserted by a sentence. The sentences "It's raining," "Es regnet," and "Llueve" all assert the same proposition.

psychoanalysis The name given by Sigmund Freud to his method of psychotherapy, eventually becoming a theory of the mind, of selfhood, and of culture, in which psychological and social phenomena are traced to their origins in the unconscious mind.

psychological egoism See **egoism.**

qualia (singular: **quale**) A term in the **philosophy of mind** deriving from the Latin word for "quality," designating the qualitative (as opposed to quantitative) features of mental experience; the experience itself of softness, redness, pleasure, pain, and so on.

radical doubt See **methodological doubt.**

rationalism The **epistemological** view that true knowledge is derived primarily from reason (or exclusively from reason in the purer strains of rationalism). Reason is conceived as the working of the mind on material provided by the mind itself. In most versions, this material takes the form of **innate ideas.** Therefore, for the rationalists, **a priori** knowledge is the most important kind of knowledge. In rationalistic **ontologies,** the mind and the world are seen to be in conformity—the real is the rational. The classical rationalists were the seventeenth- and eighteenth-century Continental philosophers (Descartes, Spinoza, and Leibniz), but the concept is broad enough to include such philosophers as Plato and Hegel.

reification The result of illegitimately concretizing that which is abstract, that which is general, or that which defies concretization. From the Latin *res* (thing), hence, to "thingify."

representative realism An **empiricist epistemology,** usually associated with John Locke, according to which the data of perception represent the external world without literally duplicating it, very much the way a photo or a painting does.

secondary qualities A term from seventeenth- and eighteenth-century **epistemology** and **ontology** designating perceived qualities (such as colors, tastes, odors) that appear to be real properties of material objects but in fact actually exist only in perception and are caused by the properties that do exist in material objects, viz., by **primary qualities.**

sense data A sense datum is that which is perceived immediately by any one of the senses prior to interpretation by the mind. Sense data include the perceptions of colors, sounds, tastes, odors, tactile sensations, pleasures, and pains. Classical **empiricism** based itself on the supposed **epistemologically** foundational nature of sense data.

skepticism (or **scepticism**) A denial of the possibility of knowledge. General skepticism denies the possibility of *any* knowledge; however, one can be skeptical about fields of inquiry (e.g., **metaphysics**) or specific faculties (e.g., sense perception) without denying the possibility of knowledge in general.

soft behaviorism The view that there is no need to include "minds" in the scientific study of humans, whether or not minds exist. The study of "behaviors" and their physical causes is sufficient for a complete psychology. Contrast with **hard behaviorism.**

soft determinism The view that **determinism** is true but that **freedom** and responsibility can exist despite the truth of determinism. Contrast with **hard determinism.**

solipsism The view that the only true knowledge one can possess is knowledge of one's own consciousness. According to solipsism, there is no good reason to believe that anything exists other than oneself.

structuralism Based on the philosophical anthropology of the contemporary French theorist Claude Lévi-Strauss (but also finding followers in all the human sciences), the view that the human mind is universal in that everywhere and in every historical epoch, the mind is structured in such a way as to process its data in terms of certain general formulas that give meaning to those mental data.

sublimation A term central to **psychoanalysis** that names the process whereby certain antisocial drives are directed away from their primary goal (the satisfaction of sexual or aggressive desires) and transformed into the production of socially valuable higher culture—art, religion, philosophy, law, science, and so on.

substance In philosophy, traditionally the term naming whatever is thought to be the most basic independent reality. Aristotle defined a substance as whatever can exist independently of other things, so that a horse or a man (Aristotle's examples) can exist independently, but the *color* of the horse or the *size* of the man cannot. The seventeenth- and eighteenth-century **rationalists** took the idea of substance as *independent being* so seriously that one of their members, Spinoza, claimed there could be only one substance in the world (i.e., only one *thing*), namely, God, because only God could exist independently. Under Berkeley's criticism of material substance and Hume's criticism of spiritual substance, the concept of substance was very much eroded. It turned up again in Kant but only as a "category" of knowledge, not as a basic reality itself.

sufficient condition P is a sufficient condition of Q if the presence of P guarantees the presence of Q. For example, the presence of mammary glands in an animal is a sufficient condition for calling that animal a mammal. (It is also a **necessary condition** for doing so.)

superego In **psychoanalysis,** the component of the psyche that counteracts antisocial desires and impulses of the **id** by attaching conscious and unconscious feelings of guilt to them.

synthetic proposition A **proposition** is synthetic if its negation does not lead to a self-contradiction. For example, "Jupiter has a square moon" is synthetic because its negation, "Jupiter does not have a square moon," is not self-contradictory (usually associated with **a posteriori** propositions; the opposite of **analytic propositions**).

tabula rasa Latin for "blank slate." **Empiricism** from John Locke forward assumed that the mind is a *tabula rasa* at birth and that all knowledge must be inscribed on that blank slate by experience.

tautology A **proposition** is a tautology if it is in some way repetitive or redundant. For example, definitions are tautological because their predicates are equivalents of the term being defined. See also **analytic propositions.**

teleological argument An attempt to deduce God's existence from the fact that there is purposeful behavior in nature on the part of nonintelligent beings. (E.g., the "purpose" of the sharp point on the bottom of an acorn is to break the surface of the ground when the acorn falls.)

teleology The study of the evidence for the existence of purpose, design, and intentionality in both human and nonhuman domains. A teleological explanation is an explanation in terms of goals, purposes, or intentions (from the Greek *telos* = goal). For example, "John closed the window because he didn't want his budgie to escape" and "An acorn has a sharp tip on its bottom in order to break the ground when it falls from the tree" are both teleological explanations because they describe behavior in terms of intentions and goals. Contrast with **causal explanation.**

Thanatos The Greek god of death, which in **psychoanalytic** theory becomes the name of a purported "death instinct" inherent in all organic matter and that is somehow more basic than its opposing instinct, **Eros,** the "life instinct."

theism Belief in the existence of God or gods.

theoretical entity A term from twentieth-century **empiricism** naming entities that exist only as parts of theories, not parts of reality. For example, "the average American housewife" is a theoretical entity.

transformational grammar A system of grammatical analysis that uses a set of algebraic formulas to express relations between elements in a sentence or between different forms or tenses of a phrase, such as active, passive, future, and present.

utilitarianism The moral and social philosophy of Jeremy Bentham and John Stuart Mill according to which the value of any action or legislation can be derived from the principle of utility, which advocates "the greatest amount of happiness for the greatest number of people."

Credits

Index